THE FLETCHER JONES FOUNDATION
HUMANITIES IMPRINT

The Fletcher Jones Foundation has endowed this imprint to foster innovative and enduring scholarship in the humanities.

*The publisher and the University of California Press
Foundation gratefully acknowledge the generous support of the
Fletcher Jones Foundation Imprint in Humanities.*

Agrotropolis

Agrotropolis
───────────────

YOUTH, STREET, AND NATION
IN THE NEW URBAN GUATEMALA

J. T. Way

UNIVERSITY OF CALIFORNIA PRESS

University of California Press
Oakland, California

© 2021 by J. T. Way

Library of Congress Cataloging-in-Publication Data
Names: Way, John T. (John Thomas), 1966– author.
Title: Agrotropolis : youth, street, and nation in the new urban Guatemala / J. T. Way.
Description: Oakland, California : University of California Press, [2021] | Includes bibliographical references and index.
Identifiers: LCCN 2020029675 (print) | LCCN 2020029676 (ebook) | ISBN 9780520291850 (hardback) | ISBN 9780520291867 (paperback) | ISBN 9780520965485 (epub)
Subjects: LCSH: Urbanization—Guatemala—History—20th century. | Youth—Guatemala—Social conditions—20th century. | Economic development—Social aspects—Guatemala—20th century.
Classification: LCC HT384.G9 W39 2021 (print) | LCC HT384.G9 (ebook) | DDC 307.76097281—dc23
LC record available at https://lccn.loc.gov/2020029675
LC ebook record available at https://lccn.loc.gov/2020029676

30 29 28 27 26 25 24 23 22 21
10 9 8 7 6 5 4 3 2 1

CONTENTS

List of Illustrations   vii
Acknowledgments   ix
List of Abbreviations   xi

Introduction: Agrotropolis   1

1 · "Power's Destiny": Political Economy and Popular Culture to 1986   27

2 · "Americamorfosis": Identities and Urbanization, 1987–1993   59

3 · "Not Fish, Not Iguana": Organized Bands and Agro-urbanization, 1994–1998   94

4 · "If Only You Could Live Here": The Emergence of La KY, 1999–2004   129

5 · "In the Jaws of These Gray Cities": Strategic Territorial Interventions, 2005–2012   165

Conclusion: "Mi País"   199

Notes   211
Works Cited   265
Index   279

ILLUSTRATIONS

FIGURES

1. Civilian Self-Defense Patrol, 1985   *41*
2. Army cocaine seizure, 1987   *51*
3. Majawil Q'ij in Encuentro Continental, 1991   *79*
4. Protest in Sololá, 1992   *81*
5. Primera Generación Records advertisement, 1996   *89*
6. Youth crowd-surfing at concert, mid-1990s   *102*
7. Young soldier defends a finca, 1995   *102*
8. Guerrillas training, 1996   *103*
9. Central Aguacatán, 2016   *120*
10. PAC turns in arms, Colotenango, 1996   *123*
11. The zotz' symbol, 2019   *126*
12. Fans awaiting Garra Chapina concert, 2002   *140*
13. "Gramático," graphic from *Supositorio*, 2002   *153*
14. Different childhoods, Panajachel, 1999   *154*
15. Toy tuc-tuc, Sololá, 2016   *163*
16. Feria, Sololá, 2016   *177*
17. B-boy Chino break-dancing, 2016   *187*
18. Pauper in Cuatro Caminos, 2016   *190*
19. Ijatz Crew banner, 2016   *207*
20. Sanick, Chino, and Lokillo, 2016   *208*

MAPS

1. Guatemala *xiv*
2. Huehuetenango Department *74*
3. Urban growth in Chiantla *96*
4. Lake Atitlán basin *152*

ACKNOWLEDGMENTS

I write in a pandemic, conscious of and thankful for my family, friends, colleagues, and fellow travelers. My gratitude and appreciation are in inverse proportion to the brevity of these remarks. I begin with the departed and missed: my parents, Frank Judge, Carol Craycraft, Patricia Pessar, Stephen Vella, Rebecca Ruquist, Shafali Lal, Nancy Yanoshak, Tani Adams, Ralph Laws, Ana Cayax, Denis Gainty, Cliff Kuhn, Doug Reynolds, Jacqueline Rouse, Alana Rosenwhite, Che Lindken, and Ricardo Stein Heinemann.

Joe Perry and Diane Nelson have slogged through drafts and are responsible for many insights and none of my errors. Thanks for input, edits, comments, encouragement, and help in many forums go to Deborah Levenson, Martha Few, Isa Blumi, Alison Bruey, Shannan Clark, Joyce DeVries, Fred Viguier, Kathleen Mallanda, Jennie Burnet, Adrienne Rosen, Héctor Fernández L'Hoeste, Mark Olsen, Michael Gubser, Dave Carey, Ingrid Castañeda Sierakowski, Kirsten Weld, and Eric Zolov. Laura Briggs is a constant source of support, ideas, inspiration, and comfort. Like Laura, others in the Tepoztlán collective helped me shape and refine my ideas; I send special thanks to Bethany Moreton, Pam Voekel, Adam Warren, Elliott Young, David Kazanjian, Josefina Saldaña-Portillo, Lisbeth Haas, Heather Vrana, and Rachel Nolan. In GALACSI—my Atlanta collective and writing group—thanks are due to all, especially Yanna Yannakakis, Tom Rogers, Lia Bascomb, Reinaldo Román, Corinna Zeltsman, Alex Wisnoski, and my colleague Julia Gaffield. From the UA/Guatemala collective, I thank Liz Oglesby, Jill Calderón, J. P. Jones, Jenn Casolo, Linda Green, Sapana Doshi, and all the Mesoamerica scholars at the University of Arizona. Finally, thanks go to Don Reitzes, Gyan Pandey, and all in the Practice of Democracy collective here in Atlanta.

Kate Marshall, Enrique Ochoa-Kaup, and Susan Silver are wonderful, as is the University of California Press team as a whole. The American Philosophical Society, GSU Scholarly Support, the GSU Department of History, and the Center for Neighborhood and Metropolitan Studies have all supported my research. I can't name all my fantastic coworkers but will send a shout-out to Jeffrey Trask, Michelle Brattain, Jared Poley, Jake Selwood, Denise Davidson, Alex Cummings, Ian Fletcher, Harcourt Fuller, Marni Davis, John McMillian, Rob Baker, Greg Moore, Lela Urquhart, Chuck Steffen, Carolyn Whiters, and Robin Jackson. This book would not exist without Paula Sorrell's constant help and good cheer; thank you!

At CIRMA, thanks go to Chris Lutz, Guisela Asensio, Thelma Porres, Anaís García, Marta Elena Alonzo, Yuddi Morán, Roxana Romero, and the team. In Huehuetenango, María Concepción Saenz and all at CEDFOG were exceptionally helpful, as was the Municipalidad de Sololá; special thanks go to Marco Tulio Zúñiga de León and Herber Ruiz. There is no way I can properly thank all who have helped me in Guatemala. Gracias to Henry, Harry, Devora, Norma, Dennis, *y toda la familia;* and Bilian Hernández, Luis Yoxón, Nicolás Ramos, Helen and Sergio Vickers, *los hermanos* Cota, Hugo Pablo, Otto Curup, Maynor González, Lucky Paniagua, Anabella Acevedo, Rigo Ajcalón, Pascale Daime, Benji Fogarty, José Carlos Payeras, Carol Loaiza, Edi Queché, Pablo Castro, Moisés Sygier, Irene Malabanan, Marco Cordedda, Yolanda Colom, Ijatz Crew, and all whose names are changed in this text.

Gabriel García heroically helped with research, as did Christian Pettersen and Steven García. Among the incredible CIRMA students, I'd like to especially mention Chelsea Halstead, Ian Philabaum, and Kara Andrade. My "GSU crew" of Suzanne Litrel, Alex McCready, and Pablo Valenzuela has always made me happy to be a historian. For inspiration earlier in my life, I thank Marty Porter, Bonnie Cousineau, and Andrea Kane. I'd also like to thank Gil Joseph, Ralph Lee Woodward Jr., Dee Woodward, George Lovell, and David McCreery. I'll end with special appreciation for *mi familia*. Here's to the Judges—Carolyn, Julia, Spencer, Marguerite, Gerry, and Kathleen—and Kate Way and Dinah Mack. I dedicate this book to Carol.

ABBREVIATIONS

ASC	Asamblea de la Sociedad Civil (Assembly for Civil Society)
CNR	Comisión Nacional de Reconciliación (National Reconciliation Commission)
COCODEs, COMUDEs, CODEDEs	Consejos (Comunitarios, Municipales, o Departamentales) de Desarrollo Urbano y Rural ([Community, Municipal, or Departmental] Urban and Rural Development Councils)
COMG	Coordinación de Organizaciones Mayas de Guatemala (Council of Mayan Organizations of Guatemala)
CONJUVE	Consejo Nacional de la Juventud (National Council on Youth)
COPMAGUA	Coordinación de Organizaciones del Pueblo Maya de Guatemala (Council of Organizations of the Pueblo Maya of Guatemala)
CUC	Comité de Unidad Campesina (Campesino Unity Committee)
EGP	Ejército Guerrillero de los Pobres (Guerrilla Army of the Poor)
FAR	Fuerzas Armadas Rebeldes (Rebel Armed Forces)
FDNG	Frente Democrática Nueva Guatemala (New Guatemala Democratic Front)

FRG	Frente Republicano Guatemalteco (Guatemalan Republican Front)
IDB	Inter-American Development Bank
IMF	International Monetary Fund
MINUGUA	Misión de Naciones Unidas en Guatemala (Mission of the United Nations in Guatemala)
NTAs	nontraditional agro-exports
ORPA	Organización Revolucionaria del Pueblo en Armas (Revolutionary Organization of the People in Arms)
PAC	Patrulla de Autodefensa Civil (Civilian Self-Defense Patrol)
PAN	Partido de Avanzada Nacional (National Advancement Party)
PCD	Plan Comunitario de Desarrollo (Community Development Plan)
PDM	Plan de Desarrollo Municipal (Municipal Development Plan)
PET	Plan Estratégico Territorial (Strategic Territorial Plan)
SIF	social investment fund
SUD	Sololatecos Unidos para el Desarrollo (Sololatecos United for Development)
URNG	Unidad Revolucionaria Nacional Guatemalteca (Guatemalan National Revolutionary Unity)
USAC	Universidad de San Carlos de Guatemala (University of San Carlos of Guatemala)
USAID	United States Agency for International Development

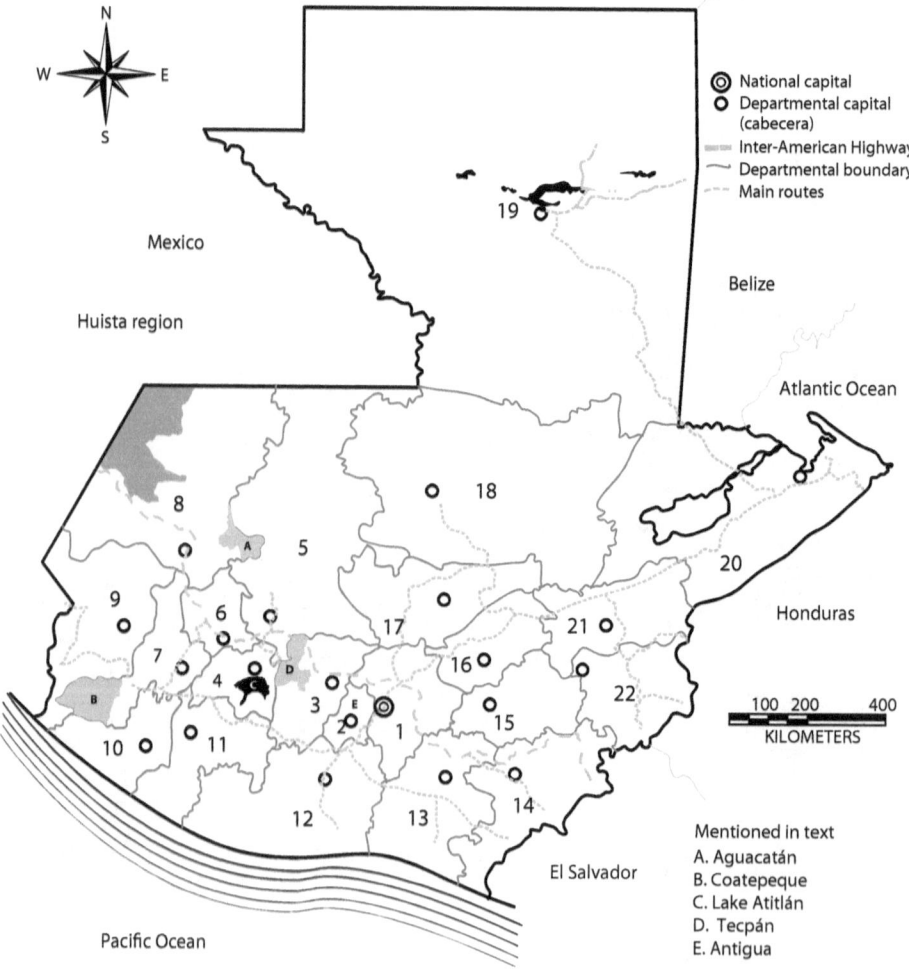

MAP 1. Guatemala.

Introduction

AGROTROPOLIS: A HISTORY OF YOUTH, STREET, AND NATION

A LITTLE BLUE-AND-WHITE BOAT called a *lancha* crossing Lake Atitlán is not an obvious setting in which to contemplate the global urban landscape. Yet that's what I'm doing in August 2016, looking at one of the most stunning natural vistas, not just in Guatemala's Mayan highlands but in the world. I'm here studying urbanization and cultural change since a baby boom that began in the 1980s made "Guate" one of the youngest countries on earth. With two companions I am on the way to San Pedro La Laguna. There we will meet Ijatz Crew, Tz'utujil Maya–speaking B-boy rappers, break-dancers, DJs, and graffiti artists. The *lancha* wallows, overloaded, toward the southern shore's skyline of three-and-a-half volcanoes. "Tono," my taxi driver and friend, points at the half volcano—bell-shaped Cerro de Oro. There's a road around it, he reminds me. It could be cool to check it out. Hugo, this book's amateur photographer, quashes this idea, using exactly the urban slang I'm studying: "Nel vos, na' que ver, allí te roban hasta los pelitos!" (Nope, dude, no way, they'll rob you down to the pubes there), he says. *A la gran puta.*[1]

Tono is from a town near Antigua, about four hours away. Hugo is local; friends call him Gokú, after a character in the anime Dragonball series. Both in their twenties, these young men are members of a polyethnic, nonagricultural working class that exploded in size with the nation's 1980s baby boom. They're from Kaqchikel Maya families, but, unlike other members of their generation, neither learned his parents' still-very-living language. Tono's wife, whose brother is a B-boy, is from San Pedro. She speaks Tz'utijil with their daughters; Tono can catch only a phrase or two.

The speaking of twenty-two Mayan languages with thousands of local dialects is just one of countless reasons that Guatemala epitomizes what Raymond Craib calls a "fugitive landscape" that escapes both the control and the gaze of the state.² There are no accurate population statistics or up-to-date maps; place-names are wrong on Google Earth. In the municipalities around the lake—Kaqchikel speaking on the shore we left, and Tz'utujil where we are headed—as in others around the nation, overlapping layers of authority and opaque structures of power make it difficult to know who, if anyone, is in charge.³

This mysterious landscape is due in part to Guatemala's history of war. Marxist guerrillas fought the right-wing state from 1960 to 1996. From the *lancha* I try to pinpoint the location of one of the last local guerrilla encampments, but I can't. The army base where people were tortured and murdered in the years around the 1981–83 genocide was just outside the departmental capital of Sololá, up the mountain and behind us. It became a university campus in 1998. Until roughly the same time, there were military garrisons in the towns. An exception to this rule was Santiago Atitlán, ahead and to our left. After soldiers committed a massacre there in late 1990, the townspeople drove the garrison out and took over "security" themselves. Security remained an issue after the war ended. As in all of Guatemala, many of today's lakeside population centers have homegrown security patrols, supposedly to combat gangs and crime rings.

Danger and celebration, like tradition and transformation, seem to be in constant friction in this land of contrasts. There are curves on mountain roads where bandits in balaclavas stop cars, swarming out of the cypress forest with AK-47s and bad intentions. Sometimes, at night, mountainside caves flicker with fire; it's a Maya holy day, and rites are being held. Tourists flocked to the lake on 13 Baktun, the end of the Maya calendar's last long count, when the world was supposed to end on 21 December 2012. They were there for Maya culture but also packed the discos. As our boat crosses the Kaqchikel Tz'utujil–language line, I show my friends the shore where all-night raves were the rage when they were just young teens. That must have been a tourist thing, Tono mused. *Nel,* said Hugo. The partiers were mostly *chapines,* slang for Guatemalans. At this moment a *lancha* passes heading the other way. We wave to the mix of tourists, artisans with bags of tools, schoolkids, and men and women commuting to work—some wearing Maya traditional dress, called *traje*. It's morning, but half the tourists look *súper pero súper* high. There's a reason locals call San Pedro "San Pedo," Saint Stoned.

Tono and I are on the last leg of a road trip through Guatemala's *occidente,* the Maya-majority west. We started in Kaqchikel-speaking Chimaltenango. Every day "Chimal" looks more like the country's capital, Guatemala City.

The *capi* bears significant blame for why the nation appears in reports in the United States, where I am from, as one of the most dangerous countries in the world. Paradoxically, Chimal's similitude with the *capi* is in part attributable to the fact that its working-class sprawl is fringed with *centros comerciales* (malls) where armed men guard the parking lots. Besides malls, Chimal is girdled by a dwindling number of maquiladoras, or factory sweatshops, most of which followed cheaper labor to Asia. Still lining the one-lane highway are brothels, where women in traje pose in front of cheap bead curtains. Also along the traffic-jammed highway are auto-parts and tire stores, office-furniture workshops, and agroindustrial fertilizer and seed outlets serving the surrounding farmland. Seeking shortcuts to that farmland, I have driven on dirt roads through fincas (plantations) in the middle of the night, only to emerge in poor neighborhoods full of alleys and dead ends. Night or day, however, no one looks at me funny when I drive through Chimaltenango. It's a city. Strangers are to be expected, and nobody cares who you are.[4]

The same cannot be said of the residents of Tecpán or Nahualá, the next stops on my road trip with Tono. Every time I go to these places, people *notice* me. These Kaqchikel-speaking population centers fall somewhere on the scale between "big town" and "small city," making them fascinating laboratories of urbanization and cultural change. Tecpán is an emerging city that grows broccoli and manufactures counterfeit brand-name clothes, but it is not so much of a city that people do not pay sometimes-scary attention to strangers. The people of Nahualá are even more vigilant. Nahualá is not quite as much of a city as Tecpán, which is not quite as much of a city as Chimaltenango, but it is coming to have a similar feel. Tono and I commented on Nahualá's urban ambience and youthful population. Teenage girls in heels and form-fitting traje and boys sporting NBA jerseys and electric-blue fauxhawks looked up from their cell phones to stare at us as we made our way to the center, where *reggaetón* and other *música urbana* blasted, and three-wheeled tuc-tucs (motor rickshaws) zipped around the streets.

Our next stop was a "real" city. We crossed into areas where K'iche' and Mam are spoken and hopscotched towns to Quetzaltenango ("-tenango" means "place of," and the quetzal is the national bird as well as the name of the currency). The historical center of the nation's "second city" still feels quiet, but Quetzaltenango is circled by suburbs, commercial districts, and poor barrios where the population is dense and engine noise and music fill the air. From there we were off to Huehuetenango, a smaller but still-sprawling city near the Mexican border, and neighboring, gang-tagged

Chiantla, which had grown to join "Huehue" in a metro region. Then we circled back east. We traversed sylvan peaks to commercializing towns like Aguacatán, where people peered at us suspiciously, but half smiling... not many gringos make it up this way. We were en route to Santa Cruz del Quiché, a place with a mazelike street market packed with informal vendors' stalls right in its center, a city-within-a-city so fascinating to both of us that we unexpectedly stayed three nights.

Tono and I stopped in Chichicastenango and Sololá before we returned to my home base in Lake Atitlán's Panajachel and then across the lake to meet the B-boys. "Chichi" is home to the Americas' oldest pre-Columbian market still in its original location. A third of the market is for tourists, but the rest serves the local population, as do the surrounding cantinas, brothels, and barrios. Next to the market is the Catholic Church. The army had turned its rectory into a torture chamber in the early 1980s. People still remember hearing the screams at night. Our last stop was Sololá, high above Lake Atitlán. In the *parque central* teenage Kaqchikel students were finishing marching-band practice and shedding their uniforms for fashionable clothes, buzzing in anticipation of a rock concert. *Feria,* the town's fair, was coming up, and the government had been sponsoring games and shows for weeks. For a moment the music helped people forget the kidnapping rings, the lynchings, and the rage that drove mobs to burn down the police station. Sololá seemed youthful, fun, and happy on the day we visited.

A HISTORY OF AGROTROPOLIS

These places, like many others in agrarian-yet-urban, provincial-yet-urbane Guatemala, form what I call an "agro-urban" landscape, this nation's variant of an emerging, global "Agrotropolis." This concept—country on one side and city on the other—is meant to encapsulate a wide range of slippages and contradictions that manifest in the nation's built environment, in ideas and discourses about it, and in its residents' changing subjectivities, identities, aspirations, and cultural expressions.[5] *Agrotropolis* is the first urban history of contemporary Guatemala to consider not just the capital city but also provincial centers and their hinterlands. Its scope is deliberately provocative. Guatemala, for decades *the* exemplar of ongoing Latin American rurality, still has a very real agrarian landscape peopled by a Maya-majority *campesinado* (poor farming sector). It has also profoundly urbanized since the 1980s.

This book traces how urbanizing rural regions, their politics, and their cultures evolved in dialogue with the changing global and national political economy as the increasingly cosmopolitan baby-boom generations grew up. It explores the dialogical and mutually constitutive ties between structural socioeconomic change, local politics and crime, discourses of identity and belonging, and cosmopolitan urban youth cultures and countercultures in the capital and the provinces.

The centers of today's urban/urbane Guatemala include not only the capital, Quetzaltenango, and tertiary cities such as Huehuetenango but also far-flung municipal seats—towns that were by any standard "rural" at the time of the genocide in the early 1980s but that were beginning to urbanize by the time the thirty-six-year war ended in December 1996.[6] Today, as diverse as they are, they have a similar look, one both common to global urban poverty and specific to Guatemala and its history. Concrete-block buildings line central streets, where formal shops, businesses, and banks (blazoned with ads: *the best place to save your remittances!*) abut informal vendors' tarp-covered stalls. Smaller *calles* (streets) and *callejones* (alleys) form warrens that lead to barrios with handmade huts and humble cinderblock homes. Around these dense central settlements is farmland, which is itself interspersed with outlying villages that duplicate the center's built environment on a smaller scale. The pattern then repeats; the agrarian fields around the villages are peppered with even poorer hamlets that are in the process of urbanizing in similar ways.

Inseparable from this expanding agro-urban network is a contested yet common field of discourse about what it means and feels like to be *from* these places. This discursive field is what Tono and Hugo would call a Guatemalan *forma de ser*, or "way of being." It arises from the lived experienced of the built environment, of its poverty, and of its registers of violence that manifest in local politics and in organized and street crime alike. This book traces the physical, social, and cultural roots of this lifeworld from the end of the genocide in 1983 to the "end of the world" on 13 Baktun in 2012. Mapping urban development and the spread of globalized popular youth cultures, such as *rock nacional,* and subcultures such as the Ijatz B-boys' rap and break-dance, it insists that places relegated to rurality, like provincial Guatemala, must be entered into the equation if we want to understand the global urbanization that scholars and policy makers around the world are noting.

In exploring this history, this book makes a series of arguments, elaborated through a set of interrelated dialectical tensions—urban/rural, transformation/continuity, creation/destruction, and inclusion/exclusion. First, this work contends that one of the planet's most iconographically rural regions, without losing its agrarian backbone, has in fact profoundly urbanized, physically, socially, and culturally. Second, it maintains that this happened as part of complex processes that both from above and below melded "new" and "old"; the constellation promoting capital expansion and neoliberal multiculturalism drew on older developmental policies and militarism, and poor people who engaged in new economic activities drew on a history of "informality" and grassroots ingenuity. Third, the book argues that culture, and particularly youth cultures, took on new importance through and after the end of the Cold War—a period when visions of communist revolution were crushed, when models of capitalist development failed to lift up the poor and middling classes, and when criminality came to pervade the body politic at all levels. Fourth, it argues that despite (and in dialogue with) ongoing marginalization, Guatemala's new, young generations have upturned age-old codes of status, identity, and belonging. In the context of an urbanizing nation and a rapidly changing global political economy, they have done so by drawing on a heritage of resistance and by tapping into and retooling cultural forms that range from the "traditional" to the global. Wittingly and unwittingly, youth are rewriting what it means to be citizens both of Guatemala and of an increasingly interconnected world. While joining a wide body of scholarship that decries the tragedies of the Cold War and its neoliberal aftermath, this work unearths a positive and overlooked achievement of Guatemala's recent generations. *Agrotropolis* culminates with the contention that the nation's urban and agrourban youth have overturned a system of *castas* (castes) that dates to the Spanish Conquest. They have rejected what Guatemalans call "servility" as a cultural form and have cocreated a bottom-up idiom of national identity, giving rise to an alternative popular nationalism.

This historic achievement is bittersweet. It shows the hydraulic cultural force of Guatemala's poor majority, but it has not ended poverty, exclusion, racism, sexism, or classism. Given the state of geopolitics, it is completely unrealistic to expect young, poor, baby-boom Guatemalans (that is, people of ages corresponding to Generation Xers, millennials, and Gen Zers in the United States) to have been able to change the terms of the system on their own. It is time to rethink the historical contributions of Guatemala's new generations of impecunious, "everyday" youth. Their militant and activist elders—including Marxist guerrillas, right-wing military types, 1960s-style counterculture participants, and even academics—dismiss them as vapid, apolitical consumers. An elite national and generalized global public sphere paints them as gang-banging *mareros,* criminals, and libertines who pump out "unaccompanied minors" and other brown-skinned "surplus humans."[7] A "humanitarian" institutional and commercial universe insists that they be ideal representatives of indigenous purity or national tradition or rags-to-riches ingenuity and relegates them to perfect-victim status even as it works to convert them into consumers of goods and loans. At the same time, their productive cultural expressions, confected in dialogue with global, national, and local conditions not at all of their own choosing, bear evidence to the many ways in which they have been challenging and rewriting age-old codes of exclusion and marginalization.

Agrotropolis is the poor, creative, pained, productive space in which we can trace the confluences between top-down and bottom-up forces. In this history, agrotropolis emerges from a predominantly "rural" weave of population centers to become an agro-urban space marked by a real-and-imagined *calle.* The growing, physical network of streets and the idea of popular "street culture" came over time to link Guatemala City and provincial centers in a new urban fabric and a new kind of national commons. This discursive national commons, in turn, evolved in dialogue with and became, and is still becoming, part of a fluid global commons. A study of agro-urban Guatemala is essential to developing a fuller understanding of global phenomena—the barrio, the hood, the shantytown, the megacity, and the terms and conditions of an urbanizing, mediatizing, financializing world that subsumes and threatens all of us. Such a study also reveals overlooked but historically significant cultural assertiveness. Guatemalan cultural critics write that their nation's poor majority of indigenous and mixed-race citizens have a centuries-long tradition of coping with their marginalization not only with a valiant history of rebellion, resistance, and revolution but also, on an everyday level, with performances of subservience, with bowed heads, evasive statements, and averted gazes. Today's working-class Guatemalans do not hesitate to look anyone squarely in the eye. This book looks squarely back.

BLURRED LINES AND HISTORY FROM BELOW

The majority of Guatemala's population is poor, and for heuristic purposes that majority can be conceived of as basically consisting of two broad groups: mixed-race, brown-skinned mestizos and the Maya. The word "Maya," however, was not historically used as an identifier. Instead, people referred to themselves as *naturales* or *indígenas* (indigenous people) or used the name of their language group; Hugo's grandparents called themselves "Kaqchikeles," for example. A diverse and not-always-in-agreement body of groups summed up as the Mayan movement popularized the identity-related term "Maya" in the 1990s.[8] An important 2008 volume on multiculturalism in Guatemala explored the process of "Mayanization" as people began to adopt this new term. Instead of covering political leaders, intellectuals, or cultural activists, this volume broke new ground because it focused on "everyday people *[personas de a pie]*, those in the cornfields *[milpa]* and on the street *[calle]*, to whose identity and culture, directly or indirectly, this ideological proposal relates."[9]

Agrotropolis salutes the scholarly turn toward studies of everyday life. It explores how ordinary, de a pie people came to self-identify not just as "Maya" or "not-Maya" but also in new ways as *Guatemalans* and chapines in the context of an increasingly neoliberal political economy and an urbanizing and globalizing landscape. This landscape included often violent "street realities" that manifested in urbanizing towns with new forms of poverty unrelated to agricultural peonage, spreading crime, and vigilante-like "security." People expressed the lived experience of street realities through evolving, creative popular youth culture—in particular, popular music produced by and for Guatemalans. In *Agrotropolis* I use this popular music as a means to sketch the contours of changing vernacular identities, styles, and subjectivities and *not* as a means to attempt to define them. To trace this polyvalent cultural history means grappling with the blurred lines between putatively opposed categories: binary structures of class (rich/poor), race (Maya/not-Maya), space (rural/urban), political economy (state-led/neoliberal), and culture (traditional-folkloric/globalized-degenerate). From a de a pie perspective, these categories are endlessly muddied by ambiguities and slippages, and it is in these gray areas that much of the meaning of having been alive during these dehumanizing times can be excavated.[10]

Agrotropolis uses a mix of archival and ethnographic research to excavate such gray areas. It maps the physical and cultural urbanization of rural population centers against a history of popular music and youth cultures and countercultures in both the capital city and the provinces, continuously rejecting clichéd understandings of *rural* and *urban*. Remaining attentive to the evolving political economy, it uses this methodological approach to analyze changing actions, perceptions, and ways of identifying one's self and others among a diverse population kept invisible by its very conditions of marginalization.

There is a great deal at stake here. Taking a bottom-up approach unearths important dimensions of the human experience of this period—making visible the "invisibilized" lives of people like Hugo, Tono, and their families. As such, it sharpens our understanding of subaltern history and of everyday practices of accommodation and resistance as armed rebellion ended and dreams of revolutionary victory took on more diffuse and sometimes subtle forms. Looking at these processes from a de a pie perspective is now possible in never-before-seen ways, thanks to spreading literacy, new media, and online self-publishing. The view from below also highlights the ramifications of the life-changing policies and programs promoted by some of the most powerful institutions on earth. Tracing the evolution of social space in this corner of the world can amplify our understanding of an urbanizing planet, of the Cold War's legacy, and the messy processes of neoliberalization. This history illuminates the securitization of society at all levels and changing senses of self, community, and nation in a new phase of capital expansion.

Capital expansion, the rise of agro-urban space, and the spread of cosmopolitan cultural expressions in Guatemala form an important part of what scholars call "planetary urbanization." This new scholarship asks us to discard the epistemology of an urban/rural divide altogether and insists, in Neil Brenner's words, that "the meaning of the urban itself must be fundamentally reimagined."[11] Faced with a vastly transformed national territory, Guatemala's government came to a similar conclusion in 2014. This was a complete about-face. For decades the state had demarcated territory and designed development plans using population-based definitions of *urban* and *rural* that defined most of the nation as the latter. Thus, one could stand with one foot in an urban center and the other in a rural village, as if straddling the equator. The 2014 national development plan, K'atun (a Mayan term for "the time it takes to bring a project to fruition"), recognized rapid population growth and rethought these categories. It claimed that terms such as "periurban" and "ruruban" better described what had become a contrast-filled, country-city "continuum." Provincial population centers had matured into a "diffuse" landscape marked by "complex and fluid processes that partially transform rural environments into urban ones." These processes, K'atun held, entailed new kinds of social, economic, and cultural behaviors. K'atun dated the nation's transition from predominantly rural to predominantly urban to approximately 2009–10 and forecast the emergence of a national megalopolis by 2032.[12]

Part of my work in this book is to convince readers that "rural" Guatemala in fact has an urban history, and that said history forms part of a still-to-be-written chapter in widely read urban studies—a body of scholarship that focuses on megalopolises so enormous that not even Guatemala City, the largest city in Central America, qualifies for inclusion. Physical and cultural urbanization in small countries such as Guatemala deserves to be considered in a vast literature referenced by texts such as Richard Florida's works on creative communities and city life and Mike Davis's on a "planet of slums," along with studies of global cities by scholars such as Saskia Sassen.[13] Guatemala's capital city, studied by several anthropologists and historians, is now, I argue, joined by the nation's provincial centers in meriting a place in conversations about urbanization around the globe and around Latin America.[14] These growing, increasingly urban and culturally cosmopolitan webs of villages, towns, and small cities came into being as an agrarian modality of what the urban theorist Emilio Pradilla Cobos describes as a Latin American variant of the "city-region"—an urban system that includes and integrates peripheral and rural areas "in a dense but not continuous weave." The emergence of city-regions implies a process of change that, as Pradilla writes, is "not just demographic or physical, but fundamentally structural, including all the spheres of economic, social, and cultural life."[15]

Few factors played a greater role in shattering and realigning Guatemala's "spheres of . . . life" than the Cold War, the crucible from which the contemporary agro-urban landscape emerged. An invasion, planned and led by the CIA, overthrew the nation's modernizing, democratic revolution of 1944–54, ushering in right-wing military rule. In the wake of the Cuban Revolution, Marxist guerrilla resistance arose in 1960. Over time, a constellation of never-united revolutionary armies battled a U.S.-backed national-security apparatus whose state-terror tools of war included torture and death squads. The war intensified in the Mayan highlands in the 1970s. The army responded to widespread grassroots resistance and organizing with unspeakable violence. Troops went from Maya village to village from 1981 to 1983, indiscriminately massacring human beings from infants to the elderly, mostly in remote areas that remain agrarian to the present day. A "return to democracy" followed with the rise of civilian rule in 1986, but peace was not declared until the end of 1996. By the turn of the millennium, two truth commissions, one led by the Catholic Church and the other by the United Nations, released voluminous documentation of the horrors. Together with the growing body of forensic evidence from excavated mass graves, these testimonials formed the evidentiary base for human rights and genocide trials, several of which continue at the time of this writing.[16] Neither civilian rule nor new attention to human rights discourses, however, erased Guatemala's legacy of war. Far from withering away, the logics and polities of Guatemala's brutal, Cold War counterinsurgency are interwoven in its urbanizing landscape. The result has been endemic violence, a phenomenon exacerbated by the neoliberal turn in the body politic.[17]

Guatemala's political economy became more neoliberal in rhythm with similar changes seen around the region and the globe. Patterns of agricultural production and labor changed in ways that, together with migrants' remittances and informal-economy workers' earnings, helped to fund the rise of agro-urban space.[18] Society and culture urbanized, mediatized, financialized, and commercialized as new generations came of age. NGOs, microcredit enterprises, chain stores, and banks spread across the landscape.[19] In the late 1990s, when a historic Maya power movement was at its height, Guatemala privatized its telecommunications and electric industries. The nation's inclusion in CAFTA-DR, the Central America–Dominican Republic Free Trade Agreement, in the mid-aughts cemented its full-blown membership in the neoliberal world economy. Just as agro-urban Guatemala asks us to rethink old rural-urban binaries, the processes that structured its emergence and evolution militate for a study not of neoliberalism as a bounded set of policies and initiatives but for what the geographer Jamie Peck calls "neoliberalization," consisting of "open-ended and contradictory process[es]" that involved a "messy hybrid" of institutions, plans, and policies.[20] Many of the NGOs and banks, both regulated and offshore, were new, as were narcotraffic rings, kidnapping rings, and other mafias. However, Guatemala's neoliberalization also drew on a long history of "development" that was funded for decades before and after the genocide by an apparatus of powerful institutions. These included not only the state but also the World Bank, the Inter-American Development Bank (IDB), the international cooperation agencies of donor nations, and scores of NGOs. This development apparatus promoted the spread of private capital and the reduction of the barely formed democratic central state. At the same time, it *also* promoted the Mayan movement and "local power" initiatives that gave rise to what has become known as "neoliberal multiculturalism."[21] This fact, along with ongoing poverty and marginalization, has caused many scholars to question just how much real power the rise of postwar Maya power has entailed.

Besides providing aesthetic cover for a state that has taken insufficient steps to help its indigenous population recover from genocide or rise out of structural poverty, the official, top-down discourses about Maya identity associated with neoliberal multiculturalism occlude complex realities and blurred lines in Guatemala's complex and idiomatic conceptions of race and class. *Agrotropolis* approaches the nation's self-described system of castas by looking at the issue from the perspective of youth, tracing how they have forged a still-emerging national cultural commons. This commons, a geographic and discursive space, spans both the capital city and provincial city-regions and includes citizens of different ethnic and class backgrounds. Guatemalans (and scholars who study the country) have long spoken of a nation divided between people who are either Maya or *ladino* (not-Maya). Ladino is a broad-to-the-point-of-meaninglessness descriptor that includes a small minority of light-skinned elites and a huge population of brown-skinned mestizos, many of whom live in dire poverty.[22] Guatemalans often refer to the bottom-of-the-pyramid, Maya-and-poor-ladino majority—the castas—as the *pueblo,* which has a positive tone. They also use racialized and class-based slurs and epithets, because, according to the anthropologist Jorge Ramón González Ponciano, the elite has inculcated the middle sectors with "its repulsion for *mestizaje indígena* [indigenous race mixing]," making them "feel the obligation to defend the structure of servile relations."[23]

González rightly warns us to problematize binary, Maya-versus-ladino readings. For example, insults such as *shumo,* which has the ring of "brown trash," might refer to either a (poor, lowbrow, tacky) Maya or ladino. Shumo joins insults such as *mozo,* meaning agricultural peon, and race-neutral terms like *cholo, cholero,* and *muco* (the first two refer to poor urban thugs; the third means gang member). González's study of Guatemala City youth culture traces a "symbolic war between a cosmopolitanism from below . . . and a cosmopolitanism from above" in battles over the right to appropriate and perform foreign styles.[24] Poor, brown-skinned youth began to invade this once-elite terrain, breaking social codes in "a nation of bowed heads . . . of obedient servants who know their place in society . . . a nation of castes."[25] González's work focuses on the persistence of caste-based social codes among youth of the elite and aspiring-to-be-elite sectors, and *Agrotropolis* takes up the issue predominantly from the other, de a pie side. Lower-class urban and agro-urban youth, this book argues, have rejected servility as a cultural form, even if some middle- and upper-sector youth still expect it of them. The Maya/ladino divide still exists, but multiple realities complicate that binary in everyday life.

The chapters ahead show how de a pie, working-class youth of varied ethnic backgrounds—in interclass and intercaste dialogue with middle- and upper-class youth—have reworked grassroots idioms of national identity and belonging in ways not always visible if viewed from above.[26] Examining rock nacional and often ludic youth countercultures may seem superfluous or disrespectful in a nation that lived through a genocide and has experienced "war by other means" ever since.[27] It is not. Youth cultures are an inextricable aspect of a changing body politic, and they provide a window on the social and cultural aspects of those changes. When teamed with an analysis of the changing political economy and of the agro-urbanizing landscape—and the recognition that such relationships are dialogical and not directly causal—an examination of youth countercultures has much to tell us about the lived experience of a period of rapid and often heartbreaking historical change.

It is in pursuit of this very human story that I find myself on a *lancha* in 2016 with Hugo and Tono on the way to San Pedro Atitlán to meet the Ijatz Crew B-boys. The children of illiterate campesinos whose own parents' lives were forever altered by war, the B-boys are young men who self-identify as Maya, as Tz'utujiles, as chapines, and as members of a national and global urban youth community that references poverty and "the street," *la calle,* wherever it appears. As I will soon discover, these youngsters cherish their elders. They also have no doubt that they hail from a very different generation.

GENERATIONAL CHANGE, IDENTITIES, AND LIVING ARCHIVES

It is hard to overstate the scope and impact of generational change in Guatemala. From the 1980s to the 2010s, increasingly cosmopolitan generations in the urbanizing provinces bespoke a changing political economy and often horrified their elders. Over time, in the face of poverty and joblessness, these young people cocreated a new vernacular idiom of national identity in complex dialogue with their capital-city counterparts. While that new idiom was rooted in Guatemala's rich body of cultural traditions, it was also globalized, embodied on the real-and-imagined space of *la calle*—a space often denoted by the end of this history as "la KY" in internet slang (the letters are pronounced *kah*-yay, or *calle*). The ways in which Guatemalan street culture manifested were on one hand ludic and baroque and, on the other, historically transformational.

In the late 1970s and early 1980s, when state terror was at its peak, globalized, anticonformist youth cultures emerged in Guatemala City. Death-metal and hard-rock subcultures, along with rap and break-dance (associated, often falsely, with the street gangs born in the mid-1980s), marked the rise of a disenchanted urban generation and formed an early chapter in the violently contested formation of a national discursive field. Though there were certainly cliques of followers in larger provincial centers, in general, youth outside Guatemala City did not have the luxury of participating in popular countercultures in these years. In the militarily occupied Mayan highlands, coerced seasonal labor on the fincas was the norm. *I, Rigoberta Menchú,* the 1983 testimonial of a K'iche' activist who later won the 1992 Nobel Peace Prize, graphically described a countryside in which illiterate campesinos were brutally exploited. The labor regime that Menchú described changed in the years ahead. By the late 1990s, a new generation of provincial youth was coming of age, many of whom were the first in their family's history who could read and write and who were also the first *not* to work in agriculture or migrate from tiny family plots to the fincas as debt-peons.[28] Their life stories coincided with the urbanization of the countryside. A 2015 USAID report on surveys of highland youth captured generational change dramatically. "While the youth and adults unanimously recognized that virtually everyone of the older generation had been (mainly subsistence) farmers," the report stated, "no one mentioned farming as work to pursue.... The young people described their grandparents with phrases such as: 'they were barefoot'; 'they were illiterate'; 'they suffered terrible discrimination.' Virtually every young person . . . was intent on becoming 'a professional.'" The report added that "the one young man who said that he wanted to be a farmer *[agricultor]* was immediately interrupted by a chorus of peers: 'No, an agronomist!' they chimed in."[29]

The USAID report stressed that parents and children alike wanted a "radical change of life" that would bring prosperity, creature comforts, and class mobility. Radical change occurred, but not in terms of up-classing, since there was "no work for this new generation of 'professionals.'" Instead, it came from "factors like urbanization, increased literacy, migration, and the mass media (especially internet and TV) [that had] oriented young people toward a life that is unknown and frightening" to their elders.[30] That "unknown and frightening" realm resides in great measure on the real-and-imagined street, la KY. Given the failures of politics and the economy, la KY is precisely where we need to look to understand this dimension of ground-level historical change in Guatemala.

The indigenous teenagers that USAID interviewed in the mid-2010s were not only confronting an extractive, brutal political economy and an exceptionally violent body politic. They were also ongoing cocreators of a newly expanded *chapín* (Guatemalan) popular youth culture that several decades earlier had been a relatively elite domain that excluded their parents and grandparents. Guatemala's now-more-multicultural popular youth culture, with its rough slang and street styles and identities, in many ways shows what Achille Mbembe calls "the baroque character of the postcolony; its unusual and grotesque art of representation, its taste for the theatrical, and its violent pursuit of wrongdoing to the point of shamelessness."[31] That is not a reason, however, to dismiss it as simply the symptom and aftereffect of a neoliberal "disease" that infected the body politic with consumerism after the right wing tried to kill off the left. Once put in the foreground of history, youthful cultural expressions take on new significance—even ones that de a pie Guatemalans will often characterize as *estupideces* (stupidities), *muladas* (dumb ass things), and *pura paja* (pure bullshit) that their classmates or they themselves grew out of but that still form the soundtrack of their lives and have residual effect in their *forma de ser* (way of being).

Far from being a ludic or tragic or inconsequential "sideshow" to the "real" story of history, popular youth culture offers a means of entry into identity formation and from-below nationalism as enacted in everyday life in a time of remarkable urbanization, capital expansion, financialization, commercialization, and a developing-world variant of what Stig Hjarvard terms "mediatization," a "process whereby culture and society to an increasing degree become dependent on the media and their logic."[32] This book examines a wide lexicon of street slang, style, and performativity—accessed primarily through the history of "national rock" and related musical forms—as a means to explore what Swati Chattopadhyay calls "provincial cosmopolitanism."[33] These cosmopolitan cultural forms were an integral element of a new vernacular idiom of popular nationalism, one with deep and multiple roots in the past but that newly came to link the "big city" and the "small city" and their citizens together in what Raymond Williams terms a "structure of feeling." This analysis of both identities and bottom up "street-nationalism" follows Frederick Cooper's exhortation not to posit a "flattening rubric of identity" but instead to focus on a mode of "self-identification" that "takes place in dialectical interplay with external identification."[34] The three-word phrase "alternative popular nationalism" summarizes a single concept that, like "agrotropolis," is meant to capture an internal dialectical tension.[35] Built from below, in rejection of, yet in dialogue with, a detested, corrupt government, this contested-but-unified set of grassroots national self-identifications references a variety of ways to *be* authentically Guatemalan, coalescing in a recognizable *forma de ser* that, for all its internal differences, universally rejects the "official" Guatemalan state and its global, neoliberal funders.[36] Guatemalans speak often of their divided society, but they also celebrate their nation's unique cultural qualities. *Agrotropolis* seeks to highlight the unity that exists despite the nation's conflicts and divisions.

The analysis here draws on a diverse archive to get at this history. Methodologically, while drawing on the insights and techniques of human geography, cultural studies, and ethnography, this study is grounded in what I hope is an innovative use of the historical method. Its archival sources (in a nation that does not archive its paperwork) begin with development-sector documents (from state dependencies and municipal governments, the United Nations, and the NGO and national and transnational banking sectors, among others) and those of the guerrilla and progressive Left, read in conjunction with Guatemalan academic production on the evolving contemporary landscape.[37] It contextualizes these sources with readings of press accounts, editorials, and essays that deal with urbanization, youth culture, and national identity. Building on this base, the work then maps a wide variety of cultural production, using memoirs, counterculture publications, novels, music and song lyrics, websites, advertisements, YouTube videos, blogs, and group Facebook pages.[38] My sources further include interviews I have conducted, as well as conversations and interactions I have documented, over nearly three decades of visiting and living in Guatemala. Finally, I also draw on my observations and experiences of the nation—its pains, terrors, and indignities; its graffiti and commerce and rites (processions, parades, festivals, protests, pyrotechnics, "traditions"); its architectonics; and its textures, noises, smell, and feel.

In short, an evolving "archive" of cultural expressions forged in dialogue with violence and marginalization lies at the heart of my analysis. The use and conceptualization of archives in this work joins that of other recent scholarship. Kirsten Weld's 2014 *Paper Cadavers* builds on the discovery of the hidden, atrocity-filled police archives in Guatemala City to explore the relationships between information, power, and memory. Explicating "archival logics," Weld argues that "we must place archives—with their histories, their contingencies, their silences and gaps, and their politics—at the heart of our research questions" and that "archival thinking... derives its vitality from outside the ivory tower."[39] An example of such vitality is found in Emily Callaci's 2017 *Street Archives and City Life,* on "popular urbanists" in postcolonial Tanzania. Callaci uses "a collection of 'urban texts' [that] might include novels, newspapers, magazines... religious books... graffiti... slogans printed on the sides of busses... oral texts... song lyrics, proverbs, and praise poems" to "examine text-making as a mode of city-making." She adds that (like the sources I deploy) "these texts can be read as unintended archives of an unmapped city" and that "each collection of texts is an unofficial 'street archive.'"[40]

Over the period covered in *Agrotropolis,* "street archives" gave rise to a contested set, or archive, if you will, of popular cultures that congealed in a real-and-imagined "street"—the contested discursive space or cultural commons now dubbed "la KY." In my reading la KY, in turn, took on "archival" status as the referent for a retooled, redefined, and newly invented national identity inflected from above but *built* from below. At all levels, these living archives were and are shot through with violence: war and genocide's legacy and "poverties" (*pobrezas,* as Guatemalans put it) old and new. They gave rise to imaginaries constructed where "first world" dreams meet "third-world" realities, where hope and rage collide.

In a historical era when guerrilla and popular-front activism fragmented in the face of the right-wing's military victory, hope and rage collided in the terrain of everyday life. Though we will meet guerrillas and writers and rock stars in the pages ahead—people whose activism and cultural production made a great difference in the archive of ideas and expressions underpinning life on la KY—*Agrotropolis* is, at its heart, a study of everyday people living ordinary lives. Some identify as Maya, some as ladino, some are from the middle sectors, but most are from the pueblo. This work is meant to complement an excellent and growing literature on Guatemalan activists, gang members, and other people doing extraordinary things. *Agrotropolis* is about de a pie young Guatemalans and about the world they inherited and changed, as it urbanized with them, under conditions no one would have ever chosen.

SCOPE OF THE WORK AND NOTES ON TERMS AND CATEGORIES

I have watched more than a few young Guatemalans grow up. I have visited Guatemala regularly from my first arrival in 1991 and since then have spent roughly half of my adult life in the nation. From 2002 to 2012 I lived year-round in Guatemala, first in the capital and then between greater Antigua and Panajachel, where I maintain a residence. Many of my best Guatemalan friends are from the *clase popular,* the working class. In part, I believe, this is because I first arrived as a young backpacker with no university or institutional affiliation. As such, I tended to meet more "everyday" people than I did activists, guerrillas, or academics. They have shaped my understanding of the nation. This work is neither biographical nor is it the story of my friends and acquaintances, but my experiences and, more important, their experiences enliven and enrich it at every level.

I have written this book with a focus on everyday life and everyday people to fill gaps in an already-existing scholarly literature. It is not intended to be either a thorough political history or an in-depth study of a single town or community, such as might be found in the anthropological literature. *Agrotropolis* complements works by other scholars that cover not only politics but also the history of formal youth and education policies and programs, of spiritual change and religious conversion, of human rights and genocide trials, and of postwar social movements.[41] It also builds on a rich and extensive historical literature on changing identities, discourses of race and indigeneity, and social citizenship in the decades and centuries before the period (1983 to 2012) under study.[42] Finally, while I believe I am providing the most thorough history of Guatemalan rock and other counterculture musical genres in the English-language literature to date, this is not intended either to be a work of ethnomusicology or an encyclopedic history of every single national band, musician, or popular style; such a work remains to be written. In using popular music as a means through which to trace chapín cultural production, slang, and idioms of self-identification, I have tried to select the most popular and influential groups and songs and have focused on a period when rock nacional went "national" in an urbanizing landscape in a newly influential way. While it is not meant to be a music history, and thus may disappoint some fans, *Agrotropolis* does have a "soundtrack" that is easily accessed through simple internet searches. Readers who take the time to look up the songs and to access pictures of the cities and towns discussed will have a much richer experience of the text.

No book can be everything, and *Agrotropolis* also points to areas for further study. A shortcoming of this work, and an area where more scholarship is needed, is in the history of the everyday life, subjectivity, and cultural creativity of working-class women in agro-urban barrios over the period. By dint of my subject-position in a highly gendered society, only men from this social class have shared their experiences with me in ways that go beyond superficial commentary, often not opening up until we had known one another for years. Compounding this problem is the fact that the popular cultural forms under review in this work are largely male-coded. After much hand-wringing, I decided to go with the strength of my fieldwork and have tried to mitigate the gender imbalance by including the stories of strong female historical actors and by analyzing both men's and women's relationships to the changing political economy.

This book's scope is national, and it references global phenomena. That said, it uses central case studies to familiarize readers with several select areas. These are found in Huehuetenango Department and its Huista region that spans high-mountain municipalities near the Mexican border, and in the departments of Sololá and (to a lesser extent) Quetzaltenango. It adds information on Totonicapán and Chimaltenango Departments, using primary research but drawing on the findings of scholars who have already studied these areas intensively. Guatemalanists will note that similar urbanization is also seen both in Maya-majority and primarily ladino regions mentioned only in passing or not at all. I hope that this work will complement the rich anthropological literature and spark further local and regional histories.

I now turn to terminology, beginning with words related to the *urban* and the *rural*. This work rejects an urban/rural binary, situating Guatemalan social space within the greater process of "planetary urbanization" and what the urban theorist Álvaro Sevilla-Buitrago calls "original extended urbanization."[43] Without deploying problematic, taxonomic neologisms such as "rururban" and "periurban," however, it is possible to write about the areas under review only by using words such as *urban/rural, city, town,* and *village*. I use *agro-urban* specifically to reference the porous boundaries between such spaces, and my use of common, readable terms should not be taken to constitute the unintentional reinscription of the categories I seek to disrupt. Many terms correspond to Guatemalan territorial divisions, which begin with 22 departments (analogous to U.S. states) and 340 municipalities (akin to U.S. counties), all with *cabeceras* (capitals or seats).[44] Cabeceras, especially departmental but also municipal, were always to some extent more "urban" than their surrounding *aldeas* (villages), *caseríos* (hamlets), and *parajes* (household clusters).[45] Some people would say that the departmental and municipal cabecera of Huehuetenango was already a "city" by 1970, when it was big but "rustic"; others would say it did not "become" one until the 1990s, by which time it had mushroomed and had new street gangs, shantytowns, stoplights, migrants, and malls. "City" is a subjective word, but it is an unquestionable, empirical fact that urbanization (physically, socially, and culturally) has occurred. *Agrotropolis* traces a process of "agro-urbanization" in which already-existing networks matured and grew and in which the metabolism between cabeceras and aldeas and *caseríos* changed in historic ways from the 1980s to the 2010s. It seeks neither to engage in debates about dated spatial typologies, nor to be read as "defining" the "urban" by a single metric or phenomenon, such as population growth, the presence of gangs and criminals, or the appearance of shantytowns, for example.

I place *youth* within the same frame of analysis through which I view the *urban;* that is, I relate this word's multiple meanings—in local, national, and global conversations—to evolving social space as perceived, conceived, and lived.[46] In framing youth as dialogically related to the urbanization of social space, this work builds on scholarship on youth as an analytical category in Latin America—a "concept," as Valeria Manzano puts it, that historically "embodied hopes and anxieties projected onto claims for change."[47] *Agrotropolis* primarily seeks to explore how young Guatemalans from different classes and backgrounds articulated, experienced, contested, performed, and dialogically defined "youth" in changing ways over time and space in an urbanizing society. Manipulated in politics, debated in public discourse, and contested in everyday life as a fluid assemblage of identities, "youth" and "youth cultures" comprise practices and imaginaries that flow through and are coconstitutive of social space. In short, they are inseparable from the urbanization of social space in Guatemala.

Just like shape-shifting agro-urban space, then, *youth* is both a real and imagined terrain. *Generations,* however, are almost completely imaginary. While I speak of generations (notably, the "revolutionary" 1960s–70s generation, the "lost" generation of the 1980s, and the "new rock/age-of-peace" generation of the 1990s, for example), it should be noted these constructs are more related to changes in the political economy and popular culture than they are to demographic realities. Siblings might span these generations, and any given person might have been *jóven* during more than one of the periods discussed. As in English-language popular music, "old" bands keep producing "new" youth culture material long after their members turn thirty. Additionally, categories of styles and tastes may appear as mutually exclusive or as fixed identities but absolutely are not. A person might be both an antimining activist and a slam dancer; a formal or de a pie Maya-rights advocate and a rapper (like the Ijatz B-boys); an Evangelical and a techno fan; a traje-wearing woman and a *reggaetón* lover who hits the disco on Saturday night; or a "youth" completely uninterested in globalized pop culture. Additionally, we should remember that people grow up; today's fauxhawksporting emo could be tomorrow's accountant wearing slacks and a button-down. I pass along a frequently heard request—both spoken to me personally and found in document after document—that we please refrain from putting Guatemalans in boxes. They are people, like anyone else.

But are they chapines? Chapín (*chapina* in the feminine) is a "good" word, not a slur; a national nickname, it is used in ways analogous to how New Zealanders call themselves *kiwis* and Costa Ricans dub themselves *ticos*. However, this moniker has racist and classist origins. The terms *chapín, chapina,* and *chapinismo*—meaning the popular body of national slang and its associated *forma de ser*—are all objects of debate among academics and activists.[48] I will risk backlash by stating that in my and my informants' opinion, the pueblo has reappropriated the word. The Ijatz B-boys use chapín to refer to themselves, and the word is in their lyrics. It appears over and over on popular culture websites. It's in TV ads; it's on the radio; it's on T-shirts.... It's ubiquitous. The worries about the political correctness of this word are genuine, but they tend to come from above, not from below. Chapinismo is at the very center of this study, and readers should be aware of the debates about this term, which I attempt to use only as it is deployed in popular culture.

Another phrase that needs to be qualified is "servility." Let me state from the outset that I in no way believe that people were ever really "servile." This book argues that young so-called castas have confected an alternative popular nationalism and have put an end to servility as a cultural form. It is critical to note that the term *servility* is not mine but—like castas—is taken from Guatemalan discourse on the subject (see, for example, the comments on "bowed heads" and "obedient servants" in the earlier discussion of shumos). As scholars such as James Scott remind us, any performance of servility would be only that, an act.[49] Discourses about servility are presented in the pages ahead. For present purposes suffice it to say that thirty-six years of armed revolution alone—and five centuries of resistance and cultural retention—should be enough evidence to debunk any idea that poor Guatemalans were ever "servile" in "real" ways.

STRUCTURE OF THE WORK

Agrotropolis takes up the challenge of conducting an analysis that integrates the built landscape, the political economy, and sociocultural change. Each chapter's title is a phrase taken from popular music that sums up the central theme that holds these moving parts together. Characters and their stories run through the narrative and tie the chapters together, as does the use of theory taken primarily from the political philosopher Enrique Dussel, Henri Lefebvre, and the scholars in *Implosions/Explosions,* the work on planetary urbanization edited by Neil Brenner.[50]

Chapter 1, "Power's Destiny," argues that in a nation built from below and sustained by the economic activity of the poor majority, the capital-city "street" became a theater on which de a pie Guatemalans began to retrench, retool, and remake identities, while historical actors in the agro-urbanizing provinces asserted new discourses of Maya nationalism even as they grappled with ongoing military occupation. It begins with basic historical background, weaving a gloss of political and economic changes and interethnic debates together with a synopsis of youth countercultures in Guatemala City and urbanizing forces in the provinces from 1950 to 1983. The urbanizing forces of war, state terror, counterinsurgency, poverty, exploitation, and genocide all structured the questions of "power's destiny" that took on new dimensions as Guatemala began its martial return to civilian rule in the 1980s. So too did economic changes, as a rural population displaced by war swelled city neighborhoods and counterinsurgent agricultural programs and the cultivation of nontraditional agro-exports (NTAs) began to change agrarian lifeways. Questions of ethnicity, class, and caste were bound up in politics, in evolving and emerging discourses of nationalism, and in idioms of self-identification. While urban subcultures such as death metal were appearing in Guatemala City, rejecting social norms, people in all corners of the nation were debating what they termed the "ethnic question." All this contestation occurred within a shattered body politic characterized as a "state without a nation," during a period in which militarism and violence were imbricated not just in the political economy but in everyday life, in overt and subtle ways. Fights over "power's destiny" in the years around the 1986 return to civilian rule have unfolded in the nation ever since, in dialogue with the neoliberalizing global and national political economies.

Chapter 2, called "Americamorfosis" after an Alux Nahual rock album, spans the years between the 1986 return to civilian rule and the new system's consolidation after a 1993 constitutional crisis. It challenges before-and-after narratives in which neoliberalism and consumer culture gave rise to an apolitical, apathetic new generation. It argues that events through the Cold War's end show less the *replacement* of developmentalist and counterinsurgent policies and discourses about socioeconomic development than they do their *dis-*

placement, and that anxieties about the "Americamorfosis" of social space were displaced on youth. The chapter begins with the dialogue between the recrudescent Left and the state, which was slowly and partially adopting neoliberal policies. It maps such changes against moral panic about *robaniños* (kidnappers of children) in the city and discourses of culturally corrupted youth in the still-warring highlands—Guatemalan variants of panics seen around the Western world as regimes of capitalist accumulation transformed. As agrourbanization and Maya political activism accelerated, panic about de a pie, youthful historical actors helped to erase the ways in which they gave life to the social and Maya power movements. Culturally assertive provincial youth began a process that would later bring idioms of resistance and Maya pride to national popular youth culture. Panic about youth, however, was not entirely misplaced; youth culture was taking antisocial and violent turns in Guatemala City. The chapter ends with a discussion of the capital's ladino, middle and upper-class "lost generation" and the brutal interclass street wars that some of its members started when they attacked casta break-dancers in the capital— wars that, when read from below, highlight cultural assertiveness on the part of urban castas analogous to that seen among provincial Maya youth.

Chapter 3 details the evolution of social space from 1994 to 1998, the years around the 1996 Peace Accords. It argues that agro-urban "city-regions" began to form in the late 1990s, when the optimism of peace was tempered by spreading crime and vigilantism, building "double negatives" into expressions of identity and nationalism.[51] The title, "Not Fish, Not Iguana," is a lyric from a song that became a national youth anthem when new-generation rock nacional leaped the capital city's borders. As this peaceful music popularized, both organized and common crime exploded. Local strongmen, often related to military or paramilitary structures, used the need for "security" to cement their power, and the phenomenon of lynching accused criminals by burning them alive began. In this violent environment, however, agro-urban and village youth asserted themselves in ways that were productive, if not always positive. They supported the Mayan movement, formed gangs, and participated in popular culture and the *libertad de expresión* (freedom of expression) of which the new bands sang. They unconsciously challenged the nation's caste system as they began to make national popular culture their own. Poor Guatemala City castas joined in this from-below cultural creativity, coming to represent a missing "authenticity" for middle- and upper-class youth, as revealed by an against-the-grain reading of rock counterculture publications. When their bands began to tour in the highlands, ladino rockers marveled at the even more authentic *chapines locales* but completely missed the significance of their cultural assertiveness. De a pie youth in the urbanizing provinces melded tradition, pop culture, and rebellion as the Mayan movement was at its peak and the optimism of peace was at a high—a time when the war-torn past was not yet over and the hoped-for future had not yet arrived.

Chapter 4, "If Only You Could Live Here," details the emergence of a discursive, national "KY" (real-and-imagined city street) from 1998 to 2004 in an age of privatization, commercialization, and mediatization. It argues that—as new democratic politics failed to express popular human will, becoming a corrupt and violent free-for-all, and as the economy failed to deliver on postpeace promises of progress—peoples' withdrawal to inner spheres gave rise to a reconfigured outer sphere. Musicians wrote songs with titles like "Interna/Externa"; Guatemala City–based essayists wrote about a society characterized by "masks" and "uniforms"; and the anthropologist Diane Nelson, in the same period, published an article called "Stumped Identities" that, among other arguments, spoke of a "phantasmatic split between public and private" in Guatemala.[52] I draw on these ideas to trace the ways in which such public/private splits instantiated involutions through which frustrated political will found an outlet in a reconfiguring chapinismo, or alternative popular nationalism, shot through with hatred for the state. Youth cultures began to "centralize" and forge a chapinismo-based national commons, providing a kind of grassroots "centralization" that unfolded in dialogue with official cultural decentralization programs. In the new millennium the liberty associated with youthful recreation contrasted with the liberty of criminals and clandestine groups that thrived under decentralization. The result was a more exciting world to live in that was (as ever, but in new ways) completely unlivable. The chapter's conclusion uses what I call "the moral economy of the tuc-tuc" to symbolize the Guatemalan variant of the gig economy. This economy relegated its ever-more-educated and capable working-class youth to a future in which the only "secure" thing seemed to be certain poverty, unless, in the spirit of "if only you could live here," they migrated to toil in El Norte.

Chapter 5's title, a rap lyric, "In the Jaws of These Gray Cities," references the emergence of the Guatemalan agrotropolis. The chapter shows how, by 2012, cultural expressions on la KY had become the archive of a retooled and more inclusive grassroots vernacular of national identity. It argues that bottom-up expressions of chapín youth culture, despite evolving in dialogue with corporate media and consumer capitalism, nevertheless formed a critical field of production through which everyday Guatemalans rejected codes of servility and gave rise to a more inclusive alternative popular nationalism. The chapter first explores how Guatemala's agrotropolis emerged in the intersections between wide-ranging economic, social, and cultural transformations in the age of political decentralization and the CAFTA-DR free-trade agreement. It amplifies the phrase "territorial interventions," which the Inter-American Development Bank used in its projects to remap the nation's political and financial landscapes, to include the reimagining of Guatemala through various types of tourism and in the memories of the diasporic community. Such maps and imaginaries came together at the level of individual bodies and subjectivities. From-below and from-above representations of identity—of beauty, sexual attractiveness, and chapín/chapina authenticity—dialogically made the pueblo into the nation in a way it had never been before. Grassroots expressions of chapinismo went viral in the age of Facebook and YouTube, as well as in the spreading genre of rap music. Cultural productivity chipped away at the hierarchy of castas but at the same time expressed the realities of a brutal and tragic world. The chapter's final section details the violence of everyday life "in the jaws" of Guatemala's "gray cities," using a case study of lynching in Panajachel to demonstrate the emotional and psychological effects of violence and exclusion, the inseparable partners of cultural productivity in agrotropolis.

The conclusion takes its title, "Mi País," from a Ricardo Arjona song that headlined a 2012 Pepsi campaign, "Guatemorfosis," designed to convince young people to save the nation by behaving better. Even though youth were still having ugly online fights about caste and status, "barrio cool" had arguably won out over "elite cool." In the Guatemalan agrotropolis—a global-but-local, cosmopolitan space that had come to include both the capital and the provinces—Mayan rap and pop joined a chorus of national, youthful cultural production. Guatemala was *"mi país"* for the popular classes as never before. Drawing on a rich history of local traditions, political resistance, and ethnic expressions, de a pie Guatemalans had created an alternative popular nationalism and rejected five hundred years of servility as a cultural form. Their victory was bittersweet. The castas won cultural power, but in the nation, as around the globe, economic and political power remained in the hands of a small elite. At the time of this writing, eight years after the "end of the world," when 13 Baktun cycled away, there is no clear path toward power for the pueblo. But Guatemalans have an extraordinary history of resistance, and their nation's younger generations, I argue, are no exception to that rule. In an age of global urbanization and neoliberalization, when popular will around the planet was thwarted and abused, they have used the power available to them in historic ways.

I

"Power's Destiny"

POLITICAL ECONOMY AND
POPULAR CULTURE TO 1986

ACCORDING TO "BLACKO" GONZÁLEZ, lead singer of the heavy-metal band Sangre Humana, Raquel Blandón de Cerezo was the "*máxima impulsora* of rock and metal in Guatemala." The soft-spoken First Lady began a tradition of holding Christmastime rock concerts for youth in Guatemala City's *parque central* in 1986, near the end of the first year of civilian rule. Blacko and the other members of a band whose name means "Human Blood" were surprised to find themselves onstage. The 1986 Concert for Peace, in Blacko's view, marked the moment when, unbelievably, capital-city counterculture groups were disinterred from the hidden "under" scene and given an unexpected national spotlight.[1]

Imagine, for a moment, the cross-section of society that was likely present at this concert. Certainly, there were sharpshooters on the rooftops and police and soldiers on patrol, as at any public gathering. Eyeing them warily were the young and not-so-young urban *rockeros* in the audience: a thirty-something generation of hippie-inflected nonconformists who had embraced a new kind of "cool" in the 1970s while their classmates went off to join the guerrillas; a "teens and twenties" generation of hard rockers and *metaleros;* and preteens who would later pioneer a new genre of Guatemalan rock that would leap the capital's boundaries and spread around the nation. University students were there, activists and leftists among them. Possibly some university-trained leaders of the burgeoning Mayan movement were in attendance, along with Maya farmers visiting the city from the provinces to sell their produce in the wholesale markets. Perhaps a general or colonel or two watched the show, no doubt with frowns.

It is entirely plausible that death-squad operatives and torturers mingled in the crowd that day. Certainly their children did, many of whom, like middle- and upper-class teens whose parents had less gruesome careers, considered themselves part of the *mara,* the in-crowd, the cool "gang." The show was free, and one imagines the tensions in the crowd as relatively well-off youth rubbed elbows with the youth from the shantytowns. The other maras, the street gangs for which Guatemala and its Central American neighbors would later become so famous, had only recently appeared in the capital city. Even though many of the first gang members were probably from lower-middle and middle-class neighborhoods, in the minds of urban upper-sector youth, the *mareros,* or "gangbangers," were impoverished, bottom-caste creatures spat out by the slums.[2]

Many residents of Guatemala City's slums had been born outside the city. The shantytowns had been growing for decades, paralleling the decay of the so-called middle class as wealth in the economy failed to trickle downward. Food-for-work programs, war, genocide, and counterinsurgency had pushed thousands more Guatemalans out of the countryside. They fled not only to refugee camps in Mexico and to the United States for low-paid jobs but also to the capital. Rural-to-urban migrants, many of them Maya, settled in the city's growing "precarious neighborhoods." At least a few of these "urban campesino/as" must have been in the audience that day, along with their children, some of whom were probably shining shoes or selling Chiclets and "loosie" cigarettes.[3] The youngest of these were the first of a baby boom that within a decade would make Guatemala one of the most youthful countries on earth. In this new democracy, in a country still at war, the question of what kind of nation these children would inherit and create was very much alive.

A Sangre Humana song, "Destino del poder" (Power's Destiny), evoked what was at stake.[4] Battles over power in Guatemala transformed after the 1981–83 genocide, as the military high command oversaw a martial "return to democracy" that resulted in the election of the center-right, civilian Christian Democrat, Vinicio Cerezo (1986–91). No one quite believed that the generals would give up their grip on the state, but Cerezo survived numerous coup attempts and completed his term. In the years leading up to his election and through his presidency, the social movements, the Mayan movement, and the armed resistance became more militant. Interelite battles pitted older agro-exporting classes against more neoliberal rivals. Sea changes in agriculture unfolded. New mafias arose, and narcotraffic began to warp the body politic. In Guatemala City, youth countercultures evidenced social change. The mid-1980s are remembered for the appearance of the street gangs, but these years also saw the flowering of heavy-metal and hard-rock subcultures. In the city's poor neighborhoods, new styles and cholo identifications tied to hip-hop appeared. These capital-city youth subcultures—like the greater, power-laden changes in the political economy—formed a part of the prehistory of social and cultural change soon to manifest around the nation as the process of urbanization in provincial population centers sped up.

As Guatemala's political economy changed through the 1980s, the role of youth in political discourse changed as well. Blandón's new Concerts for Peace were an early example of top-down promotion of youthful self-expression. Counterculture bands like Sangre Humana—excoriated in the press and popular discourse at the time as aberrant and antisocial—had every reason to be astonished at their invitation to perform. Even years later they would be remembered by commentators as representatives of an apolitical generation, one whose apathy and hedonism signaled a neoliberal turn toward mass media–driven consumer culture, which, in critics' view, foreshadowed the fall of the revolutionary Left and its project of social transformation.[5] The lyrics of "Destino del poder," full of rage, however, lend themselves to a political reading. "The sky is turning dark / It's the fault of the man / with all his crazed desire, desire for power," the song begins. "Nothing matters to him / Only getting his damned power / Who will be the next one he wants to kill? / It could be that it's you."[6]

These lyrics suggest a critique of the right-wing, the military, and militarism. In the years around the return to civilian rule, society was structured by counterinsurgency, battered by violence, and in the midst of economic and political transition. Scholars have established that militarism and barbarism born of and imposed through military conflict were smuggled into the Guatemalan body politic in ways that would make its new democracy—and later its "postpeace" period from the mid-1990s to the mid-2010s—remarkably violent. Carlota McAllister and Diane Nelson have titled their work on this dynamic *War by Other Means*. A 2015 collection of essays published in Guatemala also had an evocative title that referenced a society riddled with terrors: *Dinosaurio reloaded*. The "dinosaur" of violence refused its own extinction. Within the rubric of an ongoing civil war and in the context of a changing global political economy, militarism infected the connective tissue of Guatemalan society at its every articulation.[7]

"Power's Destiny" not only critiqued this militarism but also captured the spirit of what was becoming a struggle for power at all levels of Guatemala's postgenocide society. In the 1980s, a new phase of questioning and contesting national belonging began. These often violent debates broke along lines of class, race, ethnicity, culture, and caste, as seen both in intense political organizing and in evolving youth culture and disillusionment. Guatemala entered the 1980s with a social system of castas that were the product of centuries of exploitative relations of production and exchange. In the wake of genocide, grassroots contestation over class, caste, and belonging intensified and took unexpected turns. Everyday, de a pie historical actors began to rework the grammar of social identity, layering cultural conflict over battles about the economy and politics.

The various participants and onlookers whom we can imagine were at the first Concert for Peace in 1986 symbolize the myriad constituencies in the struggles over "Power's Destiny" that were emerging by the mid-1980s and that matured in the years ahead. The battles over power between and within these sectors of society played out in arenas ranging from the growing system of political parties, to the guerrilla organizations and the social movements, to the increasingly vibrant world of municipal governance. Importantly, however, they were *also* waged in everyday ways on the capital city's streets and in townships around the country at the very dawn of their transformation from rural to agro-urban space. In mutually conditioning, dialogical ways, the evolving and often grassroots and youthful battles over "power's destiny" reshaped the multiple valences of what it meant to be Guatemalan. Violence was bound up in the nation's road to peace, but so too were productive reactions to violence that laid the groundwork for challenges from below to the nation's caste system in the years ahead—significantly, not just from political actors but also from the de a pie members of the generations just born and yet to be born, in the city, in urbanizing space in the provinces, and in the still very rural hinterlands on the war's front lines.

The post-1986 struggles over power were grounded in a long history of war and changes in the relations between classes, castes, and the urban and the rural. The sections that follow trace these transformations chronologically, providing a brief historical overview before delving into debates over nationalism and the "ethnic question" and the militarization of the body politic in the first half of the 1980s. We begin with the arrival of rock and roll in the 1950s and the outbreak of war in the decade that followed.

EARLY YOUTH TERRITORIES, 1950S–1960S

The guerrillas of the 1960s were the third revolutionary generation of the twentieth century in Guatemala. The first had ushered in a decade of political and cultural experimentation, union organizing, and forward-looking modernist plans in the 1920s, only to be crushed in the 1930s, and the second had brought the democratic revolution of 1944 to fruition, only to be crushed by the CIA-led invasion of 1954. The intense polarization of the Cold War period, exacerbated by the United States' destabilization of the nation's politics, played out tragically in Guatemala in the 1960s and beyond. Unlike their predecessors, the revolutionary youth of the 1960s eschewed electoral politics as a means to change and also rejected the gradualism of older communists, who wanted to work within the system, modernize the nation, and oversee an evolution to socialism as a class of wage laborers grew. Instead, the new generation of Marxists, inspired by Cuba, sought to overthrow the state by force of arms.[8]

The first guerrillas were nationalistic junior army officers who staged a quickly defeated barracks uprising in 1960, protesting the training of foreign soldiers in Guatemala for what later turned out to be the Bay of Pigs operation. After two years in exile, they returned as Marxist-Leninist revolutionaries. Though always supported by an urban guerrilla movement, the first phase of their Cuban-inspired insurrection primarily unfolded in the eastern part of the country, called the *oriente*, where the relatively sparse population was mostly ladino.[9]

The military conducted scorched-earth campaigns against the guerrillas in the *oriente*, while simultaneously accelerating counterinsurgent, capitalist agricultural development initiatives around the countryside. Many of these programs were reconfigured, anticommunist versions of modernizing plans that dated to the 1944–54 revolution, including educational campaigns in literacy and agronomy. Agrarian "development zones" and army-led Integrated Community Development programs aimed to commercialize agriculture and promote obeisant forms of citizenship, while a multiyear Seminar on National Social Integration sought to identify ways in which the state could more efficiently incorporate and "civilize" the indigenous population. Guatemala City, meanwhile, a growing metropolis, was ground zero in a project to turn the urban proletariat into what the government envisioned as a "new middle class."[10]

Attempts at mixing counterinsurgency with rural and urban social-engineering programs in the 1950s and 1960s were largely unsuccessful, and the capital city and the agrarian provinces were not as separate as they appeared to be. In the years after the 1954 counterrevolution, a rudimentary highway network began to link the nation together, occasioning increased rural-to-urban migration and transmigration from the countryside. The formation of the Central American Common Market in 1960 triggered a spate of industrialization in the city, most of it spearheaded by foreign corporations. When Guatemala's thirty-six-year-long war began, its capital city was increasingly a nexus where the existing urban working class mixed with new arrivals from the countryside. Campesino migrants often maintained hometown ties, engendering a web of urban-rural interaction that linked town to city in ways that complicate a binary city/country divide. Country-city dialogue lent urban elements to outlying towns and villages and campesino culture and flavor to Guatemala City neighborhoods.[11]

Together, urban and rural working-class Guatemalans built city neighborhoods. In the markets, they provided the food that kept the population alive. They also expanded and created new levels of the bottom-up "informal economy" that over time came to represent some three-quarters of all economic activity in the nation and that increasingly tied country and city together. I have argued elsewhere that calling this life-sustaining economy "informal" is ideological; it was *the* economy, and relegating it to a secondary status hides the central role of female proprietorship and women's labor in its functioning, understates its centrality, and concords with the top-down thinking of midcentury social engineers. Similarly, discourses that reproduce a real but oversimplified ladino-Maya divide occlude the complex articulations and lived experience of ethnicity, class, and caste not just in city barrios but also in an evolving sociospatial geography that spanned and superseded the porous borders between the urban and the rural.[12]

The same logic applies to the diffusion of "foreign" music like rock and roll, which popularized in the years around the outbreak of war. While not wholly incorrect, the unexamined labeling of such cultural forms as *only* exogenous consumer culture associated with an expanding, global, capitalistic "youth market" hides bottom-up realities. To be clear, such styles were *far* from being the most historically "important" phenomena at the dawn of a war in a nation with an impoverished majority and a social structure described in Richard Adams's classic text as *Crucifixion by Power*.[13] They were simply one small thread in a changing social fabric. That fabric, however—like the nation's economy, working-class neighborhoods, and rural and urban landscape—was built from below, not from above, and following this one thread within it has much to reveal about Guatemala's class/caste relations and its invisibilized de a pie majority. Foregrounding the people in the margins and applying what Mark Driscoll calls "the methodological optic of the peripheral a priori" to this one thread of popular culture illuminates greater changes in both

Guatemala's urban/rural geography and its complex (and multilingual) grammar of ethnicity, caste, and class—changes that some three decades later would manifest as part of what Enrique Dussel calls the identity-based "irruption of new rights" that are "imposed a posteriori by the struggling movements" of "the exploited, the excluded, the nonequals."[14]

At its appearance in Guatemala, rock and roll seemed to have little to do with the exploited and the nonequals. It was associated with a foreign middle class, "whiteness," and modernity. Rock and roll erupted in the pages of the press, on Radio TGW, and in programming on the newly founded TV Channel 8, in 1957. By 1959 there were already twenty-three AM stations in the capital alone, and the city had its first truly homegrown rock-and-roll band, Los Black Cats. Soon other groups that would cover foreign songs and imitate their tones for middle- and upper-class audiences emerged, such as Los Holiday's and Los Picapiedra (The Flintstones). The music that would later be at the heart of debates about youth counterculture was, in the late 1950s and early 1960s, in line with social conformism, gender norms, and anticommunist nationalism.[15]

After 1961, when the capital's first radio station devoted exclusively to rock and roll and youth pop culture went on the air, the situation began to change. Discontent with national and municipal politics boiled over into a popular revolt early in 1962, and soon after, with the arrival of the first active guerrilla fronts, Guatemala's *guerra popular y revolucionaria* began. By about this time, historian Mario Castañeda Maldonado writes, the city's commercial market had begun to give rise to a new kind of separation of popular tastes based on class, beginning at the grassroots. Capital-city youth—among them many who threw up the barricades in the uprisings of early 1962—held rock-and-roll gatherings, called *repasos,* that split along neighborhood, and therefore economic, lines. Some *repasos* saw college and private high school youth renting salons in well-off districts. Others were held in the neighborhoods where city-born workers and new rural arrivals mixed, the working-class *colonias* and the shantytowns.[16]

In an attempt to sanitize what was happening in these lower-class city neighborhoods, the state invested in *colonia* construction explicitly aimed at the creation of a "new middle class."[17] While middle sectors grew, lower sectors exploded, as the bottom-up economy took on its contemporary form and industrialization gave rise to an age of what scholars have called "polyester," "urban loneliness," and *"modernidad a la chapina"* with a quirky mix of futuristic elements and conservative tradition. New kinds of class-based identities were in formation as the union movement grew and popular revolution spread. Middle-sector youth, often deploring their own "bourgeois" origins, began to join the resistance.[18]

Joining the guerrilla resistance was itself a form of youth rebellion, albeit a deadly serious one; Pablo Monsanto, the commander of the FAR (Rebel Armed Forces), later titled his memoir on the war in the 1960s *Somos los jóvenes rebeldes* (We are the rebel youth).[19] Primarily, however, armed rebellion was a response to structural poverty in a nation in which a democratic revolution had been overthrown in 1954. Distribution of land and wealth was grossly unequal. Agricultural labor was based on peonage, and poor indigenous campesinos—the class of people insultingly called *mozos*—increasingly had to migrate as seasonal workers to the fincas over the second half of the twentieth century. Urban workers earned substandard wages, and many ended up in the so-called informal economy. In the face of these conditions, popular resistance grew. The state increasingly used terror and technologies of surveillance and control to discipline an insurrectionary population. The United States supported state terror, notably in Operation Cleanup, which resulted in the assassination of scores of progressive, labor, social movement, and leftist leaders. Right-wing death squads appeared in major population centers, making *disappear* a transitive verb (as in "to disappear someone") by 1966.[20]

The history of youth countercultures in Guatemala is inextricably bound up with that of war and state terror. Around the same time as the death squads began appearing, nonconformist "rock" branched off from rock-and-roll. As elsewhere, rock came to be associated with hippie styles and the social subversion of drug use and licentiousness. Paradoxically, however, in a country at war, rock counterculture also provided a sector of the youth population with a way to rebel that did not involve risking one's life by joining the guerrillas or the social movements. Castañeda writes that many youth who self-identified as rockeros avoided politics, retreating to the private sphere in an era of lethal public threats. This early example of how violence permeates the relationship between the public and the private in popular culture as in social life more generally in contemporary Guatemala also manifested in urban space. The ongoing, neighborhood-based *repasos* created a Guatemala City–specific, class-based geography of grassroots economic markets where music was performed and consumed and where goods like alcohol and cigarettes and services associated with concerts and nightlife were purchased. In a landscape pockmarked with guerrilla safe houses and government torture chambers, urban youth territories based on musical styles and counterculture identities were beginning to emerge.[21]

HEIGHTS OF REVOLUTION AND TERROR, 1968–1983

Such was the scene in 1968, when a young intellectual named Mario Payeras flew home from East Germany to join the revolutionary cause. A multilingual ladino native of Chimaltenango, Payeras had studied philosophy first in Mexico and then at Karl Marx University in Leipzig, where he remained for several years after graduating. When Payeras returned to Guatemala, the revolution was shifting gears, and his career in the years that followed traces the major changes in the war. He was among the founders of a new guerrilla army whose emergence bespoke ideological divisions on the left, as would events later in his life. He was a protagonist in opening up the major fronts of war in the nation's Mayan highlands, as was his life partner, Yolanda Colom, whom he met in the Cuchumatanes Mountains of Huehuetenango Department in 1974. The stories of this guerrilla couple intersect with many of the major historical changes in Guatemala's battles over "power's destiny."[22]

By 1969 scorched-earth campaigns had effectively defeated the fledgling guerrillas in the *oriente*. They regrouped in Guatemala City, from where, in the 1970s, they spread into the Mayan highlands (the west, or *occidente*), beginning a politically charged Maya-ladino encounter that profoundly conditioned later iterations of grassroots nationalisms. A new guerrilla contingent by this time was the Guerrilla Army of the Poor (EGP). Mario Payeras, who helped to form the EGP in the years before it announced its existence, was a commander, and used the nom de guerre "Comandante Benedicto." The new EGP cadres joined the older FAR and, within a few years, another new group, ORPA (Revolutionary Organization of the People in Arms) as one of the three major combatant forces.[23]

In 1969, when the nearly defeated guerrillas were planning the move into the highlands, young Guatemalans attended "Woodstockito." The authorities had come to regard youth counterculture as subversive, and the concert was held against police wishes. New rock bands like Apple Pie and SOS performed. After this concert Rony de León, the vocalist of SOS, got arrested on dubious charges of conspiracy to kidnap the Haitian ambassador. He gave concerts in prison before his release early the next year. Police and paramilitary teams in the early 1970s cut off young men's long hair in the street and hassled women for wearing miniskirts. Under Gen. Carlos Arana Osorio (1970–74), youth rebellion, countercultures, and drug use assumed their lasting place in national political discourse, particularly after a 1971 report on youth and the family sparked an antidrug campaign.[24]

Both rock and revolutionary folk music popularized over the 1970s in spite of state oppression. Rock bands such as Plástico Pesado, Abraxas, and, later in the decade, "Caballo Loco, Pastel de Fresa, Banda Clásica, Ataúd Eléctrico, Aeroplano de Jade" had a "more acid, more underground" sound with "aggressive distortion" inspired by bands like Grand Funk Railroad, The Who, and Led Zeppelin. Young people following these bands were called *onderos* (*la onda,* a term that came from Mexico, roughly translates as "the vibe") as opposed to "square" *fresa* youth who listened to pop music, dressed properly, and believed in the system.[25] As drug culture spread, the onderos, packing concerts in the thousands, increasingly came to characterize the capital's youth music scene. In 1974 a huge concert called Lámpara de Acuario (Lamp of Aquarius) portended the spread of ondero counterculture. It was held at a finca in the Kaqchikel Maya municipality of San Juan Sacatepéquez, a place soon to urbanize and become part of the capital-city metro region. Lámpara de Acuario was attended by the capital's Radio Juventud, by "'Karishnanda,' the spiritual guide of the Templo Yoga of zone 8," and by foreign hippies.[26] Hippies and onderos, however, did not lay sole claim to popular youth culture in the 1970s. Many leftists followed *trova,* revolutionary folk music related to the *nueva canción* movement.[27] La Estudiantina, a student music organization at USAC (University of San Carlos of Guatemala, the national university), promoted *trova* with songs like "La Samba del Che," "El plebeyo" (The plebeian), and "Defiendo mi tierra" (I defend my land).[28] Singer-songwriter José Chamalé, who later, in 1988, helped found the prorevolutionary Círculo Experimental de Cantautores de Guatemala (Experimental Circle of Guatemalan Singer-Songwriters), was an early champion of *trova*. Crafted in dialogue with Radio Cuba, *trova* became an important genre that would outlive the war itself. A far greater influence, however, came from the ondero movement, which ultimately paved the way to national rock.[29]

In popular and academic history alike, onderos are not remembered largely for participating in politics, yet the lines between this counterculture identity and political action were likely more blurred than any simplistic story suggests. For example, the cynical guerrillas portrayed in *Los compañeros* (Comrades), Marco Antonio Flores's 1976 work hailed as starting the age of the new Guatemalan novel, inhabited a world filled with drugs, sex, and vulgarity. Flores's novel both cautions us to avoid binary distinctions between groups such as onderos and political youth and reminds us that much of the street slang commonly associated with the turning millennium had been around for quite some time.[30] So too had many of the 1970s' "new" wave of ondero rockers. The bands who played for the onderos were often led by veterans of 1960s rock. They helped to give rise to a new generation of *pesados* (heavies) who liked hard rock and heavy metal.

These changes unfolded over the course of the 1970s, a decade that marked a major turning point in Guatemala's war. The guerrilla movements reached their height, the social movements unleashed the greatest period of activism and protest in the nation's history, and the moving of the theater of war to the Mayan highlands occasioned an impactful and historic encounter between urban and rural Guatemalans. Many of the organizers and guerrillas who moved into the countryside hailed from the middle and upper classes. One such guerrilla was Yolanda Colom, who worked with the EGP as an educator, helping to open fronts in the wilderness while specializing in literacy training and political formation with the rank and file. It was in a guerrilla camp, in 1974, that she met Mario Payeras.

Yolanda Colom's memoir speaks to the ladino-Maya encounter in guerrilla camps. It also bears evidence to the deep divide between ladinos and Mayas that made the intricacies of indigenous society—cosmovision and beliefs, internal class and caste differences, systems of local self-governance, and a history of resistance and rebellion—invisible to their ladino compatriots. Colom was working in remote villages, far from the cabeceras, where the educated indigenous elite, for centuries "hinge-men" to the ladino state, had been building on the unfulfilled promises of the 1944–54 revolution to remake local politics and to begin to take over mayoralties.[31] Colom commented on none of this. She wrote of indigenous campesinos' dire poverty and of their deference to the local ladino leaders and *finqueros*. She saw how indigenous *compañeros/as* treated their ladino guerrilla comrades with a similarly servile attitude, changing their verbs from informal *vos* to formal *usted* and staying silent when they disagreed. She noted that, far from thinking themselves as unified "indigenous people" (the term "Maya" was not yet in currency), local ethnic groups, such as Ixiles, did not even self-identify as "Ixiles." Instead, they identified by villages, and intervillage rivalries and feuds abounded, she wrote, as did machismo, forced marriage, and polygamy. In guerrilla camps and solidarity movements, by Colom's telling, all this slowly began to change. Women were at least discursively given equal status to men in the guerrilla hierarchy; they began to question patriarchy. Colom's narrative positions guerrilla squadrons as sites where people began to break down deeply ingrained social codes. A new generation of militant Maya youngsters began to look their ladino peers directly in the eye and dream together with them of social and economic justice. Ladino-Maya encounters in guerrilla camps—the encounters that Colom lived personally—certainly contributed to cross-ethnic dialogue and to the diminution of so-called servility. Far more influential in this regard, however, was grassroots Maya activism itself, in an era when liberation theology–inspired, Catholic Left organizing in indigenous communities was building a powerful and deeply rooted network of social movements. Organic leftist organizing and rising Maya politics affected challenges—to the caste system and its performances of servility—that later generations would bring to fruition.[32]

Yolanda Colom had already been working for about three years to open guerrilla fronts in Huehuetenango and El Quiché Departments, when a devastating earthquake hit in 1976. It left millions homeless, swelling the city's shantytown population and the ranks of the leftist movements alike. By that time the Left felt that victory was within reach. The North Vietnamese had defeated the United States, revolution had broken out in El Salvador and Nicaragua, and stagflation was afflicting the global capitalist economy. The 1976 earthquake accelerated two significant, rural-urban and Maya-ladino encounters that were already underway: one, exemplified by Colom's experience, between an educated, urban revolutionary vanguard and Maya villagers in the provinces and another between urban proletarians and campesino rural-to-urban migrants in the capital city's slums. Encounters between leaders of Maya leftist movements and ladino guerrilla leaders were soon to follow. Although it was not apparent to anyone at the time, the already-porous boundary between urban and rural Guatemala—falsely dichotomized as ladino on one hand and Maya on the other—was beginning to significantly break down, even as the leftist popular and guerrilla movements ramped up.

The 1976 earthquake was an urbanizing force, driving the displaced to the capital and larger regional cabeceras. Rebuilding also shaped the look and feel of devastated highland towns; concrete block replaced traditional adobe or mud-brick structures.[33] Beyond striking in the context of accelerating armed and peaceful resistance that cut through significant sectors of society, the quake also intersected with ongoing changes in agriculture that would profoundly affect both urbanization and youth culture in the years ahead.

By the middle of the 1970s, Guatemala was suffering a severe crisis in what are called "basic grains." Shortages of corn and beans threatened famine. As the military occupied the highlands to fight the guerrillas, it took control of maize harvests, and the Agricultural Science and Technology Institute (ICTA), its USAID-supported scientific agriculture wing, experimented with hybrids and affiliated local maize-seed producers. By the end of the decade, farmers affiliated with the ICTA produced 90 percent of the maize-seed crop; the ICTA itself produced the rest. The military state had colonized the very heart of Maya agriculture.[34]

Over the course of the 1970s, in an early example of neoliberal change in Guatemala, another, related phenomenon in highland agriculture was underway, with the introduction of crops known as "nontraditional agro-exports," or NTAs. Over time the NTA portfolio came to include crops such as broccoli, cauliflower, cardamom, snow peas, French beans, macadamia nuts, and flowers. The rise of NTAs in Guatemala was financed by foreign assistance, private capital, and the state. In 1970 USAID seed money jump-started the Latin American Agribusiness Development Corporation (LAAD), a "private investment and development company."[35] In 1971 LAAD used foreign assistance funds to found ALCOSA, Alimentos Congelados—bought by the U.S.-based Hanover Foods a few years later—to freeze fruits and vegetables in Guatemala. The military-run state injected funds into this mix of foreign-assistance money and private capital through the ICTA, BANDESA (National Agricultural Development Bank), and other agencies. Most significantly, the state promoted the formation of agricultural cooperatives throughout the highlands that would become key to commercializing agriculture in the years ahead. By the middle of the 1970s, export vegetable production was underway. ALCOSA-Hanover opened channels to U.S. markets, and, in what was to become the Cuatro Pinos cooperative in Santiago Sacatepéquez, not far from Guatemala City, a Swiss NGO helped to provide access to Europe.[36]

The Maya farmer of the 1970s was in the crosshairs. The rural population was growing and with it the class of landless agricultural laborers. The high price of green-revolution fertilizers and pesticides forced more and more Maya to migrate to coastal plantations for seasonal work, even as those chemicals "burned" the earth and poisoned the water in their hometowns, as counterinsurgency-based development and military control of basic grains inserted the state into the deep cultural relationship of the Maya to maize and to the land.[37] Over the same period, NTAs were grown on company farms worked by landless laborers. Later in the decade, ALCOSA began to contract production to medium-sized fincas, typically owned by ladinos, and, slowly, it began giving contracts to cooperatives. The system broke down in 1980. ALCOSA had contracted more than it could sell. As it rebuilt its field operations in the years ahead, it began contracting Maya smallholders directly. New forms of agricultural production for the global market soon propelled urbanization and generational change in the highlands.[38]

As NTAs were working their way into the economy in the 1970s, the revolution reached its apogee. The last three years of the decade saw union victories, guerrilla victories, and, notably, the rise of the tremendously influential Maya organization, the Campesino Unity Committee (CUC), renowned for its spokesperson, 1992 Nobel Peace Prize–winner Rigoberta Menchú. Rural and urban unions launched more job actions in 1977 than in any other year in history, and protesting, Mam-speaking miners from San Idelfonso Ixtahuacán in Huehuetenango held a "Glorious March" to the capital. More than one hundred thousand supporters joined them along the way. Activism continued the next year, and in May 1978 the military opened fire on unarmed civilian protesters in the town of Panzós, Alta Verpaz, an event that many have seen as the harbinger of the mass violence to come. In 1979, a year celebrated on the left for the historic Sandinista victory in Nicaragua, the guerrilla group ORPA went public. The 1980s began with the much-remembered "Spanish Embassy massacre." CUC activists occupied the embassy, and, when the Guatemalan police violated international law and stormed it, a fire started and thirty-nine people died. Massive agricultural strikes and protests around the nation followed as political violence escalated.[39]

In 1981 the army struck back. Among other victories they effectively eliminated the EGP's urban contingents in Guatemala City, which by that time were under Mario Payeras's command. According to Payeras, troops then moved against the guerrillas in the rural regions of the Pacific coast, after which they marched on the Mayan highlands.[40] The genocidal campaigns that ensued began under the rule of Gen. Romeo Lucas García (1978–82), who also created PACs (Civilian Self-Defense Patrols), in which male villagers from the prepubescent to the elderly were forced to march around and turn in guerrillas to the army. The village-to-village slaughter continued and came to a head under Gen. Efraín Ríos Montt, who overthrew Lucas and ruled from March 1982 until his own ouster in August 1983.[41]

Besides wounding society in ways that will take generations to heal, the violence of the early 1980s left a legacy of militarization that structured the nascent agro-urban social and physical landscape. The state militarized the

FIGURE 1. A Civilian Self-Defense Patrol (PAC) stands at attention, 20 July 1985. Fototeca Guatemala, Archivo del Diario El Gráfico, CT-CIRMA-FG-086.

countryside over the 1960s and 1970s in measures that came to a final paroxysm after the genocidal campaigns of 1981–83. This was not just true of the hundreds of remote, indigenous hamlets high in the mountains and accessible only by footpath, where many of the fiercest battles of the war were fought and mass graves are found. Departmental cabeceras and the towns and villages just around them—the areas soon to urbanize—were also under direct military occupation and subject to state terror and mechanisms of social control.

The army kidnapped local boys in a system of "forced recruitment" that would not end until 1997, and its troops gang-raped girls and women around the highlands. The military also set up systems of surveillance and control that penetrated the social and political fabric, with effects that lasted for decades after the end of the war. Thousands of military *comisionados* served as the hingemen who tied local neighborhoods and clusters of families to the army apparatus. Many of these also served as auxiliary mayors and as leaders of the PACs. By the time that Gen. Óscar Humberto Mejía Víctores (1983–86), Guatemala's last military ruler, was consolidating the counterinsurgency apparatus—preparing the country for its "return to democracy" from mid-1983 to the end of 1985—the state had put in place overlapping layers of military-led bureaucratic oversight in a countryside dotted with "Development Poles" and concentration camp–like "Model Villages." The system was called Inter-Institutional Coordination (IIC), and its goal was to create a counterinsurgent dragnet through which, in theory, no citizen could possibly escape. The IIC system used technologies of governance and control that had matured through Guatemala's age of developmentalism. As counterinsurgent, authoritarian anticommunism began to morph into multicultural, neoliberal democracy in the years of Guatemala's military-to-civilian transition, the IIC morphed with it, smuggling militarism into the new body politic.[42]

At the dawn of the new democracy in 1986, when Sangre Humana sang of "Power's Destiny," questions of the destiny of power were profoundly structuring provincial communities. *Comisionados,* PAC leaders, and other local constituencies that had allied with the army were later loathe to give up their local power. They had prestige. They had control over resources. They could grant life or impose death. Their presence, like the persistence of forced recruitment, deeply colored not only municipal development but also the families, the consciousness, and the *being* of young people growing up in this environment—so too, however, did the history of consciousness raising and of participation in the revolutionary popular war and in the largest and most militant social movements in the nation's history. Scholars generally agree that, beyond all other reasons, the Guatemalan military systematically massacred whole villages in the highlands in the early 1980s because what had once been a relatively containable, ladino guerrilla movement was fast becoming a Mayan cause, with all the dread possibility of a race war that a general indigenous uprising entailed. Indeed—while we should pause to underscore that not all highland Maya were involved in either the insurrection or the social movements and that some in fact oppressed and fought the Left—the rise of the Maya in left-wing organizations marked a watershed in the nation's history. Through a period of extreme violence, what Guatemalan left-wing leaders dubbed the "ethnic question" became a matter of national debate and contestation.

NATIONALISM, THE ETHNIC QUESTION, AND SUBCULTURES IN THE 1980S

The ethnic question was debated in politics, development discourse, and in the weave of everyday life in urban and rural regions alike. Like violence and militarism, it was imbricated in the postgenocide process of physical and cultural urbanization and in the associated "street cultures" associated with the spread of globalized youth culture in the years ahead. Maya cultural and political activism profoundly shaped the consciousness of youth born in the 1980s who would come of age in a rapidly urbanizing landscape in the years around the 1996 Peace Accords. Indigenous activism, as it had emerged from the genocide, had given rise by that time to what might be termed a full-fledged Maya power movement, an example of what Dussel calls the "irruption of new rights."[43] While Dussel's analysis applies to the aftermath of a successful bourgeois revolution, his point nonetheless opens a window on events in Guatemala, where sustained state terror and genocidal violence resulted in a wan, elite-dominated, and far-from-democratic "return to democracy" in 1986. The negotiation of "a posteriori rights" unfolded on the level of high politics, but their sociocultural *reality* was negotiated at the grassroots. The ethnic question, which also crossed lines of class and caste and identities new and old alike, was contested among the de a pie Guatemalans, the taken-for-granted poor majority—Driscoll's "peripheral a priori"—in productive but often violent and endlessly chaotic and open-ended ways.

The ethnic question was bound up in politics, in idioms of self-identification, and in evolving and emerging discourses of nationalism. Brutal counterinsurgency in the city and the countryside alike over the late 1970s and early 1980s in the never-united nation engendered what scholars characterize as a state without a nation. In her work on student activism at the national University of San Carlos, for example, Heather Vrana writes that, "by 1980, student nationalism extended beyond justice, rights, and fraternity, which had characterized previous decades." Distorted by a state terror, "it became a nationalism without a state."[44] As we will see in the chapters ahead, from the "return to democracy" forward, the state, aided by the development apparatus and private capital, has continuously attempted to foment a hegemonic nationalism, with partial success at best. Instead, kaleidoscopic strands of nationalism have arisen from the grassroots. Just as the economy that sustained human life in Guatemala was built chaotically and by hand from below, and just as the political movements that despite unspeakable oppression indelibly conditioned the body politic arose from the grassroots, new and contested iterations of identity and national identity—that is, of national belonging and of nationalism—came up from the fields and the streets and the *barrios* through waves of generational change in a society atomized, and beginning to urbanize, through violence.

Understudied youth cultures and countercultures, evolving in the fringes of these political changes, bear evidence to how what Dussel calls the "cultural field" that (among others) intersected with the "political field" in the period from the late 1970s to the mid-1980s.⁴⁵ Guatemalan rockeros remember the late 1970s as a time when their art form was nearly wiped out by state and police oppression. "By 1979," writes the musician Paulo Alvarado, "a shyly budding *rock chapín* (that is, *rock guatemalteco*) had been all but annihilated. Only a few bands survived into the early 1980s, including Pirámide, Panivers, Rocks, and Terracota. The sole exception to this unfortunate pattern," Alvarado adds, referring to a band of which he was a founding member, "was Alux Nahual." Alux Nahual (pr. a-*loosh* nah-*wahl*) was a "bridge band" between the rock bands of the 1970s and the groups that would form later, after the national returned to civilian rule. Formed in 1979, the group released its debut album on the DIDECA (Discos de Centroamérica) label in 1981. Inspired by Kansas, The Eagles, and Boston, Alux Nahual remained popular for decades. Some critics at the time complained that the lyrics were apolitical, despite the group's Mayan name (which the band translates as "spirit of the music"; a nahual is also a Maya spirit guide). "I don't have any qualms about admitting that we were insufficiently class-conscious to leverage our position as musicians into *líderes de opinion*," Alvarado later wrote. "But at the same time," he added, "I believe that it is fair to stress that while none of us pretended to possess an acute social awareness ... it is also fair to say that Alux Nahual's music had very little in common with disposable pop songs and attitudes either."⁴⁶

Alux Nahual represented a middle ground between "disposable pop" and new, anticonformist subcultures found primarily in Guatemala City. By the 1980s members of the anticonformist generation had come to be referred to as *pesados*, youth who liked hard rock and heavy metal. They embraced the occult, drug use, and free sex and had reflected a growing attitude that Guatemalan scholars later dubbed *valeverguismo*, from *me vale verga* or *me pela la verga*, phrases that mean "I don't give a fuck."⁴⁷ As Guatemala moved toward democratic rule, writes Manuela Camus, this urban generation rejected values and discourses of politics and class that dated to the 1940s. High on marijuana and hallucinogens, they embraced consumeristic social codes, engaged in class and status warfare, and in general displayed what she calls "militant anti-conformism." Over the course of the 1980s, as the "new [neoliberal] economy" congealed and education was gradually becoming "mercantilized" through a growing welter of private institutions, class antagonisms sharpened.⁴⁸ Mass media played a role in this process, especially for the lucky few who could afford a satellite dish (and later in the decade, cable) to be able to enjoy MTV's arrival in the 1980s. These were also the years of

AM-to-FM transition, not just in Guatemala City but around the country, and televisions had spread; even the military's TV Channel 5 was broadcasting foreign rock and heavy metal. Metal, Guatemala's longest-lasting counterculture sound, was the era's best example of "militant anti-conformism." It was viewed as "satanic" and antisocial well into the new millennium.[49]

Sangre Humana, one of the earliest and most influential Guatemalan metal groups, was founded in 1979. Singer Roberto "Blacko" González briefly ran a Sunday-night radio show in 1982 on Radio "La Voz del Hogar." Its "metal massacre" theme soon got it canceled for antisocial excess, but it did help to popularize the genre in Guatemala City. After its 45 rpm album in 1983, the band's songs over the rest of the decade included "Satanás ésta es tu canción" (Satan, this is your song) and "Muerte dónde estás" (Death, where are you). Sangre Humana was a leader in the new subterranean heavy-metal and *rock pesado* wave that included older ondero groups like Panivers and Rocks as well as newer ones such as Crucifix and Machine. "Their members had long hair and wore black and/or leather clothes," writes María Escobar Urrutia. "The musicians were carried to the stage in coffins."[50]

In-depth studies of the metal scene are needed, and they need to take into account its ladino, middle-class devotees' schools, neighborhoods, and family ties to the political economy and the counterinsurgent state. Lyrics like those of "Power's Destiny"—"Who will be the next one he wants to kill? / It could be that it's you"—belie a reading of the genre as either apolitical or as purely symptomatic of a tuned-out, anticonformist generation. Here I analytically situate Guatemala's metal and *pesado* subcultures as part of the greater matrix of contestation about identity and belonging in the early 1980s. I do so in part because metaleros and other *pesados* unleashed street warfare against brown-skinned break-dancers later in the decade, an issue covered in chapter 2. Primarily, however, I do so because I believe that there is a fruitful discomfort produced by analyzing extravagant and ultimately marginal youthful expressions in the same frame as the more-studied, historical arguments over race and class that Guatemalans were generating in their violence-shattered state-without-a-nation. If we are going to understand the history of the de a pie, even in glimpses, we need to lean into the disjunctures—the everyday collisions of life and death, of serious and ludic, of being and becoming—that shot through real peoples' lives and that have left a residue we can trace in popular culture, just as we can trace it in politics.

In politics, the already-roiling ethnic question became acute in the wake of the massacres. In August 1983, as Mejía Víctores was unleashing the coup that unseated Ríos Montt and put the nation on its martial road to a "return to democracy," the EGP published an interview on interethnic relations in its newsletter. "Emiliano"—his nom de guerre—was Q'anjob'al Maya, "the son of exploited campesinos." He was born in Huehuetenango Department near the Mexican border and traveled across it with his parents to look for jobs. They found them all over Mexico, working in a lock factory, for example. Back in Guatemala, still in his teens, Emiliano ended up in the banana fields. As everywhere, the job paid only pennies. Later, when the guerrillas recruited him, he had been dodging the police for years, trafficking contraband medicine home from Mexico.[51]

The EGP published this story in response to virulent debates that were breaking out. Had ladino guerrillas exposed the highland Maya to extermination? The guerrilla armies formed the URNG (Guatemalan National Revolutionary Unity) umbrella group in 1982, but they remained fundamentally divided, especially over the ethnic question—a question exacerbated by the genocide and championed by groups in the growing Mayan movement, which was broadly divided into overlapping, yet distinct spheres: *clasistas,* who worked with ladino groups on issues of class, and *culturalistas,* who focused on Maya identity.[52]

Divisions in Guatemala's constellation of guerrilla groups over the past years had focused not just on differences of ideology and the struggle of young combatants against gerontocracy, but also over the ethnic question. Upon its formation, for example, ORPA had vowed to take indigenous issues more seriously. Ideology, strategy, and attention to ethnicity were all among the reasons why in early 1983, in self-imposed exile with other guerrilla leaders in Mexico City, Mario Payeras, "Comandante Benedicto," resigned from the EGP. Payeras critiqued the EGP's leaders' triumphalism, verticalism, and misguided adherence to *foquismo* (Che Guevara's *foco* theory of warfare that depended on small, mountain-based guerrilla groups led by an elite revolutionary vanguard). In his opinion, these factors had caused them to grossly underestimate the enemy, to ignore advice and input from within, to neglect political organizing, and thus to expose the highland population to slaughter.[53] According to Yolanda Colom, EGP leaders saw all critique as dissent.[54] When Payeras quit, the EGP high command responded by accusing him of having both vague theories and personal ambitions to be commander in chief.[55] By Colom's account, however, others rallied to his side and convinced him to start a new movement. Called Octubre Revolucionario (OR), it was born in early 1984. Its members claimed to be determined to do the hard work of political organizing, to foment internal democracy, and to address, once and for all, the ethnic question.[56] They established a working group that produced papers on this topic for the rest of the decade. Ultimately, they concluded that, despite the URNG's efforts to take the ethnic question into account, the large guerrilla movements, cleaving to dogmatically Marxist class-based analysis, had failed to undertake a deep enough analysis of racial and cultural issues.[57]

From a class-based position, the Left's only viable option was to put its differences aside and fight as a unified front. As Emiliano put it in his 1983 interview, the answer was to call for class solidarity between the ladino and indigenous poor. "I have in my mind," he said, "the exploitation and the discrimination against *mi pueblo indígena,* but I know that to triumph, we have to struggle and die together, indígenas and ladinos."[58]

To some extent ladino and Maya activists did struggle together as the 1980s progressed. Many Maya joined guerrilla cadres or participated in Catholic Left groups, such as the CUC, or both. Some, however, formed indigenous separatist organizations that both the state and the ladino Left rejected. These included the Movimiento Revolucionario del Pueblo Ixim (MRP-Ixim) and the Movimiento Indio Tojil, which formed military fronts and later gave rise to MAYAS, the Movimiento de Acción y Ayuda Solidaria, which called for an independent Maya republic.[59]

Extraordinary documents bear witness to the divisions of the day. "The *pueblos indígenas* of Guatemala declare and denounce before the world: more than four centuries of discrimination, negation, repression, exploitation, and massacres committed by foreign invaders that continue to this day in the hands of their most savage and criminal descendants," began the CUC's "Declaración de Iximché," a prorevolutionary, anti-ladino, anti-imperialist, race-based 1980 manifesto that many Maya groups to follow would reference.[60] In 1982 the *Revista del Movimiento Indio* denounced massacres, atrocities, and U.S. and Israeli support for the Guatemalan military; it also railed against tourism and the "folkloricizing" of indigenous culture through fake, state-sponsored holidays and events.[61] MRP-Ixim struck a different tone in its inaugural 1983 newsletter, expressing hope that the URNG could provide revolutionary unity.[62]

Could the Maya and the ladinos live together? Did they share common goals? The much-cited August 1983 manifesto, "Guatemala: From the Centrist Bourgeois Republic to the Popular Federal Republic," held that "indios and ladinos need to decolonize their relations"; that "Guatemala is not a nation but a society"; and that the "ladino community [constitutes] a 'nation' without a national consciousness." The formation of a "chapín" national identity was thus impossible. In Guatemala the *"communidad mayence"* was both ethnic, made up of nationalities (the various language groups), and "pan-ethnic, or pan-Indian." The *mayences* were "nationalities or a nation without a State." The problem with the Marxists in Guatemala and all over Latin America, the document held, was that they still had not recognized "the need for liberation of the *pueblos colonizados*." Even those ladino guerrilla groups in Guatemala that had been struggling with ethnic complexity and who conceived of locally rooted *"pequeñas nacionalidades"* were ideologically blind and always returned to the "necessary national integration of the indigenous ethnicities."[63] The authors rejected such integration. "The Maya Republic will be a grand multi-ethnic nation," they wrote, "and as such, it will have a multinational State constructed so that each one of its ethnic components is itself a nation, which delegates a part of its autonomy to the State." The federal republic would have *"países Maya y Criollo,"* with a "plurality of 'regions'" inside the Maya *país* (country). They saw this federalist solution as more "viable and moderate" than "Indianist" calls for total independence and separation.[64]

According to Santiago Bastos and Manuela Camus, the URNG dismissed this idea of a federal republic out of hand.[65] At around the same time, the PGT-6 de Enero (the fraction of the communist party that was allied with Octubre Revolucionario) was propounding its own solutions to the ethnic question: the use of Spanish as a language of national unification (along with bilingual education and state-led antidiscrimination campaigns in the provinces) and the establishment of the revolutionary "unitary and multiethnic National State."[66] Stripped of all its revolutionary content, this multicultural vision would later come to characterize the state project in Guatemala.

In the 1980s, however, the idea of indigenous revolutionary nationalism continued to spread.[67] By early 1984 the Movimiento Indio de Guatemala was explicitly calling for the formation of three separate nations—the Nación Ladina, the Nación Negra, and the Nación Indígena.[68] "It is demagoguery to say that Guatemala is indigenous and equally unreal to affirm that in Guatemala there exists one single nationality," the April 1985 manifesto of the Movimiento Indio, Nacionalista y Revolucionario declared. Marxist-Leninist groups were unable to grasp the deep religious and spiritual roots of Maya communities, and what was needed was a Mayan nation. This nation would be built only through years of revolution, but the group vowed to begin constructing it immediately through education, arts, and cultural revival.⁶⁹ It would turn out to be through these routes that Maya nationalism evolved in the decades ahead.

Revolution, however, was still an option in 1984. In the same year, the Liga de Resistencia Popular Awesh (LRP-Awesh), a group formed in 1979 that had functioning guerrilla cadres, excoriated the "dominant racist ladino class" but maintained that "ladinos and mestizos are brothers of *mayense* descent."⁷⁰ Without ladino-indigenous unity, LRP-Awesh proclaimed, the people's movement could never win. While the URNG represented a possibility for such an alliance, that alliance "had broken up significantly." They called for "strategic unity," an end to vanguardism, and social revolution. They vowed to work for these goals and to develop bilateral relations with other Latin American and Caribbean organizations. "There are shortcomings of the past that have recurred, and this means that some of the 'old' organized sectors are unable to permanently group the oppressed and overexploited popular sectors together," the group wrote. "Sadly, at the moment, the *youth* [emphasis added] of LRP-Awesh do not have the ability to achieve this goal either."⁷¹

Although neither revolutionary unity nor revolutionary victory ensued, Awesh's invocation of youth was important. The rise of Maya nationalism and the ascendance of the Maya in local politics deeply colored consciousness and everyday life in the nascent agro-urban areas. Together with a heritage of leftist revolution, these factors also fostered pride and defiance in later generations of indigenous and mestizo castas. Like their predecessors, however, those later generations would prove unable to overthrow the structural conditions of poverty.

"The ethnic-national question can be solved only through revolution," concluded Octubre Revolucionario's analysts in the mid-1980s, tying the problem to capitalist exploitation. Indigenous leadership and participation was key to that revolution's success. The goal would be not only to usher in a new society but also to create an entirely new culture, one based in Guatemala's roots and expressing "the values that the indigenous have cultivated and preserved throughout their history."⁷² Octubre Revolucionario's conclusions about a whole new culture—like Awesh's cry to rejuvenate politics through youth—would be prophetic, if not in the optimistic way either group envisioned. In the decades following the 1986 return to democracy, de a pie youth used culture as a productive field of contestation, taking up and appropriating globalized styles even as they retooled and revitalized local traditions. The new meanings with which everyday people infused culture soon bore evidence of rapid, generational, cultural change.

OVERLAPPING FIELDS AND SLY TRICKS
IN A MILITARIZED BODY POLITIC

Generational change in Guatemala is inextricable from its history of war. At the national, regional, and local levels, contestation over "power's destiny," to borrow Sangre Humana's title, was embedded in the change from military to civilian rule and in economic transitions that deeply conditioned the relation between the rural and the urban in Guatemala. In a constellation of chaotic, bottom-up examples of how, as Dussel writes, economic and cultural fields intersect with the political, the Guatemalan landscape evolved in ways that showed not only the effects of greater globalizing forces and elite-dominated politics but also those of militarization, displacement, and violence.

At the time of the transition to civilian rule, Guatemala was still at war, and huge sectors of the population—at least a million people—were displaced. Refugees crowded camps on the Mexican side of the border, and whole communities fleeing violence were living in resistance in the mountains. Other displaced Guatemalans moved to the capital or regional cabeceras to rebuild their lives, and thousands of war orphans became Guatemala City street children. Forces both military and paramilitary jockeyed at all levels for power, and new constituencies appeared, among them the first of the narcocartels and the street gangs. Every intersection in this complex landscape was infected with militarism and violence, which worked their way into the weave of the evolving body politic and the process of rural-urban change.

Discourse about narcotraffic provides an excellent example of how political, economic, and cultural fields intertwined and overlapped. While information on the rise of the major Latin American cartels is readily available, and has even become the subject of Netflix telenovelas, little is known about the early stages of drug trafficking in Guatemala. Besides filling in a spotty history of the national cartels that transport narcotics to the north—the Guatemalan chapter of a global history linked to the Andes, the battlefields of Vietnam, the CIA's covert drug-smuggling activities in the Contra War, and the like—further research is needed on the *internal* drug trade in Guatemala, tracing the still-unknown story of how the products associated with the rise of drug culture in the capital and secondary cities were produced and distributed. We have clues, but few answers. Following the threads of this story, however, provides insight into the transformations underway in the 1980s.

FIGURE 2. The army seizes cocaine valued at $500 million on the Atlantic coast, 29 September 1987. Fototeca Guatemala, Archivo de Juan Rolando González Díaz (photographer), GT-CIRMA-FG-160.

In 1980, according to the press, a man called "El Coyote" established a drug-dealing network in Guatemala City's Barrio El Gallito, one of the nation's most notorious slums.[73] Over the same general period, we know that high-ranking military officers were buying up fincas in the Petén and elsewhere in what is called the Franja Transversal del Norte (FTN, Northern Transversal Strip), an area soon to become a hub of the new national cartels.[74] As such investments were underway, however, the state used narcotraffic as an excuse for counterinsurgency, in an example of the kind of discourse soon to link youth "delinquency" to social-cleansing campaigns. In early September 1985, for example, army troops raided the USAC campus, under the pretext that it was a center of narcotraffic and subversion.[75] The raid on USAC, however, was less about narcotraffic than it was a response to violent bus-fare protests in the city. Sparked by students from a downtown high school, the protests soon became a generalized uprising; Deborah Levenson writes that "these urban demonstrations in the mid-1980s were the last in the twentieth-century" with the "kinds of 1970s left-wing politics" of cross-class solidarity. The September 1985 bus-fare protests are also remembered as the public debut of the capital city's new maras—gangs that at the time were far less violent than the ones we know today, but whose participation in the protests resulted in "massive publicity." "This new discourse concerning unruly urban youth," Levenson writes, "not only furthered the silence surrounding state violence in the 1980s, it put into motion an astonishing reversal of truth, a lie that was part of the war: youngsters were the source of violence and other dangers from which the state would protect its good citizens in order to create a new social reality."[76]

"Reversal of truth" is a phrase that encapsulates a great deal of what was happening in Guatemala in the years around the transition to civilian rule (itself a good example of how militarism and elite rule continued under another guise). Consider, for example, the mixed effects of NTAs in agriculture. NTA cultivation—an economic activity that USAID was promoting around the developing world—helped to generate profits for Maya smallholders, who sometimes gained land at ladino planters' expense.[77] They used those profits to build new urban neighborhoods and businesses and to send their children to school. As we will see in later chapters, many of those children, members of the new agro-urban generation, grew up wanting to work in *anything* except agriculture. At the same time, NTA-growing Maya smallholders provided work to landless laborers who far preferred to work locally than to migrate seasonally to the ladino-owned, agro-export fincas. Thus, besides being a factor that helped to give rise to new generations of children, of whom many would be the first in their families' five-hundred-year history to work in labor regimes that had not been traditionally connected to the agrarian economy, NTAs also instantiated regional population growth and internal "rural-to-less-rural" migration. This, in turn, spurred the need for more commercial goods and services, such as banks, supermarkets, and the like.[78]

At the same time, however, NTAs were bound up in other processes that fueled or conditioned the process of agro-urbanization. They contributed to the emergence of a more commercial land market, although land distribution as a whole remained starkly unequal. Agrarian land became more expensive, even in areas where NTA cultivation did not take root, benefiting large landholders and a handful of small producers but hurting the majority population of renters and tenant farmers. As cabeceras and the aldeas right around them began to grow, over time, many landholders engaged in a process known as *lotificación*, cutting what was once their milpa lands into urban plots that sometimes were developed by their own family members but that often went to renters or working-class buyers as well. Farmland turned into towns, later to turn into agro-urban cities.[79]

Rural-to-urban conversion was wrapped up in greater flows of commercialization and economic change, which were riddled with militarism, in classic examples of Guatemala's "reversals of truth." NTAs spurred Maya proprietorship, but they had their roots in military-run agricultural programs and were promoted by production cooperatives linked to the counterinsurgent IIC program. Many of these cooperatives interfaced with a growing constellation of NGOs, a relationship that accelerated in the mid-1980s, when cooperatives began to be charged with devoting profits to providing essential services such as education, in part relegating to humble farmers the responsibility of providing or paying for services typically associated with the public sector. As they assumed this responsibility, farmers took on risk, because NTA exporters contracted for less produce than they expected to need and then bought the excess on the open market. Thus, elite exporters displaced the capricious price swings of the global commodity market downward. They did so at a time when the national economy was teetering, marked by falling exchange rates and high inflation.[80] Despite the inherent instability they engendered, state-led plans to turn Guatemala into an agro-industrial nation and diversify its crops through public-private alliances continued throughout the decade, while plans to alleviate poverty met intransigent elite opposition.[81]

The presentation of the kind of commercialization seen in the NTA sector in development literature as a purely positive force is a classic "reversal of truth." NTAs did produce gains but were also intimately related to the downward displacement of capitalist markets' risks. It should also be noted that not all NTAs were legal; they also included understudied crops such as heroin poppies, whose cultivation near the Mexican border prompted the Drug Enforcement Administration to fumigate with Paraquat and other deadly chemicals in the mid-1980s.[82] Commercialization entailed the maturation of complex webs of business interests from high to low and from legal to illegal in a war-torn body politic that was shot through with militarism.

"Youth" both discursive and real were caught up in this process. As Levenson notes, "massive advertising campaigns aimed at the urban youth market" were underway in the mid-1980s, part of a "relentless multinational crusade to get youth from all social classes and ethnic backgrounds to desire goods that formed part of a fantasy 'world youth culture.'"[83] Such commercialization was not just a top-down process, however. Just as they had built the economy from the bottom up for decades, working-class Guatemalans confected vernacular varieties of commodified youth culture. Indigenous entrepreneurs created cottage industries that bootlegged the brand-name hoodies and sports jerseys for which global industry and media had created a demand.[84] Youth, meanwhile, deployed globally inflected cultural forms and styles in their own sometimes violent and sometimes inspirational contestation over caste, class, ethnicity, and national belonging. The first iterations of a Guatemalan "street" that was linked to an emerging planetary street culture were seen in the capital city, with its new "anticonformist" generation, its new maras, and its growing constellation of subcultures. Like all other forms of change associated with the new era of commercialization in Guatemala, however, emerging street cultures were inseparable from the militarization of the body politic and society as a whole.

Popular historical memory evidences these connections. Metaleros weren't just in Guatemala City in the early 1980s, "Alhazred" blogged on the website *Rock Republik* (pronounced "República," using the *kah* sound as in KY for *calle*) in 2011. They were also in the army. Military heavy-metal fans "brought to the war the violence that metal in theory implied," Alhazred posted. "In fact," he added, "many of the razed villages in the west felt death coming under pitiless fire from helicopters in which today's classic metal bands were playing."[85] Perhaps this singular piece of historical memory in Guatemala's efforts to grapple with its violent past was little but the transposition of a movie scene—*Apocalypse Now* with Wagner changed for Metallica—or perhaps it referenced the media coverage of the U.S. military's use of heavy metal against foes like Saddam Hussein. The heavy-metal lovers who added their thoughts on this topic to the blog, however, did not note such connections. Instead, they had a vibrant historical debate. They mused about the relationships between the army and youth counterculture and about the political meanings of different musical styles. In their 2011 posts, they pondered the role of mass media and foreign cultural production in the city and the country during the days of genocide. Those days had passed over a quarter of a century before but continued to haunt their world.[86]

The very title of the website, *Rock Republik,* bespeaks an imagined national identity related to transnational youth culture, just as Alhazred's imagery asks us to consider how war and violence worked their way from the torture chambers and killing fields into consciousness and society at every level. Alhazred's greater point was that the country's military rulers had "allied" with rockeros and metaleros in the early 1980s. They put the music on TV and allowed it on the radio. Why? Because hard rock and metal were styles completely opposed to hippies and their lyrics of "peace, love, and reconciliation," Alhazred claimed; the generals used these genres to win over a generation of middle-class ladinos. Youth's soundtrack changed to one more compatible with scorched-earth policies. The programming on the military's Channel 5 mixed concert scenes of bands like KISS and Twisted Sister with combat scenes of the elite attack forces, the Kaibiles.[87]

Alhazred sparked debate on *Rock Republik*. Did the army help to promote an "anti-cool" that made youth look down on social protest? What did these videos from their childhood mean? "Ramses" wondered if rock had really been a part of a greater project of class warfare. If so, he asked, could it really be true that an army whose foot soldiers were mostly impoverished campesinos committed genocide while blasting heavy-metal music?[88]

The online discussion of 2011 formed part of a larger discourse linking the army to virtually all aspects of life in Guatemala. The military has been connected to everything from street gangs to international drug trafficking. Alhazred's and Ramses's ruminations speak more to how the war conditioned life for years to come than they do to hard facts. Did soldiers really use rock and heavy-metal music as a weapon and a tool of social engineering? Probably not, but the very fact that the army-metal connection is plausible illuminates how shot through this society was (and is) with violence. The pervasive violence comes not just from the war-torn past but from an economic regime and its webs of power that run through Guatemala's smallest corners and on a larger scale link it to an extractive global system.

The dead can be counted by exhumations, but no number of exhumations can count their multiplier effect—the million "everyday deaths" they occasion in consciousness, in political action or inaction, in endless chains of mundane decisions over time. A good example of this appeared on *Rock Republik* in 2011. In response to Alhazred, "Mike1701" chimed in that there had been few documented massacres—leftists had falsified the data—and that reports of the violence were overblown. Mike1701's inaccurate comment prompted "Gerardo Perez" to weigh in with firsthand testimony about both counterinsurgency and heavy metal. "Well, I'm from the interior of the republic, and as a child I lived through those days when the army took the town, surrounding it with armed personnel carriers and everything," he posted. "Lots of times I heard people say that the army used hard-rock music as a type of psychological torture against some of the villagers and also when they were doing forced recruitment."[89] Gerardo's later comments date his teens to the mid-1990s, and his memories testify to the ongoing military occupation and attacks that persisted for years.

"What I am going to write now is personal," Gerardo blogged, remembering his childhood and a music video released in 1994:

> I remember watching Channel 5 as a kid and waiting for, Saturday I think it was, for this metal music segment, to see one of the videos that I liked the best and that they put on the most ... Megadeth, "Train of Consequences," the one where these babies are hung all along the road, and then, exactly, right, all these images of the army that you saw that made you want to be part of it, and I remember that when the *militares* came I ran to be able to see them ... *que trance va buen juego sicológico* [what a scam, right, good mind game]. I've meditated on this for a long time and, well, Channel 5 was part of what it was that made me like metal, even though I was only maybe ten and didn't even know what this kind of music was.... Thank God for metal ... [which] since I was a child made me have a different vision of this existence.[90]

Gerardo's memory speaks to a morbid fascination with violence seen again and again in Guatemalan youth culture and popular practices.[91] It evokes the affective bond that humans have with artistic forms and how music reciprocally shapes our realities. The way Gerardo mixes memories of years of dictatorship with those of civilian rule indicates that these political beginnings and endings are less defined in real life than they are in historical narratives. His use of urban street slang and his early-childhood love of metal underscore the importance of transnational countercultures, not just in the capital city but also in the provinces. The two-syllable word *trance* (pr. *trahn*-say) literally means "trance," as in English, but the slang phrase *que trance, ¿va?* has the street sense of "what a scam" or "good trick, right?" While used in a variety of contexts, it often appears in de a pie historical memories and in black-humor critiques of rich people, politicians, and other *cerotes* (pieces of shit). For example, *"el cerote de Kjell* said he wanted campesino cooperatives to get the leaders to come out of hiding so the army could kill them. Que trance, ¿va?" Or "supposedly they gave us 'democracy' in 1986, but the *militares* and *los ricos* ended up with all the money and power. Que trance, ¿va?" Or "the First Lady started those concerts, *vos*, so the *jóvenes* would keep listening to rock and getting stoned instead of joining the guerrillas. Que trance, ¿va?"[92] In Gerardo's blog post the *trance* consisted of the army's airing a Megadeth video—"Train of Consequences," in which a train passenger sees a woman by the tracks hanging babies like laundry on a clothesline—side by side with its own promotional material. The combination of propaganda and heavy-metal pop culture made a wide-eyed little boy want to run to admire the troops and be a part of them when they invaded town. Que trance, ¿va?

The *Rock Republik* blog indexes the everyday "train of consequences" that connects Guatemalan popular youth cultures to the nation's polyvalent battles over identity, the ethnic question, and "power's destiny." Light-skinned and long-haired, and typically from the middle classes, the rockeros and metaleros of the 1980s represented only part of what was happening in grassroots counterculture. Break-dancing and hip-hop also emerged on the urban scene. Early 1980s hip-hop was originally enjoyed only by the upper and upper-middle classes, who had access to MTV and films like *Breakin'* and *Beat Street*. Gradually, as local radio stations gave airtime to the genre, it became more popular. It made its way to youngsters called *choleros*—a male-coded epithet that denoted poor city boys who wore counterfeit brand-name clothes, donned earrings, had gold teeth with hearts in them, and got tattoos. Most of these young people came from poor and working-class *colonias*, as well as from shantytowns and land invasions.[93]

In the 1980s the use of slurs like *cholero*, *shumo* (brown trash), and *muco* (shumo gangbanger) that relegated poor, brown-skinned, casta youth to new, urban subcategories became more widespread.[94] Rounding out this evolving taxonomy were the maras, the street gangs that appeared in roughly 1984 and 1985. By the 1986 return to democracy, the street, *la calle*, with its *fresas, onderos, metaleros, shumos, mucos,* and other youth groups, had become a theater on which de a pie Guatemalans in the capital city began to retrench, retool, and remake identities.

La calle was a site that showed the everyday interweaving of cultural conflict with political and economic struggles for power. It emerged as such in a still-warring state structured for counterinsurgency and a nation structured by a caste system that was being renegotiated in a revisiting of the ethnic question after the genocide. Violence, militarism, and state terror formed a connective tissue between politics, economics, and cultural change. They penetrated not just the political economy but also historical memory, popular consciousness, and popular youth culture, as the metaleros' memories on *Rock Republik* attest. In the corpse-littered capital city filled with mushrooming slums, land invasions, and street children, some young people rejected all narratives of propriety and progress. They did so as terror deployed against the Left proved that the state's only legitimacy resided in its power over death.[95] In the agro-urbanizing towns and villages around the country—towns where NTA profits and *remesas* (migrants' remittances) joined the displacements and divisions of war in remaking the physical and social landscape, towns like the one where the young Gerardo Perez would soon fall in love with heavy metal—the army was *everywhere*. The urban *calle* is inseparable from the barracks, the battlefield, the agrarian hinterland, and the rural and urban killing grounds in Guatemala. Like a "train of consequences," Guatemala's bloodbath simply would not go away. As Gerardo put it later, remembering the seductive power of the Special Forces' videos, the ways in which militarism and violence inserted themselves not just into politics but also into everyday life were not only overt but also sly and subtle. Que trance, ¿va?

2

"Americamorfosis"

IDENTITIES AND URBANIZATION, 1987–1993

OVER TOO MANY GALLO BEERS, a Guatemalan friend told me my *análisis* of changes through the Cold War's end was *pura paja*, bullshit. He was on board with the "que trance, ¿va? / good scam" line of thinking, but overall, he said, I was making a simple story way too complicated. He drew me a three-decade, comic book history titled *¿QP Pasó?* (WTF Happened?).[1] In the 1970s panel, a revolutionary stick figure cried *"¡Hasta la victoria siempre!"* A cowboy hat–wearing campesino, referencing the arrival of new export crops, wondered, "What's cardamom?" The 1980s had a caption: "Welcome to Your Genocide." First: *Silencio*. Then Youth said, *"Pasáme el flex vos:* pass me some glue to sniff," adding, once high, "Democracy's great!" Enter Uncle Sam: "I'm just beginning to *chiquitiarte*" [a very strong verb meaning "to penetrate you anally"]. The final 1980s figure was a kid (running from Tío Sam and from another stick figure trying to beat him down): "I just want to break-dance." The 1990s panel featured characters saying, "McDonald's ... cool!" "Eat shit," and "We've signed peace!" The last, downcast *chapín* announced, "I'm going to the USA." My artist-analyst friend added an epilogue: one stick figure bending over another for forced penetration from behind. *Así es vos*. That's how it is. Write your book already.

I share this de a pie history not to be scatological but for good reasons. This cocktail-napkin cartoon, drawn by an indigenous-descended ladino with an eighth-grade education who grew up in an agro-urban land invasion, both reproduces and subverts before-and-after narratives of change through the end of the Cold War that this chapter argues against. Such narratives are a commonplace in popular discourse and are subtly reproduced in academic analysis, which tends to overlook everyday social actors like the cartoon's working-class creator. These narratives hold that "neoliberalism" and "consumer culture" occasioned an antirevolutionary body politic personified by an apolitical, apathetic new generation. In the cartoon we see the before-and-after story in the arc from revolutionary to migrant, peopled in the middle with the breakdancer and the McDonald's eater. My friend also complicates and subverts this story, however. He highlights, as academics do, changes in agrarian production *(What's cardamom?)*, the atomizing effect of genocide, and U.S. interference. He also sketches a democracy you have to sniff glue to believe in. Interestingly, however, break dancing appears in his rendering not as the *product* of a foreign invasion but as an *escape*, both from Uncle Sam and from another violent and unidentified figure. On a related note, what most impresses me about the cartoon is that it was drawn in the context of genuine debate between friends from entirely different worlds and backgrounds. Like the escaping break-dancer, this friendship bespeaks a working-class self-assertiveness—a willingness to share what James Scott calls the "hidden transcript"—that I believe we can understand in new ways by rethinking the transformations through the Cold War's end.[2]

Given that de a pie analysts and academics generally agree that Guatemala's Cold War conflict did not really end but instead took on a new form (que trance, ¿va?), it is worth pausing to discuss periodization and political history before delving into the subject at hand. There are real bookends to the before-and-after story I wish to complicate. Politically, in Guatemala, these include the 1986 return to democracy and a 1993 constitutional crisis, after which civilian rule was consecrated and the capitalist elite won the day. This fate was not preordained, however. In part emboldened by the return to civilian rule, the social movements and guerrillas revivified. Their activism pushed the state under Vinicio Cerezo (January 1986 to January 1991) to team pro-business policies with ones that stressed social spending. The beginning steps toward peace dated to Cerezo's term, but the process accelerated significantly under Jorge Serrano Elías (January 1991 to June 1993). Serrano was forced into exile after a May 1993 "self-coup," in which he dissolved Congress. Fears of an army takeover were allayed when the human rights ombudsman, Ramiro de León Carpio (June 1993 to January 1996), emerged as head of state. Civilian rule and the peace process were cemented by year's end.

According to Serrano's memoir (and self-defense), his ouster also cemented neoliberal, private-sector domination of the state. He writes that it was his insistence on forging public-private alliances instead of fully privatizing state enterprises that ran him afoul of his wealthy friends, whom he contends drove him out of office.[3] As Serrano's claim indicates, the first years of civilian rule were marked by intense contestation over the political economy. At the turn of the decade, however, the terms of the debate changed in dialogue with global reconfigurations: the rise of Solidarity in Poland and the fall of the Berlin Wall in 1989; the "war on drugs" and the United States' invasion of Panama in late 1989 and early 1990, followed by the Sandinistas' electoral defeat; the first U.S. Gulf War in 1990–91; and the Soviet Union's 1991 dissolution. Many Guatemalan guerrillas retired, and those who remained fought not for victory but for strength in the peace negotiations, principally by staging preannounced armed actions in a public relations campaign waged less on the battlefield than in the media.

This profound switch in strategies among the guerrilla Left was one aspect of the more general commercialization of social space that characterized the period and is associated in memory with a new generation of youth. Consider two Alux Nahual songs that also bracket this period. The first, from 1987, is the title song of the group's fifth album, *Alto al fuego* (Cease fire): "Hold your fire, cease fire! In all of Central America!" "The foreign armies pulled out / But the fools and the guerrillas remained," it lyricized. "Everybody wanted to raise a new flag / And exchange dreams of liberty for checkbooks."[4] Such antiwar lyrics help to explain why the band went down in history as being "apolitical," as did, unfairly, a generation of young people as a whole. Accused of being the ones who wanted the checkbooks instead of liberty, the new generation would be remembered for its focus on identity rather than on social solidarity. In 1993 Alux Nahual released an album called *Americamorfosis* (stress on the second-to-last syllable: *-more-FOE-cease*). One of its tracks, "500 Años," referenced the five-hundredth anniversary of Columbus's landing. "Half a millennium of survival *[sobrevivencia]* / Of living in our *inconciencia* / Half a millennium of such *violencia* / 500 years of *adolescencia*," it sang. "Today in the ship of imagination / We travel with the wind of our reason / To discover and then to conquer / This new land called identity."[5]

Before-and-after stories of this period of "Americamorfosis" foreground "this new land called identity." Supposedly, identity politics replaced Cold War "big politics." Consumer culture replaced revolutionary consciousness. Generational change reflected so-called neoliberalism. An up-close examination, however, complicates the *que trance ¿va?* sly trick through which one era reappeared as another. Events in Guatemala through the Cold War's end show *displacement* more than they do *replacement*. Politicians, pushed by the Left, instituted new consensus-forging mechanisms associated with neoliberal development, discursively displacing, but not replacing, older forms of counterinsurgent development. Nationally, moral panic displaced anxieties about the horrible and silenced aftermath of genocide and a changing political economy onto "youth" as a discursive field, in ways analogous to how a generation of black- and brown-skinned youth was criminalized in the United States' "war on drugs" over the same period. In the militarized highlands, where the historic Maya power movement was underway, discourses of revalorized tradition displaced anxieties related to agro-urbanization—and, more broadly, to what the urban theorist Álvaro Sevilla-Buitrago calls a planetary process of "original extended urbanization" that moves in rhythm with expanding regimes of capitalist accumulation—onto youth as well.[6] Far from just reflecting corrosive consumer culture and neoliberal change, youthful cultural production over this period was *generative*. It was sometimes creative and sometimes destructive, but it was always productive. It evolved in the context of a process of urbanization—global, national, and local—in ways that disturbed elders in agro-urban Guatemala and shocked the national consciousness with its violence in Guatemala City. The cultural assertiveness of Maya and casta youth, while sometimes "consumeristic" and sometimes violent, was an essential and underappreciated element in the formation of social space. In both the agro-urbanizing provinces and in Guatemala City, young people began to lay the groundwork for a later cultural commons that would cross over lines of caste, class, and race in historic ways.

NEOLIBERALIZATION, RESISTANCE, AND PANIC

Guatemala's political economy began to neoliberalize in the context of ongoing war, a transformation coconstitutively tied to changes in capital accumulation and the phase of "original extended urbanization" that was underway nationally around the globe. The nation's moves toward neoliberalism in the mid to late 1980s were slow, incomplete, and at times contradictory.[7] In hindsight, neoliberalization—privatizing, weakening the central state, investing insufficient amounts in public services and a safety net, embracing multicultural politics, and using public funds to subsidize private-sector growth—seems such a fait accompli that it bears remembering how contested and far from predetermined these measures were. Liberalizing policies were created in dialogue with a resurgent Left on one hand and changing global ideology on the other. A series of what I call *displacements* wrapped older structures up in new formations that appeared to replace them. The complex processes that in aggregate underpinned the commercialization of social space in this time of transformation entailed physical displacements, which condensed in the built environment of urbanizing agrarian population centers, as well as emotional displacements that condensed in moral panic.

In the realm of policy, historical memory provides an example of the teleological rewriting of the intense contestation over neoliberalization. From the vantage point of 2010, IDB analysts called the 1987 Esquipulas II Accord a watershed in Central America's acceptance of the Washington Consensus. In this short accord Central American presidents committed to solving conflicts politically and democratically and pledged to "accelerate development to achieve more egalitarian societies free of misery." In the IDB's backward-looking analysis, the accord envisioned regional economic integration and marked a move away from protectionist import-substituting industrialization, laying the groundwork for neoliberal reforms.[8] In reality, Esquipulas II had done no such thing. More than anything else, its language showed the strength that Sandinista Nicaragua, under attack in the Contra War, still had at the bargaining table. The URNG originally saw the agreement as a "positive step," although they quickly denounced the government for failing to live up to its terms.[9]

As the URNG noted, Cerezo's policies in general favored the business elite. The president infuriated the private sector, however, when he announced that the state had a "social debt" to its citizens. His 1987 Plan de Reorganización Social called for increased public-sector spending, especially in health and education, and for aid to landless campesinos.[10] While the state did not and would never provide sufficient resources for such measures, the steps it did take were the product of dialogue with the Left. Social activism and leftist militancy were revivifying after a postgenocide downturn. In part, despite ongoing repression, this was an effect of the political opening that civilian rule afforded. Early in Cerezo's first year in office, Octubre Revolucionario (OR)—Mario Payeras's and Yolanda Colom's split-away guerrilla group—noted increased coordination between urban and rural social movements as well as ladino and Maya cooperation in a range of growing social movement webs that included unions, the Grupo de Apoyo Mutuo (GAM, the Mutual Support Group that advocated for the families of the disappeared and massacred), and the Campesino Unity Committee. The CUC expanded and announced its support of the *"lucha popular"* in 1986, and unions and labor confederations grew. In 1987, in a massive display of class solidarity, the public sector held a general strike from April to June. Cerezo declared the strike illegal, but it ended only when his government legalized sixteen unions, conceded pay raises and benefits, and promised not to privatize the National Electrification Institute (INDE, the electric company).[11]

The guerrilla organizations worried about social-movement advances achieved without a revolutionary vanguard at their head. They also debated the value of the hit-and-run victories that they themselves began to score during the Cerezo presidency. Were lightening-strike operations, such as occupying fincas for an hour or two to deliver a pedagogical talk to the workers, more media events than effective military strategy? In 1989 OR held that such operations retarded the task of building a properly organized popular movement back up by inviting repression, especially of Maya activists. The URNG concurred, conceding that this kind of militancy gave the state an excuse to repress popular movement leaders who were not linked to the revolution. Still, the operations continued.[12]

The popular movement's activism through the late 1980s, meanwhile, helped to win it a place in a process of "national dialogue." This began in 1989, with the formation of the National Reconciliation Commission (CNR), of which the future president Jorge Serrano was a member. Although the CNR's creation had been mandated by Esquipulas II, it appears that it came to belated fruition in part because of pressure from the Left.[13] An essential part of the quest to forge a "social pact," multisector roundtable negotiations based on the CNR model were soon a permanent feature of Guatemala's political landscape. Over time such roundtables became arenas in which opposition sectors had a voice. It was a circumscribed voice, however; blocs of powerful businessmen functioned as what the Guatemalan analyst Adrián Zapata calls "veto players" who overruled any out-of-the-mainstream proposal.[14] Elite-dominated, but arguably at least in some measure a product of leftist activism, the CNR and the similar multisector forums founded on its model were an integral element of the neoliberalization of the Guatemalan body politic and, later, of local governance and development—in short, of agro-urbanization.

Agro-urbanization was also fueled by new, neoliberal funding mechanisms that circumscribed the central government, as Guatemala slowly adopted "social investment funds" (SIFs). Like roundtable-style negotiation, the SIF model was integral to the practice and financing of "community-driven development" later at the heart of agro-urban politics. The World Bank created Latin America's first SIF as an emergency measure to speed humanitarian aid to Bolivia, which was undergoing economic shock therapy in the middle of the 1980s. The World Bank never envisioned SIFs becoming part of its plans to liberalize economies elsewhere. Yet in Guatemala that is what happened. According to a World Bank internal report, the Bolivian SIF piqued Cerezo's interest. His government petitioned to institute a similar plan, but the World Bank rejected the proposal. First, since one of the main goals of Bolivia's SIF was to bypass the central state and rush funds to local governments and NGOs, it claimed that Guatemala had no need for such measures. The bank also noted that Guatemala was already decentralizing, having dedicated 8 (and later 10) percent of its tax revenues to municipalities. The Cerezo administration rewrote the proposal and won the loan, but Congress voted down the legislation at the end of his term. By that time, however, the bank had rethought its position, and in 1990 it loaned the outgoing administration US$15 million to draft new legislation to form the nation's FIS (Fondo de Inversión Social). "Neoliberalism" did not just change Guatemala; Guatemala changed "neoliberalism."[15]

Serrano picked up where Cerezo left off. He created FONAPAZ, the National Fund for Peace, a social investment fund that brought public and private investments together to aid agrarian communities hard-hit by the armed conflict. FONAPAZ and later related social funds so eloquently encapsulate the changing relationships of public and private through the last years of the Cold War that it is worth jumping slightly ahead to see how they ultimately emerged. Unlike FONAPAZ, which was run by the president's office, Guatemala's FIS was autonomous and governed by its own statutes, making its creation a matter of great political debate. Indeed, Congress did not pass the law creating the FIS until July 1993, when Serrano was in exile and de León Carpio was head of state. Following the World Bank's philosophy of bypassing government "line ministries," the FIS acted as a facilitator. It did not carry out projects. It contributed funds and streamlined the efforts of municipalities, communities (who had to chip in), international cooperation and development concerns, and NGOs (of which there were more than two hundred in the nation), with the ultimate goal of hiring private-sector actors to get the work done.[16] Through the FIS, funding bypassed a potentially regulatory central state and flowed to the private sector. By the mid-1990s the FIS and other social funds were channeling significant amounts of aid.[17] They became a major force in shaping development and the process of agro-urbanization. According to Jennifer Schirmer, both FIS and FONAPAZ programs resembled those carried out in the army's Development Poles of 1983–84. They funded and worked with Peace and Development

Committees rooted in the counterinsurgent PACs. "Ironically," Schirmer concludes, World Bank funding brought to a head "the army's decade-long attempt to see to it that their development-qua-security project be consolidated, financed, and hence legitimized, even if indirectly, by the global economic community."[18]

The roundtables and social funds reacted to the Left's demands and provided "humanitarian cover" for a still-oppressive state. They also dovetailed with what Guatemalans call the "NGO-ification" of their body politic during a time of capital expansion. In her case study of how NGOs were taken up and engaged from below, Erin Beck details their profusion and their role in diminishing the centrality of the state in the 1980s and 1990s.[19] Over the same period, as traced in Kedron Thomas's study of counterfeit brand-name apparel workshops in Tecpán, "informalization" of the economy and new networks of illegal or semilegal production and exchange arose in the highlands.[20] Both these works highlight the contested, dialogic, and improvisational ways in which neoliberalization unfolded. There was connective tissue between the before-and-after narratives in which state-led development morphed into neoliberal developmentalism and attempts to eliminate or incorporate the so-called informal sector morphed into a new, neoliberal focus on "microenterprise." The development apparatus and the structures of "democratic" politics in Guatemala did not so much work to replace older structures of control as it to displace, or reposition, them.

Other displacements were unfolding around the globe that we will reference here only in passing. Narcotrafficking channeled funds into money-laundering operations and unregulated and offshore banks, elements of the extralegal world explored by Carolyn Nordstrom in *Global Outlaws*.[21] It also sparked the highly lucrative and politically useful "war on drugs" that outlived the Cold War. Washington did not just build a "consensus" in Central America. It used extralegal means to fund its Contra War against Nicaragua. When the United States unleashed Operation Just Cause and invaded Panama in late 1989 and early 1990, it sent a double message. One was that the drug trade could justify war even in the absence of communism. The other, aimed particularly at Nicaragua but not unnoticed elsewhere, was that the "democratization" referred to in Esquipulas II was going forward, *or else*.[22] At the same time, as its own cities were devastated by crack cocaine, the United States modeled how to use the drug problem to wage war against one's own population while curtailing social spending. Policies began to congeal that would result in the imprisonment of disproportionate numbers of African Americans, and moral panic roiled over "welfare queens" and "crack babies."²³

Guatemala also lived through moral panic that devolved on the poor and the young, as the economy changed and crime exploded. Panic unfolded as the government foregrounded youth in new policy initiatives. Besides debuting rock concerts, the Cerezo administration created CONJUVE (National Council on Youth), a council that was part of its greater National Plan for Youth. After signing Esquipulas II—which was dedicated to Central America's *juventudes*—it sponsored a toothless Youth for Peace program for Central America as a whole.²⁴ At the time, poor Guatemalan youth were facing a humanitarian disaster, and they increasingly became its face in political and popular discourse alike. Alux Nahual's 1987 song, "Como un duende" (Like an elf), which remained a hit for decades, is about a street child. "He's a gray-skinned boy / With nobody, no home, sleeping on the sidewalks / Waking up without having dreamed," the second verse begins. The chorus chants, "He's like a duende ... / Child with no childhood or birthday cake." Tens of thousands of orphans flooded the city in the 1980s. Tens of thousands of more were displaced, swelling the ranks of the hopelessly disenfranchised in the inflationary economy. There's "just one world," "Like a Duende" intoned, but "they leave [us] the third [world], nothing more.²⁵ As *delincuentes*—young delinquents and most especially the members of the new and spreading street gangs—came to symbolize the problems that plagued the nation, street waifs, Alux's *duendes,* became the mascot of misery.

In the late 1980s the homeless *duendes* were at the center of growing terror about *robaniños* (people who stole children) and traffic in bodily organs. In mid-1987, the URNG accused high-ranking military officers of colluding with clandestine baby-selling rings, which the guerrillas alleged had been operating since 1982. The clamor on this topic had gotten so loud by 1988 that the U.S. consul in Guatemala promised to personally investigate, and the European Parliament condemned Guatemala for trafficking in children and bodily organs. Fueled by the proliferation of street children and the spike in transnational adoptions, stories of "missing bodies" filled the press in the mid to late 1980s. Guatemala City stories told of girls and boys vanishing into worlds of adoption, organ harvesting, prostitution, and child pornography, as kidnapping became a daily reported crime.²⁶ The *robaniños* panic continued into the 1990s, by which time "gringos" were the suspected kidnappers, a belief that motivated violent mob attacks on foreigners as well as on the police, who were suspected of collusion in the crimes. The panic and violence came to a peak and finally ended in 1994, as detailed in a study by Daniel Rothenberg, who argues that "the motivating power of the *[robaniños]* tales as the catalyst for the panic was bound to the way the stories encoded a focused and compelling counter-narrative to the promises of peace and the democratic transition in Guatemala," expressing "uncertainty, fear, and deep-rooted mistrust."[27]

When the *robaniños* panic began in the 1980s, the supposed perpetrators were not brazen foreigners who wrested children out of their parents' arms but unidentifiable, occult Guatemalan forces discursively related to the security state and corrupt foreign trade in babies and bodily organs. The panic can and should be read as a popular reaction in a war-torn body politic to Guatemala's martial transition to democracy. It was also, however, part of a worldwide phenomenon in which anxieties related to the sea change in global capitalist accumulation—and thus to the contemporary phase of planetary urbanization—condensed around children and youth. In the same decade, a moral panic about pedophiles, pornographers, and the satanic ritual abuse of children swept through the United States, and from there around much of the English-speaking world and northern Europe.[28] Latin America's child-abduction and organ-stealing allegations were seen in "Argentina, Bolivia, Brazil, Chile, Colombia, Costa Rica, the Dominican Republic, El Salvador, Guatemala, Honduras, Mexico, Paraguay, Peru and Uruguay," writes Rothenberg.[29]

In Guatemala, as in many places around the globe, moral panic broke out as the "age of development" was slowly, painfully transmogrifying into what would soon be recognizable as the age of "neoliberal multiculturalism." This transformation itself was intrinsically related to the discursive ascendance of so-called identity politics as the politics of class solidarity were seen as waning—a shift with an attendant vocalization in popular culture, as expressed by the changes sketched out in my friend's historical cartoon and given voice in the arc from Alux Nahual's 1987 "Cease Fire" to their 1993 *Americamorfosis* album with a track that sang of sailing to "this new land called identity." The condensation of anxiety around youth—and, as we will see, popular youth culture—was bound up in the post-Fordist wave of planetary urbanization that, in Sevilla-Buitrago's words, "entailed the condensation of urban patterns of sociospatial structuration in the countryside."[30] It was a chaotic, contested, and often violent process.

AGRO-URBANIZATION, RESISTANCE, AND PANIC

In April 1990, as presidential campaigns were ramping up, the URNG issued a report on conditions around Guatemala. It said that social protest was exploding because of a 110 percent rise in the cost of living, sparked when Cerezo eliminated price controls on basic foods at the beginning of his term. With 85 percent of the population of some nine million living in poverty, Guatemala was one of Earth's most unequal countries. It was also one of the planet's youngest, the URNG noted, claiming that over 45 percent of the population was under the age of fifteen; the average age overall was twenty-two. Interestingly, although the URNG analysts noted both a growing population and rising population density in key highland areas, they claimed that the nation was still nearly 70 percent rural and closer to 90 percent in many areas. The guerrillas underscored the preponderance of small towns of under five thousand inhabitants, which, like even smaller villages, had seen no change in urbanization or services. "The quantitative relation between the rural and urban populations has practically not varied over the past forty years," they wrote.[31]

In fact, both the quantitative and the qualitative relationships between urban and rural populations were changing in ways that were already becoming visible but that would not become obvious for another ten to twenty years. The URNG's statement speaks to the "invisibility" of the agro-urban landscape that was emerging. Through the return to democracy, modernizing development brought roads, electricity, telephones, and new technologies such as cable television to agro-urbanizing territory, most of which was still under military occupation. As these infrastructural grids were expanding, families were moving from small villages into municipal cabeceras, and from municipal to departmental cabeceras, causing the population to grow in urbanizing centers.

The informal sector grew as labor regimes changed. The social, economic, and cultural metabolism between small rural villages and hamlets and their regional centers took new form. This "Americamorfosis" of rural space was underway at the same time that the new and semiprivatized development regime epitomized by the idea of the social pact and the mechanism of the social investment fund was taking shape. By the time that neoliberalized, "community-driven" development plans formalized in the mid-1990s, many of the "rural" areas they addressed had begun to look, socially and culturally, more akin to poor Guatemala City neighborhoods than they did like "traditional" country towns. As the URNG's 1990 assessment reminds us, however, provincial Guatemala, despite the urbanization around the Cold War's end, still appeared overwhelmingly rural to observers.

This agrarian landscape was an arena of active politics and ongoing irregular warfare. After military offensives in 1987 and 1988 drove them out of their bases in the remote mountains, the guerrillas—like significant proportions of the agrarian population itself—moved major operations both into the capital city and into economically important agrarian centers, many of them located on or near the nation's few main highways. From 1989 to the mid-1990s, agro-urbanizing cabeceras were on the front lines of a war that, like the neoliberalizing political economy and the moral panic in public discourse, at once reflected and helped to constitute the "Americamorfosis" of social space.

One protagonist in this process who later wrote a memoir was Comandante Santiago of ORPA, a guerrilla group founded in the late 1970s with the mission of taking indigenous people and their issues more seriously. Santiago Santa Cruz Mendoza arrived in the highlands in 1980, later than Yolanda Colom and Mario Payeras had. Like them, however, he was a member of the urban generation whose "national encounter" with the highland Maya would color the tenor of later agro-urban culture and race relations. The squadron he led, the Frente Javier Tambriz (FJT, Javier Tambriz Front), was active through the 1996 Peace Accords. It was a key combative force that brought the war to central areas, making its history a veritable tour of the complexities of life in the agro-urbanizing highlands.

Like all guerrillas, Santa Cruz had experienced the nation's "ethnic question" in the ranks. In the 1980s, as the front's members were writing their campfire anthem to the tune of the Beatles' "Yellow Submarine," tensions arose. Influenced by Maya nationalist movements, a combatant demanded that the indigenous members be in charge of the front. This "reverse racism," in Santa Cruz's words, damaged fraternal bonds. He had the (urban) ladino leaders take on workaday tasks and ceded authority to the (rural) Maya members. This didn't work, since the Maya *compañeros* could not read and write and were lacking logistical training. After several weeks the FJT combatants decided that they needed to put aside their differences, train each other in their respective areas of expertise, and labor side by side—to live together, as it were, in their "yellow submarine."[32]

The squadron was a microcosm of greater social changes on which the documents are silent. Guerrilla camps were not the nation's only "yellow submarines" in which people from different backgrounds and ethnicities mixed and in which indigenous people refused to be subservient. Over the same period many Maya were moving not only to the capital city's barrios, where they would come into closer contact with poor ladinos, but also to municipal and departmental cabeceras.[33] Far from being spurred just by labor demand and the market's invisible hand, however, such relocation was also driven by the military campaigns that pushed the guerrillas into more central areas in the late 1980s. Over the same period, displaced populations of Maya villagers, many with children who had grown up in hiding in the wilderness, began coming down from the mountains. After reindoctrination sessions at army posts, many of these displaced campesinos ended up in agro-urbanizing villages and slums and thus back in the center of the war once again. The populations they entered were larded with military Civil Affairs officers whose job was to spread anticommunist ideology and root out and turn in potential subversives. Civil Affairs also provided the high command with "social intelligence" that it passed on to the executive branch so it could effectively target its development and counterinsurgency campaigns.[34]

Development campaigns, counterinsurgency, a relocating population, and new forms of economic activity were all factors in the agro-urbanization of the areas into which the guerrillas moved. The process of bringing the war to economically important centers, Santa Cruz writes, dated to 1986 and accelerated in the years ahead. The EJT's focus in 1988 was Chimaltenango Department. By the beginning of 1989, ORPA was active not only in this NTA-growing area but also in municipalities in Sololá Department around Lake Atitlán, where tourism was important, as well as along the Atlantic Highway in Suchitepéquez and Escuintla, in the heartland of traditional agro-export fincas. The army pursued them from its massive, nearby bases. ORPA guerrillas briefly occupied the municipality of Ciudad Vieja in early 1990 and took over the cone of Volcán de Agua, audacious moves that showed they were in the country's very center. These areas border Antigua, the onetime colonial capital and the national epicenter of tourism, located just outside Guatemala City.[35]

The guerrillas finally created a coordinated Unified Front (Frente Unitario) in 1991, early in Serrano's term. By this time they were fighting an impossibly uphill battle. With the end of the global Cold War, the Left's strategy turned away from trying to win militarily and toward negotiating a political settlement. To do so from a position of strength, they needed shows of force. The guerrillas had two problems. One was that counterinsurgency had left them unable to live among the population in highland villages. The other was that recruitment had become next to impossible. "The popular, worker, and campesino organizations weren't responding to our calls," Santa Cruz remembers. "Members of three generations of the same families had participated in the war. Many had grown up ... immersed in war, and ... they were retiring from the regular columns and becoming part-time combatants. This would let them tend their plots of land and take care of their nuclear families."[36] As we will see, the children of those families, growing up in a radically reconfigured municipal landscape over the course of the 1990s and into the 2000s, were protagonists in Guatemala's physical and cultural transformation from rural to agro-urban.

As the weakening guerrillas warred to negotiate peace, their hit-and-run operations in the economic heartland became high-stake media events. "In the worst-case scenario," wrote Santa Cruz, by 1991 "the guerrillas risked becoming part of national folklore and being exploited for tourism."[37] They continued to fight in urban areas like Mixco (part of Guatemala City) and in important secondary centers.[38] One such action came in August 1991, when the FJT shut down Escuintla. They announced their action on AM and FM radio, took over residential neighborhoods, and blocked the highways for several hours. Not a single combatant died in the ensuing firefight. On the same day preparatory meetings for peace talks were underway in Caracas, Venezuela. Reportedly, Serrano tipped his hat to URNG commander Gaspar Ilom, saying, "We know what your boys did in Escuintla."[39]

In October the URNG planned to follow up on this success by having the FJT take over Antigua itself. If it had succeeded, this action would have been less a military victory than a magnificent media event, a show of force broadcast around the world. After a long march to San Lorenzo del Cubo, a town on Antigua's fringes, the guerrillas were exhausted and hungry. They sent a *compañero* to go buy them Pollo Campero fried chicken. When he got to Antigua, the *compañero* turned them in to the army. The army encircled the guerrillas, who lost eight members as they fought their way out. The heartbreaking irony of communists dying because in a very human moment they wanted some Pollo Campero (from a company owned by one of the nation's wealthiest capitalists) reminds us of the blurred lines between the supposedly separate spheres of political activism and popular consumer culture.[40]

Such blurred lines characterized public discourse in the provinces, where anxieties about generational change, consumer culture, and corrupted youth were bound up in the process of agro-urbanization. Far away from Antigua and

Guatemala City, along the Mexican border, in the Huista region of Huehuetenango Department, a local newspaper was founded in 1991 that promoted the Mayan movement, militated for peace, documented modernizing change, and fretted endlessly about the new generation of teenagers. Though the writers in the Jacaltenango-based *El Regional* were deeply disturbed about youth and mass media, their paper itself was a prime example of how mass media diffused in Guatemala at the end of the millennium. Published in Spanish and Jacalteco Maya, the local language, *El Regional* grew quickly. In the years ahead it spread to Huehuetenango and Quetzaltenango, adding supplements and printing articles in a variety of Mayan languages. Its founders made distribution deals with major national newspapers, and Mayan-movement leaders such as Rigoberta Menchú lent their names to its masthead.

When *El Regional* began publishing, forced recruitment, PACs, military commissioners, and counterinsurgent development still defined community life. Its first editorial, however, "Time to Be Born," spoke not of armed conflict but of a generation lost. Their region, the editors wrote, was under "continual bombardment from huge media like radio, newspapers, and television, that little by little are inculcating [our youth] with foreign values and replacing our own elements of local culture." The *jóvenes,* they held, "feel ashamed to be children of this land." Youth were shunning their native language, way of dressing, and local music in favor of imitating "foreign ways" they were exposed to through mass media.[41]

A sidebar to "Time to Be Born," titled "Crisis and Identity," noted how youth were "enslaved" to foreign phrases and styles in a "cruel reality" of "alienation." "It's not uncommon to see 'gringo getups' [*disfraces gringos*], to hear words that don't belong to the Spanish language," the author mourned. "This [foreign cultural] invasion," he continued, "has brought social consequences that seem to have no possible solution. [They] have caused mistrust that makes communication impossible between the *urban and rural populations* [emphasis added]; they have created a barrier between the people who share the invading ideas and those who do not share them or who have not had the opportunity [to get to know them]."[42] The author differentiated between young indigenous villagers and more "gringo-ized" youth in and around the municipal cabecera—youth not unlike the future *Rock Republik* blogger Gerardo Perez, who would later remember the period to the tune of Megadeth's "Train of Consequences."

In the early to mid-1990s, the Huista region was in the throes of modernization. Road construction and rural electrification were proceeding at a

Huehuetenango Department

1. Huehuetenango
2. Aguacatán
3. Chiantla
4. Malacatancito
5. Santa Bárbara
6. San Sebastián Huehuetenango
7. Todos Santos Cuchumatán
8. San Juan Atitán
9. San Rafael Petzal
10. San Gaspar Ixchil
11. Colotenango
12. Santiago Chimaltenango
13. San Pedro Necta
14. San Idelfonso Ixtahuacán
15. Tectitán
16. Cuilco
17. La Libertad
18. La Democracia
19. Santa Ana Huista
20. San Antonio Huista
21. Santiago Petatán
22. Unión Cantinil
23. Concepción Huista
24. Jacaltenango
25. Nentón
26. San Miguel Acatán
27. San Sebastián Coatán
28. San Rafael La Independencia
29. San Juan Ixcoy
30. San Pedro Soloma
31. Santa Eulalia
32. San Mateo Ixtatán
33. Santa Cruz Barillas

◎ Departmental capital (cabecera)
〜 Departmental boundary
— Municipal limit
○ Municipal seat (cabecera)
▨ Huista region

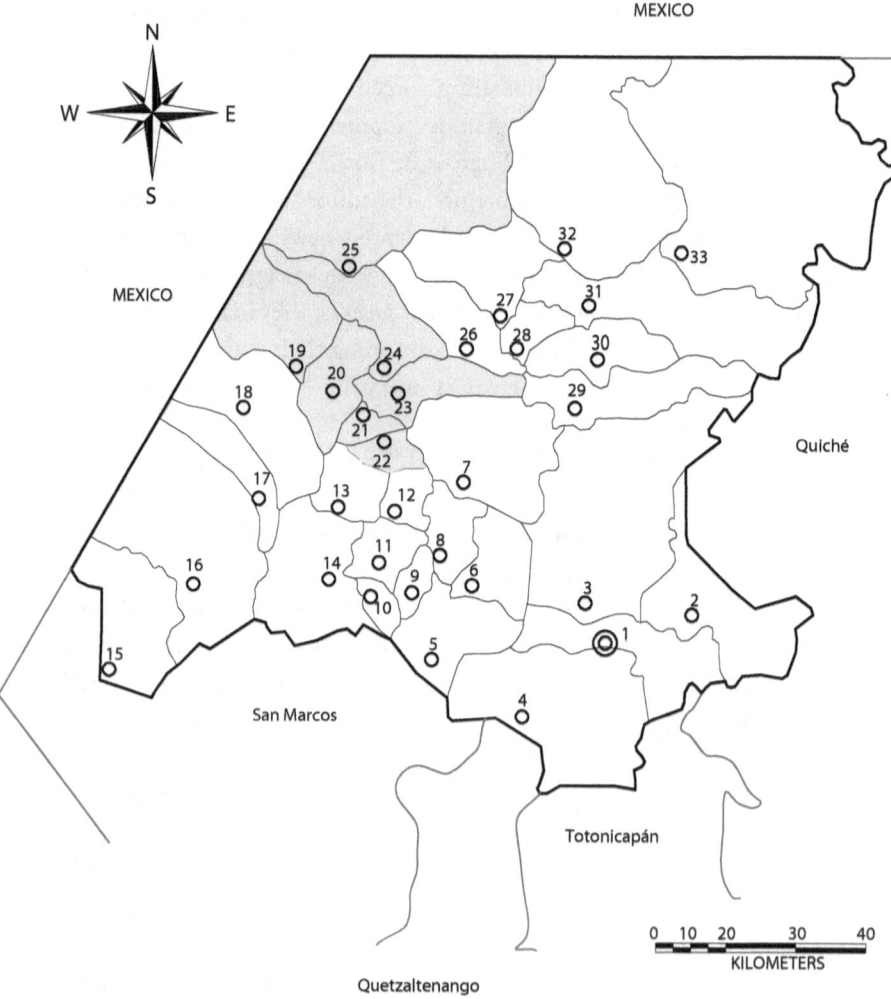

MAP 2. Huehuetenango Department and its Huista region.

rapid pace, phenomena that nearly all analysts have connected with the state's counterinsurgency mission. Telephones were just starting to come to many towns, in the form of one public phone somewhere in the center. The first informal cable TV companies emerged in cabeceras, and the rich had access to the boxy wireless telephones of the era. As everywhere in Guatemala, Protestant Evangelical sects were proliferating in a sea change in faith not unrelated to the armed conflict. Agriculture was being reconfigured through the introduction of NTAs and an intense focus on crop commercialization. Migration to the United States was becoming a huge issue, one to grow in the years ahead, as remesas (remittances) remade the landscape. Too, common crime was on the rise, and not just in crowded departmental cabeceras. Drunken youth were to blame for the rise in crime in San Antonio Huista, said the town's mayor in June 1991, even as what would be an ongoing panic over how pornography was warping young minds broke out in *El Regional*'s pages.[43]

"Sing with me, joven!" implored a letter to the editor and poem sent into *El Regional* from Costa Rica by a Huista-region refugee in 1992. The letter writer was worried about "youth in a world of crisis," crushed by poverty and consumer culture and seduced by capitalism, fashion, music, and mass media. Drugs, alcohol, and the allure of prostitutes awaited them. We should not criticize these lost youth, the author contended. We should help them. And to do so, he wrote them a song. "Sing, sing, sing *joven* / who are yourself a song," it read. "They've told me here / that in you, there's just drug addiction / that in you, there's just prostitution / but I know, that in you there is love. . . . Sing, sing, sing, joven / who are yourself a song / 'cause depending on you is the happiness / of a corrupt world."[44]

The world's corruption was a major topic in agro-urbanizing Guatemala. An *El Regional* story, for example, documented Maya prostitution. "Now Maya women have become part of the guild," the sensational two-page spread lamented.[45] The paper reported on child pornography and "practices" such as "homosexuality, bisexuality, [and] drug use" that "exist in our community more than we believe." It also covered AIDS (HIV was not yet a term in use).[46] Although there had not been a single case in Huehuetenango by the end of 1993, AIDS received far more coverage in *El Regional* than cholera, which spread in epidemic waves in the first few years of the 1990s.[47] When cholera broke out in Huehuehtenango, *El Regional*'s reporter went to investigate, only to find an urban hellhole. The neighborhood where the disease had broken out had no running water or drainage system. It was full of open sewers, its streets were prowled by feral dogs, and the water people drank was rank with feces.[48]

The threat of future HIV-AIDS eclipsing the present reality of cholera is a displacement that, like panic about youth, reflects ground-level anxieties about changing conditions in the time of "Americamorfosis," many related to urbanization. In growing tertiary cities like Huehuetenango, as in expanding municipal cabeceras throughout the highlands, agro-urban Guatemala's habitus (in Pierre Bordieu's sense) was undergoing rapid change. In these centers (though less so in their outlying villages and hamlets), youth participation in "foreign" cultural forms was in and of itself nothing new. People from Quiché and Chimaltenango, for example, remember having followed bands like the Rolling Stones and Led Zeppelin in earlier decades. There were parties and bars in the 1960s and 1970s where people danced to rock in Quetzaltenango and Huehuetenango.[49] Throughout the highlands new bands playing more traditional but popular and still-very-living country-music styles (akin to Mexican *ranchera*) arose throughout the mid to late 1900s. Foreign *música tropical* styles such as *bachata*, personified by the popular Dominican musician Juan Luis Guerra, found highland followers of all ages.[50] The focus of adults, such as those writing in *El Regional*, on youthful cultural corruption had more to do with transformations in the political economy, social changes wrought by the shock of genocide, and the urbanization of social space as poor, "yellow submarine" barrios and shantytowns spread than they did with anything actually terrible or new that young people were doing. Just as the conglomeration of neoliberalizing policies, institutions, and ideologies came together dialogically and improvisationally, so too, in related ways, did discourses about corrupted youth.

Few commentators concerned about "crisis and identity" stopped to think about exactly *why* they found it so concerning. Nor did they contemplate, deeply, what it was *like* to come of age under these conditions. They did not consider that in the face of poverty, in areas under military occupation, and in a society torn through with wartime violence, it took cultural assertiveness for youth to experiment with foreign styles and forms shunned by society at large. More remembered is another kind of cultural assertiveness, one associated with the Mayan movement, of which *El Regional* itself was an expression. Youth played a major role in the Maya pride movement of the 1980s and 1990s. They demonstrated in the streets, filled cultural events, and ultimately grew up to be members of the first generation to refer to itself unselfconsciously as "Maya." Many of them ended up erased from this history of "traditional" cultural revival, however (and unfortunately), when they *also* adopted foreign forms and ways. Thus, in ways analogous to how democratic "participation" helped to erase a not-so-democratic democracy in the age of "Americamorfosis," not-Maya-enough youthful cultural assertiveness in the age of the Maya-led local power movement helped to erase a major constituency that gave the Maya-power movement life.

IDENTITY, LOCAL POWER, AND MUNICIPAL METAMORPHOSES

Maya leaders spearheaded the *poder local* (local power) movement to win more autonomy, power, and funding for municipal governments. They mixed ethnic and cultural issues with their political demands. Their efforts won support from the development apparatus, ranging from huge organizations such as the World Bank, which promoted "decentralization" globally, to progressive NGOs that supported indigenous demands. Their vibrant politics would soon become absorbed, at least in part, by official neoliberal multiculturalism. This was far from the case through the Cold War's end, when Maya activists created new political strategies to revivify old political structures.

Such structures were hidden to the ladino gaze. From its 1984 formation Mario Payeras's and Yolanda Colom's Octubre Revolucionario studied Maya Guatemala's complexities. One of OR's internal work papers gives a guerrilla's-eye ethnography of San Miguel Acatán, a Q'anjob'al municipality in Huehuetenango's Cuchumatanes Mountains. It detailed a multilayered, complex web of *cargo* systems—a "civil-religious hierarchy"—that was "virtually the entirety of the social structure of [the] indigenous municipality." Community governance was conducted not by the official municipality, OR claimed, but by traditional indigenous systems headed by the K'amol B'ey, an elder who arose through the *cofradías,* or church lay confraternities. Traditional indigenous leaders came under attack in the early 1980s, after the townspeople became militant participants on the left. The army slaughtered them and replaced them with compliant PAC leaders who reported to the local military commander. People fled. OR estimated that some four thousand Acatecos were in Los Angeles, with many more in refugee camps in Mexico. State institutions (part of the interinstitutional web of organizations related to counterinsurgency discussed in chapter 1) flooded in. The result, OR concluded, was not just the replacement of one set of indigenous leaders for another. It was the deliberate tearing up of local power and the imposition of counterinsurgent state power, a frontal assault on the very way of life of the indigenous population.[51]

On this point the newly emerging organizations of the Mayan movement could not agree more. The Consejo de Comunidades Étnicas Runujel Junam (CERJ) arose in 1988 to promote Maya culture, to advocate for human rights and take victims' testimony, and to protest counterinsurgency.[52] Two years later, in the same period as important organizations such as the Council of Mayan Organizations of Guatemala (COMG) were appearing, a group called Majawil Q'ij (meaning "new dawn" in Mam) was born.[53] Drawing together traditional leaders such as *sacerdotes mayas*—Maya priests, or shamans— Majawil Q'ij organized around the highlands and participated in events such as the Segundo Encuentro Continental de Pueblos Indígenas, the Americas' second international meeting of indigenous peoples, which was held in Quetzaltenango in 1991.[54] Together with other organizations in the flowering movement, Majawil Q'ij demanded a voice for the Maya in the peace talks and promoted a history of popular resistance that dated not to 1962 but instead to 1524.[55] The organization also underwrote the costs of forming the Defensoría Maya in 1993.[56] The Defensoría was one of the organizations in 1994 that formed part of a new and influential umbrella group, COPMAGUA (Council of Organizations of the Pueblo Maya of Guatemala). This organization participated in the newly created Assembly for Civil Society (ASC), founded by the government, along roundtable lines, to give various sectors of civil society a nonbinding voice in the peace process. By advocating for the Maya in the ASC, COPMAGUA became the movement's main representative in the peace process.[57] The Mayan movement was gaining ground internationally and nationally, arising from very local bases.

The movement wanted authority and autonomy in those local bases. Understanding the process of forging poder local requires looking at the complex politics that OR studied in San Miguel Acatán. Maya activists remade and revitalized systems of governance that dated to the 1500s and that had been evolving since. In few words, the Habsburg Crown's República de Indios (a separate legal structure for indigenous people established in the 1570s) had created parallel and subordinate indigenous-led governmental bodies—a sort of "control the head, rule the body" strategy. The *alcaldía indígena* (indigenous mayoralty) survived waves of liberal attempts to eliminate it over the centuries. Over time, to simplify, many municipalities came to have two mayors, a Spanish one who really ruled and a Maya one, from a

FIGURE 3. Majawil Q'ij participates in the Segundo Encuentro Continental de Pueblos Indígenas in Quetzaltenango, 12 October 1991. Fototeca Guatemala, Archivo de Juan Rolando González Díaz (photographer), GT-CIRMA-FG-160.

privileged sector, who served as a hinge-man between the two worlds. The remnants of this system, where it still existed, came under attack in the 1980s.[58] In general, it was in the 1990s, through intense Mayan grassroots organizing, that the "official" municipality, where it was still under ladino control, became a *municipalidad mixta* (that is, mixed between ladinos and Maya), although in some municipalities the Maya takeover happened earlier. Meanwhile, the alcaldía indígena, the secondary Maya mayoralty, revived and took on new importance. Though it remained unrecognized by the state, the alcaldía indígena worked alongside the official city hall and with leaders in the communal cultural and religious cargo system. The result (to summarize a highly varied landscape) was a three-layer system: an official *alcaldía* increasingly run by Maya mayors; an unofficial alcaldía indígena; and a mix of traditional cargos, including councils of elders and *cofradías*, with leaders chosen at the grassroots. Later, in 1996, this rich and complex mix of polities, with officials both elected and appointed, would assemble in Sololá to create the Guatemalan Association of Indigenous Mayors and Authorities (AGAAI).[59]

Perched on a mountain above Lake Atitlán, Kaqchikel-speaking Sololá is the cabecera of the municipality and department of the same name. It was one of several important centers where grassroots political actors remade municipal and ethnic politics throughout the Cerezo, Serrano, and de León Carpio presidencies. Agrarian Sololá was also urbanizing over this period. Its central neighborhoods swelled. Its residents invested in package stores, coming to own informal chains of *tiendas* around the nation.[60] As in the Huista region, Sololatecos engaged in discourses about lost youth, foreign invasion, and cultural cosmopolitanism. Unlike the writers in *El Regional*, who blamed mass media for their wayward young, Sololatecos blamed tourists and foreign expatriates. This is not surprising, because just below Sololá on the lakeshore lies the heavily touristed, hippie town of Panajachel. Bohemian "Pana" was a music town full of live-rock venues, bars, and discos. As tourism began to revive during the peace negotiations, Pana built on its long-established profile as a "gateway" town where Guatemala City counterculture artists met eager audiences of fans not just from abroad and from the capital but also from the highlands.

In a 1992 *cabildo abierto* (open town-hall meeting) in Sololá, residents railed against the corrosive effects of this bohemian enclave. "Tourists destroy our cultures," one said. "Our municipality of Panajachel has already lost all its values." This comment, punctuated with cries for "no more hotels!" and "no more typical [folkloric] centers!" prompted a response. The kids are doing drugs, lamented the next speaker. They are smoking cigarettes, drinking, and thinking of "other things," all because of the foreigners, who, he added, get rich on all this tourism while we stay poor. Another Sololateca chimed in. These outlanders don't just come with drugs, she said. They're also spreading prostitution and AIDS.[61]

The Sololá town meeting demonstrated the militancy of highlanders determined to assert their rights. Not long before, in Santiago Atitlán, across the lake, the outraged population had forced the local army outpost to with-

FIGURE 4. The story behind the *cabildo abierto* in Sololá was a battle over the fate of a lakeshore finca occupied by people from the area, who were violently evicted by the army and police. This protest of the eviction occurred on 8 April 1992. Fototeca Guatemala, Archivo de Juan Rolando González Díaz (photographer), GT-CIRMA FG 160.

draw after soldiers massacred twelve demonstrators at the end of 1990. Sololá's *cabildo abierto* of 1992 and the demonstrations that prompted it formed one small chapter in this greater history of resistance. Young people in Sololá, as around the Mayan highlands, were hardly just smoking cigarettes and thinking of "other things" in the early 1990s. They were also participating in historic grassroots movements to end military occupation, forge local power, and assert Maya pride—pride that years later would manifest itself as an essential element of a new popular nationalism.[62]

The grassroots struggle in the years leading up to peace was polyvalent. It was a battle to get rid of the army bases, break up the PACs, and stop political murder. It was also a fight to validate Maya culture and to assure that the genocide of the 1980s was not forgotten. In the same year that Sololatecos bemoaned the corrosive influences of foreigners on their children, a team of forensic anthropologists was working in the neighboring department of El Quiché, accelerating a project of exhuming mass graves that had begun in 1988. By 1992—the year in which Guatemalans were electrified by the awarding of the Nobel Peace Prize to Rigoberta Menchú—these exhumations were promising remembrance and portending possible justice for the military's crimes. Also coming into view were "hidden" indigenous systems of local rule that had been driven underground during the violence.[63]

The process of forging local power played out differently in the hundreds of highland municipalities. In Sololá, according to studies by Rigoberto Ajcalón Choy and Timothy Smith, the indigenous mayoralty took the lead in the early 1990s.[64] Supported by left-wing groups at a time when guerrillas were still active in the area, the alcaldía indígena led the community—including its youth—in the fight against army commissioners and secret police, military conscription, and the PACs. As the protest movement grew stronger and as more villages and hamlets began to participate in organized politics, local leaders split the religious cargos off from the alcaldía indígena (also called the *municipalidad Maya*), an organization in which they had traditionally been important members.[65] This was an important step in the evolution toward today's three-level system, in which the official *muni*, the Maya *muni*, and the traditional leaders work together, and sometimes fight one another, in a complex mix. It freed the *municipalidad Maya* to focus on political issues, and by 1992 its members were secretly plotting to take over the *alcaldía oficial*, which was controlled by the ladinos and penetrated by the army. The year 1992 began with waves of protest against military oppression as indigenous municipal representatives were being elected. To better unite themselves, Sololá's leaders formed a Committee to Support the Maya Municipality, which worked to coordinate the efforts of participating groups, including the CUC and Majawil Q'ij. In mid-January, the committee held a huge protest against forced recruitment, and a week later it presented the army with a petition to end the practice. Sololtecos continued organizing and protesting in the years ahead. Their *municipalidad indígena* was a powerful local political force by 1994, and committees and subcommittees flourished as the Maya *muni* became more institutionally sophisticated.[66] In the next year's election, Sololatecos would bring to power an "official" mayor who was Maya, a historic milestone. By 1996, as we will see, both the "official" and the "indigenous" city halls were in Maya hands. Unfortunately, however, other powers remained on the scene.

The reconfigured municipal structures seen not just in Sololá but, with many variations, around the highlands were constructed in resistance to and in dialogue with the administrative structures of counterinsurgency. Military *comisionados* and PAC leaders reappeared in many places as *alcaldes auxiliares*—the auxiliary mayors who represented aldeas (villages) and *caseríos* (hamlets) in their municipal centers, where military Civil Affairs officers were active. Local factions tied to the army and to the atrocities gained and held power in numerous locations (que trance, ¿va?). Where they lost elections, these right-wing local strongmen sometimes formed rival factions that fought the mayor for power.[67] The structures of insurgency and counterinsurgency further divided Maya polities that were already divided. In some areas, Maya leaders were linked to the political party system, which their forbearers had joined during the democratic revolution of 1944–54. In others, grassroots leaders had nothing to do with such structures of officialdom; these were exemplified by but hardly limited to the *sacerdotes mayas,* by councils of elders "elected" at the neighborhood level, and by the *cofradías*. Finally, Maya activists as a whole fell into two broad camps, the *clasistas* and *culturalistas*. Local politicians would have to navigate all these constituencies.[68]

Seen from above, local politics trace a historic transformation as activists popularized Maya identity and indigenous politicians wrested mayoralties from ladinos. Seen from below, however, they reveal a messier "Americamorfosis," in which everyday people contested power and identity in far more complicated ways. They did so in an agro-urbanizing and "Mayanizing" body politic cut through with changing striations of caste and class.[69] A friend of mine, "Estuardo," for example, was born in an agrarian hamlet of Sololá, but his mother moved the family to a shantytown in the center after a PAC member murdered her husband. Estuardo's memories twine discourses of powerlessness and empowerment. He regularly encountered his father's killer in the market but had to keep his silence. Too small to prevent his alcoholic stepfather from beating his mother, Estuardo would stand outside the handmade hut as she screamed, throwing rocks at its flimsy metal roof. He was only just in puberty when he demonstrated against the army in the early 1990s, but he recalls it as the first moment in his life when he felt empowered to *do* something about the world around him. At this phase of life, like so many in his generation, he was just beginning to self-identify as Maya. His new ethnic self-awareness was born in the force field of grassroots activism *and* in the social space of the agro-urban barrio—the space in which teenagers were "smoking cigarettes" and thinking of "other things." Some kids from his barrio, "tough guys" who "wanted to be somebody," adopted cholero "bad-boy" street styles; other girls and boys defied their elders simply by flirting, fraternizing, and hanging out in the park. Later in his teens Estuardo briefly dated a ladina, a violation of community norms he compounded by refusing to marry in his early twenties. Significant numbers of the first Maya generation were people who strained against tradition while at the same time giving life to ethnic politics based precisely on vindicating and valorizing tradition.[70] This internal tension infused bottom-up identity politics in a population variegated in transforming ways by caste and class, by powerlessness and empowerment, and by the urban and the rural.

The agro-urbanization of Guatemalan social space cannot be understood without taking de a pie indigenous people into account and remembering that a great deal of the discourse about them was related to the widespread moral panic about youth, which later worked its way into historical memory. Highland youth did not just adopt foreign and city styles and vices because of some invisible hand of neoliberalism or consumer culture. They confected their own homegrown and hybrid modalities of what Philippe Bourgeois calls the "oppositional style" of the "street culture of resistance."[71] That they did so bespeaks their active participation in identity politics, in their towns' agro-urbanization, and in "planetary urbanization."[72] Very shortly, as Guatemala City bands began to regularly tour in the highlands, these Maya youth, and their younger brothers and sisters, would become more *visible* participants in chapín countercultures. Later, after peace and into the new millennium, many would blend their Maya pride and their cosmopolitan iterations of "cool" into self-identifications that entered the mix of idioms that ultimately contributed to the rise of a bottom-up alternative popular nationalism. Though we lack nonpanicked documentation on how provincial youth took up "foreign ways" in the late 1980s and early 1990s, before ladino rockers from the capital city appeared in the highlands, an against-the-grain reading of the available sources strongly suggests that they were already active historical and cultural actors who melded "Maya pride" and "foreign cool." This point is important because it resists two narratives: one in which provincial youth became apolitical dropouts and another in which they abandoned Maya ways once they were seduced by pop culture. Neither foreigners nor ladino kids from the city brought globalized tastes to provincial youth (as, for example, the Spaniards brought smallpox and Christianity to the Americas). Indeed, inasmuch as their "oppositional styles" embedded Maya pride, provincial youth, not city youth, were the *leaders* in forging what would later grow into a bottom-up alternative popular nationalism. Far from being only a sign of the commercialization of society and of the spread of neoliberalism, the ways in which young Guatemalans produced, contested, revived, and remade culture show legacies of resistance and everyday idioms of expressing youthful identity that took shape as the grand political narratives of the Cold War era unraveled and were rewoven into transforming social space.[73]

The end of the global Cold War occasioned significant changes in Guatemala in 1992. The Serrano administration began to repatriate refugees from Mexico. The returnees' arrival profoundly impacted the process of agro-urbanization in the areas in which they resettled, and the outflow from the refugee camps deprived the guerrillas of their one remaining source of new recruits. ORPA's Comandante Santiago remembers that, in 1992, the already-excruciating process of recruitment became virtually impossible.[74] The URNG high command publicly declared that peace was its main objective.[75] The war entered its ramp-down phase.

Still-militant guerrillas had to make life-changing decisions. At the end of October 1992, Octubre Revolucionario's members voted to dissolve their organization. Forming a new group called Citizens for Democracy, they came out of clandestine resistance and began to work within the law as members of civil society. In an "absolute minority," Yolanda Colom and Mario Payeras opposed this transformation. They also opposed the whole idea of a negotiated peace, believing that, without force, the Guatemalan elite would never enact meaningful change. But worn down by years of war and confronting a new planetary geopolitical reality, a generation of guerrillas was beginning to join the mainstream.[76] As OR dissolved, Santiago Santa Cruz's FJT shrank to a mere twenty-seven combatants and retreated to its camp on Volcán Atitlán in Sololá Department near Lake Atitlán. It saw few successes through 1993, and by the end of the year Santa Cruz had had enough. He visited the URNG high commander in Mexico City and quit. The thirteen-year ORPA veteran was off to Georgia and Texas to build another life.[77]

A generation of warriors confronted a new geopolitical reality, but on the ground anticommunist geopolitics continued apace. In Huehuetenango, for example, there were 3,000 soldiers and a quarter of a million members of the PAC in place to fight an estimated 135 guerrillas. When an *El Regional* reporter asked the military zone commander if he didn't think that was a bit excessive, the commander explained that the PACs' job was not to fight the URNG but to provide the citizenry with *security*.[78] As the process of agro-urbanization continued to unfold in this violent body politic, youth would increasingly become the object of "security" measures as they came to stand, discursively, for society's degeneration. Young Guatemalans at the grassroots, however, continued to contest and transform idioms of identity in agro-urban space. In so doing, they wrote their own chapter of national battles over authenticity, caste, and "the ethnic question." At the time, these questions were exploding in violence on the streets of Guatemala City.

GUATEMALA CITY AND THE FIRST LOST GENERATION

"La puta lucha de las clases" (The fucking struggle of the classes), whined the apathetic, nihilistic, middle-class antihero of *Ruido de fondo* (Background noise), Javier Payeras's stunning short novel about coming of age in Guatemala City in the first half of the 1990s. There was a war going on, but at least one social segment of spoiled kids in the capital city chose to pretend that there wasn't. "The armed conflict," the fictional narrator said, "I didn't see it, I didn't live it, until who knows how a copy of a book by Mario Payeras made its way to me (I don't remember the title)." There is inside humor in this line; the guerrilla Mario Payeras was the novelist Javier Payeras's uncle. In Javier Payeras's book, the antihero's mother hated the guerrillas. His father was ambivalent. He remembered his university friends who had joined the *compas* fondly, but he got mad when he found his son reading Mario Payeras's book. "When I found out about the war, it was already over," the nameless narrator said.[79]

The war was not yet over in the early 1990s, but on many levels the master narratives that had driven it had already lost their sway. The cynicism and solipsism of *Ruido de fondo*'s young antihero reflected—as did urban counterculture and street violence in the capital in general—the total erosion of developmental narratives of progress and the associated visions of the future that had underpinned the discourse of the Left and Right alike for decades.[80] In fact, the antisocial, antipolitical attitudes of this supposed new generation had *also* been building up for years, if not for decades, but, nonetheless, the late 1980s and early 1990s youth of Guatemala City became (not without reason) the national mascot of *bad attitude*.

For many reasons the youth coming of age around the turn of the 1990s were seen and remembered as what might be called Guatemala's "first lost generation." Javier Payeras's short novel is a devastating critique of the era's soulless youth. The middle-class narrator remembers the "pusher" who sold drugs in high school. He says of his first girlfriend that she "fucked like a demon; it's all she knew how to do, the only thing she was good for," adding that "it's not bad—some people aren't even good for that." He tells of the meaninglessness of classes in the university and waxes on about his boring "bureaucrat" parents. He speaks of a shabby, filthy city in a country forever doomed to be "third world." "A quick tour of the Historic Center [of Guatemala City]," he quips: "transvestites, cokeheads, thieves, rapists, children of rapists, whores, sons of whores, and police—sometimes all in the same person."[81]

Payeras's iconic young hater represents a generation that would be remembered for embodying Guatemala's turn away from revolutionary consciousness and toward consumer culture. According to scholars who have studied urban, middle-class youth in this general period, these youngsters displayed an attitude known as *valeverguismo* (not give a shit ism). They came up in an era when racialized slurs like *shumo* ("brown trash," in loose translation) were gaining currency on the streets, as caste- and class-based distinctions sharpened in rhythm with the spread of forms of distinction linked to consumer capitalism.[82] For young people these distinctions were lived both in a physical geography—in a web of schools and private schools and neighborhoods that every day reflected acute divisions of wealth and status more sharply—and in an associated and similarly variegated semiotic universe of slang, style, and song.

Spreading FM radio and cable television, especially MTV, played foreign music and styles that Guatemala City youth drew on in their own musical and cultural production. Many popular genres and bands came from the English-speaking world, but Spanish-language groups were increasingly popular. Ricardo Arjona, Guatemala's first pop star to make it big on a global stage, exemplified the continental rise of *rock en español* in the 1980s. Ironically, by the time he was famous, Arjona had moved to Mexico; he had been unappreciated at home.[83]

Though Guatemala City was far from being a major center in the Spanish rock explosion, its homegrown subculture music scene became more commercial over the end of the 1980s and into the 1990s. Death metal popularized and gave rise to a thrash and trash craze, showing the exodus of a musical form from an "under" youth counterculture to a more widespread youth culture. Bands like Yttrium, Bathory, Abbadon, and Extasis were so popular that, despite Guatemalan society's ongoing rabid rejection of the genre, Radio Metro Stereo felt obligated to play them, along with new metal releases from abroad. Meanwhile, the term *rapero* entered everyday language, as youth shyly began to experiment with the new genre and break-dance in the streets.[84]

It was with good reason that the government's youth council focused on music as an important ground of cultural production. CONJUVE continued to promote rock and hold concerts; one in the city's central park in 1989 drew a crowd of more than forty thousand fans. By that time radio DJs were beginning to give more airtime to rock genres that previously had been distributed largely hand to hand in the form of bootleg cassettes. Metro Stereo 102.9's show, *Revolución Rock,* for example, sparked the formation of club-like groups such as the Consejo Supremo de Metal.[85] Of greater effect was the new Central American grunge sound beginning to emerge in the 1990s; *Religiones,* a 1993 album by the Costa Rican group 50 Al Norte, helped to popularize the genre.

Religiones, a pioneer album in Central American rock, was released by Primera Generación (First Generation) Records. The label and studio's owner, the producer Giácomo Buonafina, had opened Primera Generación in his hometown of Guatemala City in late 1991 when he was twenty-five years old.[86] Primera Generación was a well-named company. Later, in the mid-1990s, it became the principal organization that nurtured and promoted a new strain of rock nacional that youth around the nation adopted as the soundtrack of the reconfigured, bottom-up chapinismo they were unwittingly constructing. In the first years of this new label's existence, however, popular youth music and countercultures were far from being unifying.

From the late 1980s to the early 1990s, brutal, youthful turf wars broke out in Guatemala City. Upper-caste, light-skinned rockeros and metaleros, who called themselves "antibreaks," attacked lower-caste, brown-skinned break-dancers and *raperos.* These interclass battles revolved around antigang sentiment, musical styles, and challenges to the unwritten codes of the system of castas. Primarily, the street fights were wars over status, access to foreign cultural forms, and the right to perform culture in public space outside of the confines of a barrio. In this sense they formed part of the contestation over ethnicity, class, belonging, and "power's destiny" seen at all levels in Guatemala. On one hand, the street wars can be read as an expression of the generalized violence of a society disfigured by state terror. They illustrate the realities that underpinned the moral panic and politics that displaced youth to a pathologized sphere and displaced counterinsurgent violence into a reconfigured rubric of *security* and social cleansing. On the other hand, seen from below, the street wars give evidence of a new kind of cultural assertiveness among the city's casta youth—urban kids who dared to dance in public

FIGURE 5. This advertisement for Primera Generación Records appeared in early 1996, in a rock magazine that Giácomo Buonafina published (see chapter 3). *Hasta Atrás*, no. 4 (ca. January 1996): 9. Archivo Histórico de CIRMA, Colección Lucía Escobar, GT-CIRMA-AH-98-027.

at a time when they came to stand, symbolically, for the problems that plagued the nation.

The antibreak street wars, while never disappearing completely, unfolded in two distinct waves. The first dated from 1987 to 1989. The second wave erupted in 1992, reportedly coming to a head in a huge battle in October 1993.[87] The street wars finally died out by around 1994. Seen as a whole, these battles give evidence to sharpening caste distinctions in a city where gangs were proliferating, common crime was spiraling up, and the spread of private schools accompanied consumer culture in helping to commercialize and "class" or "brand" youth by social status.[88] Regarded in stages, on the other hand, the two waves of antibreak wars show significant changes in how urban youth were *contesting* their caste status in ways that augered greater national transformations in culture and identity to come. The street wars of the 1980s were powerful-on-powerless events. In the 1990s, the castas fought back.

The pressure behind the street wars had been building up for several years. In Zone 1's Plaza Vivar and Centro Comercial Capitol shopping centers, break-dancing competitions—reportedly between local gangs, or maras—began around 1984. Break, like the maras, was a new phenomenon in Guatemala's popular classes. It swept into the barrios along with other styles such as "popping," a Californian urban street dance with jerky and robot-like motions, at the same time as the new gangs were forming. Maras began to attract national attention in 1985, when their members participated in bus-fare riots. Mara 33 and the Mara Plaza Vivar Capitol were born in the same year, the latter created by a group of friends planning a break-dancing competition.[89]

Break dancing and the musical styles associated with it had originally been the purview of wealthier kids with access to cable television. These elite and "wannabe-elite" youth did not appreciate the down-market voyage of the genre, and neither did they look kindly on the exodus of bracelet-wearing, sneaker-sporting, move-busting "breaks," "cholebreaks," and "cholos" from the city's marginal zones into the city center to perform their art, especially as public panic over gangs began to spread. Claiming to be fighting the spread of gangs, elite and upper-middle-class youth formed "antibreak" clubs that had their origins in the capital's wealthy private schools.[90] Their targets were supposedly delinquent "breaks," or *mareros,* kids who "wore hair short in front and long in back; an earring in the left ear, moccasins or All Star sneakers, and pants cut wide at the bottom," writes María Escobar Urrutia, who, as an undergraduate anthropology major, produced the most fine-grained piece of research on the break wars written to date. She added that those fashion-based attributes soon ceased to be as important, however, as simply "dressing badly, living in a poor neighborhood, studying in a public school, and having physical traits associated with indigenous people."[91]

By roughly 1987 the first antibreak hunts, called *cacerías,* had begun. Devotees of *rock pesado* and heavy metal, these youngsters attacked the choleros with depraved indifference for human life. Drunk and high on cocaine and pot, they would fall on the break-dancers in the city center and beat them, sometimes to death. By some accounts they gang-raped the young women. Though purportedly antigang, they resembled gangs themselves, roaming armed, even with guns, in packs after school.[92]

The antibreaks were also indirectly and directly related in hard-to-trace ways to the counterinsurgent structures of militarism that were in the process of metamorphosing into structures providing so-called security and espousing an ideology of social cleansing. Escobar's informants told her that the sons of military officials and paramilitary death-squad leaders were participants in the antibreak wars and that they also had connections to underground mafias.⁹³ Among paramilitary organizations, gangs and juvenile delinquency provided cover for political social-cleansing campaigns. By the time that the first wave of break wars died down, circa 1989, the government had created a special military-police wing—SIPROCI, the System of Citizen Protection—to "protect" a citizenry ever more worried about security. Besides going after delinquents, it also reportedly attacked members of the social movements, the guerrillas, and even military officers opposed to Cerezo.⁹⁴ Serrano renamed this force "Task Force Hunapú." In the period when the second wave of anti-break wars erupted, its "military-police patrols," writes Schirmer, "'cleansed' street gangs and demonstrating students and unionists."⁹⁵ The term *social cleansing* does not quite capture the barbarity of the murder and torture that authorities perpetrated on poor, young gang members and street children.⁹⁶ In one scandal, police were accused of making glue-sniffing youngsters rub the flammable inhalant on their palms and fingers and then setting their hands on fire.⁹⁷ Social cleansing was presented in the press as the barbaric application of medicine to a real social ill. There was a plague of children.

The apolitical "lost generation" lived these politics on the streets. The jaded, hateful narrator of *Ruido de fondo* was driving through "the ugliest city in the world" one day with his private-school friends, when they saw a "break" on the sidewalk. From the backseat, he made a joke about messing the kid up. His friend in the front passenger seat threw his door open to hit the cholero, while the driver swerved toward him on the curb. The narrator saw the break's backpack flying through the air and his *"cuerpo infeliz,"* his "unhappy body," lying prone on the street. His friends cracked up. Maybe they had killed him.⁹⁸

This gruesome scene dates to the city's second-wave street wars. The first-wave wars had been events in which middle- and upper-middle-class youth attacked the poor. According to Escobar, in the 1990s, some lower-middle-class ladino youth from less expensive private schools joined the vigilante bands, along with a small number of poor, brown-skinned castas who had previously been the *victims* of antibreak violence. The most significant change, however, was not this attempted up-classing but the new assertiveness of the castas—the so-called *choleros* and *shumos* and *indios* of the barrios. Far more so than they had in the 1980s, the lower-class break-dancers and rappers began to fight back. They formed roaming patrols and initiated attacks on youth dressed in black, the uniform of the antibreaks, even as they armed and organized themselves for the growing rumbles in the city center.⁹⁹ The caste wars were still on in Guatemala City, but this time the castas were taking the initiative.

It is hard not to cheer for the underdogs from the barrios, yet we must bear in mind that the scene was ugly. These teenagers came of age in a remarkably violent atmosphere. Usually held on Friday afternoons after school, street battles were, as in the late 1980s but even more so, the sites of wanton violence. Antibreaks reportedly wore Rhino-brand steel-toed boots as a required part of their all-black uniforms. The goal was to make their enemies "eat cement," breaking their teeth and jaws by stomping their heads into the sidewalk.[100]

"They called us antibreaks because we were against that shit music *[esa música cerota]*," wrote "Safiroth"—whose posts always began with a friendly "Hail Satan"—on the *Rock Republik* site in the 2010s, in a discussion thread on the "underground." Metaleros, he said, hung out at a McDonald's near Plaza Vivar, where their lower-class enemies, the breaks, were dancing. The hunts of the early 1990s began "clandestinely," he claimed, but events came to a very public head in pitched battles on Sexta Avenida in the city's Zone 1. "En la Plaza 6–26 hubieron varios muertos unos break's jajajaja" (In Plaza 6–26 there were lotsa dead breaks ha ha ha), he posted. After the violence the hunters would go eat at Pizza Grizzly and play video games.[101] Like Javier Payeras's antihero, they seemed simply not to care.

Javier Payeras, on the other hand, was a member of the city's "lost generation" who cared very much indeed. The fact that he later wrote this novella evinces another, creative and critically thinking side of the generation that grew up through the end of the Cold War.[102] Statistically speaking, very few young people were either gangbangers or street warriors. Youth involved in destructive and antisocial activities are the ones *remembered* from the period, but they were not the norm. *Duendes* and delinquency joined organ-trafficking and child-porn rings to feed moral panic. This panic facilitated the displacement by which youth became a ground for political intervention and social cleansing alike. Most young people, however, grew up with these things happening in the background of their lives. Many poor, young Guatemalans shared their stories with me in the capital city and in the provinces in the early 1990s. They told me that *fear* was their number-one emotion. They spoke against the police and the army, shared family histories of torture and disappearances, and related their experiences in antimilitary demonstrations. They also worried that they were branded as delinquents for their musical tastes and style choices.[103] They taught me my first phrases of chapín street slang. I did not know it at the time, and neither did they, but under terrible conditions culturally assertive young people and their everyday iterations of being chapín were reinforcing the nation's caste hierarchy and also reconfiguring and undermining it. De a pie youth cultures and self-identifications, as well as discourse about youth, as they developed from the late 1980s to the early 1990s, invisibly began to bring "urban" and "rural" spheres into closer dialogue, blurring the lines of that divide.[104]

What was it like to be a young person in this violent, poor society? The *trova* singer-songwriter José Chamalé wrote a poem in 1994 that captured the emotional landscape of the era of "Americamorfosis." In the poem, "An Island in the City," the author sits in a park and watches what is going on around him: glue sniffing, prostitution, someone reading newspaper headlines: "Urbanization Underway," "Street Child Murdered." The music of Los Bukis plays in the background. "Everything seems bleak in modernity and/or postmodernity," reads the text. "The park in the afternoon after the rain ... apart from our world and still a part of it, without a visa, nothing more than dreams, if it can be that any remain hidden in the twisted ruins of skepticism and despair." So appeared the world as Guatemala warred its way toward peace. "An island afire with voices and beggars," afire "with miracles, magic, ritual and frustration."[105]

3

"Not Fish, Not Iguana"

ORGANIZED BANDS AND AGRO-URBANIZATION,
1994–1998

A HUGE ROCK CONCERT HELD IN GUATEMALA CITY in December 1994 stands out in the popular memory of how youth culture turned from expressing "the twisted ruins of skepticism and despair" to calling for peace and singing lyrics that spoke of "miracles, magic, ritual and frustration." The show was called Libertad de Expresión ¡Ya! (Freedom of Expression, Now!). It came to symbolize the cry of a generation.[1]

Rony de León, the lead vocalist of the 1970s band SOS, opened with his group Liverpool. Channeling Woodstock and Jimi Hendrix, they played a rock version of the national anthem. The most remembered bands onstage, however, were youthful and recently formed. Libertad de Expresión ¡Ya! brought these 1990s-born groups out of the garages, high school gyms, and small venues of the capital and put them on a national stage. The young musicians were astonished that they could play their own music in front of thousands of moshing fans. Not long later they would be gigging for moshing fans in the provinces, where the desire for freedom of expression was spreading and where the new rock nacional was becoming the soundtrack of the "peace" generation.[2]

Bohemia Suburbana was the most famous of a group of bands born in the early 1990s that forged a new and lasting sound. Coming out of Guatemala City's well-heeled private high schools and universities, this "new" form of already-existing national rock would soon come to stand for the whole and be dubbed rock nacional. Rockeros of this generation developed a "Guatemalan groove"—a distinctive, rough yet lyrical, grunge sound that remained characteristic of *rock chapín* in the decades ahead. The rock of the early 1990s was about getting over class differences and class warfare in the streets, said Giovanni Pinzón, the vocalist of Bohemia Suburbana, when interviewed for a 2010 documentary. It was also about ending the armed conflict. "Our cause was to live in peace," he stressed. "No more war."[3]

After intense negotiations, Guatemalans signed a "firm and lasting peace" accord on December 29, 1996. *El Regional*'s headline used the Mayan movement's name for the nation: "Paz en Iximulew!"—Peace in the Land of Maize.[4] In the idiom of youth, whether what was to come would be a remade "Guate-mala," a reimagined "Guate-buena," "Guatemaya," "Iximulew" (seen also as Ixim Ulew), "Chapinlandia," or—as a T-shirt popular with hip chapines and young tourists alike would phrase it some twenty years later—"Guatever" remained to be sorted out. Throughout the 1990s fear and insecurity continued to shape everyday life, "NGO-ification" colored neoliberal change, popular culture became more streetwise and urbane, and urban space expanded in an age of commercialization and increased financial flows. In the middle of the decade, at the end of a thirty-six-year-long war, Guatemalans began reimagining their nation, even as that nation morphed before their eyes, often in unspeakably violent ways.

In the years around the Peace Accords explored in this chapter, from roughly 1994 to 1998, the agro-urban landscape evolved rapidly. As the processes of agro-urbanization (detailed in the previous two chapters) reached critical mass, provincial population centers began to function as what are called "city-regions." Secondary cities grew, followed by departmental capitals that turned from "big towns" to "small cities." Smaller municipal cabeceras soon began to transform as well.[5]

As the metabolism between city, town, and village changed, the dreams and hopes of the growing young population in this landscape changed as well. Many youngsters would be the first in their family to learn to read and write, the first who never suffered seasonal work in the fincas, and the first to come of age in a municipality whose mayor spoke their native language. A few would be the first to join a street gang. Many more would be the first to dance in a mosh pit as the new touring bands came to entertain them. In an expanding but still brutally extractive economy, it remained to be seen exactly what the members of this new generation would *do* with their lives. An era had ended, people felt, but a new one had not yet begun.

The most popular rock anthem of the decade captured this feeling of being in between, neither one thing nor the other—a state of double negation called *ni fu ni fa* in popular language. Bohemia Suburbana first released "Peces e iguanas," "Fish and Iguanas" on their 1993 album *Sombras en el jardín* (Shadows in the garden), produced by Giácomo Buonafina at Primera

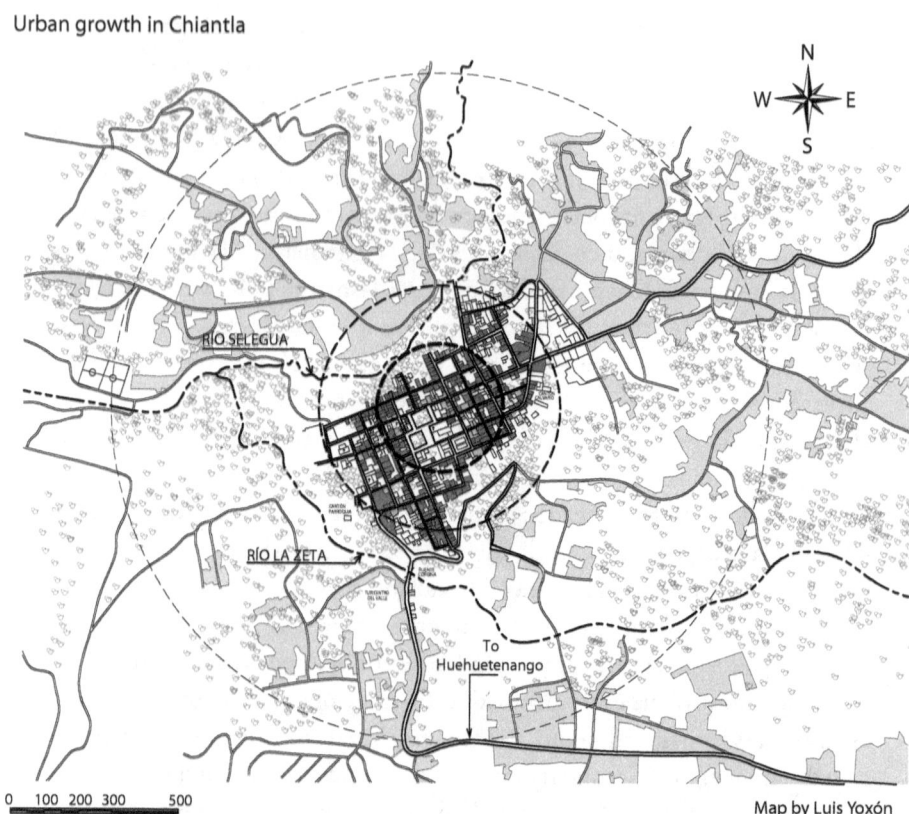

MAP 3. Chiantla, a municipal cabecera with a population of roughly 105,000, neighbors the departmental cabecera of Huehuetenango, with which it has formed a city-region (described in chapter 5). The circles approximate growth over time, with 1954 in the center. The second circle shows growth by roughly the mid-1990s, and the outer circle, by roughly 2010. The shaded areas show urban expansion.

Generación. Three years later the grunge-rock song was the top track on the hit album *Mil palabras con sus dientes* (A thousand words with their teeth), produced in Miami. "How will you know whether you're a fish or an iguana," the chorus asks, "if you never try *[pruebes]* either *tierra* or *agua,* earth or water, land or sea?" It was a chorus crowds could sing and chant: "Not fish, not iguana / Not earth, not the water."[6] On this track and others, Pinzón's raw vocals gave voice to the hopes, fears, and frustrations of youth who could see, but never quite have, something better, something more.[7]

The lyric *"ni pez ni iguana, ni tierra ni agua"* captured the zeitgeist. It poetically expressed an *anti-identity* that over time, I argue, became an *identity*—but a far-from-monolithic identity composed of a set of antithetical identities, identities of *I am not* massed in a conflictive yet paradoxically cohesive bunch. Beyond alluding to the factionalism at the heart of Guatemala's evolving alternative popular nationalism, *ni pez ni iguana* also captured the stark binaries and double negatives of the period, popularly remembered as a time of neither peace nor progress.

This chapter argues that dialectical double negatives were built into Guatemalan iterations of identity and nationalism at a time when agro-urban city-regions emerged and the optimism of peace was tempered by spreading crime and vigilantism. The youth who helped me with this project and I borrowed a phrase used in a guerrilla document to sum up social change in this period: "organized bands." Our punning double entendre encapsulated both the *bandas organizadas* of the new rock nacional and the exploding criminal and vigilante bands to which the guerrillas were referring. In the years around peace, what I refer to as a phenomenon of lawless "warlordism" arose; organized and common crime spread, and people started to burn alleged perpetrators alive in the street, bringing the word *lynching* to the vernacular. Over the same period there was tremendous optimism, cultural creativity, and hope for the new generation. What lay in store for that new generation, however, was yet to be determined. A brutal past had ended, but no bright future had yet appeared.

POLITICS, IDENTITY, AND ORGANIZED BANDS

A quick slice-of-life tour of the Huista region shows a society in transition as 1994 waned into 1995—while in Guatemala City the new generation of rockeros celebrated in Libertad de Expresión ¡Ya! and the antibreak wars came to an end. A center opened in Huehuetenango to counsel youth with drug and alcohol addictions. Scammers claiming to work for a congressional representative tricked some two hundred desperate Jacaltenango-area campesinos into buying lots on a fake finca. The coyotes, dodging stepped-up border security, began ferrying more migrants through La Mesilla, near Huehuetenango, than through Tecún Umán, closer to the coast. Hundreds of undocumented migrants started streaming through the Huista region; neighbors petitioned the governor for help in setting up security patrols. The Mayan movement held a peace march in Quetzaltenango. MINUGUA, the recently arrived Mission of the United Nations in Guatemala, came to

Barillas and fell afoul of the locals when they unwittingly rented a home owned by an ex-PAC *comandante* and military *comisionado* for their office. Some everyday events were happier, however. Manuel Santos Montejo Camposeco ("Santos Montejo" on YouTube), a young Jacaltenango songwriter, singer, and guitarist, released his first cassette, which featured two songs in Jacalteco Maya. His "testimonial music" included tunes like "La Tierra de los Abuelos" (Land of the ancestors), "Hace 500 Años" (500 years ago), "Niño Pobre" (Poor boy), and "Hombre de Maíz" (Man of maize). Somewhere, perhaps in the same part of the highlands, a preteen future blogger named "Gerardo Perez" was, with morbid attraction, watching soldiers troop through town as Megadeth songs ran through his mind. As 1994 wound to a close in the Huista region, the URNG blew up electric towers near the army base, throwing the barracks and surrounding towns into darkness. Two days later, in faraway Marrakesh, on New Year's Day, the World Trade Organization was born. Two weeks after that, Mario Payeras died in Mexico. Change was afoot in Guatemala.[8]

The international community became increasingly invested in this process of change, as the guerrillas, the military, and the state negotiated a series of Peace Accords in talks monitored by the United Nations and a group of "friendly nations" in places like Oslo, Norway. MINUGUA arrived at the end of 1994. The UN mission was set up to last for three months but remained until 2004. Like the already-large constellation of international cooperation agencies and NGOs it joined, MINUGUA had a tremendous influence on the changing political, economic, social, and cultural politics of Guatemala.[9]

In March 1995 the first MINUGUA director, Leonardo Franco, submitted his initial report. It was a chilling document. The Verification Mission had begun to follow up on more than one thousand allegations of human rights violations that it had received in just a few months. Mayan movement activists were in the crosshairs. Assailants murdered two Mayan movement leaders in Quiché, and waves of death threats continued. In Chupol, five men beat the CUC leader's fifteen-year-old son nearly to death and left him bleeding in the road.[10] Beyond individual cases, however, the report portrayed a society permeated by terror and violence. Threats, abductions, and executions were pervasive, and torture on army bases was systematic. MINUGUA estimated that some five hundred thousand illegal firearms were in circulation. Their bearers were protected by the police, who were supposed to be disarming society. Members of the PACs (which for years had officially been called CVDCs, or Civilian Volunteer Defense Committees, a term no one used) formed tiny local armies. Together with the newly demobilized *comisionados*, with the military's support, they were asserting authority in town after lawless town. Conflict seethed. As refugees returned, land invasions and agrarian disputes increased. Crime was rampant, and in the absence of trusted authorities, people were taking "security and justice into [their] own hands."[11] Criminals were also getting creative, disguising themselves as rebel combatants or military men. One group marauded through a town dressed up as guerrillas and even blew up an electric tower to make themselves look more credible. The URNG then pledged to MINUGUA that their combatants would refrain from undertaking any actions that "had no direct impact on the armed conflict" (such as blowing up electric towers that didn't power army bases, presumably).[12]

At the time of MINUGUA's arrival, the ASC (founded by the state in 1994 for the peace process) was circulating a document to be much cited in later years: "Strengthening Civil Power and the Function of the Army in a Democratic Society." It declared that "the multiple violations of human rights, such as kidnappings, disappearances, torture, intimidation, and assassinations of popular, democratic, and progressive leaders, as well as the forced exile of thousands of Guatemalans, are but one sign that civil society has been permanently unable to emerge and develop." The document then detailed the complete military penetration of nearly every branch of state. It called for decentralization, demilitarization, and an end to paramilitary structures such as the PACs.[13] The ASC, meanwhile, weighed in with a proposal for what would later be the Accord on Socioeconomic Aspects and the Agrarian Situation, noting that the "current neoliberal tendency" exacerbated the "hegemonic, exclusionary, authoritarian, classist, ethnocentric, and patriarchal" nature of the Guatemalan State. They advocated for an end to privatization efforts, for open migration, and for a greater voice for small producers in trade agreements, including any future trade agreement with North America.[14] Given the huge ideological divides, it was a testament to the sincerity of all sides that four key peace accords had already been signed by the time that MINUGUA appeared on the scene.[15]

Embedded in the peace process—particularly in the work of the ASC and, within it, of the Mayan movement's umbrella group COPMAGUA—were ideas that envisioned remaking society and politics from the bottom up. COPMAGUA's original proposal for what would be the historic Accord on the Identity and Rights of the Indigenous Peoples (AIDPI) demanded recompense for three "holocausts": the conquest, capitalism, and counterinsurgency.

COPMAGUA's political demands were not met in the accord signed later, but the agreement did embrace their vision of a pueblo whose members "self-identify as Mayas" and within which women played a "transcendentally important" role in transmitting identity.[16] The AIDPI, signed in March 1995, defined the nation as "multiethnic, pluricultural, multilingual." It was the first time that the modern state recognized structural racism, promised to address discrimination, and embraced the idea of a "Pueblo Maya," but many of the Left's political demands, seen in COPMAGUA's proposal, had been toned down, leaving cultural issues in the fore.[17]

Just after signing the AIDPI, the URNG released a lengthy "Proposal to Society" that spelled out its political program and foreshadowed its later platform as a registered party. Among other things the proposal called for Maya enfranchisement, decentralized government, modernized agriculture and increased access to credit, and educational reform. All these measures would come to pass in years ahead, but in ways that fell short of most people's hopes for socioeconomic and political empowerment and tinged with identity-based concessions for indigenous people that in some ways created a variegated form of citizenship based on an identity to which not all members of the group adhered.[18]

"National identity" and "Maya identity" were center-stage questions in Guatemalan society in the mid-1990s.[19] Some positions were extreme in their blindness to (and reproduction of) structural racism against the Maya. A ladino op-ed writer in *El Regional* claimed that Mayan movement spokespeople were sophisticated individuals, "educated in the United States or Europe," who "fly around in airplanes as often as a real indígena *[indígena de verdad]* rides a bus." Repression hit poor ladinos just as hard as it did the Maya, he wrote, and "in the *maquilas,* a ladina *muchacha* is exploited the same as another of 'Maya' origin.... This thing of speaking [as some do] ... of '*indígenas* and *no indígenas*' reminds me of the discourse of Hitler, when he referred to the pure race, the Aryans."[20] Some indigenous citizens also bristled at the term "Maya," albeit for very different reasons, but it was embedded in the peace agreements, it dovetailed with the discourse of the growing pan-indigenous movement, and it also became a revitalized identity and source of pride for many. In particular, it took hold at the grassroots in youth culture, in ways to which the later rise of Maya pop would attest.[21]

In the middle of 1995, pulsing grassroots energy filled the Mayan movement. Its leaders formed new groups that organized a virtual Maya takeover of highland municipal politics. They also teamed up with the FDNG (New

Guatemala Democratic Front), a left-wing political party founded in July 1995 that was in favor of decentralization. At the same time, the URNG guerrillas were unleashing spectacular actions, "harassing and attacking military units," in MINUGUA's words, even assaulting the army's prestigious Honor Brigade in the capital and occupying hamlets around Quetzaltenango. The battle to win negotiating power in the peace process inspired the retired guerrilla, Santiago Santa Cruz Mendoza, to leave his self-imposed exile in the United States and take up arms again. Blows between the army and the guerrillas continued as he worked his way back to Guatemala while the contentious election season unwound in late 1995. By the time of his early December arrival, Guatemala had seen a political opening. The FDNG had put forth a slate of candidates, and Maya politicians were poised for a major acceleration in their slow and steady takeover of "official" municipal government even as they were reviving the alcaldía indígena. The state also began the messy process of demobilizing the military *comisionados,* signaling that the war was winding down.[22]

The inauguration of Álvaro Arzú (1996–2000) occasioned a race to finalize the peace process. Both sides made concessions as battles continued. In Arzú's first week in office, Santa Cruz's front staged actions on and around the Inter-American Highway near the road for Patzún-Patzicía, striking a major economic artery in the Chimaltenango altiplano. Soon the squadron moved south and attacked the important sugar-growing regions in Escuintla.[23] Such militancy helped the URNG negotiate the important Accord on Socioeconomic Aspects and the Agrarian Situation by May. As with the AIDPI, however, this accord emerged as a faint shadow of the ASC's original proposal. The government promised to devote unspecified amounts of resources to rural development, health, education, and other social programs, as well as to aim for an annual GDP growth of 6 percent. The main thrust of the agreement, however, boiled down to municipal autonomy and further decentralization of powers to the municipal level, policies that—not unlike the Maya cultural language in the AIDPI—turned out to be a double-edged sword.[24]

As peace approached, the URNG formed "political life and propaganda and communication" teams that worked in relative cooperation with the state.[25] Before taking over a town or finca, the rebel leadership would inform the police, the mayor, the military zone commander, and the media. The generals kept the troops in check. Noti-7 TV news crews and *Prensa Libre* reporters scuttled out of the capital to catch the action. None of the changes

FIGURES 6, 7, AND 8. Varying experiences of youth in the mid-1990s. In figure 6 (top), a Maya youth crowd-surfs at a Bohemia Suburbana concert in Panajachel. In figure 7 (bottom), an indigenous young soldier of about the same age—perhaps one of the army's many forced recruits—defends a finca in Santa Lucía Cotzumagualpa, Escuintla, 1995. Figure 8 (opposite) shows guerrillas training in 1996; the young woman in the foreground may also be Maya. Female guerrillas found it difficult to readjust to the norms of patriarchal society after demobilization. Credits: Figure 6—"Concierto de Bohemia Suburbana en Panajachel, Sololá, 1996–1997." Fototeca Guatemala, Archivo de Kurt Zierlein (photographer), GT-CIRMA-FG-170. Figure 7—"Indigenous Guatemalan soldier, carrying his AK47 rifle," 1 February 1995. Fototeca Guatemala, Archivo de Juan Rolando González Díaz (photographer), GT-CIRMA-FG-160. Figure 8—"Guerrilleros en entrenamiento," 1996. Fototeca Guatemala, Archivo de Moisés Castillo (photographer), GT-CIRMA-FG-078.

in the terms of war seem to have surprised Comandante Santiago. He knew his war was now a war for peace and that as such it was largely a public relations battle. The need to win "hearts and minds" at home and on the international stage also explains why the army allowed the guerrillas to hold their events. Far more than the establishment's bows to the Left, what the veteran guerrilla found most astonishing upon return to his homeland was just how *different* the new generation of combatants was from older ones. Back in the revolution's glory days, he wrote, young recruits had picked noms de guerre that harkened to Cuban heroes, such as Fidel and Camilo. During the genocidal 1980s biblical names became popular: Aarón, Abraham. In the mid 1990s, under Hollywood's thrall, the kids were choosing names like Antonio Banderas and Mike Tyson.[26]

Santiago Santa Cruz was not alone in noticing how the younger generation iterated identity in dialogue with ever-more-widespread mass media and global youth culture. When speaking of Maya youth, ladino observers often associated this change, and even the use of modern technology, with the supposed loss of culture. The political scientist Francisco Beltranena, for example, saw the harbinger of profound generational change in the fact that the children of traditional furniture makers in the Kaqchikel towns of San Juan and San Pedro Sacatepéquez were now running their parents' rustic businesses with computers. "The problem," he wrote, "is how to sketch [*perfilar*] a Guatemalan society that already lacks the indigenous component, which has been appropriated by the white man."[27] Like the use of technology, new globally inflected articulations of consumer culture and youth culture were no longer primarily confined to small elite circles or counterculture cliques in Guatemala City, or even to ladinos as a whole. They were spreading across the landscape in an era of contested politics and contested identity, leading to the further discursive linking of youthful cultural change with spreading criminality.

Crime had spiraled out of control by the time of the "firm and lasting peace."[28] It is difficult to overstate the impact of this danger on people's everyday lives. The father of one petty thief ended up in the pages of *El Regional* for issuing a general call to his neighbors. He had counseled his son over and over again not to rob, he said, but to no avail. The kid was just no good. If you see him, the father announced to the public, please kill him.[29]

The "kill my son" call, while extreme, was not mere rhetoric. Waves of lynchings began in 1996. Usually, what Guatemalans called *lynching* consisted of dousing people with gasoline and burning them alive. But sometimes suspects would be beaten to death or murdered by a mob in other ways. One *El Regional* front-page photo showed a man going up in flames as a crowd stood watching. Among them was a campesino in a cowboy hat, with his hands on the shoulders of his little son who stood in front of him, absorbing the lesson. Often the victims were accused of minor crimes. In a village near Soloma, Huehuetenango, a lynch mob set two minors afire for stealing a TV. Reporting on lynchings in six departments, MINUGUA noted, "There is no question that the population's profound lack of confidence in the effectiveness of the institutions in charge . . . offers fertile ground for engendering such acts."[30]

Reports on these horrific acts underscored the spread of common crime, organized crime, street gangs, and kidnapping and extortion rings as the forces driving mob violence. Shadowy forces lurk within these narratives. Beginning a trend that would escalate until the present day, neighbors in rural, urban, and urbanizing areas alike formed security patrols, some of which would conduct "social-cleansing" campaigns. As patrols, bands, and criminal rings proliferated, society began to cast around for someone to blame. The FDNG (the new left-wing party) accused the army of being behind paramilitary and criminal bands. Others agreed, adding that the PACs (CVDCs) and demobilized *comisionados* were the main drivers both of mob justice and small-town terror.[31] Finally, and disturbingly, some commentators on the barbarism of lynching attributed it along racial and cultural lines to the Maya and, in particular, to groups practicing *derecho maya* (traditional Maya law), which had functioned for centuries in small communities to settle disputes and impose conformity with social and cultural norms. As *derecho maya* came ever more into the headlines in the Maya renaissance of the 1990s and the first decade of the 2000s, and as MINUGUA, NGOs, and some political leaders clamored for it to be legally recognized and validated by the state, Mayan movement spokespeople increasingly had to point out that the community elders who ran this system were not the ones responsible for burning accused criminals alive.[32]

"Warlordism" and generalized violence increasingly came to characterize Guatemala's social landscape. MINUGUA reported in July 1996 that, thanks to its lobbying efforts, the new Arzú government was taking steps to break up organized crime rings headed by high-ranking military officials and, in some cases, by the police. Some success in arresting drug traffickers and heads of car-theft and kidnapping rings was noted, but it was only a small dent in an escalating problem. Meanwhile, in swaths of the national territory, MINUGUA documented "the emergence of various [armed] civilian organizations that carry out surveillance patrols, establish curfews and make arrests." PAC (CVDC) members and ex-*comisionados* were turning themselves, often by violent means, into local authorities (and, not infrequently, into lynch-mob leaders). They continued meeting with military zone and area commanders and were also starting to reconfigure themselves as "peace and reconciliation committees," "community development committees," and the like. Many would cash in on the NGO-development boom that had been building up for years, but that escalated significantly after the peace accord was signed.[33]

Fear, crime, and insecurity all grew through the time of peace. Peace was *ni fu ni fa, ni pez ni iguana, ni tierra ni agua*. New "organized bands" wrestled for power in society's highest levels and its smallest corners. In 1996, the year of peace in which Bohemia Suburbana's *Mil palabras con sus dientes* came out, the URNG wrote, "The dimensions of the politics of terror in Guatemala are so deep and long that historians of the future will have great difficulty registering their magnitude."[34] A track on *Mil palabras*, "Aire," put it this way: "*aire, me falta el aire / miedo, me sobra el miedo* (Air, I need air / fear, I'm too full of fear)."[35] These words resonated in a country where people were quite literally going up in flames and where identity, belonging, and the imagined future were being rewritten by the day.

ROCK, COMMERCIALIZATION, AND
THE CRISIS OF AUTHENTICITY

The fact that youth around the nation made "Aire" a hit—just as they did with "Peces e Iguanas"—opens a window to the commonalities between the different-yet-related life experiences of young people in the city and the provinces in a time of violent transition. The rock scene in the capital in the mid-1990s was related to the rise of cliques and castes seeking the cultural power that comes from distinction, but it was also a sphere of grassroots cultural creation that gave voice to a generation's hopes, dreams, frustrations, and fears in ways that resonated far outside the capital's borders.[36] Both the "style snob" and "dreaming for more" sides of this equation were related to the overall trend of commercialization in the era.

In *Ruido de fondo,* Javier Payeras's novella about the 1990s, as in popular memory, commercialization resulted in meaninglessness, in a society (in the antihero's eyes) where everything was cheap and fake and stupid. Only Guatemalan rock got a partial pass. "Rock and roll is the most *yankee* vile lie," the narrator asserted. "Here we're its supposed sons, and we're the worst represented ones . . . savage little dwarves from the worst generation of twentieth century, the worst century of them all." After this introduction, however, Payeras's hater had something good to say. "For me," he held, "Bohemia Suburbana is the nineties. . . . There's no good football, no good booze, no good TV, no good governments, but at least we had good rock groups. Rock," he claimed, "saved our minds and condemned us a little."[37]

Capital-city youngsters like Payeras's fictional protagonist had access to the new bands of the 1990s in their early years, before the 1994 Libertad de Expresión ¡Ya! concert. Much of the new music had started in elite schools like Colegio Americano, Colegio Maya, and Colegio Alemán. Many of these bands never made it big—groups like Crow's Nest, John Doe, and Reagan's Colon Surgery. But others did. Ricardo Andrade, in future years the famous vocalist of Los Últimos Adictos, formed a group called Stress (later changed to Spanish, as Estrés) in the early 1990s. It was a *fresa* (meaning "yuppie" or "snobbish") band, Últimos Adictos bandmate "Taz" would later write in his memoir. Viernes Verde, soon to become wildly popular, was born as a school band named Blind Spirits. In 1994 La Tona, another group bound for fame, came out of the high school scene. The private Universidad Rafael Landívar was home to Bohemia Suburbana.[38]

Though some of these new bands signed with the traditional label DIDECA, many were propelled to fame by Giácomo Buonafina's Primera Generación Records, the business most responsible for promoting the new sound at home and abroad. The groups began to tour around the country in the mid-1990s, performing for their growing base of fans in the provinces. In Guatemala City, Primera Generación became a hangout where young artists of all stripes came together. Rock nacional, later critics agree, opened a discursive space for the creative class around the nation, helping to occasion an explosion in the visual arts, dance, theater, film, photography, and literature.[39]

In October 1995—a month whose violent events included a military massacre in a returnee camp and brief guerrilla takeovers of *colonias* in the capital city's outer regions—a slick rock fan magazine appeared in Guatemala City.[40] *Hasta Atrás*, published by Primera Generación, later became a hard-to-find collector's item, an artifact of the golden age of rock nacional and of what is known as the *under* chapín—the chapín "underground" counterculture (borrowed from English and pronounced *oon*-dare). *Hasta Atrás* was just as professional a publication as any found on the newsstands of New York or Berlin. Tabloid-size, printed in four colors on thick stock, the magazine by all appearances had been designed on a Macintosh with the latest software. Its title, the slang phrase *"hasta atrás,"* translates literally as "ahead to the past" or "forward to backward" but also means something along the lines of "shitfaced": drunk, high, twisted. *Hasta Atrás* was an important mouthpiece for the new rock generation; the publisher, Giácomo Buonafina, appeared on its masthead, although without a title. So too did a twenty-year-old young woman whose later career in vanguard counterculture media brought her to the very center of spreading urbane national youth culture. Her name was Lucía Escobar—nickname: "La Lucha" (meaning the fight, the struggle). Some two decades later she would donate *Hasta Atrás*, along with her other publications, to a historical archive.[41]

Among the foreign bands covered in the premier issue of *Hasta Atrás* were the Red Hot Chili Peppers, the Beastie Boys, and Björk. Guatemalan groups included the Fábulas Áticas and Bohemia Suburbana, who provided an interview. The issue's editorial complained that listening to "Paleozoic" Guatemalan radio was "something like being trapped in a bar full of nostalgic bureaucrats." FM radio in Guatemala, the editors mourned, featured tunes from a woeful low of Barry Manilow to a best-case scenario of Carlos Santana. "Poor us who want to hear 'excentricities' like reggae, funk, techno, jazz, metal, punk, ska, or grunge! We're just a bunch of 'fashion victims,'" the piece continued. The editorial concluded that "rock is a part of the culture of any civilized country, and it's a very serious business."[42]

Rock nacional was becoming a serious business, changing from a collection of Guatemala City subcultures to a national genre that soon formed part of the soundtrack and fabric of everyday life for a new generation. Primera Generación released its CD of Libertad de Expresión, ¡Ya! in 1995. This was an important step in disseminating the music that was beginning to gain a notable following outside the capital-city area. Guatemalan bands were gaining attention not only in the provinces but also around the world, riding the wave of the Latin rock explosion that got mass-market fuel when MTV Latino debuted in the United States in 1993. Bohemia Suburbana, for example, recorded their first album with Primera Generación; *Mil palabras con sus dientes* was produced by the independent RadioVox label in Miami. RadioVox had been started by an Argentine exchange student, Gustavo Menéndez, and his partner, Rodolfo Castillo, a Guatemalan-born music producer—a pair who scooped up talent from around Latin America and, notably, Central America and brought their music to a hemispheric and global market. "Mainstream" rock bands like Bohemia Suburbana and Viernes Verde would begin to tour internationally in the mid-1990s.[43]

Like rock, Guatemala's still-thriving, flamboyant heavy-metal counterculture was commercializing as well. Rotting Corpse, formed in 1992, had originally been "all about blood," but by the time they talked to *Hasta Atrás* reporters in early 1996, they were "more into perverse sex and critiquing society."[44] Late that same year Sanctum Regnum—soon to be known for burning Bibles in their concerts—came together, joining groups like Sádica, Noctis Invocat, Sore Sight, Rottenness, and Putrid Child. *Hasta Atrás* columnists touted the revels of the *trasheros,* celebrated "the whirlwind of violence that is Black Metal," and welcomed groups like Mexico's Foeticide, who entertained the mara with songs like "Putrefact Corpse."[45] Metal, like rock in general, formed part of a continually commercializing music industry. This subculture continued to grow, as did the related *trashero* scene, when the more mainstream, "grunge-like" rock nacional began to attract its following.[46]

Guatemala's music scene was becoming more sophisticated and professional, and, as part of this process, genres and their fan bases increasingly crossed over with one another. The "melodic hard rock" band Yttrium, for example, opened for the Mexican pop-rock, world-beat band Maná at a Guatemala City concert and soon signed with the national label, DIDECA.

As Guatemala City became a "world-tour" stop for big foreign acts—Luis Miguel and Juan Gabriel, for example—opening for a headline band became a life-changing gig. Rock's becoming a business in Guatemala helped to normalize genres once considered "radical" and to homogenize, as well as commercialize, the music counterculture scene.[47]

At the same time, rock nacional became truly "national," as bands started to tour the provinces. As we have seen, this was hardly the first entry of globalized music to the highlands. Foreign genres such as *bachata* and other *música tropical,* Mexican *ranchera,* and English-language rock were already very much a part of the provinces' soundtrack. Radio stations in larger secondary centers, such as La Voz de Huehue and Stereo Mam, began supplementing their playlists with an occasional homegrown rock or pop group to cater to new youth demand for *rock chapín*.[48] *El Regional,* joining a national trend, introduced a "Contacto juvenil" section to cover pop and rock music. It reported the rise of new Guatemalan stars such as singer-songwriter Fernando Scheel, who released his first solo album, *Por dentro y por fuera,* in 1995. The importance of emerging national rock to social and political discourse was confirmed when the government invited Scheel to write the official theme song for the signing of the Peace Accords, "Hablemos de paz" (Let's speak of peace). The countryside began giving rise to "must-play" touring stops for Guatemalan rock bands. Antigua, Panajachel, and Quetzaltenango were the three main destinations, but the list soon expanded to include growing departmental cabeceras such as Huehuetenango and smaller rural centers as well.[49]

Band members spoke of their experiences in the "interior" in ways reminiscent of how an older generation of urban, middle-class guerrillas remembered their forays into "deep Guatemala." They discovered a side of their nation they had only read about or seen on TV and were amazed to find fans in the hinterlands who already loved their music and knew the lyrics. Their words about these encounters with the provincial *"chapines locales,"* captured in the rock documentary *Alternativa,* speak volumes about the grassroots creation of a youth idiom and of alternative popular nationalism from below.[50] Leaving aside any given band member's attitudes about race (because some may have been quite progressive), the capital-city ladino amazement at finding something "modern" and "chapín" among the provincial population—who, far from being different, deferent, and servile, wanted to attend a rock concert—demonstrates the race-and-caste-imbued worldview of a class raised to view indigenous people as backward *indios,* as servants and *mozos* (agrarian peons). At the same time, their astonished admiration for these kids—youth who were not just rock fans but also de a pie leaders in a grassroots Maya-pride movement—shows the frisson of transformative transcultural experiences that ultimately made cracks in the nation's caste system. Over time such experiences would coalesce in a new idiom of national identity on the discursive ground of Guatemala's expanding urban/agro-urban city street. As had been the case in the guerrilla-Maya encounters of a previous generation, and building on their legacy and still-ongoing work, Maya youth asserted themselves in this cultural process and made it their own. What band members experienced as an encounter was really a new chapter in an evolving grassroots national dialogue.

For capital-city rockeros in the mid-1990s, "deep Guatemala" represented an escape from the globalized consumer culture they themselves were unwittingly helping to spread. The musical youth scene in Guatemala City was already evolving from a space in which young people could assert an alternate identity (and perhaps choose sides in interclass street wars, as happened in the late 1980s and early 1990s) to being "mass merchandise." The very publication of *Hasta Atrás* bespeaks the commoditization of the genre. Just as happens with all fads and styles in a consumer-capitalist marketplace, this dynamic gave rise to a constant quest for "cool." As soon as today's cool ended up on MTV, it no longer satisfied the "vanguard"; they had to find something new. "Discovering" an "interior" full of indigenous kids, *chapines locales* who loved the music, however, added a different dimension to this dynamic for the small group of Guatemala City's middle-class rockers in ways that mapped onto the national dialogue as a whole. In the interior was the *real* Guatemala, a painful place, but one that still had authenticity in an ever-less authentic world.[51]

If Guatemala City was "real" for middle- and upper-class youngsters, it was real in the sense of being a car wreck between late-capitalist consumer culture and what they themselves derided as "third-world" squalor. The capital city in the mid-1990s was the epicenter of the phenomenon of capital expansion that changed the country so dramatically in the epoch. The first postmodern malls sprang up, as franchises such as Pizza Hut, McDonald's, and Payless Shoes opened around the city. Land invasions and shantytowns spread as the urban lower class expanded. This was a metropolis increasingly characterized by gated-off spaces for the well-to-do, by ever more murderous street gangs, and by children who lived by picking through garbage in the dump.[52] "Cities in the late twentieth and early twenty-first century," wrote a columnist in *Hasta Atrás* in a 1995 review of a Fábulas Atícas concert, "seem to project themselves as ideal sets: supermarkets, retail outlets, fast-food restaurants, and endless rows of buildings in functional housing blocks." In this landscape (one more characteristic of upper-class Guatemalan vacation destinations, such as Miami, than of chaotic, grimy, and far-from-functional Guatemala City in 1995), "technology lives alongside savagery" and "the streets have lost their significance as part of an urban historical tradition.... Now, as in a futurist-punk film, there are only tribes and territories."[53]

These words, *tribes* and *territories*—if one vows to use *tribe* only in its social sense and to strip it of any tinge of racist association with the resurgent indigenous population—serve to capture much of Guatemala in the era of peace. For our presumably upper-middle-class author, probably a university student, "all order and reason become meaningless" as "space-time fragments." Rock expressed the fragmentation that youth experienced and gave voice to the "void" of (post)modern life for a certain *clase de gente* ("type" or "class" of person). "The few of us who made it to the Fábulas Áticas's carnivalesque gig," the author held, "now know that geography is misleading. What back in more innocent times we called reality, and even fantasy, was really a circus act all along."[54]

Guatemala's interior, for the few young rockers who were able to tour, offered a world that was more than just a circus act. Ironically, however, so too did the squalid corners of the capital itself—the barrios where the breaks lived. In this city of tribes and territories, no end of "popular-class" antifresa chapines had great disdain for middle- and upper-class youth. They saw them as a stuck-up *clase de gente*—self-styled "maras" who thought they were cool, who had the money to get into rock concerts, and who'd had time as teenagers to skid skateboards down handrails in front of condominiums while other people had to work. Their privilege made the lower sectors jealous of them, but, interestingly, youth from the more moneyed sectors also expressed (in muted tones), a jealousy of the lower class, who, not unlike the predominantly indigenous *chapines locales* of the interior, over time seemed to have more of a claim to the *authenticity* that was so lacking from their lives.[55]

An essay published in *Hasta Atrás* just after Arzú took office opens a window on this double-sided jealousy. It covered a Semana Santa holiday. The story, in the author's tone and voice but shortened, translated, and paraphrased, went like this: Dad, a pathetic, potbellied bureaucrat, takes the family to the seashore. The tacky, slutty sister buys a twenty-quetzal used bathing suit with menstrual stains on it. The stupid, spastic brother gets coconut oil all over his shorts in the car. The mother buys avocados and tortillas to save money on going out to eat; the nasty, cheap hotel room stinks of them. The father tries to play a dumb family game on the beach; only the sister joins in, just to show off her body to the mara. Swarms of teenage girls in bikinis get Dad hot and bothered. He makes a lame excuse and brings Mom to the room to get it on, sliming up the sheets and worsening the odor. Everything is stained. Everything is cheap. Everything smells. Kids from El Mezquital and La Bethania, our author says—meaning kids from the impoverished, "popular" neighborhoods of the capital—have an "I'm poor, but it's all good" attitude. Not me, man. Dad only had the money for three days at the beach, and at the end all he had left was forty quetzals to buy the gas to get back to the city. Back home, back to school, back to normal. My brother will grow up to be just like Dad and my sister just like Mom. Me, *I'm outta here* as soon as I can be.[56]

The author's loathing of his own class status is complemented in this piece of writing by a bow to the authenticity of the "popular"-class kids, kids who weren't part of the cool "mara" but who dealt with maras of a very different kind. One of these youngsters was named Ángel Cañas. Also known by his street-rap names of "Señor Rima," "Ekis Ekis," and "Joker," Cañas would later blaze a trail that crossed with that of Javier Payeras and other well-off capital-city youth, with young fans in the agro-urban highlands who were still toddlers at the time and with NGOs and foreign filmmakers. None of this seemed likely in 1996. In the era of the Peace Accords, the story began in a "land invasion" in the urbanizing periphery of Guatemala City.[57]

A young, homeless *marero*, Cañas was making his way in early 1996 from the inner-city slums of central Guatemala City to a land invasion in the suburb of Villa Nueva. Known as Mario Alioto López Sánchez (Mario Alioto for short), this settlement had sprung up at exactly the same time as the first issue of *Hasta Atrás* was going to press, when workers from the city's nearby maquiladoras, or export-assembly plants, took over the land. These were people who were not even "lucky" enough to be living in shantytowns like El Mezquital and La Bethania and who certainly could not take their children to the beach for a three-day vacation. The impoverished squatters, when not working their shifts in the factory sweatshops, bit by bit built their neighborhood. They named their settlement after a student-movement leader beaten to death by the police for participating in bus-fare protests in November 1994. Soon a Mormon missionary named Miguel Gaitán arrived in the ghastly slum from his highland posting in Totonicapán. With the help of the human rights ombudsman's office, he started a children's theater group, later to be called Iqui Balam. When fourteen-year-old Ángel Cañas drifted onto the scene, he already had experience with rap and break dancing. Soon he joined the theater group, which was becoming an arts and recreation center, where hundreds of inner-city children gathered. Cañas and his little brother "MC Plenno," both participants in Iqui Balam, were active hip-hop artists by 1997, performing in the neighborhood and doing "stomp" on city busses. Their group ultimately took the name Alioto Lokos, after the neighborhood in which it was born.[58]

In the new millennium, the Cañas brothers and Alioto Lokos would become virtual poster boys for the creativity of inner-city youth, playing a role in the assertion of lower-caste pride and the diminution of so-called servility as a cultural form. The group's rise to fame, as we will see, was in large measure thanks to NGOs and funded community organizations like Iqui Balam, with which they remained loosely related. No one, however, would have seen this coming circa 1997, as the group remembered in a 2010 song and video called "Qué pasó?" (What happened?): "Recuerdo [I remember] Iqui Balam . . . the homies, the DJs . . . // Filling whole notebooks with sick verses . . . // For real, they hated the Alioto Lokos back then" (obvio que vió con odio a los Alioto Lokos en este episodio).[59]

The group was the expression of an urban geography as unequal and divided as any on the planet. It emerged out of an cityscape in which gang violence had taken on legendary proportions, in which middle- and upper-class youth relentlessly chased the symbols of consumer culture and its distinction, only to find them empty, and in which thousands of families were so desperately poor that land invasions continued to mushroom even as postmodern malls and gated communities sprang up. Advancing a musical genre that had been at the center of antibreak wars of the late 1980s and early 1990s, the Alioto Lokos were yet another expression of the endless divisions of class, caste, and race that characterized society as a whole. A band member named "Maskota" ("Pet," because he was small and the youngest) remembered years later that "you couldn't just *be*. If you dressed nice you were homosexual, if you dressed in black you were a rocker, and if you wore baggy clothes you were a gangbanger. . . . They made you join a gang."[60]

If the *Hasta Atrás* kids lived in what they saw as a futuristic, unreal, and postmodern world, the world that the Alioto Lokos kids and those like them lived in was all too real. Popular youth culture bore evidence at every level to inequality, social violence, and the profusion of "tribes and territories." Yet youthful cultural production also speaks to the *ni fu ni fa, ni tierra ni agua* dynamic of the era of peace. In the midst of generalized social warfare, youth were unknowingly carving out a cultural space in which an alternative popular nationalism was being germinated. They did so in dialogue with their on-the-ground conditions. The reality of NGOs and a body politic colored by a resident UN peacekeeping force overlapped with that of changing commercial and media regimes and with the terrain of evolving everyday life in the impoverished nation. Endogenous and exogenous forces mixed. Within that mix, in the sphere of urban youth culture, the nature of popular nationalism—of expressing "Guatemalanness" and a sense of national belonging—began to change. That it did so is precisely because "urban" youth culture stopped being a field of cultural production solely associated with the capital city (and of course also with elite cliques in major secondary centers). It became generalized—national—as urban space spread. In the years ahead, the urban beats of hip-hop groups like the Alioto Lokos would find widespread followings and would inspire new bands in Guatemala's provinces, just as the 1990s ladino rock nacional of bands like Bohemia Suburbana, Viernes Verde, and La Tona was already doing. The first steps in this process were already well underway. In the middle of the 1990s, agro-urbanization accelerated.

YOUTH, GANGS, AND AGRO-URBAN CITY-REGIONS

Before hip-hop spread around the country, cities, slums, and gangs spread, as did foreign media and consumer culture. Agro-urbanization accelerated, with its *ni pez ni iguana* mix of rural and urban, old and new. Over the course of the 1990s, local customs reflected these transformations. For example, in *convites*—traditional street dances held in honor of the Virgin of the Conception and the Virgin of Guadalupe as well as of major religious holidays—costumes with pre-Hispanic and colonial roots became complemented and even outnumbered by Mickey Mouse, "Escubidú" (Scooby Doo) and "Winipú" (Winnie the Pooh) getups. Drunk men, dressed up half as guerrillas and half in drag, danced to booming techno beats behind the sacred floats.[61] Rural Guatemala had been tied for generations to the global, capitalist economy through agriculture and peonage, and its "world-upside-down" *convite* dances made reference to its brutal web of client-patron relations. Now, however, in complex ways, the impoverished population was being reincorporated and was reincorporating itself outside of the agrarian economy as exporters, cultural producers, and, most of all, as a *market* of consumers in a landscape of expanding capital. While many were no longer peons, the tragedy of this transformation is that many Guatemalans remained in the status of surplus humanity and had to scramble for pennies; they were *ni pez ni iguana*.

Economic changes, inflows of money, and new technology accelerated this transformation. In many places, NTA cultivation was reconfiguring economic relationships; in others, the booming tourism industry provided monetary inflows that changed local socioeconomic relationships. Migration to the United States and the consequent inflow of dollars caused no end of class-status shifts; poor villagers used their remesas (remittances) either to build on site or to move to the cabecera, accelerating urbanization and population growth. Meanwhile, a flood of funding from donor nations, state agencies, and NGOs worked to remake the economy. In early 1997, as the guerrillas were turning in their guns, governments from around the world, working through the Inter-American Development Bank, pledged just short of $2 billion by the end of the decade to help Guatemala live up to the accords' provisions. At the same time, the first ads relating to the internet appeared in *El Regional*. The internet—accessed more easily as low-cost internet cafés opened around the country—would propagate in the years to follow across a landscape where mass media, tourism, and crime were spreading, along with global youth culture and its associated *desmadre* (chaos attributed to the loss of good customs). Touring Guatemalan and foreign rock bands, increased FM radio and cable TV footprints, the cell phone, the internet, and a new wave of foreign and internal youth tourism would all help to shape life in populous municipalities around the nation. Increasingly, these areas began to have problems that looked a lot like those seen in the capital city and in many other places around Latin America and the globe.[62]

From the mid to the late 1990s, a new modality of city-regions began to emerge around Guatemala.[63] This wave of urbanization unfolded in a landscape still dotted with tiny hamlets accessible only by footpath. In the nation's center a "greater Guatemala City metro area" further developed, a phenomenon also seen in Quetzaltenango. In the provinces, large tertiary centers, such as Huehuetenango, Chimaltenango, and Escuintla, for example, became recognizable as small cities. Meanwhile, larger regional towns—rural municipal cabeceras—began to urbanize in significant ways. This nationwide process of agro-urbanization was violent and painful, but it was also—*ni tierra ni agua*—creative and ebullient at the same time.

The greater capital-city area garnered the most attention from planners interested in urban problems in the mid-1990s. Guatemala City, as evidenced by the land invasion in Villa Nueva, where the Alioto Lokos arose, was both spreading beyond its borders and becoming the nucleus of a conglomeration of outlying, urbanizing areas. The city's integrated urban development plan of 1995, titled *Metrópolis 2010*, recognized the integration of surrounding municipalities into an AMG (Área Metropolitana de Guatemala) and envisioned a significant role for private capital, international cooperation, and the NGO sector in fomenting "sustainable urban-rural" development plans.[64]

Many plans would follow, but sustainability would not. Interclass tensions, not unlike those seen in Guatemala City, would be one "symptom" of the messy, painful process of agro-urbanization, as outlying villages morphed into towns and from there into a web of small urban centers. The Guatemalan NGO PAMI reported in early 1996 that a new urban-rural divide was emerging in growing agrarian areas not far from the city. In San Miguel Petapa, for example, a village-based proletariat of underage, illiterate construction workers was swelling. Discriminated against and laughed at, this class of poor masons was ever more desperate for money so they could afford the consumer goods for sale not just in the capital but also in the very same expanding and urbanizing centers they were building. Frustrated, these youth tended to become alcoholics, according to PAMI, and squander their measly pay in brothels. While PAMI's report overlooks regional complexity and reproduces the standard story of indiscipline seen in the development literature, it still shows how growing class distinctions were geographically conditioned. Youth in towns and villages that had primary schools and were closer to either to the capital or to more developed cabeceras where secondary education was available did better as a whole. Other children suffered terribly. Some ended up working for slave wages in fireworks "factories," really informal and lethal cottage industries. Some joined gangs. The worst off joined the growing ranks of street children.[65]

Similar phenomena were seen in the provinces. Quetzaltenango also became the center of a growing metropolitan area. National franchises opened, and local developers built minimalls, expanded chain stores, and constructed *residenciales* (housing developments). In Quetzaltenango local developers included Ramiro de León López and Sara Cohen Alcahé, the husband and wife founders of the La Democracia minimarket. They had been early "pioneers" in bringing brands such as "Colgate, Kern's, Ducal, Gerber, Ideal, Café Incasa, Nabisco, Cristal and the whole line of Foremost pasteurized products and Kerosene gas" to the region. Their chain of Delco stores later expanded to twenty-four branches, and they were working with real estate developers in building housing complexes.[66]

As Quetzaltenango grew, so did its urban problems. *El Regional* reported in late 1997 that most of the thirty-odd youth street gangs in Quetzaltenango, like the King Boys and the Ángeles Caídos (Fallen Angels), were informal groups of teenagers. Several, however, were offshoots of more organized and sinister Escuintla-based gangs. One was led by an adult woman wanted for murder who went by the street name of "La Pantera" (The Panther).[67] "Solutions" to such problems rose to the level of social cleansing. So-called death squads formed in Quetzaltenango in late 1997 to rid the streets of gangs; reportedly, the city morgue suddenly filled up with the corpses of tattooed teens. Social anxiety ran high; at around the same time, there was a moral panic in the city about the possibility that transvestite prostitution was on its way. In examining social cleansing, MINUGUA reported that these organized-yet-disorganized waves of chaotic terror targeted not only crime rings and street gangs, but also other supposedly undesirable groups such as squatters and homosexuals. The process of urbanization involved a panoply of unwelcomed social phenomena.[68]

Foreign Moonies, for example, caught the public's attention when they "invaded" Quetzaltenango, San Marcos, and Totonicapán in late August 1997. These Japanese and Brazilian members of the Unification Church, followers of the Korean Reverend Sun Myung Moon, were recruiting for the mass marriage of 3.6 million couples worldwide in a ceremony to be officiated in Washington that coming November (which happened, but with only about thirty thousand couples). By the time the government ejected them two months later, they had given the "pre-matrimonial blessing" to some four hundred couples in the highlands. While both spectacular and indicative of the globalized dimensions of Guatemala's exponentially changing sociocultural landscape (*Really?* Four hundred couples in the occidente signed up for mass marriage?), the Moonies were the least of the problems facing the pueblo. Criminal rings, social-cleansing efforts, and lynch mobs all grew and proliferated.[69]

This generalized violence was related to the social urbanization taking place in the context of a changing political economy and of urbanizing social space. While the capital and Quetzaltenango grew to become centers of cityregions, so too did larger departmental cabeceras such as Huehuetenango, Chimaltenango, and Escuintla. Huehuetenango, which was hanging stoplights in 1998, and where new shopping centers were opening, is an excellent example of this phenomenon.[70] "Huehuetenango is undoubtedly a city like many others," wrote a columnist in the local magazine *Controversia* in 1997. The older generation couldn't have seen this coming, the author explained;

they could not see that "in just a few decades this city would no longer be the little city trafficked by horses, carts, and people on foot."[71] Residents alarmed by the pace and violence of this change formed a committee to organize a departmental "citizen security plan" in early 1997. The area, they said, was plagued by organized and common crime and riddled with gangs, and lynching was on the rise.[72] Crimes like kidnapping, extortion, and rape were noted, and no sooner did bank agencies and national chain stores open—a key element of agro-urbanization—than they were set on by organized bands of thieves.[73] Serious worries and moral panic mixed, especially concerning youth. Even if they were not involved in crime rings or gangs, public discourse held, youth were too involved in sex, drugs, and rock and roll, getting terrible grades in school, and showing the influence of foreign imports like "violent films and pornography."[74] Adults could not understand these kids, and even used English to dub them "Generation X."[75]

In agro-urban Guatemala, poor, brown-skinned members of "Gen X" were showing a culture assertiveness that drew and built on the nation's history of rebellion and resistance and that helped to break down the lower-class performance of servility as a cultural form. In popular discourse, however, these youth were overwhelmingly associated with the criminality that was spreading as they came of age. Populations around Huehuetenango were so beset by crime and insecurity, *Controversia* reported, that entire villages were rising up in protest.[76] In Jacaltenango, narcotrafficking had sparked local drug sales, and addiction was fueling street crime. In Jacaltenango and Barillas, another growing town in the area, street youth gangs were making rape an everyday occurrence, according to *El Regional*. The same report noted an uptick in teenage suicide.[77]

Smaller municipal cabeceras such as Jacaltenango and Barillas were also becoming centers of new, still-very-agrarian modalities of city-regions, as the socioeconomic relations between the countryside's urban nodes and their outlying villages transformed. Regional cabeceras had been local centers of government and commerce since colonial times, but their role changed in the 1990s, evolving to be more similar to what bigger, departmental cabeceras had been before. These cabeceras increasingly became centers of mass-merchandise retail, education, banking, and medical services. They were places to get a car repaired, buy a motorcycle or a fridge, find building and plumbing and electrical supplies, shop for a wedding dress, get a cavity filled, or put a down payment on an electric guitar and amplifier (goods needed more by charismatic Evangelical churches, to be sure, than by budding provincial rockeros). The already-existing metabolism between cabeceras and nearby villages took on a faster pace as it commercialized and economic networks filled with mass merchandise and new service-sector endeavors. In the second half of the 1990s, central Barillas had about eighty households wired with cable television, and private telephone service was spreading. The municipality struggled to bring these services to outlying villages, but not even the center's radio stations (one Evangelical station and one Catholic) had footprints that could get over the mountain peaks.[78] Getting the advances of the cabecera to the outlying aldeas, then, was a challenge, and the cabecera itself was a destination of choice for migrants from the villages. The nation's rural-urban divide had moved to the very heart of its rural hinterland.

The municipality of Aguacatán, "land of garlic and onions," is located in the Cuchumatanes Mountains, deep inside the department of Huehuetenango. It is the only place in the country where Awakateko Maya is spoken. Traditions were down and delinquency was up, reported the debut issue of *Ye' Qatanum: El Aguacateco,* a local newspaper founded in early 1998. Youth bands kept robbing people at gunpoint. In the aldeas neighborhoods organized patrols. Sadly, the paper's editors held, the groups who were "shouting to the four winds for the rescue of Maya tradition" had yet to organize a cultural festival to keep said traditions alive. Boys wearing "outlandish sneakers, baseball caps ... and earrings" thus had little option but to listen to "boring" pop from new, peace-era Guatemalan groups like Innercia.[79] The paper painted a picture of everyday life in a growing muni, where satellite cable TV was spreading and youth gathered to eat pizza and play pool in a hangout in the center of town. They also played far-from-servile pranks; an editorialist excoriated masked youngsters for handing out obscene, satirical flyers defaming the "basest passions" and licentious exploits of local politicians.[80] Too, *Ye' Qatanum* noted the contrast of new and old commerce in town. The patron saint's feria (fair) saw all the artisans come out to sell the local handcrafts on the streets. They set up their stalls on the sidewalks around the expanding "slew of *tiendas,*" where imported bicycles, electronics, and appliances were on sale.[81]

Much of the urbanization in Aguacatán had been and was being paid for with the remittances of war refugees and migrants making a living by processing chickens at the Case Farms plant in Morganton, North Carolina. The local economy, heavily reliant on exporting garlic and onions, was reeling as cheap imports from Mexico and China drove down prices, making remesas from the United States ever more vital. In North Carolina workers from Aguacatán faced harsh conditions. Together with their Q'anjob'al neighbors

FIGURE 9. I took this picture as Tono and I were pulling into central Aguacatán in the 2016 road trip I describe in the introduction. Aguacatán was far less built-up in the 1990s; most of the construction and commerce in the shot are more recent.

from the mountains of Huehuetenango, along with workers from elsewhere in Latin America and other local allies, they unleashed waves of labor activism in the first six years of the 1990s that won them both a union and a central role in Leon Fink's fine-grained labor history, *The Maya of Morganton*. Fink's work details how Maya workers overcame the regional rivalries and feuds that, like language barriers and a history of civil war, separated them back in Guatemala.[82]

Remittances helped to sustain and grow local economies and even to keep community and family ties alive across national boundaries. But they also caused problems at the grassroots. In the Q'anjob'al-speaking municipality of Santa Eulalia, Huehuetenango, over US$2.5 million arrived in the form of remesas in 1995 alone. Over time, this huge influx of funds gave rise to a new local elite and exacerbated class differences in the municipality.[83] A string of statistics gathered from 1994 to 2004 show that the *casco urbano,* or urban center, of this place—where electrification outside the center was still spotty and many villages were still accessible only by footpath in the middle of the first decade of the 2000s—show that, while the population and population density grew by 42 percent, the central area did by 239 percent. "Formal houses" made of cinderblock and *casas improvisadas* (shacks) sprouted up, while the number of traditional mud-brick *ranchos* declined. The *casco* was home to one *caserío,* or cluster of homes with a population of two thousand to four thousand people in 1994; by 2004 there were nine. Small, family-owned agricultural plots, or "microfincas," grew in number, but since so many were leased out, the overall distribution of land remained as or more unequal than it had been for decades. One statistic, however, remained steady over the period. Whenever anyone counted, nearly half of the growing population was under fifteen years of age.[84]

As the first, big wave of Guatemala's postgenocide baby boom came of age, street gangs erupted not just in urban but also in agro-urban territory. Some were offshoots of the major, transnational gangs seen in Guatemala City, Honduras, and El Salvador. Others were homegrown affairs arranged by local adult criminals. A house-to-house search in the border regions of Tecún Umán and Ocós, San Marcos, for example, broke up a gang of sixteen- and seventeen-year-old robbers, many of them from the same private school, who were working for local adults.[85] Most, however, were the spontaneous creations of local youth who were growing up in a time when it was completely unclear what the future had in store for them.

A plague of grassroots "gangs" hit the nation in the mid to late 1990s, many of which may have been more like "clubs" of *muchachos traviesos* (mischievous boys) than sinister gangs.[86] The mass outbreak of small, informal youth gangs confirmed the fears of elders, who throughout the decade had viewed the rise of rap, hard rock, drug culture, and foreign media invaders such as "Superman, Rambo, and the Ninja Turtles" with alarm.[87] Many of the new wave of "barrio gangs" were named after cartoon and video-game characters from global media. In Jacalteco-speaking San Antonio Huista, a letter writer to *El Regional* claimed, the first teenage mara to *hacer bronca* (make trouble) was called "Los Simpson," after Matt Groening's animated comedy created in 1989. They were followed by "Los Raiders," a band of "patojos que no saben ni por donde orinan, pero sí como fregar" (little squirts who don't even know where they're peeing but sure know how to screw around). "Los Dragones" appeared soon after, painting skulls all over town.[88] In Aldea San Lorenzo, Huehuetenango, a village dedicated to growing maize and fruit and where cottage-industry tailors sewed quilts and sheets for export to El Salvador, a teenage gang so terrorized the 10 percent minority of Catholics left in the population (the rest had become Evangelicals) that they hid the statue of the patron saint lest it be stolen.[89] There were at least eight small teen gangs—groups with fewer than twenty members—operating in greater Huehuetenango in late 1997, *El Regional* reported, but that number was dwarfed by those found in the surrounding rural areas. Their names included "Los Kaibiles," after the Green Beret–like special forces of the Guatemalan army, and "El INDE," after the much-hated state electric company, which was fast on its way to being privatized. Reportedly, they robbed, painted graffiti, and caused disturbances in fiestas. All around the Huista region, residents formed neighborhood-watch committees.[90] Similar phenomena were documented elsewhere, reflecting new realities and exaggeration and moral panic all at once. In 1998 there were fifty youth gangs "whose members consume drugs" in the growing town of Coatepeque, Quetzaltenango, according to local sources.[91]

"Organized bands" characterized the new agro-urban landscape. They ranged from young pranksters in gangs like Los Simpson to groups of corrupt local politicians to transnational crime rings. "The main burden of violence and insecurity is caused by organized bands, whose origins make it difficult for the authorities to completely disband them," wrote the URNG in a 1997 tract. "What is certain is that the complexity of this panorama shows that lowering the levels of violence is going to take the effort of all society," they added.[92] To people living through this postwar conflagration, it seemed as if the state did nothing other than rely on NGOs and international cooperation agencies to fill the void left by its own negligence. What it *did* do did not work; replacing the corrupt National Police with a new National Civil Police, a process that began in 1998, for example, just put one problematic group in the place of another, United Nations reports claimed.[93] Guatemala had terrible problems and would have them for years to come. It also, however, had tremendous promise, and not just because it was heavily populated with young people full of hopes, dreams, and creative drive. The mid-1990s were years of optimism, activism, and Maya pride.

FIGURE 10. People—many youth among them—watch the disbanded PAC turn in its arms. Armanita Gálvez, "Entrega de armas utilizadas por las Patrullas de Autodefensa Civil (PAC)," Colotenango, Huehuetenango, August 1996. Fototeca Guatemala, CIRMA, Archivo de MINUGUA, GT-CIRMA-FG-103.

LOCAL POWER, MAYA PRIDE, AND THE AMBIGUITIES OF PEACE

Despite the endless coverage of youth gangs—a real phenomenon but at the same time a hyped-up one—the majority of youth who came of age in the mid to late 1990s in predominantly indigenous areas were most notably active or passive participants in the Maya pride movement and in the activism to end army occupation and counterinsurgency. Growing up in "Iximulew," in a municipality with a mayor and officials who looked like you and spoke your language, and having issues that affected your community taken seriously (even if without concrete results) at the national and international levels had an inestimably powerful effect on popular consciousness. The push for local power and local autonomy came to its apogee in the years around the signing of the peace accords. The lived experience of local politics was one of insecurity, powerlessness, and danger on one hand and of resistance and empowerment on the other.

The end of the armed conflict was a watershed in young people's experience of their nation and in local politics alike. In televised ceremonies in 1997—starting on "D-Day," the twenty-third of March, and continuing in the months ahead—the guerrillas came out of hiding, stood in line, and handed in their guns. (Where they buried the caches of the ones they kept would be an endless source of rumor for decades.) The state bought three fincas on which to house some of the guerrillas and lodged others in hostels around the nation; more would return from abroad in 1998 with the help of the UN high commissioner for refugees and other organizations. The newly created Fundación Guillermo Toriello was dedicated to training ex-guerrillas, helping them find jobs, and assisting their reintegration.[94] This goal, difficult in its entirety, was especially difficult to achieve with women, who as combatants had enjoyed a measure of gender equality and who resisted assuming traditional gender roles upon return.[95]

Many of the reintegrated guerrillas joined the vibrant, leftist political movements that were operating both nationally and locally. In Sololá, for example, they joined the network of groups that were rewriting both national and municipal politics. They helped to support the transformations that were already well underway at the grassroots level in both city hall and in the alcaldía indígena. Like other highlanders, Sololatecos had made history in the late 1995 elections. They elected Pedro Iboy Chiroy, the first Maya "official" mayor in their postconquest history, a crucial step in making real provisions in the 1985 Constitution that called for political decentralization and municipal autonomy.

The 1995 elections had done much to change the country's political landscape. The presidential results disappointed the Left, given the strong victory of the center-right PAN (National Advancement Party) candidate, Álvaro Arzú. Majawil Q'ij, like many of its partners in the Mayan movement, had supported the new left-wing political party, the FDNG (Frente Democrática Nueva Guatemala), whose presidential candidate, Jorge Luis González del Valle, had come in a distant fourth. The FDNG, however, had also championed slates of local Maya candidates, who took 60 percent of the contested *alcaldías* (mayoralties) in 1995, up from 40 percent in the 1990 elections.[96] Notably, Quetzaltenango elected Rigoberto Quemé Chay, who held office until 2004.[97] Many of the Maya mayoral candidates had been put forth by an advocacy group formed in 1995 named Nukuj Ajpop, which worked with municipal political actors even as it joined groups such as Majawil Q'ij in promoting a "democratic, pluricultural, and multilingual" Guatemala at the national level.[98] In particular, Nukuj Ajpop worked to train local populations to form civic committees, which allowed neighborhoods to promote candidates through grassroots democracy without affiliating with a political party. The official parties, Nukuj Ajpop claimed, were "linked to impunity, corruption, illicit enrichment, the sacking of the country, and the misery and dispossession of the Maya people."[99] Solola's Pedro Iboy Chiroy came from the civic committee SUD (Sololatecos United for Development); the SUD candidate also won the elections for the alcaldía indígena, the Maya city hall, which worked hand in hand with the traditional elders and community leaders.[100]

The SUD alcaldía and alcaldía indígena in Sololá were so successful that by 1998 MINUGUA highlighted them as being exemplary in reviving traditional forms of indigenous governance and promoting grassroots democracy.[101] SUD had the help of the FDNG and national groups such as Majawil Q'ij and Nukuj Ajpop, but, most significantly, they also had widespread grassroots support, buoyed—for the time being—by the participation of demobilized guerrillas. Through demonstrations and negotiation Sololatecos forced the army to close its enormous base, which became a local cultural center and was soon reopened, with a great deal of support from international cooperation agencies and NGOs, as a provincial campus of the Universidad del Valle, a private university from the capital.[102]

SUD-led programs urbanized space in Sololá's center with transportation, electricity, and drinking-water improvements and work with cooperatives modernized agriculture with new irrigation and fertilization programs in the aldeas. Besides beginning to provide desperately needed infrastructure, Iboy focused on "education, indigenous rights, and cultural events," writes Timothy Smith. "He was instrumental in revitalizing ... the Kaqchikel Mayan language, ethnic dress, Mayan cosmology, and the practice of Mayan spiritual leaders."[103] Iboy and other members of the Maya majority also made great efforts to help the ladinos feel welcome and heard, fomenting a historic and peaceful change in interethnic relations in the region.

All this activism wove itself in ways hard to quantify through the social fabric. Rigoberto Ajcalón Choy, who grew up in Sololá and was a preteen at this time and who later wrote an anthropology thesis, for example, dated to this period the proliferation of the symbol of the bat, the *zotz'* (in Kaqchikel), in Sololá. The bat symbol was embroidered on the back of men's jackets in the

FIGURE 11. The zotz' symbol as seen in Sololá, 2019.

town's traditional traje. SUD popularized a version of it seen on signage all over town. The zotz' came to stand semiotically for the cultural revival itself, Ajcalón says, noting its preponderance in public space, on park benches and city walls and fences that surround overlooks of the lake, even decades later.[104]

Sololá's cool-looking, geometric zotz' also serves as a wonderful and simple example of how popular youth culture picked up on and incorporated the "traditional" as it came in force to the highlands in the 1990s. In the years ahead the zotz' that the SUD officials began to popularize in the era of peace appeared as the logo of pickup bands from Sololá who play in the bohemian rock center of Panajachel, just down the mountain on the lakeshore. On the streets, among the set that was smoking "cigarettes" and "other things," the zotz' made its way to numerous decals and even the occasional tattoo. The bat served as the logo for several boys' and girls' sports teams; in 2017 one example could be found on the Facebook page of Sololá's "Bat Cave" soccer team. Youth culture in the region was and is just as open to incorporating and revivifying time-honored symbols and traditions as it has been to embracing new forms—to melding "old" and "new" in fluid idioms that speak to the fertility of local power as not just a political force but as a living set of social and cultural movements.[105]

The flight of the zotz' bespeaks similar *ni pez ni iguana* reconfigurations of "traditional" and "global" that were seen all around Guatemala's just-emerging agro-urban landscape. *Ye' Qatanum,* for example, celebrated the diversity seen in Aguacatán's feria. It was a day to go shopping not just for handcrafts made of wood and clay but also for "bikes and imported appliances.... [But oh!] *El corazónnnnnnn ... La chalupa ...* the lotteries that give the characteristic feeling to the *feria de mi pueblo,*" waxed the columnist.[106] Lottery *(lotería)* is a bingo-like card game with roots in colonial Mexico. A staple at saint's-day fairs and Christmas parties, *lotería* is played with cards reminiscent of a tarot deck, sporting characters like the drunken "Borracho," the brave "Valiente," and "El Corazón" (The heart). "La Chalupa" (The canoe) is rowed toward an unknown destination by a pretty maiden named Lupita. The cultural transformations manifesting in the postpeace years of poder local in Guatemala, as elsewhere, were captured decades later by Mike Alfaro, a U.S. citizen of Guatemalan descent, who redid the *lotería* deck in 2017 after a visit to his parents' homeland. His new deck featured figures like "La Feminist," "El Nerd," and "La Student Debt" (personified as Atlas holding the world on his shoulders). "La Chalupa" was reborn as "El Uber" and Lupita as the Volkswagen bug–driving gig-economy worker. "'El Uber to me is hilarious,' the creator said. "La Chalupa is now an independent woman making some extra cash on the side."[107]

Guatemala's local power movement unfolded in tandem with the planet-changing forces that have brought us the gig economy, the economy of crisis after crisis, the economy of "the 1 percent," the economy in which "making some extra cash on the side" is synonymous with independence. In its early years, when demobilized guerrillas were joining the grassroots politicians in the push for municipal autonomy, the poder local movement looked so full of promise. *El Regional* debuted a *Poder Local* section early in 1998. One of its banner headlines summed up the impatience for local rule: "Decentralization: When?" Key to empowerment, the paper's writers thought, was the growth of the "development committees" that were beginning to proliferate in municipalities, but to date "with few results."[108]

The results would soon be many, and few would be what anyone had hoped for in the optimistic years just after the end of the thirty-six-year-long war. In a nation that was still struggling to construct a stable, civilian-led, democratic state, "organized bands" of all sorts vied for power, many in the most violent ways imaginable. They did so in a rapidly urbanizing milieu that was full of young people. In 1998, Huehuetenango celebrated the opening of its first real mall. Police in Coatepeque, Quetzaltenango, arrested four young leaders of a gang called Los Chicharrines, who were having street wars with their rivals, Los Silleros, in the Centro Comercial Internacional.[109] Sololá, a leader in the local power movement, held town-hall meetings on turning the army base into a university campus; meanwhile, an NGO reported that youth from the town largely identified not so much as "Maya" but as "human beings" who liked rock and pop music, cartoons, and action movies.[110]

Perhaps a few, whose parents were protagonists in staging a Maya revival and in militating for *poder local*, were listening to *rock chapín* bands and getting a zotz' tat, unselfconsciously chipping away at servility as a cultural form.

For all their different lifestyles, backgrounds, and economic situations, what Guatemalans young and old alike had in common in these years was arguably a sense of optimism in a rapidly changing world. But the word *optimism* has to be qualified. Poverty, crime, and insecurity were out of control, but a thirty-six-year-long war had ended. Five hundred years of oppression of the Maya appeared to be on the wane, thanks to vibrant activism. The world cared enough about this long-suffering place to have sent in the United Nations to monitor its transition to peace. And the youth! The new generation was, well, *new* ... different. They wanted Libertad de Expresión ¡Ya¡ They saw new and better possibilities and longed to actualize them, to try, to borrow Bohemia Suburbana's words, both *tierra* and *agua* and to figure out who and what they were and where they were going as an all-new kind of future unfolded. A cultural space was emerging whose discursive power joined the urbanizing mountain villages and the city's popular neighborhoods and shantytowns as the seat of Guatemalan "authenticity" in the mid-1990s in ways that exploded in popular culture and grassroots nationalism in years ahead. In invisible ways in the agro-urbanizing nation, the land invasions like that of the city rapper Ángel Cañas and the sylvan-yet-urbanizing streets of the highlands began to come together in a time of not peace/not war, not urban/not rural, not the past/not the future, not fish/not iguana.

4

"If Only You Could Live Here"

THE EMERGENCE OF LA KY, 1999–2004

"*SI AQUÍ SE PUDIERA VIVIR*" (if only you could live here), lyricized one of the Guatemalan rock star Ricardo Andrade's best known songs. His bandmate "Taz" later used this phrase for his title when he wrote Andrade's biography, also a memoir of Los Últimos Adictos. Like Bohemia Suburbana's *ni pez ni iguana,* this lyric expressed the contradictory emotions and experiences of life in turn-of-the-millennium Guatemala. The line, from the ballad "El Norte," captures a woman's mixed feelings of love and mourning for her absent partner, a migrant working in the United States. Taz's book was both a tribute and ballad of mourning as well. In 2002 narcos shot Andrade and his fellow musician Gabriel Rivera dead. It was probably a case of mistaken identity. In the same year that Andrade senselessly died, the journalist, essayist, and publisher Gerardo Guinea Diez wrote a piece titled "The Fire That Consumes Us." Covering state terror, corrupt politics, neo-anarchy, and neoliberalism, it held that "Guatemala is living through a strange phenomenon: its old society hasn't finished dying and the new one hasn't finished being born, like one world fading away and another that refuses to be named."[1]

The years from 1998 to the mid-aughts are remembered for privatization, commercialization, decentralization, and co-optation. Postpeace optimism gave way to cynicism, despair, and anger, much of which has been attributed to events related to rapid neoliberalization. The state privatized its assets, most notably the telephone and electric companies. Microlenders and onshore and offshore banks spread alongside chain stores and malls. Academics and activists mourned the fall of COPMAGUA, the Mayan movement's representative in the peace negotiations, as well as the co-optation of vibrant local politics by "neoliberal multiculturalism." According to some observers, the peace process died, and so did "socialism as a historic project," when the URNG guerrillas became a legal political party.² Musicians and fans bemoaned the demise of rock nacional at the hands of corporate sponsors and radio stations. Meanwhile, corruption, crime, and violence increased and deeply colored the long-awaited decentralization of government.

By 2005, when Guatemala ratified CAFTA-DR, the Central American–Dominican Republic–Free Trade Agreement with the United States, MINUGUA had gone. After the UN mission's 2004 departure, Guinea Diez wrote an essay titled "What Will Become of Us?" Holding that "the Guatemalan case is only comparable with the tragedy of the Jewish people . . . ex-Yugoslavia . . . or some African countries," it eulogized MINUGUA's attempts to mitigate "social processes in which the practice and symbolic *internalization* of violence were seen as an inherent part of our way of life."³ The subtext was that, despite MINUGUA's best efforts, the multiple forms of violence entailed in a thirty-six-year-long war had not gone away but instead had taken on new shapes—a point on which all analysts, myself included, agree. Guinea Diez, however, also joined a turn-of-the-millennium chorus about the "death of everything"—the peace process, the Left, the Mayan movement, good rock, youth unmediated by consumerism—that needs to be rethought. While there was some truth in the "death" narratives, the social movements and the Left fought on, Maya pride popularized at the grassroots, and the kids were okay. Youth engaged in productive ways within the parameters of what was possible in a time of national and global neoliberal transformation. Social and cultural changes bore evidence to the end of older narratives of justice and liberation, but they also showed the legacy of generations of struggle.

Young Guatemalans had not only "internalized" violence and exclusion, as Guinea Diez and others would have it; they had also internalized a history of popular militancy that they were in the process of "externalizing" in new and significant ways. The internalization of violence was accompanied by multiple externalizations, as the logics of public and private, of visible and invisible, transformed. Enrique Dussel locates liberation in the revolutionary moment in which "Exteriority," the alterity of the oppressed, "bursts into history." Guatemala lived through that process in one way in its long years of war and in another in its postwar transformations. In postwar Guatemala what Dussel calls top-down power, or *potestas,* shape-shifted from older semi-feudal and developmentalist forms to new, neoliberal ones.⁴ As this happened, youthful street culture, with its marbled and fascinating mix of "old" and "new," joined ongoing activism to become an avenue through which strangled bottom-up power, *potentia,* could make its way from inside out.[5]

From roughly 1998 to the middle of the following decade, "the street"—"la KY," in internet slang—began to become a real-and-imagined territory on which, against which, and through which youth around agro-urban Guatemala expressed and represented themselves in newly cosmopolitan and assertive ways. This was an important step in the emergence of agrotropolis—not just an interwoven network of agro-urban conglomerations but a national urbane "territory" that was the lived environment in which young people, with evolving and competing identities and sense of self, ultimately gave rise to a national commons. La KY took form—or, more precisely, *se encarnó,* from *encarnarse,* to become incarnate—as a discursive construct related to vernacular national identity. In all its concrete and fantastical manifestations, la KY was a ground on which the social self was simultaneously constructed and validated even as it was neglected, marginalized, threatened, and made invisible *(invisibilizado).* Cultural forms related to la KY manifested the dynamics of internalization and externalization so remarked-on during the period—the experiences and emotions and terrors of a *mundo al revés,* a world upside-down and inside-out. La KY was a "chapín" place, but one that made people wish "if only you could live here."[6]

PRIVATIZATION AND *EL MUNDO AL REVÉS*

As a new generation came of age and "street culture" coalesced *(se encarnó),* city slang, cosmopolitan styles, and counterculture all popularized, leaving their stamp not just on young people's leisure activities but on their inward subjectivity and outward public performances of identity. Contributing to this phenomenon, in part, was the cat-let-out-of-the-bag ebullience of a population that had been under varying degrees of military occupation for twenty-some years. Here we trace a variety of *mundo al revés* dynamics—a series of convoluted inversions of the public and private spheres in the political economy and youthful street culture. Privatization and neoliberalization were dialogically related to the national discursive emergence of a real-and-imagined KY as city-regions matured.

Part of the process through which agro-urban city-regions took form was cultural—both in terms of the Maya-pride movement and in terms of cosmopolitan youth culture. In the "rockumentary" *Alternativa,* Taz remembers gigging in indigenous-majority towns he had never even known existed, like Jacaltenango, the Huista-region home of the newspaper *El Regional*. It was "unimaginable to arrive there," he remembered, to find large crowds—*"un chorro de gente"*—who were avid fans and knew the lyrics. He was amazed that Los Últimos Adictos's music, like that of other national rock bands, had made it to such remote locales, even ones reachable only by dirt roads. *Alternativa* cuts from Taz's "deep Guatemala" recollections to footage of a 2001 concert in the hinterlands. Onstage is Sobrevivencia (Survival), the first Maya rock-fusion group to later "go big," and one of the longest-lasting. Musical director–guitarist Alex Job Sis explains that youth in remote pueblos were listening to rock nacional in the mid to late 1990s. Tellingly, he says they felt *inquietude* (restlessness, worry) and *ansiedad* (anxiousness) about engaging with music that alarmed their parents and had the potential to call unwanted attention from the military. Still, Job Sis says, kids not just in cabeceras but also in tiny aldeas were desperate for the new bands to arrive; he remembers having met Viernes Verde and other groups before he cofounded Sobrevivencia. Culturally curious and assertive youth like Job Sis and everyday fans in the provinces made the homegrown music that Guatemala City Spanish speakers called *rock en tu idioma* into the first true rock nacional.[7]

Sobrevivencia came together in the mid-1990s and took its name circa 1998—in the same era as youth gangs like Los Simpson were proliferating. Its hometown was San Idelfonso Ixtahuacán, Huehuetenango, a community famous for grassroots activism. Sobrevivencia's Mam-speaking founders were young men who liked to shoot hoops and have *chamuscas,* pickup games of *fut*. Singing in Mam, Spanish, English, and later adding lyrics from a variety of Mayan languages, Sobrevivencia developed an updated, Guatemalan "rockabilly" sound that fused pop rock with local *son* and marimba, reggae, and U.S. *"música country."* The band's original goal was local, members said. They involved youth in community projects and wanted to break down cultural barriers and turn "the street" into a space of celebration. "La KY was about theater, music, friendship, *'feeling'* [in English], stories, creativity, nicknames, and every possible celebration," a reporter quoted Job Sis as saying years later.[8]

The structure of feeling around the public space of la KY coalesced as the process of privatization came to a head in Guatemala, culminating in 1998. Three events in the political economy mark this year as important, and all were underpinned by IDB and World Bank programs.[9] First, the government sold the bulk of the telecommunications and electric sectors. Cell phone providers and usage exploded, with inestimable cultural impact.[10] As

Guatemalans embraced their newfound connectivity, they began a decades-long struggle against monopoly control of the power sector, at first by Spanish transnationals. Astronomical prices and abominable service prompted them to dub it "the second conquest" and epitomized the parasite-host relationship that the economist Michael Hudson says is characteristic of the neoliberal regime.[11] Second, the state created Banrural, a private-public bank. Banrural joined an expanding universe of private banks, from eight in 1989 to thirty-four in 1998. While 70 percent of Banrural was capitalized by the private sector, its public-sector *accionistas* included the state, cooperatives, indigenous and campesino organizations, nonprofits, small- and medium-sized business associations, and women's groups. Like the social investment funds, with their progressive-looking mix of private and public funding, Banrural exemplified reconfigured, "multiculturalized" developmentalism. Decades-old attempts to formalize the "informal economy" morphed into plans to promote "microenterprise" and entrepreneurialism, occasioning the spread of microcredit and a new focus on "small and medium-sized businesses." Banrural soon became the nation's largest microlender, and the ethos of the new, entrepreneurial "professionalism" entered the weave of factors influencing everyday lives and expectations on the emergent KY.[12]

The third event that marks 1998 as a turning point was a financial crisis. One source calls it a "financial earthquake," but other nations were harder hit than Guatemala. Ecuador, for example, was suffering an inflationary crisis that led to the "dollarization" of its economy three years later, a measure that El Salvador would also take in 2001. The Asian financial crisis that began in 1997 and the Russian one of the following year occasioned defaults on sovereign debt that dried up global credit markets; Brazil was one of the first to suffer in the Americas. This shock hit Guatemala just as export prices were falling and as massive amounts of currency were flowing in from the post-peace aid extended by donor nations as well as from the privatization of the telecommunications and power sectors. Hurricane Mitch, which ravaged the highlands in late 1998, dealt another blow. The quetzal was teetering, and the central bank raised interest rates and took other measures to save the exchange rate. Three major coffee-export houses went bankrupt, several banks had to be "intervened," and the market for private-sector debt diminished. Bigger banks began to absorb less stable ones in 1999, portending troubles ahead.[13]

Banks, both in their profusion of their provincial branches and in their increasing links to the deregulated Wild West of international robber-baron finance, were just one part of a complex web of public-private initiatives and transformations that joined popular culture both traditional and mediatized to coalesce in a physical and affective KY. Funding from the World Bank, the IDB, the state, and donor nations shaped the physical side. The IDB led a multistage Financial Sector Modernization Program accompanied by investment in roads and infrastructure, in education and public health, and, perhaps most significantly, in political restructuring.[14] On the cultural side forces included the further spread of foreign media and technology: the radio stations and CD-cloning enterprises and homegrown cable companies that helped to disseminate the music of Guatemala City rockers to places like Ixtahuacán and inspire Maya-fusion groups like Sobrevivencia. Most important was the bottom-up economic activity of the growing population. *Lotificación*—cutting up private landholdings into lots and building on them—changed sylvan pathways, always *called* streets, into public "KY." La KY, as a real and imagined space, evolved in dialogue with the political economy as streets and alleyways further filled with "entrepreneurial" enterprises and gave rise to mushrooming agro-urban retail labyrinths.

The policy-driven and discursive rebranding of street vendors and artisans from their old status as problematic denizens of the "informal economy" to their new identity as entrepreneurs with microenterprises—undertaken in great measure to loop them into the global-banking and credit economy—is emblematic of the ways in which the privatization that was underway reconfigured social space. Privatization, writ large, describes a complex, nested series of phenomena that permeated the economy, politics, and everyday life. Guatemalans expressed their experience of this time of transition in terms of a *mundo al revés,* a world upside-down or inside-out—of an old time dead and a new time not yet born. Just as it was unclear what one was supposed to *do* to make a living, it was unclear what one was supposed to *be*. Little wonder, then, that in this time of instability, so many Guatemalans spoke of *death* in multiple spheres, ranging from the political to the cultural to the personal.

National political developments in part explain why so many Guatemalans spoke of the "death of everything" in increasingly hopeless tones, even as there were new reasons for hope in the years around the turn of the millennium. The URNG registered as a political party in 1998. This event promised representation for the Left, but one observer called it the death of "socialism as a historic project."[15] In April of the same year, the archdiocese released a report that documented massacres and human rights violations during the armed conflict. Just forty-eight hours after the report was released, however, assassins brutally murdered its patron, Archbishop Juan José Gerardi Conedera.[16] When, nearly a year later, the parallel report of the United Nations' truth commission declared that the military state had committed acts of genocide, there would be no stopping these hidden crimes from coming to light. The newly won "visibility" of the Mayan movement resulted in indigenous politicians gaining power in the fast-decentralizing municipalities, but the movement suffered a setback in 1999, when a referendum to modify the constitution to include the Peace Accords' definition of the nation as "multiethnic, pluricultural, and multilingual," among other measures, was defeated in the polls.[17] Just months later Alfonso Portillo (2000–2004) won the presidential election. As the candidate of the right-wing Guatemalan Republican Front (FRG) party, he was widely seen as the puppet of the party's founder, congress representative and general Efraín Ríos Montt, who had been head of state during the height of the genocide (March 1982–August 1983). "El Pollo Ronco" (the hoarse chicken), as Portillo was called, turned out to have a populist streak, and, like Serrano Elías (the president unseated in the 1993 constitutional crisis), he soon ran afoul of some of the country's elite power brokers. In 1999, however, no one saw that coming. His victory, along with the FRG's new congressional majority, prompted leftist observers to declare the death of the peace process.[18]

The rightward turn, along with the much-discussed "death of socialism" and "death of peace" evinced what Dussel calls a "political field" that was "like a minefield full of networks and nodes ready to explode over conflicts about unfulfilled demands." In the immediate postpeace period, *mundo al revés* dynamics saw inversions and involutions between Guatemala's never-healthy and already terror-ridden public and private spheres. As politics turned toward an aesthetic embrace of multiculturalism, *power* became more concentrated in the hands of the wealthy elite, nationally and globally. Dussel calls this dynamic one in which power, and "all of politics [becomes] *inverted*, or fetishized." Dominating institutional *potestas* splits off from community-based *potentia,* power rooted in the will of the pueblo to live.[19] On Guatemala's budding KY, the latest chapter in this long-ongoing process unfolded with a contradictory mix of "celebration" and violence.

The years in which socialism was said to die and hopes for a just peace faded away were most directly experienced on la KY as securitization, at once clandestine and very public. Life in the public sphere was increasingly mediated by the growth and institutionalization of "clandestine groups" that putatively worked to keep communities safe in a time of lawlessness and popular rejection of state authority. The populace increasingly saw the police as corrupt, and in 1999 the government legalized the growing constellation of local "security" posses.[20] MINUGUA stressed such groups' private and local articulations. Any given group, they wrote, could include "members of former military structures," along with "persons linked to current State structures, including, increasingly, local governments and municipal security forces." Also involved were "persons linked to private interests, including private security firms and neighborhood committees," as well as "persons linked to organized crime."[21]

Security groups that blurred the lines between public and private, internal and external, were extremely varied, but in general the municipality was *the* ground on which they arose and on which political and social conflicts unfolded. In Zacapa, for example, "coordinated, planned actions to kill persons ... [considered] to be criminals or socially undesirable" in outlying towns showed "features typical of 'social cleansing' operations," and private forces reputedly linked to the mayor murdered the leader of the municipal workers' union. In the highlands the acting mayor of Quiché, accused of misappropriating funds, fell prey to "three armed individuals wearing balaclavas" who "burst into his home and murdered him in front of his wife."[22]

Such was the private tenor of local politics as, with very public support, governance continued to grind its way toward decentralization and municipal autonomy. Urban and Rural Development Committees were now the "axis of development," declared the 1999 Strategic Municipal Plan of Barillas, in Huehuetango.[23] An early example of what was to be a spate of such documents, the Barillas Plan, like others to come, was produced by a municipal team trained and supported by the Spanish international cooperation agency, Agencia Española de Cooperación Internacional para el Desarrollo, which worked with the IDB, the World Bank, NGOs, and other donor nations. In municipalities around the nation, AECID promoted what on paper looked like grassroots participatory democracy. Besides the legacy of war and associated atomization, however, there were two large-scale problems with this approach. First was that decentralization worked as much to reduce the role of the state and increase that of what the IDB called "private operators" as it did to foment local democracy.[24] Second was that by creating complicated networks of committees and workshops and the like, the development apparatus pushed a kind of "participatory" democracy—again, not the kind of democracy that had the power to advocate for the kind of structural change its constituents actually wanted—more suited to tiny rural villages, where people hypothetically knew one another, shared common goals, and got along than to busy agro-urban centers, where people were working as hard as they could to make a living. (Imagine going to a dozen meetings to compete for running water or garbage collection.) Still, meetings became the order of the day. MINUGUA considered Sololá, with its Spanish-trained Municipal Technical Planning Unit (UTMP), to be the best example in the country of how this process could be successful.[25]

Sololá's UTMP illustrates how internationally supported municipal political-training programs were the local level of the larger project of state building and state reducing in which series of consensus-forging yet elite-dominated roundtable negotiations were held on the national and regional levels.[26] Its work was a prequel to the decentralization soon to come. The UTMP started by convening neighborhood meetings, using the SWOT formula ("strengths, weaknesses, opportunities, and threats") to earmark development priorities.[27] Over the years ahead SWOT-structured meetings, and the Community Development Plans (PCDs) that resulted from them, came to have a stultifying, template-imposed sameness. The PCDs of the late 1990s and early 2000s in Sololá, however, early texts in this genre, still had some "vox pop," with moments that sound like something people in the region might actually say: "Threats: Rising drug addiction, paying lots of taxes, rising *delincuencia,* family disintegration." Problems in the barrios were "television and consumption" causing loss of "cultural values"; too many NGOs; the terrible Sololá hospital; dogs, pigs, and feces in the streets; "parents not speaking in both languages [Spanish and Kaqchikel] with their children"; alcoholism, maras, violent films and pornography; teachers smoking and drinking; and kids not doing their homework.[28]

Sololá's threats and weaknesses were common problems in much of Guatemala, and they show in very real terms how youth, urbanization, and politics coincided. For example, parents from outlying areas, who were nearly all illiterate, had to send their children to the cabecera to study beyond the sixth grade.[29] Once there they were exposed to the drugs and the porn and the maras, including "big-gang" offshoots and local iterations like Los Simpson. Youth also traveled in search of work, and such movement—not new but accelerated and increased—helps to explain the small-village excitement about rock nacional that both Los Últimos Adictos's Taz and Sobrevivencia's Alex Job Sis described as being novel and historic. A new kind of "public" identity and idiom of being young came to the "private" space of the hamlet, even as politics in those places, fresh from war, were seeing the early institutionalization of a mesh of systemized chaos. In intimate dialogue with these trends, provincial and capital-city youth began to join together on the terrain of a real-and-imagined KY. Over time, cultural expressions on this KY would take on more and more aspects of what Achille Mbembe calls the "baroque character of the postcolony." While this process was often ludic, it was also significant. As Dussel reminds us, popular culture—"mythical stories" and "expressions like theater"—can be an expression of the bottom-up "community of wills."[30]

A mosh pit in the Mayan highlands is an example of such productive theatricality. At the time of this writing, the Facebook page of Radio Sacmixit in the village of Sac Mixit, Totonicapán, still showed the eerie legacies of war. Its banner photo depicted Kaibiles, army special forces, in camo and war paint; one soldier, in the foreground, stood arm and arm with a young woman in traje.[31] Taz remembers traveling over "frankly scary dirt slopes that not just any vehicle could get up" to gig there in 2001. In a bow to intergenerational tastes, Los Últimos Adictos learned that they were going to "take turns [playing] with Fidel Funes y su Marimba Orquesta (and we had heard Checha y su India Maya Caballero in the street just a little bit before)," Taz wrote, making reference to "old-folks" bands. "It was a curious *toque* [gig]. First Fidel would play, and all the *gente adulta* would dance, and then we'd come on, and all the young people would *moshear*."[32] The Sac Mixit moshers exemplify the intergenerational change underway in highland culture, which, in dialogue with physical modernization, was giving rise to a KY that encompassed village, cabecera, and capital city alike. We can only guess, though, what this meant to the youngsters who slam-danced—how they internalized (to borrow Guinea Diez's phrase) not just urban ladino-global popular culture but also the violence around them, the hopefulness of the years around the Peace Accords, the dreams born of being a first generation to learn to read and write, and then the bitter disappointment when prosperity failed to materialize. However it articulated in any given person's consciousness, that *internalization* has to be understood as an integral element of the *externalization* that gave rise to baroque street cultures and the contested KY in the years ahead.

Taz remembers the 1999 Atmósfera Omplog concert in the capital ("omplog" as in "unplugged"; Atmósfera was a radio station) as the best jam in the history of Guatemalan rock. The big 1990s bands played, including Los Últimos Adictos, Viernes Verde, and Viento en Contra. One of La Tona's contributions was "Interna Externa." It captured the youthful subjectivity of the dynamics of internalization/externalization, private/public, democratic/

authoritarian, old/new of the day. Starting as a spoken poem, the song speaks of turning into the four elements but as a result having to "contemplate elemental attacks": "So I should turn myself to stone ... Or maybe air ... Perhaps fire ... Possibly water," each of the first four stanzas begins. "But I'd keep being limited / my end would be marked by the beginning of the other."[33] "Elemental attacks" of every imaginable kind were changing relationships between *interna* and *externa* around Guatemala at the turn of the millennium, as debates about national identity took new turns in the neoliberalizing body politic and social fabric.

MASKS, ADSCRIPTIONS, PROSTHETICS, AND NATION

Paradoxically, given their newfound national following, the musicians interviewed for *Alternativa* remember the turn of the millennium as the twilight of golden-age *rock chapín*. Corporate sponsors colonized concerts, they claimed, and radio stations were extortionate. The Garra Chapina—a national rock festival and concert held in Guatemala City—was born in 1999. It marked the increased interest of corporate sponsors in rockers who had formed their bands in urban garages and school gyms less than a decade before. "Underground" became "aboveground." The commercialization of Guatemalan rock was symptomatic of the larger process of commercialization seen in culture, society, and the political economy. Grassroots cool—not just in music but in slang and style and street identity—was becoming more mainstream, starting its journey toward billboards and TV spots. Political and ethnic movements, now embraced by the development apparatus, were seen as morphing from "uprising" to "institution." "Youth," a category as imagined as it was real, continued the long march we have traced since the 1980s to its status as both the object of policy intervention and a social identity related to global trends. All the while poverty, lack of opportunity, outmigration, crime, and insecurity inflected the spheres in which life force became inextricably bound up with commerce, only to be marketed back to the impecunious actors who had generated it in the first place. All this commercialization, however—as disheartening as it was, and as cruel as the global economic logic that underlies it is—had a flip side. The huge new generation was coming of age, and—in dialogue both with all these forces and with the vanguardist youth of the 1980s and early 1990s, whose cultural production continued to have outsized influence—they were reconfiguring identity in

FIGURE 12. Fans await the start of the Garra Chapina concert, September 2002. Fototeca Guatemala, Archivo de Moisés Castillo (photographer), GT-CIRMA-FG-078.

ways that went far beyond what officialdom and commerce were pushing. To celebrate their cultural creativity is *not* to celebrate neoliberalism. Instead, it is to look back at a period remembered as the time when "everything died"— tradition, values, good rock, the Mayan movement, the Left, you name it— and excavate what lived, and lived with great consequence.

In an era of commercialization, culture played direct and indirect roles in changing the ways in which Guatemalans self-identified and conceived of themselves as a nation. In many iterations they described their identity as an *anti-identity*, one composed of masks, prescribed performances, and sets of antithetical and oppositional caste-based statuses. Popular youth culture injected new identifications into this mix, adding a street-level dimension to greater debates about ethnicity, identity, and nation. Everyday, bottom-up, microlevel identifications multiplied, in dialogue with lived experience in the urbanizing environment—that is, in dialogue with la KY's youthful celebrations as well as with its new perils. The emergent, discursive KY was both a product and a constitutive element of this cultural change, and embedded within it were the seeds of a reconfigured chapinismo, an alternative popular nationalism. This vernacular nationalism unfolded in a time of plans and projects devoted to "decentralization," but it paradoxically showed a kind of bottom-up "centralization" as from-above and from-below cultural creativity became increasingly interwoven, nurturing a polyvalent chapín identity that crossed lines of caste. Before delving into regional case studies, we begin in Guatemala City with writers, artists, and sponsored cultural projects, exploring how the grammar of what it meant to be chapín and chapina transformed as popular culture came to the fore.

Popular culture was coming to the fore around Latin America and the world. Reflecting on the new millennium, the Spanish-born, Colombia-based philosopher and cultural critic Jesús Martín-Barbero wrote, "In Latin America... we face a structurally broken society, but at the same time a society in which its cultural communities ... are becoming a crucial setting for the re-creation of a sense of the collective, the reinvention of identity, a renewed use of heritage, a productive linkage between what is local and what is global." Despite "the most brutal processes of economic recession, inequality and exclusion," he held, Latin Americans were "living the global transformations that combine a new method of production with a new method of communicating... [that] converts culture... into a direct productive force."[34]

The idea of culture as a "direct productive force" in a cruel, meaningless world was gaining sway in Guatemala early in the new millennium. In January 2000, Guinea Diez published an article called "Saldos del siglo" (Balances of the century) that excoriated "the commitment to the market in its most radical and absolute expression" and "the absurdity ... of reducing the size of the State, in a country still under construction," calling it "Kafkaesque." A new generation was coming up, he wrote, one born in a neoliberal time of "unbelief, cloning, fast food, forgettable loves and made-to-order ideas *[ideas a pedido]*." So what was left of the twentieth century? "*La cultura, sobre todo la cultura* [culture, above all, culture].... The poets, the musicians, the popular traditions. In sum, that inveterate vocation of humans to invent beauty and not to cry before their own defeats."[35]

Affirming the "inveterate vocation" was the goal of a group of Guatemala City writers and artists, most of them born in the 1970s, who published a magazine called *La Chalupa* in 2000—*La Chalupa* after the lottery card with Lupita rowing her canoe. The creative team comprised top young Guatemala City talent. *La Chalupa*'s editor, Maurice Echeverría, later became a noted newspaper columnist and prizewinning fiction writer. Like Echeverría, many *La Chalupa* contributors were members of the Casa Bizarra, a literary and arts center founded in the city's historical center in 1996, and many were affiliated with Editorial X, founded in 1998 to promote alternative literature.[36] The writers started the magazine with a list titled

"Why We Decided to Make *La Chalupa*. . . . To criticize the fixed position, the orthodox and the reactionary . . . to affirm the lyrical and underground Guatemala . . . because Gerardi is dead . . . because the official culture drowns another that's more vibrant and more in agreement with our generation . . . *porque sí* [just because]." They picked their title, they wrote, because Lucía Escobar—who had previously written for the rock magazine *Hasta Atrás*— had won *lotería* with La Chalupa in Todos Santos, playing with "drunk indígenas and cretin tourists."[37]

Even the new generation in places like the traditional and touristed Mam-speaking town of Todos Santos Cuchumatán, Huehuetenango— a generation that included kids forming gangs called Los Cholos and Los Rockeros—would have been scandalized by *La Chalupa*.[38] The magazine's cover image was a close-up drawing of a woman's fingers penetrating her vagina. A comedic ad showed a 1920s flapper getting high under the tagline "Smoke Good Pot." Lucía Escobar's article on the capital's gay bars was titled "Queens Go for Cocktails Too." The next page featured a (heterosexual) oral sex how-to, "Penis/Mouth Procedure," with take-ups on how to have the *"versión chapina"* of sex ("Don't say 'I wanna fuck'; say 'I'm nervous!'"). The columnist Andrés Zepeda satirized Universidad La Landívar, the writers' alma mater; Byron Quiñonez (previously the bassist of the thrash-metal band Sore Sight) wrote about the experimental California group Mr. Bungle. A piece on literature covered Ginsberg, the beat generation, and Tangiers; another featured a photo of a man masturbating (full frontal) next to the Ezra Pound poem "Commission": "Go, my songs, to the lonely and the unsatisfied / Go also to the nerve-wracked, go the enslaved-by-convention / Bear to them my contempt for their oppressors."[39]

La Chalupa's creators were members of a generation whose publications in the first decade of the 2000s marked a new era in Guatemalan literature, a creative turn that was matched at the grassroots on la KY.[40] The author and literary critic Mario Roberto Morales, born in 1947 and with deep ties to the revolutionary Left, cast a jaundiced eye on youthful creative expressions in both their elite and bottom-up iterations. The commercial new literature, he wrote, was "little more than a faithful reproduction of older neovanguardist experimentation" that "followed the contours of 'the alternative' in the U.S."[41] In the provinces, meanwhile, a "popular-consumerist resignification of urban space" was underway: "the *muchachas* (and this is nothing new) wear their native traje, although nuanced with western ornaments like factory-made sweaters, high heels, earrings, and plastic headbands. And the *muchachos* dress in North American style, with their baseball caps on backward and T-shirts with gringo emblems and logos, probably contraband smuggled in from the Panama Canal or made in the maquiladoras of San Juan Sacatepéquez, where various indigenous families have gotten rich on the maquila, using local indigenous labor."[42]

For all its much-maligned commercialization, the new generation, despite being divided by literacy and caste and class and ethnicity, was confecting a cultural commons. That commons, a unity of antitheses, *se encarnó* in the form of la KY. The commercialization of culture—but at the same time its revivification and reinvention—swept around the landscape in a time of a media revolution, of exploding webs of finance, and of thwarted dreams of social and economic justice.

As this transition occurred, ideas about being and becoming, expressed in thoughts about heroism, citizenship, and identity, became prevalent tropes. "The tired heroes / have tired of being heroes," wrote Maurice Echeverría in an untitled poem in *La Chalupa*. "They work monumental shifts / cleaning the kitchens, the bedrooms, / the slow sitting rooms of the world, // . . . to discover the next day that all has gone to shit again."[43] For him the age of heroes was over. In a 2001 essay on identity and anti-identity titled "Máscaras" (Masks), on the other hand, Guinea Diez held that Guatemalans had "civic heroism." However, it didn't correspond to an "institutionalized republican body politic. . . . And how could it be otherwise, when several generations had been exterminated," often by masked men, so that "authoritarian power could reproduce itself?" The result was that "the relationship between democracy and civic virtue is remote, torturous, and precarious. And the man on the street remains distrustful" of the state, unwilling "to believe in anything." Oppression had devolved into a war of "all against all" in a "country of people who mask themselves *[un país de enmascarados]*." Hope and struggle were relegated to interiority; exteriority consisted of hiding while performing. Hence "our inveterate custom of covering things up: account books, identities, our virtues, and our miseries." Guatemalans "lied to survive" and lived in a world structured by "anecdote" and black humor. "No society is as preoccupied with identity as ours is," Guinea Diez wrote. "Perhaps that's because we don't have one, and that forces us to use our respective and opportune masks."[44]

In an essay in *La Chalupa,* Maurice Echeverría also referenced the "masks" and "adscriptions"—the modalities of servility—in Guatemalan society. His piece, "De uniformes y uniformados" (On uniforms and the uniformed), illustrated with pictures from the armed conflict, examined the uniform as something that inspires fear and obedience, that provides a kind of social cohesion, and that, in the form of fashion, kills originality. It could be corporate, professional, or "aseptic," as when an employer makes the housekeeper wear western dress instead of traje. It could be a "quasi-uniform" that marks belonging: the clothes that bodyguards wear, school uniforms, or the jersey of a favorite soccer team. "Perhaps we will arrive in the future to another kind of stadium," Echeverría concluded, "superior and naked, in which there will be no uniforms, masks, facades, or adscriptions."[45]

Merriam-Webster defines *adscription* as "the quality or state of being added, annexed, or bound: *adscription* of serfs."[46] In one of its valences, *adscription* in turn-of-the-millennium Guatemala was certainly the "adscription of consumers"—the branding, "masking," if you will, of bodies attached to the global web of expanding capital, whether through Pepsi or Gallo beer, Marlboro cigarettes, counterfeit Levis and Tommy Hilfiger apparel, or even globalized rock-pop music. Yet in a country characterized by what its own citizens call "castes," distinctions that were over five hundred years old and that were woven into the social fabric through performances of servility and dominance, "adscriptions" had another valence. The consumer-culture styles and fads that the young Guatemalan literati called stifling were more liberatory for the once-but-no-longer *mozos* asserting themselves in city barrios and agro-urban towns as participants in global and national youth culture. In agro-urban Guatemala, youth—drawing on generations of struggle and full of Maya and regional campesino pride—made "urban" culture their own. Their creative adoption and *aldeando* (villaging-up) of pop culture—working, however unharmoniously, in dialogue with the cultural creation of poor youth from the city barrios *and* of the authenticity-seeking middle-class and upper-caste ladinos—cocreated la KY on a national stage. Together with the Maya revival, baroque youth cultures, ranging from the theatrics of the metaleros to the poetic strains of the Ginsberg-loving, university-trained vanguardists to the rap and the hoodies and even the informal gangs of la KY, bore evidence to the cultural force that Guatemalans, struggling against and at the same time deploying adscriptions and uniforms and masks, unleashed in the age of neoliberalization.[47]

That powerful cultural force, striated by caste and distinction as it was, occasioned an unremarked-upon cultural "centralization," the unintentional formation of discursive national commons that was the *indirect* result of culture as a "direct productive force." This process was largely driven from below, but the state and donor nations contributed to it, ironically, through decentralization initiatives. The Ministry of Culture's Support for Cultural Decentralization program, Aporte para la Descentralización de la Cultura (ADESCA), sponsored folkloric arts around the provinces, promoting traditional Maya dance, music, artisanal arts, and rurality.[48] A growing set of public-private initiatives helped to bring from-below and from-above together throughout the aughts. Spain, for example, cosponsored an urban arts festival in October 2000 called Octubreazul, organized by Javier Payeras, the performance artist Regina José Galindo, and the painter José Osorio. Octubreazul built on a legacy of cultural events associated with Casa Bizarra, which had broken up in 1998. It brought together a wide range of ladino and Maya artists. In turn this event inspired the formation of a group for teens and children called Caja Lúdica. The project set up shop in Correos, the historical central post office, and became a meeting ground for a remarkably cross-class selection of creative urban youth, including many from the poor *barrios marginales*.[49] B-boy break-dancers spun on their heads in the same hallways where ballerinas went en pointe. Beyond spawning Caja Lúdica, which would later have a large influence on agro-urban youth, the 2000 Octubreazul festival also inspired festivals around the highlands, some involving the same organizers. It was an important early contributor to a historic explosion of the arts, and in particular of youth arts, throughout the first decade of the 2000s.[50]

Also playing a role in Octubreazul, and soon to tour the provinces, was Iqui Balam, the theater group from the Mario Alioto land invasion with which Ángel Cañas and his rap group Alioto Lokos had an ongoing relationship. Both Iqui Balam and the Alioto Lokos were on their way to fame, and the story of how that happened illustrates how NGOs, foreign aid, national artists, the state, and local youth came together in ways that impacted national culture. After Hurricane Mitch devastated the highlands in late 1998, German international cooperation provided funds for, among other things, transnational youth arts encounters. The Iqui Balam kids soon found themselves in Hanover and, not long after that, onstage in Octubreazul. Their linkage with Iqui Balam helped the Alioto Lokos get "discovered" and become a band of choice for film soundtracks and other high-visibility projects. They formed a new group in the mid-aughts, Bacteria Soundsystem Crew, won album gigs, and influenced a generation of B-boys around the highlands—youth like the Tz'utujil young men of Ijatz Crew in San Pedro Atitlán, whom we met in the introduction.

There is a reality TV–like, game-show "Slumdog Millionaireness" to all of this. Plucking a few kids out of the land invasions and turning them into stars is completely characteristic of both reality TV and neoliberal cultural policy. Even as the state was working to "domesticate" impoverished urban youth and "absorb" and "mainstream" their street cultures—turning city urchins into a stereotyped mascot—it was also working to integrate provincial Maya youth into an as-yet-to-be-woven national fabric. In honor of a 2001 visit by the Mexican novelist Carlos Fuentes, the president's communications team produced public relations videos of children singing the national anthem in Mayan languages, a historic first. For people familiar with Guatemala, Maya versions of the anthem have a haunting effect, given the violent relationship of the state with the singers. On one hand, the videos celebrate diversity and Maya culture; on the other, they erase the Maya de a pie and promote a real, but also essentialized and stereotyped, way of being Maya.[51]

The palpable disjunctures one feels when watching such videos speak to the contradictions and slippages that were a lived reality for people growing up in this transitional time. If working-class capital-city street artists (Maya or ladino) were inspired and in some way integrated by the NGO-fueled validation of inner-city art forms, they were also aware that they were far more likely to be killed in a clandestine social-cleansing campaign than they were to be whisked off to perform onstage somewhere as if by the Mago de Oz.[52] And young Maya in the highlands, singing the national anthem in school in an official version of their language as they may have been, were coming up in an atmosphere in which violence proliferated and the population came to reject the state ever more stridently. The media and cultural projects had huge effects, but those effects were articulated in dialogue with the brutal conditions of everyday life. The ways in which youth culture unfolded in Guatemala, urban and agro-urban alike, show harmonic convergences between official culture (promoted by NGOs, the state, and private capital, glomming onto what was happening at the grassroots), as well as screeching dissonances that speak to the sometimes heartening but often violent cultural, political, and social changes underway in the urbanizing highlands.

Nationalism was at stake in those convergences and dissonances. What was *lo guatemalteco* going to be in this country that was rewriting ethnic relations, privatizing its public sphere, reducing a state just barely in formation, and, locally, rejecting what little was left of that state? Todos Santos is as "picture postcard," iconographically "Maya Guatemala" a place as can be imagined; its All Saints' Day drunken horse races rank with Chichicastenango's market as a number-one ethnotourism destination. A historic Maya takeover of local politics and the local economy was underway in Todos Santos, but spectacular violence indicated deep instability in the region's social and political fabric. April 2000 saw the lynching of a Japanese tourist—one of twenty-three visiting that day—and one of the group's Guatemalan drivers. "The former," MINUGUA reported, died "as a result of multiple and brutal blows from rocks and a hatchet, and the latter [was] ferociously beaten and burned by 500 local people.... The mob accused them of attempting to steal a child for Satanic sacrifices."[53] With the lynching of a tourist, a horrific pain that was *interna* suddenly became very *externa*. Was *this* "Guatemala," and not tradition, horse races, and women in traje?

Diane Nelson's 2001 article, "Stumped Identities," serves as a scholarly and primary source on turn-of-the-millennium Guatemala's identity crises. It described "national, ethnic... and gender identities" as "stumped, in the sense of being incomplete, wounded, and rudimentary, as well as being baffled and unsure." Nelson's analysis situated "the Mayan woman, or la *mujer Maya*," as a "prosthetic," a "discursive construct" that "covers an opening" and "overcomes a lack of presence." Like "wounded bodies," "identifications" such as "nation, ethnicity, and gender" relied "on supports like the imagined Mayan woman in order to exist," Nelson argued.[54] Her piece framed "the multiple interchanges among nation, ethnicity, modernity, tradition, and gender" as an "articulation that changes and constitutes the elements involved through their joining." After linking this articulation to body imagery, dialogically changing ladino identity, and the extractive political economy, Nelson underscored the relegation of the *mujer Maya* to tradition and domesticity while Maya men "hacked" modernity and the state, a gendered divide "produced through ... [a] phantasmatic split between public and private."[55] Here, building on this point, I argue that the polyvalent public-private splits in Guatemala referenced by La Tona's "Interna/Externa," Guinea Diez's "masks," Echeverría's "uniforms," and Nelson's "mujer Maya" manifested in an involuted set of processes through which *potentia* found its outlet in a multivocal, contested-yet-unifying, already-existing-yet-all-new chapinismo. The elements of this chapinismo—an articulation, in Nelson's sense—consisted of a generative and expanding set of prosthetic-yet-real identifications, ranging from Maya and *ladino* to *rockero, metalero, cholero, jipi, burgués, fresa,* and the like. They were constructed on, and constructed, la KY. A positive expression of creative human will, of direct and indirect productive force, KY-chapinismo was rooted and articulated in dialogue with violence, as the security patrols and the lynchings remind us. It evolved as a grassroots nationalism, but a nationalism shot through with danger and hatred for the state.

Rejecting state authority was a widespread phenomenon, MINUGUA reported in 2002. Pueblos threw out the police to protect marijuana farmers. They warred with the police to make them hand over accused criminals for street justice. They rose up in arms to force corrupt mayors to resign.[56] In one incident "villagers in Sayaxché, Petén, responded to news of a robbery by organizing themselves into patrols, capturing a man and two boys, and then torturing and fatally shooting them."[57] At the same time as events like these bore evidence to the disintegration of state authority and control, SEGEPLAN (Presidential Programming and Planning Secretariat) was publishing its Path of Peace (El Camino de la Paz) development plan, which emphasized decentralization in rural areas, and UNICEF was starting to send the slumdog-millionaire Iqui Balam kids around the highlands to give workshops on how to build a future of peace and democracy.[58] The decentralizing state and the development apparatus that aided it glommed onto la KY's youth cultures as a "prosthetic" to "overcome a lack of presence" in a fragmenting and violent body politic.[59]

Top-down, prosthetic uses of culture, however, were a reaction to already-ongoing grassroots cultural change, which itself served a different but related prosthetic purpose. As it had been since the days of the ethnic question in the guerrilla ranks, since the struggles for "power's destiny" in the genocide's wake, since the new cultural assertiveness of the *duendes* in the late 1980s and early 1990s, and since the *ni pez ni iguana* years around the Peace Accords, *identity* remained a central and fiercely negotiated issue in the turn-of-the-millennium era of commercialization. At a time when it seemed like politics were relegated to *"cultura, sobre todo la cultura,"* the direct and indirect productive force of youth culture and counterculture provided prosthetics through which ordinary people generated bottom-up, KY-based chapinismo—a vernacular idiom of belonging, an alternative popular nationalism.

The rock nacional band Viernes Verde provided a song about this bottom-up nationalism with such lasting resonance that nearly every youth I interviewed in the 2010s mentioned it to me—"Requiem en E," released on the 2001 album *Remedios para el alma* (Soul remedies). Its refrain chanted, "Soy chapín de sangre / Vas a respetarme / Si no crees en mi / Pelame la verga / Soy chapín de sangre / Vas a respetarme / Si no crees en mi / Comé mucha mierda" (I'm chapín by blood / You will respect me / If you don't believe in me / I don't give a fuck / ... Eat loads of shit.)[60] Requiem's hard-rock tone was very different from the Maya folk-rock fusion of Sobrevivencia's music, but both bore evidence to the end of servility as a cultural form and joined in a grassroots reworking of the historically racist and exclusionary concept of what it meant to be Guatemalan and who got to lay claim to chapín nationalism. "Cultural decentralization" may have been the well-meant goal of the ADESCA program, but at the grassroots level a transformational kind of centralization was underway that bore evidence to ongoing, historic shifts in expressions of identity and iterations of national consciousness.

A WORLD IN LIBERTY

The KY-based cultural centralization that, I argue, resulted in a contested-but-unifying chapinismo, was extraordinarily messy. Grassroots chapinismo reflected all the conflictivity of the body politic, and it evolved in dialogue with a free-market world. It was unifying, but it was a unity of opposites—a cultural recentering built around myriad decenterings. It expressed new freedom of expression in a time when freedom, globally, implied the freedom of capital to move unfettered—a neoliberal triumph paradoxically *encarnado* in agro-urban Guatemala through political decentralization and municipal autonomy, an ongoing process of legal and administrative reconfiguration that was in its penultimate phase at the end of the 1990s and beginning of the 2000s. In this creative and destructive period, new liberty collided with new unfreedom, *I am* relied on *I am not,* and youthful hope and rage generated la KY's mix of festivity and violence.

Sobrevivencia's first album, *Twi'Witz* (On the mountaintop), released in 2001, was full of hope for a better nation. "La Juventud" sang that "youth have the keys to this society, because they have a lot of energy for change / In their fresh minds they have new ideas for how to build and live in a better world." So "Why isn't it possible to build / Un mundo sin barreras / Un mundo sin odio / Un mundo! / Más humano / Un mundo sin conflictos / Un mundo inteligente / Un mundo! / En libertad?"[61]

This kind of a world—a world without barriers or hatred or conflict, a more human and intelligent world, a world in liberty—was not what existed or awaited. Liberty in the new millennium was chaotic, contradictory, and polyvalent. The barely held-together democratic state began a new chapter in what Guinea Diez called the "Kafkaesque" process of decentralization in 2002, and the *mundo en libertad* came increasingly to involve the "liberty" of local power groups to oppress their neighbors and rob resources, institutionalizing the "warlordism" that had been percolating since the 1980s. Once achieved, local liberty dovetailed with the partial domestication of Maya politics and the "systematization" of SWOT-based development planning. Such liberty was largely, if not entirely, performative. Municipalities built infrastructure, but real political power was out of their reach. Performativity in the political economy was matched with performativity in popular culture. As the economy failed to produce jobs, youth culture became even more baroque, and *libertad* included not just gangs and turf wars but also libertine "playworlds" that evolved in dialogue with the neoliberalizing political economy—playworlds expressed in rave culture, drug use, and free sex, as well as in hybridized, bohemian, and traditional expressions of identity.[62] As playworlds popularized, so too did reactions against them: *I am not that*. Guatemala's *"mundo en libertad"* was not just ludic. It also meant, for many young people, the liberty not to work as migrant farm laborers, to study, and to aspire to be "professionals," despite the lack of work for professionals after graduation. It could mean the liberty to be straightlaced, to be Evangelical, to be an economic refugee, to lynch delinquents, or to get involved in local government and piggyback on generalized corruption. Many Guatemalans chose to exercise their liberty in demonstrations against the globalization and neoliberalization that was making so-called freedom so unfree in their nation and around the world.

Given that neoliberalization, it is little wonder that Guatemalans remember the turn of the millennium in "death of everything" terms that this analysis seeks both to complicate and to put into larger historical context. The 9/11 attacks on the United States in 2001 marked the beginning of the end of the gush of international aid that had been flowing into Guatemala, as international aid flows redirected to the Middle East. Some three months after 9/11, Argentina's running battle with the International Monetary Fund (IMF) came to a head when massive riots forced the president to flee the country. In the same year, in Guatemala, Comandante Santiago Santa Cruz Mendoza quit the URNG in disgust, feeling that the guerrilla group–turned–political party had been co-opted by all the worst of politics. In 2002, as Guatemala's new banking laws attempted to deal with, among other things, the proliferation of offshore banks, President Alfonso Portillo was in an escalating battle—one he would lose—with the neoliberal elite. The neoliberalization and "death of everything" came putatively to include the Mayan movement; in 2001 COPMAGUA broke up. The movement's fall had a human face when Antonio Pop Caal, a leader of the movement and cultural revival for decades, was kidnapped in late 2002 and later discovered dead; it was in this same year that Charles Hale published "Does Multiculturalism Menace?," an article arguing that state multicultural policies in Guatemala were fully compatible with a neoliberalizing mission.[63] The most significant steps in that neoliberalizing mission came through a series of 2002 laws that finalized the process of municipal decentralization. While this looked at the time like a victory for Maya politicians, neoliberal ideology was ascendant, and corruption infiltrated every level of politics as the Mayan movement—at least according to contemporary commentators and to academics who later studied the subject—lost its radical edge. Thanks to commercialization, chroniclers hold, the golden age of Guatemalan rock ended too; Primera Generación Records closed its doors in 2002. Los Últimos Adictos tried to move to Los Angeles but failed, and their last concert was held in Pana Rock in Panajachel on Lake Atitlán. Ricardo Andrade was murdered by mistake just weeks later.

Meanwhile, the price of coffee plummeted. The economic backlash of this blow was only one of the reasons that Guatemala exploded in social protest in 2003, as campesinos joined the teachers, who were on a fifty-three-day-long strike early in the year, in closing the ports, the airport, and the highways.[64] The victory of the probusiness, neoliberal Óscar Berger (2004–8) in the presidential elections at the end of the year was a surprise; perhaps it was helped in part by the United States' sudden decertification of Guatemala, under Portillo, in the war on drugs. By that time Latin American headlines in global resistance to neoliberalism included Bolivia's gas and coca wars that paved the way for the later rise of Evo Morales, a landmark in the history of the "pink tide" and the pan-indigenous movement. Guatemala was never to find the cohesive force that congealed in Bolivia. Its path to *"un mundo en libertad"* was fragmented, performative, and contradictory—anarchic and bureaucratic, full of killing and playworlds alike.

"The ecstasy!" remembers "Nene," a self-described Maya Kaqchikel from Panajachel. He speaks of the drug but evokes the emotion. "The techno! The deep house! The progressive trance!" He is waxing nostalgic about the all-night, full-moon raves of the early 2000s, held at rented chalets outside of San Pedro La Laguna. Nene grew up poor on a *callejón* (alley); he got to attend these parties in his early twenties because he was hired to help organize them. Promoted by a rocker called "Carpeta" who had moved to Panajachel from the Pacific coast, the full-moon raves were a local iteration of a playworld born in Guatemala City at the end of the 1990s, when a group called Fosa Común (meaning "Mass Grave"—no comment) started organizing "moving clandestine parties" with musical hosts including DJ Chronic

MAP 4. Population centers of the Lake Atitlán basin.

and DJ Megadose.⁶⁵ An annual Rave del Castillo, held in Palencia (a semiagrarian municipality in the Guatemala City metropolitan area) began in 2000 and was active until 2008.⁶⁶ Fosa Común published a magazine for the raves called *Supositorio* (Suppository). Many of the same writers associated with the Casa Bizarra, Editorial X, and *La Chalupa* wrote for it. Maurice Echeverría penned "MDMA for Beginners" (MDMA is ecstasy), and Lucía Escobar contributed a short story on cheating partners and second loves.⁶⁷ Some *Supositorio* writers probably road-tripped to the lake to attend the fullmoon parties with local youth like Nene, another example of the contacts that brought urban and agro-urban Guatemala into closer dialogue.⁶⁸

Contacts both global and national added new dimensions to iterations of identity in the *mundo en libertad*. Cultural hybridization was especially pronounced in bohemian enclaves like the lake, where hippie globalism had been making inroads for decades. On *Rock Republik*, Alhazred posted about the

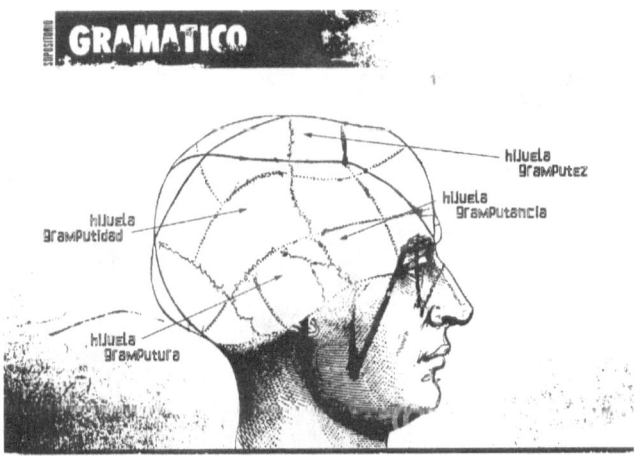

FIGURE 13. This graphic from the rave magazine *Supositorio* plays with the phrase, "hijo de la gran puta." "Gramático. Entre neologismos e hijos," no. 14, fiesta 26 (16 February 2002): 15. Archivo Histórico de CIRMA, Colección Thelma Porres, GT-CIRMA-AH-40-551.

lasting legacy of Panajachel's hippie nude-beach scene of the 1960s and 1970s.[69] But the lake was not the only place where hippie styles took root; *El Regional* called the Huista region's Maya-hippie style "new symbols of Maya identity"; long-haired men wore sandals, traditional shirts, and assumed Maya-language nicknames.[70] Sometimes the adoption of the hippie look was strategic; *"tengo que trabajar de jipi"* (I have to work as a hippie), a young man told me, sadly, at the lake when I asked him why he was looking atypically shaggy. He could sell better to tourists if he looked the part. Around the lake in the early 2000s, children and teens—most of whom sported the latest KY fashions—were speaking of *"mi cultura maya."* But not all agreed with this discourse of pride, with the political affiliations of the Mayan movement, or with the use of the word "Maya." A good number of youth were straightlaced, especially but not exclusively those from the ever-growing number of strictly observant Evangelical families. Both Evangelicals and Catholics tended to reject counterculture as *delincuencia* and Maya spirituality as *brujería* (witchcraft). Forming the flip side of this rejection was a *longing* for a stronger Maya identity, especially among KY-savvy youth like Nene, whose parents spoke Kaqchikel but who had never learned themselves—youngsters who embraced a "Guatemaya" with a reggae offbeat but mourned a heritage lost.[71]

FIGURE 14. Different childhoods, shown by this Panajachel street scene from 1999. A Maya boy carries a load on his back with a tumpline, passing another child wearing a baseball cap and a pop-culture T-shirt. Fototeca Guatemala, Archivo de Kurt Zierlein (photographer), GT-CIRMA-FG-170.

Iterations of identity, like debates about them, did not unfold in the peaceful and productive environment that Sobrevivencia wished for in "Juventud." Instead, they arose as a very human, *interna/externa* response to a changing political economy. On one hand, those changes involved the violent mysteries wrapped up in postpeace realities—the mysteries embedded in what Raymond Craib calls a "fugitive landscape" that escapes the gaze of the state.[72] Around

Lake Atitlán at the time, denizens of this landscape included highway bandits and much-rumored groups of "unknown men" whom people said lived in the mountains and periodically descended to deliver street justice to local criminals. "Who knows what's in the *monte*," one teen said to me, gesturing at the wilderness.[73] Closer to home the fugitive landscape that was coconstitutive of evolving identities included intertown, youth-on-youth violence and street gangs that broke out at the grassroots—themselves phenomena related to the corrupt and corrupting body politic as decentralization moved forward and gave rise to the neoliberalized free-for-all of the *mundo en libertad*.

Since the late 1990s intertown rivalry on la KY in Panajachel and Sololá had been taking violent turns. In Sololá's *convite* (traditional procession or dance) for the Virgin of the Conception, an event called Tabal, young men and boys from these two towns began donning demonic-looking, "modern" masks and blowing one another up with homemade bombs.[74] The pyrotechnic wars of Tabal started to send youth to the hospital and the morgue at the same time as Sololá-versus-Panajachel rumbles were breaking out. Memories vary, but most accounts agree that the Panajachel kids declared the Sololá boys persona non grata. Fights broke out at sporting events and on Saturday nights, when Sololatecos came down the mountain to go to Panajachel's discos, bars, and music venues like Pana Rock, the number-one center in the highlands for rock nacional since its founding in the mid-1980s. One of the most common accounts traces the battles to rivalry between basketball teams. A more interesting story blames the turf wars on sexual competition related to tourism, holding that the Panajachelenses wanted exclusive access to foreign women partying in the discos.[75]

Tabal firefights and the rumbles related to sports, or libido, or both, caused less local alarm than did the threat of gangs, in the Sololá Panajachel region as around the agro-urban highlands. Both a real and deadly social phenomenon and the source of moral panic, gangs were a constitutive element of the violent, anarchic *mundo en libertad* that congealed at the turn of the millennium. Panajachel's relatively peaceful gang history shows an unnoticed, bottom-up side of this story that contrasts with the more well-known history of murderous transnational gangs. Homegrown gangs, while pestiferous and antisocial, could also earn a place in local folklore, forming part of regional identity and the KY-based history of agro-urban towns.

According to some sources, both MS-13 and Mara 18 had members in Sololá and Panajachel in the late 1990s; others disagree. (One informant, "América," told me she had dated the Sololá leaders of both these gangs.) If there had been such "real" gangs, though, locals say, residents broke them up. Everyone agrees, however, that at around the turn of the millennium, a youth gang emerged in Panajachel called "Los Pokemones," after the Japanese Game Boy video games, TV shows, and anime films.[76] The gang was led by a Kaqchikel adolescent nicknamed Koki, a neighbor of Nene's. Los Pokemones didn't disappear until Koki was murdered in the early 2000s (circa 2003), according to several sources, for having disrespected a fellow inmate during a stint in prison. Koki is half-fondly remembered as a sort of folk (anti)hero. Not a single one of the many working-class people to whom I spoke about Los Pokemones remembered Koki with hatred. He was not the world's worst guy, and the kids in the gang were *"pendejos"* but okay. Indeed, Los Pokemones lived on in some strands of memory as having been a *relief*. These guys weren't Mara 18 or Salvatrucha killers from the city; they were the neighbors' kids. They smoked pot, snorted coke, and painted graffiti but didn't do anything worse than "steal the schoolhouse bell." If there had to be gangs, Los Pokemones—for better or worse a chapter in one town's history—wasn't the world's worst gang to have.[77]

The informal gangs of the early 2000s, like Los Pokemones, moved in a different milieu than those of mid-1990s, like Los Simpson, which, though similar, can be read as a reaction to the end of military occupation. Los Pokemones were more in dialogue with decentralization. The Peace Accords had a new kind of body politic, one attentive not only to ethnic diversity but also to needs of an impoverished population that could finally participate in the construction of a hegemonic state. It did not materialize. Instead, Guatemalans lived a combination of lawlessness and institutionalization. As Dussel reminds us, *law*—a functioning legal system—is at the center of a legitimately functioning political system that reflects *potentia*. In the age of decentralization, Guatemalans got a *mundo en libertad* in its stead.[78]

The devolution of government to the municipal level accelerated after the 2002 laws reformed the municipal code, formalized development councils, and mandated the general decentralization of state economics, finances, and administration.[79] To read the documents of the day is to get the (false) impression that whole towns and villages mobilized, forming committees, forging consensus, and engaging in profound participatory democracy. Yet, as with the gangs and the drugs and the raves, most people experienced municipal decentralization as *ruido de fondo* (background noise), although it came to have outsized impact on their lives. Just as was the case with the shifting markets transforming agriculture and the financial modernization and privatization programs, decentralization was Guatemala's chapter of a global phenomenon being pushed by the World Bank, the IMF, donor nations and other powerful entities. Similar projects were underway around the planet and in Latin America were noted in countries such as Brazil, Chile, Peru, and Colombia, where they had primarily served to alleviate the state's responsibility for providing essential services and infrastructure.[80]

Municipal decentralization generated a mess of bureaucratic institutionalization and intensified anarchic, corrupt, and conflict-ridden power struggles. The new laws created nested development committees—(Community, Municipal, or Departmental) Urban and Rural Development Councils (CO-DES)—named COCODES, COMUDES, and CODEDES at the community, municipal, and departmental levels, respectively. As these gradually came into being in the years after the 2002 legislation, they joined city hall, the alcaldía indígena, NGOs, neighborhood committees, and security committees and patrols (not to mention the police, churches, gangs, and organized crime rings) as local seats of power in a body politic that was anything but peaceful.

In Sololá serious political conflicts had unfolded over the years in which the muni's first Community Development Plans, finished in 2002, were being prepared. These problems were primarily the result of the Left's splitting in two when the URNG became a political party in December 1998. What had been a unified local bloc supporting Sololá's SUD civic committee divided. SUD found most of its support in the *casco urbano* and the also-urban San Jorge area, while URNG support came from the municipality's more rural villages. SUD-URNG frictions came to a head in the 2001 elections for the alcalde indígena. SUD won, but the URNG alleged fraud and ultimately threatened to burn sixteen people alive, including the indigenous mayor-elect. The alcaldía indígena closed for over a month and reopened with the URNG candidate in office.[81]

Despite its conflicts, Sololá was an example of *successful* municipal management. Other areas were far less cohesive, as decentralization hit. In looking back at Totonicapán, the anthropologist Stener Ekern later highlighted the monumental achievements of local political actors. However, the "problem," he concluded, was "to construct a legitimate Mayan authority at the apex of a system designed to share the burdens of subordination."[82] Given the already-weak and now retiring state, the *mundo en libertad* continued to evolve as a *lucha libre*. In Barillas, for example, urban-rural conflicts not unlike those seen between the SUD and the URNG in Sololá arose. Unlike in Sololá, however, where the two groups worked things out (albeit messily), a huge percentage of Barillas's population became disgusted and indifferent to the political process.[83] In Huehuetenango Department, *conflictividad* was so high that a Conflict Commission was set up. Resistance to the police, demonstrations against expensive electricity (including burning regional offices of DEOCSA, the Spanish-owned electric company), battles over market locations, and, most of all—given the high number of returned refugees in the area—land conflicts were all out of control. In October 2002 already-high crime statistics spiked all around Guatemala, and the press noted an outbreak of lynchings. In Cobán the Mayan movement leader Antonio Pop Caal was kidnapped. At the same time, campesino organizations were spearheading massive protests against the Plan Puebla Panamá and the Free Trade Agreement; they repeatedly blocked the highways and briefly shut down the border crossings.[84]

As the October 2002 protests were beginning to escalate, Ricardo Andrade and Los Últimos Adictos, recently back from the United States, were touring the highlands with the Diablos Negros, a Honduran group. Los Últimos Adictos gave their last concert on October 12, the same day that the massive antiglobalization protests unfolded. The venue was Pana Rock in Panajachel. Two days later Andrade and fellow band member keyboardist Gabriel Rivera were caught in the crossfire at Andrade's girlfriend's house in Sanarate, El Progreso. Andrade died in a Guatemala City hospital on October 20, nine days before the full moon.[85] In homage, in bars and restaurants and cantinas all around the country, the strains of "El Norte" rang out: *si aquí se pudiera vivir* (if only you could live here).

THE MORAL ECONOMY OF THE TUC-TUC

Los Últimos Adictos existed no longer, but their music lived on, both on la KY and in Guatemala's historically booming arts scene. Art and expressiveness, both elite and popular, evolved in dialogue with poverty, death, corruption, and criminality in the early 2000s. In these artistically fecund years, Guatemalans were representing themselves in more diverse, sophisticated, and media-driven ways. Much of what they reflected on was a corrupt, criminal state and body politic; a cruelly impoverished society; hidden desires and perversions; and a weave of sociocultural change with traditions both beautiful and shameful, as the world turned inside-out but its structures of poverty and exclusion marched on. In the articulations between "published culture," political culture, popular culture, and material culture, we can begin to see the nodes in what Carolyn Nordstrom, in her book on criminal networks that links a nine-year-old Angolan war orphan selling loosie cigarettes on the street to trillionaire crime syndicates, calls the "series of power grids that shape the fundamental econo-political dynamics of the world today."[86]

Corrupt "power grids" were a major theme in the new-millennium arts explosion. An excellent example is the 2003 Casa Comal film, *La casa de enfrente* (The house across the way), whose soundtrack included Los Últimos Adictos song "Blues" and tracks from Bohemia Suburbana and other rock nacional bands. Supported by Norwegian international cooperation, *La casa de enfrente* stars the writer Maurice Echeverría as an idealistic fresa accountant who works for the government. His character discovers a vast embezzlement scene and ends up falling in love with a prostitute in a strip joint, whom a higher-up has secretly hired to distract him from justice seeking and dirty him up. On the face of it, *La casa de enfrente* is about the corruption of Guatemalan politics and its social fabric, but it ultimately ends being much more about the prostitutes and their pimp. Like so much cultural production of the era, it languishes on quasi-pornographic and scatological heterosexuality, bearing evidence of a generation that hadn't had a lot of Libertad de Expresión. Despite its shortcomings, however, the film was testimony of the spectacular corruption of the body politic.[87]

Spectacular corruption permeated all levels of society and culture. MINUGUA's 2002 human rights report described a body politic infiltrated with clandestine groups but credited President Portillo for attempting to combat corruption.[88] Praise for Portillo's scandal-ridden administration would not last long. Two years later, after the probusiness, center-right Óscar Berger (2004–8) assumed the presidency, Portillo was accused of embezzlement and money laundering. He began a long road of trials that ultimately would see him extradited to the United States in 2013, where he spent a year in prison. Byron Barrera Ortiz, Portillo's secretary of social communication, later wrote a defense of the ex-president. Without denying Portillo's corruption, he attributes his downfall to populism that cost the nation's neoliberal power brokers money.[89] Barrera was joined in this view by ex-president Jorge Serrano, who writes that as soon as he heard of Portillo's allowing imported sugar, cement, and chicken imports to drive down domestic prices, he knew that the *"dueños"* would "never forgive him."[90] Along with sugar, cement, and chicken, Portillo let Brahva beer into the country (produced by Cervecería Río, a subsidiary of the Brazilian beverage company Ambev), ending the Castillo family's Gallo beer monopoly.[91] Given crippling price inflation, many people appreciated these moves, although some wore sexist T-shirts that read, *"mi mujer es Brahva, mi cerveza es Gallo"* (my woman is vicious; my beer is Gallo)—a misogynistic example of how economic and political battles filtered down to street culture. Greatly affecting lived reality on la KY was the Fiscal Pact signed early in Portillo's term. The Pacto Fiscal had been hammered out by representatives of over 130 groups. It included progressive measures, such as a promise to increase tax revenue to 12 percent of GDP, which would have required collecting more taxes from the wealthy. It also laid the groundwork for the sweeping municipal decentralization measures of 2002 with "fiscal decentralization," facilitating a free-for-all of corruption.[92] Soon the metaphorical *casa de enfrente* could be found—legalized—in municipalities around the nation, as greed and scandal formed the connective tissue that held the *mundo en libertad* together.

There are three main points here. The first is that the world of Guatemalan politics is so byzantine that it beggars belief. The second is that no matter the extent of Portillo's populist and nationalist leanings, globalization and international finance could not be stopped. Underwritten by the IDB, the World Bank, and donor nations, the neoliberalization of the economy and body politic proceeded under both Portillo and Berger. The third is that the "series of power grids" at work in this process articulated throughout society and the body politic, manifesting in culture and everyday life.[93]

Agro-urban Guatemala was a zone of expansion for capital. Opening it up as such involved significant investment in reconfiguring institutions and policies. The deeply paradoxical process through which corrupt chaos was institutionalized was spearheaded by the IDB, which, by the end of Portillo's term, had become the largest donor in the Consultative Group on Guatemala. The extension of credit was critical to the IDB's Financial Modernization Program. At the municipal level the IDB wove public-private alliances to lend money to city governments to "promote a larger and more competitive supply of services and financing from the private sector."[94] At the same time, the bank ramped up its focus on microfinance, working with the government to craft policies, guidelines, and legislation to streamline development. To make new debtors creditworthy, it complemented its loans with training programs for both municipal workers and microcredit "entrepreneurs," many of them in the NTA sector.[95] Over time these projects "arced together," bringing corruption from below in contact with corruption from above (*"es mi microempresa,"* joked a preteen who was trying to sell me pot in the street). Corrupt mayors and microcredit scammers abounded, and the financial industry benefited by new markets for credit at fantastically usurious rates.

Tecpán, Chimaltenango, is an exemplar of how these forces came together in agro-urban space. In their study of this broccoli-producing "semi-urban place," Edward Fischer and Peter Benson link the "desire" of poor Maya farmers to get ahead *(superarse)* and have *"algo más"* to global economic webs. Broccoli trucks also ferried drugs, for example. Tecpán had new gangs, which were real but also "larger than life." It had become a place where kids used the internet to follow Pokemon and watch porn. The mayor, from Ríos Montt's FRG party, had a new house and a shiny red BMW; he barely escaped alive when a vigilante mob burned his dwelling, his vehicle, city hall, and the police station (they also stripped the police naked, dragged them through the streets, and beat them).[96] Besides "private-sector actors" like the still-poor but aspiring broccoli farmers and "public-private actors" like the mayor, Tecpán also housed numerous counterfeit-clothing entrepreneurs. Kedron Thomas's study of this small city opens with the image of young guys having a *chamusca* pickup soccer match and lounging around town, wearing brand-name hoodies over "gel-drenched hair," hoodies produced in the "pirate" factories of the town itself. She notes how "branded fashions" fit into a broader rubric of a "colorful and loud" world of "style," one that comprised highly decorated retooled U.S. school buses, fireworks, music-blaring loudspeakers, and logos on counterfeit clothes that were "reiteration[s] of an effusive aesthetics that makes life in the region visually arresting and baroque." Part of that "aesthetic effervescence" was the tuc-tuc, the three-wheeled moto-taxi that arrived from Asia early in 2001 and was ubiquitous by mid-decade.[97]

In many ways the tuc-tuc serves as a metonym for greater processes at work in Guatemala, as they were globally. It traversed the overlapping realms of formal and informal, legal and extralegal, global and local, and old and new in the economy and lived environment. Seen from above, the "immoral economy" of the tuc-tuc ultimately benefited corporations, intermediaries, and relatively wealthy fleet owners; it tied poor workers in barrios to global networks and linked them to economies of extraction that were sanctioned, "gray," and outside the law, the sorts of multileveled networks that Nordstrom describes. Seen from below, through the lens of what I call the "moral economy of the tuc-tuc," the moto-taxi symbolizes the ways in which Guatemala's popular class adopted new technologies and forms of work in its ongoing assertion of the "right to subsistence," as James Scott phrased it in *The Moral Economy of the Peasant*.[98] The tuc-tuc provided employment and cheap transportation to the poor majority; it slotted in perfectly to the web of grassroots economic relationships that kept the nation alive. The tuc-tuc quickly became an integral element of agro-urban life and the baroque cultural aesthetics of its KY.[99]

It is almost impossible to imagine agrotropolis without the *tuc*. Their noisy ubiquity (the name *tuc-tuc* comes from their high-decibel *puttt*) so typifies the agro-urban landscape that citizens at the time of this writing were amazed to remember that their arrival was so relatively recent. The tuc-tuc has achieved timelessness. Checha y Su India Maya Caballero, the still-popular marimba orchestra that Taz remembered from Sac Mixit that had been capturing the texture of everyday life in grassroots Guatemala since the 1950s, wrote a tune about it: "El Tuc-Tuc." *"El tuc-tuc se mira por aquí / El tuc-tuc se mira por allá,"* its catchy tune goes. *"Se está poniendo de moda* [it's getting fashionable] / *En todo de Guatemala."* Locals came to call the three-wheelers *toritos* or *toros con tres llantas* (little bulls, or three-wheeled bulls); *"muy chiquitito y gracioso"* the song went: itty-bitty and funny! *"El tuc-tuc bip bip!"*[100]

The diffusion of the tuc-tuc from its birthplace in India throughout the Global South exemplifies changes underway in the locally articulated global economy. Grossly overpriced, the imported tuc-tucs cost around $5,000 apiece. Manufacturers, shippers, and importers were all getting their cut. Fleet owners, meanwhile, tended to be wealthy locals—intermediaries, some already rich, but some who had built up small fortunes from owning public bathroom concessions and *tiendas* and other such businesses.[101] Besides having to house and maintain the fleet, they also had to negotiate the corrupt politics of getting the *toritos* licensed; most towns have far too many, thanks to mayors who couldn't say no to a bribe.

If fleet-owning intermediaries crossed the fuzzy divide between the formal and informal sectors, drivers were thoroughly in the latter. Seen from above, these brown-skinned boys and men were right where they ought to be: serving others and making very little. (In Guatemala's highly gendered society, they were also almost exclusively male.) The *tuc-tuquero* existed in a Guatemalan age-old but brand-new version of the gig economy—his own boss, not making a living wage but at least doing something and able to freelance on the side. Drivers rented the tuc from the owner, typically for a hundred quetzals a day. If on some days they made money, on others they were lucky just to break even after paying for gas and minor repairs. In Panajachel and Sololá, the *tuc-tuqueros* of the first decade of the 2000s tended to be teenage boys and single young men who were supplementing their families' overall income. They adorned their *toritos* with bull horns, decals, flashing lights, and sometimes even sound systems. They would drag-race in the streets and compete to be

FIGURE 15. For Hugo, who took photos for this project, these children playing in a toy tuc-tuc in the *parque central* of Sololá captured how deeply the mototaxi has become a part of local culture. Photo by Hugo Pablo de León, 2016.

first in line outside girls' schools at dismissal time. The moral economy of the tuc-tuc—not just about the moto-taxi but about life and labor generally in the new/old—wrapped up local life, its family-based strategies of grassroots survival, and its rituals of courtship in baroque street aesthetics.

This "moral economy" unfolded, however, in the context of grinding poverty. By the 2010s the "immoral economy" side of the dialectic predominated. For the most part immiserated, middle-aged *dons* replaced youth as the largest group of drivers, at least in Panajachel and Sololá, using the tuc-tuc not to supplement parental income but to attempt to support a family. Agro-urban life was hard. Nene briefly drove for one of the first owners in Panajachel in the early 2000s. The income was low and he moved on. His career trajectory would lead him to self-directed study of Maya culture in hopes of being a tour guide (this didn't work out); to the police academy (he graduated but wasn't willing to be posted to some remote locale); to driving a delivery truck; to chef's school at INTECAP, a national trade school (there was no regular paying work); to the municipality (where he worked as a traffic cop and garbage collector for less than a living wage); to working for a tourist–shuttle bus company as a driver. Nene finally just accepted he could never earn more than minimum wage, but minimum wage was still more than what could be made driving a tuc-tuc.

In 2003 I first met a young Kaqchikel man, whom I'll call "DJ" because of his love of making mixtapes. He was selling beer at his mother's *caseta* near the beach. Next he worked at his Tz'utujil girlfriend's parents' banana-bread store in the foreign hippie district of San Marcos La Laguna but had to quit when they decided he wasn't good enough for her. He was contemplating suicide when he became a *tuc-tuquero* back in his hometown of Panajachel. DJ's memories run olfactory. He remembers the hippies' "stench of armpits and *¿cómo se llama? . . . ¡patchouli!*" in the banana-bread store. The smelly moto-taxi exhaust irritated his nose and eyes, and he got carpal tunnel syndrome and a bad back from driving all day and night. His grandmother died during his tuc-tuc-driving years. The family could afford only a rustic coffin; DJ gagged on the smell of her decomposing body on the way to the grave. All he wanted was to get ahead, get married, and have a family. Later jobs included handyman and hardware-store helper, before he was able to finish vocational high school as an electrician. He had a "second childhood" back in school, joining the marching band and soccer team and living the teenage world in his late twenties that he had missed in adolescence. But after he graduated there was no work. DJ converted to prosperity-gospel Evangelical Christianity, got a translation of *Rich Dad, Poor Dad,* and became an unsuccessful salesperson of Amway products. He married a nurse and, at the time of this writing, has two children and a minimum-wage job with the municipality.[102]

Both DJ and Nene, born of the 1980s baby boom, love Guatemala and love their hometown on Lake Atitlán. They could have gotten a coyote and migrated *bajo agua* but didn't. Both played Viernes Verdes's "Requiem en E" for me as they helped me with this book: "Soy chapín de sangre / Vas a respetarme." Both are doubly castas, as indigenous people and as the class referred to as *shumos* or *nacos* in certain circles. Yet both are proud citizens of "Guatemaya" and "Guatebuena," and it is here that they have chosen to raise their children, to live and die. The daily struggle to make ends meet, however, takes its toll. "Look," said DJ, "I'm not from the *clase de gente* that gets to travel all over the world and see other places. But from what I hear, this place is pretty beautiful. 'If only you could live here.'"

5

"In the Jaws of These Gray Cities"

STRATEGIC TERRITORIAL
INTERVENTIONS, 2005–2012

IT WAS EARLY OCTOBER 2005, and my friend DJ was in the handyman phase of his career. Tropical Storm Stan had just stalled over the highlands, killing more than 1,500 people.[1] DJ, his ladina boss "Bea," and I were among the many volunteers in the Panajachel gymnasium-turned-shelter. "I don't know what to do with him," Bea whispered to me. "He does his job, but he's just not . . ." She searched for the word. "He's not deferential," she said. "He isn't *servile*."

DJ's laudable lack of deference, like lower-caste youthful cultural production as a whole, was evidence of historical changes in Guatemala's social structure, caste system, and national self-image in the years when "agrotropolis" matured. The nation's *tejido social* (social fabric) showed dialectics of cohesion and atomization, and tradition and novelty, in a time when—in the culmination of a years-long process—social codes changed while still remaining somehow the same. The strength of Guatemala's tejido social, as well as the challenges to it, were on full display in the aftermath of Stan. There was looting, house robbing, and price gouging in Panajachel right after the storm, but neighbors quickly organized and put an end to such crimes. With bridges and roads out, outside aid could not get in, but locals made sure that everyone was housed and no one went hungry. Just over a month before, images of New Orleans after Katrina had filled the airwaves, and the contrast with the Atitlán region could not have been greater.

An umbrella group of western highland Maya organizations, the Movimiento Tzuk Kim Pop, published a trenchant analysis of the storm under the title "Why So Much Destruction?" It arced back to the colonial period and glossed centuries of distorted capitalist development, culminating in a government working in favor of the private sector, a landscape dense with microfincas, and a population turning increasingly to migration to make a living. The result was a "perverse spiral of economic growth with *nuevas pobrezas* [literally new poverties] for communities and regions." The real heroes, the report concluded, were ordinary citizens, whose actions "let us be optimistic about the change toward solidarity, creativity, and citizenship despite a tejido social wounded by thirty-five years of repression and intolerance, as well as by the current security crisis [the crisis of citizen security patrols]."[2] Diaz Negros, a locally known Panajachel band of Kaqchikel hard rockers, came to the same conclusion. They used pictures of people volunteering, of locals rescuing neighbors, and of Sololatecos carrying supplies down the mountain, for the video of their song "Fuego a mi favor" (Fire on my side), referring to local, everyday "heroes" with *"corazones de fuego."*[3] Yet in a country—and, as we will see, a town—where "fuego" was more and more associated with vigilante lynching by burning alive, counterculture youth like the metaleros of Diaz Negros were often associated with the degeneration of the tejido social, with nuevas pobrezas, and were still rarely celebrated for their "solidarity, creativity, and citizenship" in the mid-aughts. From above, social engineering attempted to domesticate and remake youth like them through development and enlist them in citizenship-building projects, while, from below, social cleansing cast them as the internal enemy. By the 2010s the discourse had changed. Maya rockers, rappers, B-boys, and pop artists—men and women alike—together with the ladino urban poor, came to form the face of a reconfigured national image. Nuevas pobrezas locked fingers with a new, more inclusive chapinismo.

In a new, yet continued, chapter in the evolution we have explored since the early 1980s, changes in the tejido unfolded in tandem with changes in the political economy and culture: the effects of CAFTA-DR, the free-trade agreement that came into force in July 2006; the making real of municipal decentralization after decades of planning and preparation; the maturation of new-generation social movements, particularly those opposing mining; the ongoing historical arts explosion; the spread of the internet and the rise of social media, especially Facebook; and the related "mediatization," in Stig Hjarvard's sense, of identities and the diffusion of cosmopolitan countercultures. Through the end of the Berger administration and the presidency of Álvaro Colom (2008–12), Yolanda Colom's brother, official youth discourse became more corporate and mediatized as self-identifications and their associated "imagined communities" flourished. Selfies and self-publishing helped to popularize grassroots aesthetics of beauty and creativity; youthful, technological interventions in the tejido social spread casta self-esteem in dialogue with mass media and political youth interventions.[4]

Over the period youthful cultural assertiveness paradoxically achieved a bottom-up version of what the state had envisioned in its 2005 *Política nacional de la juventud*, a CONJUVE plan that focused on "constructing unity in diversity."[5] Youth brought this project to a head in dialogue with the changing political economy, social fabric, and built environment. This chapter traces how, from the mid-aughts to the end of 2011, historical processes long underway coalesced in "agrotropolis"—on one hand a constellation of urban-yet-agrarian/urbane-yet-provincial city-regions linked to the capital city and the planetary urban landscape, and on the other hand a discursive, cosmopolitan social space that, like the national commons of la KY, was no longer divisible into a Guatemala City–versus–Everywhere Else" binary but was national and encompassed both. Like this work as a whole, it argues that ground-level expressions of urban and agro-urban chapín youth culture, despite evolving in dialogue with corporate media and with the extractive economy, nevertheless formed a critical field of production in the conjuncture of forces through which everyday Guatemalans brought an end to performed servility and gave rise to a more inclusive alternative popular nationalism. They did so in a period of breakneck capital expansion, a time when violence, exclusion, and terror—hard as it is to believe, given their previous dimensions—all escalated.

THE CAFTA EFFECT AND TERRITORIAL INTERVENTIONS

Tropical Storm Stan left the mountains of the western highlands raked as if by giant fingernails as a result of what geologists call *lahars,* avalanches of rocks and soil. Both volcanic and deforested mountainsides are prone to lahars, putting Guatemala's poor, the only people who settle on such slopes, at particular risk. The lahar is an apt metaphor for changes in the political economy in the middle of the aughts, when what Guatemalans call the "CAFTA effect" ripped through the body politic and the nation's tejido social, exacerbating what Tzuk Kim Pop called "nuevas pobrezas" in a landslide of capital expansion.[6]

The ripping asunder that had characterized the economy since the mid-1980s turn toward the Washington Consensus came to a crescendo in the

CAFTA era. By 2006, according to the Bank of Guatemala, migrants' remesas had become the nation's "most important single source of foreign exchange."[7] Despite this fact and the human suffering that underpinned it, and despite the $980 million-dollar shock of Stan, the IDB reported in mid-2006 that Guatemala's economy was "buoyant." Notable because it didn't have an IMF austerity program, Guatemala boasted the lowest debt in Central America. The IDB praised the nation's anti-inflationary monetary policy, noting only in passing that the government was "passing on oil price increases to consumers," who thus felt incredible price inflation. With its "disciplined fiscal policy" and "strengthening financial sector," the bank stated, "Guatemala is doing a good job."[8]

Crisis hit the financial sector just five months after the IDB released its report. Bancafé, a major private financial group and bank, went bankrupt in a spectacular case of fraud, corruption, and money laundering.[9] The government intervened and worked with other banks to absorb Bancafé's holdings, a move observers quickly linked to self-interested elites and institutions in the byzantine world of Guatemala's ruling class. Meanwhile, foreign-exchange Forex houses, one with a parallel offshore bank, started crashing, and a flurry of financial mergers and acquisitions followed.[10] Just before Christmas, the banks ran out of money: not deposits, but cash. ATMs ran dry, and cash withdrawals were limited; anyone without a checkbook, credit card, or neighborly credit was out of luck. The central bank took responsibility. They hadn't ordered new currency from the printing house, but a partial run on the banks after the Bancafé incident didn't help. The situation was resolved in early January, but Guatemalans rang out 2006 without cash in hand and with every reason to worry about the stability of their banking system.[11]

Waves of mergers and acquisitions continued in the years ahead, along with a series of bank frauds that totaled in the millions of quetzales.[12] They were exemplary of the CAFTA-effect frenzy of foreign and national investment. "The demons are running free," commented Gerardo Guinea Diez on the speculative rush.[13] The "demons" had roots in the financial modernization that had been underway since the 1990s, and they thrived in a deregulated, lawless environment. Even the IDB summed up the problem as the "weak rule of law" and expressed concern over the growing number of "unregulated domestic subsidiaries of the banks" and those offshore.[14] Besides the lust for banking secrecy and a plague of money laundering, the IDB stated, fear of being kidnapped and held for ransom was an important factor driving the growth of offshore banks, where money could be hidden away.¹⁵ "These unregulated entities," the IDB reported, "carry on a level of financial intermediation in Guatemala that *may be as large as that carried out by the regulated entities.*"¹⁶ Despite measures in 2008 to tighten financial supervision, frauds and scandals in the sector continued. The number of offshore banks lessened from ten in 2006 to seven in 2013, but mostly because of mergers and acquisitions.¹⁷

The CAFTA effect—really the maturation of decades of neoliberalization—spread far beyond the financial sector. Cheap imported corn and wheat hurt local growers, and even the NTA sector saw bumps in the years ahead; a few NTA-growing smallholders gave up in despair and went back to growing corn and beans.¹⁸ The greater matrix into which these dynamics fit, however, was the weave of development that worked to decentralize Guatemala, pit its people further against one another, create agro-urban slums, "offshore" more and more citizens to the United States, and spread alienation and hopelessness. The Guatemala City ska-pop band Malacates Trébol Shop, one of the new-generation groups born in the 1990s, captured something of the zeitgeist when they remade a video of their song "Ni un centavo" for a 2007 Walmart TV special. The tune sang of being penniless and disillusioned and drinking alone while waiting for life to end.¹⁹ Although neither Nene nor DJ is a big Malacates fan, the song's title gives voice to the condition they faced, as did scores of young people like them in neoliberalizing Guatemala. They chose the tejido social and were among the "heroes" who put "fire on my side" after Stan. They didn't migrate. Both express a mix of profound rootedness and love of place as well as a deadening, soul-numbing alienation. This all-alone feeling, in these two cases and doubtless many others, does not relate to social isolation. It relates to *ni un centavo,* to the powerlessness of being unable to provide for oneself or one's family. These nuevas pobrezas—new modalities of an overarching poverty, metapoverty, that repeats and repeats itself for century after century, putting new clothes on a still-battered body—are part of the remapping of the tejido social and the realms both physical and affective that characterize the globalized, cosmopolitan commons that gradually began to unite the young in cities and agro-urban territories alike.

Besides popular youth culture and empty wallets, what these places had in common was an underlying lahar of capital expansion that had its fingers deeply entwined with those of the state and the development apparatus. Top-down strategies arose that built on decades of previous plans that fomented "community" while simultaneously atomizing it, in ways that reached new levels of sophistication and were aided in their effectiveness by the corrosive, life-draining realities of the new economy.[20] Economic changes and development programs worked together in a kind of self-perpetuating feedback loop. For example, consider a program called Vamos Guatemala. The IDB noted that "under [this] Economic and Social Recovery Program for 2004–2008 ... the government designed a rural strategy, Guate Solidaria, which targets municipios characterized by high risk for food insecurity and chronic poverty"—problems exacerbated, if not directly caused, by economic policy. "The strategy is comprehensive and intersectoral in nature," the IDB reported, "and involves territorial interventions (at the community and municipal levels) in three simultaneous areas (family, community, municipios), to be implemented through existing programs that will be aligned with the methodology of comprehensive and participatory intervention."[21]

Territorial interventions is a phrase that encapsulates sets and webs of policies, corporate and capital moves, tax-dodging financial flows, and growing and new diasporas. At the ground level, decentralization was the most overt, physical manifestation of this multifaceted process of redefining territory. Early in the new millennium, development agencies quite literally remapped Guatemala, in the first phase of a process of redistricting for political decentralization. They delineated new and politically significant "regions" and "microregions" within the already-existing geography of departments and municipalities. As development teams drew up these new boundaries, they sometimes administratively conglomerated villages that were not even connected to one another by footpaths, much less roads, and that spoke separate languages.[22] Such remapping continued into the first decade of the 2000s with the further waves of districting needed to create the COCODES, the development committees based in the communities that made up the various microregions and regions. By the time this new political map morphed from on-paper plan to reality, in the second half of the aughts, the process of decentralization had given rise to new geographic territories with very real political and economic ramifications.

Although development organizations billed territorial reorganization as facilitating local democracy and the poder local that the Mayan movement had long been demanding, its effect was just the opposite. Besides becoming part of a free-for-all of graft and corruption—subjects to which we will return—community-based committees institutionalized and professionalized. The Municipal Development Plans (PDMs) of the mid to late aughts, though ostensibly crafted through grassroots FODA-SWOT exercises, had a very different voice from the pioneering documents produced just five years or so earlier, in which the voices of real people could be discerned. The newer plans tended to conclude that what was needed was *more* decentralization, *more* microcredit, and more of the same neoliberal medicine denounced by Maya leaders not long before. The plans bespoke an authoritarian political economy in which the words of development experts and technocrats were put into the mouths of local actors.

Besides disempowering Guatemalan communities under the guise of empowering them, decentralization's development plans also defined larger territories, adding layers of complexity to an already-chaotic system. The PDMs were wrapped up in higher-level strategic planning, which dictated their template and also generated a series of Strategic Territorial Plans (PETs).[23] The PETs were in part a reaction to growing agro-urban city-regions that spilled over municipal boundaries. To address this new territorial reality, the government joined agro-urban municipalities together in commonwealths, or *"mancomunidades."* The one in the Lake Atitlán region was called the Sistema Urbano Mancomunidad Mankatitlán.[24] Similar reorganizations were seen around the nation. The department of Chimaltenango, for example, had so rapidly urbanized that its PET mapped out distinct "Agro-Productive, Agro-Eco-Touristic, Coastal, and Industrial" territories.[25] Development and urban growth were remapping the Guatemalan agrotropolis in coconstitutive dialogue in the era of decentralization.

As the final phase of decentralization came to fruition, Guatemalans were further drawn into the banking and credit economy. This happened deliberately and was brought to fruition through sustained public-private cooperation. The IDB worked with the state to regularize financial administration and public investment and to spread microcredit networks, in part by providing loan guarantees for private lenders.[26] Microcredit enterprises exploded, and direct-to-consumer credit became available to the working class. An important step came in 2007, when the Mexican Banco Azteca opened credit-granting branches in its sister company's Elektra appliance and electronics stores in Guatemala. Provincial Elektra outlets in Guatemala had recently proliferated as part of agro-urbanization, and being able to get an on-the-spot loan, typically to buy electronics, was the first entry of many working-class Guatemalans into the credit economy, entailing high interest rates that few understood.[27]

The ultimate effect of the web of territorial interventions in politics and finance was to make impoverished individuals and communities compete with each other for scarce resources. In historical perspective this was the genius of the system. Instead of contesting the state and the structures of power, citizens became embroiled in a *lucha libre* of *competencia* among themselves. Little wonder, then, that on-high efforts were underway to make the nation and its citizens more *competitive*. By the end of 2006, the Economy Ministry's PRONACOM (Programa Nacional de Competitividad) had forty-five community promotion groups of small-business leaders who were working in nine departments to help identify or create potential investment opportunities for private capital.[28] PRONACOM had three overarching goals. Besides the vague and undefined endeavor of turning Guatemala into the "logistics center for Mesoamerica," it aimed to increase the nation's role as an agro-export powerhouse and to turn it into "the tourism, ecological, and cultural destination of Mesoamerica."[29]

The idea of Guatemala as a "cultural destination" was intimately related to its identity as a real-and-imagined "territory." As such, it opens a window on polyvalent territorial interventions that went far beyond development projects and that formed the ground-up side of the CAFTA effect. Internal tourism, ladino-Maya cultural encounters, and the *aldeando* (villaging-up) of popular culture and KY-chapinismo bespoke the emergence of a much-competed-over but still newly unifying national commons. At the same time, the marketing of "Guatemaya" to foreign audiences entailed not only transnational encounters but also the articulation of identities that simultaneously drew on and influenced cultural changes underway at the grassroots. In the context of the spreading credit economy and nuevas pobrezas, meanwhile, Guatemala as a territory also increasingly came to be inscribed with meaning in the minds of its migrants and their children, who now formed a multigenerational diaspora found mostly in the United States. The CAFTA effect did not just involve territorial interventions on the part of most powerful organizations on earth. It also involved a dialogical and messy process of rethinking and contesting of the meaning of Guatemala on multiple levels in a globalized world and society.

As an entry into these multifaceted territorial interventions, let us begin in bohemian Panajachel. In 2006 Lucía Escobar, "La Lucha," the writer whom we have met through *Hasta Atrás, La Chalupa,* and *Supositorio,* moved to "Pana," a relocation that is itself an example of the attraction that the "authentic" highlands had for the nation's cultural vanguard. She and her partner, Juan Miguel Arrillaga, founded a local magazine called *Ati: La Revista del Lago,* which covered local culture and promoted touristic, ecological, and cultural projects.[30] The very existence of *Ati,* which published from early 2006 to late 2010, bespeaks not only an economy that was able to support it (though hardly luxuriously) but also evolving interclass, intercaste dialogue. *Ati* was a microlevel example of macrolevel changes, as the territories of city and province, of ladino and Maya, and of top-down chapinismo versus KY chapinismo melded in the emergent agrotropolis.

Upon moving to the lake, "without even realizing it," Lucía Escobar wrote, "I became an adolescent again, when arriving in Panajachel always became a party, a trip, an adventure.... I learned a lot about drugs, about music, about *amores* there.... This town, polluted, dirty, backward, full of hippies and drugs, full of art and strong vibes, represented for me more than the liberty of a quick escape, much more."[31] Such encounters and cultural mixing played out differently for different people in the bohemian culture that thrived around Lake Atitlán, a touristic "cultural destination" where the scramble to sell services and an "authentic" experience to tourists was a major part of the economy. By far, most young Guatemalans in the area simply went about their lives, perhaps working in hotels or restaurants but also becoming construction workers or accountants or "bilingual secretaries" or schoolteachers, just as youth all around Guatemala were doing, showing generational change but ignoring and tacitly rejecting the touristy *desmadre* going on around them. Other local youth, like the Diaz Negros, hybridized heavy metal and Kaqchikel KY culture. Still others got wrapped up in hippie counterculture, marketing Mayan handcrafts or earthy authenticity in an atmosphere where a craze that *Ati* dubbed *"rastafarismo"* was underway.[32] This mix of local culture, national generational change, and globally inflected hybridization in bohemian tourist destination makes the lake area a fruitful, microlevel case study of how such forces interacted in society at large.

The phenomenon by which poor Maya and ladino castas came, in contested ways, to stand for authenticity in the nation as a whole was particularly pronounced in the reshaped world of tourism in Guatemala. Starting from the time of the Peace Accords, Guatemala turned from a destination that primarily drew travelers attentive to human rights (including Peace Corps and Witness for Peace volunteers and socially conscious backpackers) into a party destination. In this transformation we can see the intersections between homegrown rockero culture and its related internal tourism, the global tourist economy, the drug scene, and evolving Maya youth identities in agrotropolis. The competitiveness that PRONACOM and economic planners in general sought to promote in the tourist sector increasingly involved, in the real world, making drugs available and throwing after-parties.

New levels of female-on-male sex tourism entailed providing vacation romance with "your Latin lover," *moreno, clase-popular,* barrio-authentic hot boys. "Lover Boy promised to give a workshop on how to seduce tourists without the need to intoxicate them," read a satirical article on the "Macho Alfa" in *Ati*.[33] The foreign hunger not just for fun but for ethnically coded *authenticity* often led to confusion about who was available and who was not; tourists sometimes chased deeply religious, happily married, or sexually conservative Guatemalans who were intent on ignoring the *desmadre*. We can only imagine how individuals internalized such sexualized transnational encounters. What is certain, however, is that in places where tourism thrived, its external articulations added another dimension to Guatemala's myriad debates over identity, as the representation of the national self to the foreign other took on a commercial edge that in tentative and contested ways valued barrio authenticity and casta beauty over that of light-skinned elites.[34]

Officially sponsored ethnotourism, which had a boom in the mid-aughts, was another "competitive development" and "strategic response" to tourists' hunger for authentic experiences, as well as a means through which Guatemalans represented themselves and their culture to a foreign market.[35] Ethnotourism's new iteration germinated at the intersection of progressive NGOs, humble communities, and the development apparatus. The projects of the first decade of the 2000s were community based and community run and often mixed ethnotourism with ecotourism. Tourists could go river tubing through the sacred Candelaria Caves in Alta Verapaz; on Lake Atitlán, *Ati* reported on a fishers' tour in San Juan La Laguna, where local producers sold organic soaps and shampoos to visitors. Ex-guerrillas turned one of their state-granted fincas into a tourist destination.[36] In the remote hamlet of Río Negro, Alta Verapaz, meanwhile, the grown-up child survivors of a 1982 massacre returned to found the Centro Histórico y Educativo Riij Ib'ooy. Guides lead groups up the mountain, retracing the events of the day when the PAC tormented and then killed nearly all the women and children (the men had been murdered earlier, having been summoned to a "political meeting"). Visitors pass the tree where the PAC made the villagers listen to an anticommunist ideological talk, then the place where the gang rapes occurred. The hike ends in the excavated mass grave on the mountaintop, where a guide narrates how as a little boy he hid in the brush and witnessed his mother and sisters being slaughtered with machetes.[37]

Río Negro was the setting for the documentary film *Discovering Dominga,* which tells the story of one of the massacre's survivors. Denise Becker, née

Dominga Sic Ruiz, was adopted by a family from Iowa; her return to her birthplace turned her and her family's world upside-down and resulted in a profound questioning of her identity.[38] Like the Riij Ib'ooy memory center, *Discovering Dominga* is a haunting example of the multiple registers of memory and community that joined other factors making territorial interventions in the emergent Guatemalan agrotropolis. Other types of "ethnomemory" communities were developing as well. Maya immigrants in Los Angeles founded a group that aired a web and radio program called *Contacto Ancestral*, in which Sobrevivencia's music regularly aired. "Through the construction of an audible 'community archive,'" writes Alicia Ivonne Estrada, "Contacto Ancestral creates a space from which Mayas can maintain an audible local and hemispheric memory, which is simultaneously attuned to contemporary Pan-Indigenous, immigrant and human rights movements."[39] Affective communities of memory and multiple *contactos ancestrales* accompanied, articulated with, and overlaid global/local KY culture in the construction of agrotropolis as a territory in the age of the CAFTA effect. Guatemalans, in their struggle to survive, were marketing their culture in ways that ran the gamut from *desmadre* tourism to life-changing memory- and ethnotourism. In large measure, however, their survival was aided by the sweat and sacrifice of migrant relatives who could not make a living in their ancestral homeland—a homeland whose agrotropolis barrio poverty and ethnic diversity were the very factors that the nation marketed as it imported tourists and exported its own citizens.[40]

In the age of the CAFTA effect, new poverties joined decentralization and what the IDB summed up as "financial modernization" to make drastic territorial interventions in the Guatemalan body politic and its tejido social, even as that lifeworld was being transformed by "in-the-middle" and bottom-up cultural and social phenomena associated with globalization, generational change, and the retooling of grassroots identities. "Community archives" were found not just in projects like *Contacto Ancestral* but in multiple spheres of life. The Spanglish, internet slang tagline on a homemade Sobrevivencia video that a fan uploaded to YouTube, *"este es mayan pride 100% 4 life"* bespeaks the transnational and migration-inflected dimensions of the interrelated cultural forms coalescing in a contested national commons in Guatemala.[41] A new grammar of national identity was taking form in the time of the CAFTA effect and territorial interventions—one that mixed Mayan pride, casta pride, and the pride of chapines abroad for their lost homeland. Building on historical processes long underway, and in dialogue with the globalizing, extractive, and violent political economy, Guatemalans began to represent themselves in transformed ways to one another and to the world.

CHULO TU CHUCHO AND BARRIO NATIONALISM

The reconfiguration of personal and national identity played out in urban and agro-urban barrios in which city life and street culture brought a commonality to the lived experience of new generations of young Guatemalans. If the progressive Mayan folk music of bands like Sobrevivencia formed an audible archive for a diasporic community of ancestral memory in the United States, in Guatemala it formed part of a popular-culture archive that referenced the multiple grassroots identities proliferating on la KY. In drawing on that archive of cultural forms, ordinary Guatemalans gave rise to a barrio-based nationalism. On one hand, this bottom-up, contested-yet-unifying field of cultural production bespoke the pride and assertiveness of a casta population that was rejecting the servility that had been expected of people of its station in Guatemalan social relations for hundreds of years. On the other hand, the barrio-based chapinismo of the new millennium was evidence of how performativity—ludic, comedic, vulgar and baroque—came to take on an outsized role in a system built on human exploitation and misery.

These factors came together in the lived experience of ordinary people, whose stories reveal the deeper levels of pain and dislocation that underpin their performative KY-chapín street styles. Consider, for example, internal migrants. While migration to the United States is the best-known manifestation of the nuevas pobrezas, significant numbers of Guatemalans also moved to Guatemala City or agro-urban cabeceras in search of work.[42] A Panajachel *tuc-tuquero* named "Ángel," for example, was earning just uphill of *ni un centavo* in the middle of the aughts. Still, he sent money to help his family, who lived on the far side of the mountain in a hamlet near Patulul, working as tenant farmers and seasonal workers in rubber-processing plants on the Pacific Highway ("you can't imagine what those fumes do to you," he said, his face twisting; *"Eso... no"*).[43] Internal migration could also take the form of minidiasporas, as was (and is) the case of Sololatecos, who own chains of *tiendas* around the nation. Children from Sololá would tend these stores, sleeping in little rooms at the back. Often internal migration also took the form of "offshoring" a child who might not make anything but at least would

FIGURE 16. Hugo, the photographer, took this picture at Sololá's feria because he felt that the image evoked the many dimensions of the "world upside-down" theme discussed in this chapter. Photo by Hugo Pablo de León, 2016.

be one less mouth to feed. "Luis," from the town of San Andrés Semetabaj, was fourteen when a carney from the feria (saint's day festival) offered him work as an assistant as the circus-like team traveled around the country. His parents let him go without even having met the man. Luis remembers two years of sleeping under trucks and being hungry; what else happened to him, he will not say.[44]

Luis's odyssey of poverty was one that could have taken place in the 1970s, or 1920s, or even in prior centuries: *kid runs off with carneys*. It was also a tale of a changing era. This was because of why and how it unfolded—no remesas coming in from the United States "yet"; an absent, semiemployed alcoholic father just sixteen years his senior who had been raised to be an illiterate agricultural peon but now cleaned the streets for the muni for a pittance, a gig he got only when his party's mayor was in power; a depressed "I think she's sick with sadness" mother who let him go without meeting the señor who took him; a traditional feria now turned big business, full of video games and electric rides, but where people still played *lotería;* and a barely remembered semisubsistence economy of corn and beans that had been dying for decades and was now all but nonexistent. Luis, poster-boy target for youth-saving initiatives of all stripes, had a childhood that at once referenced Guatemala's old poverties and its *nuevas pobrezas*, one that absolutely referenced the territorial strategies at play at all levels in the age of CAFTA.

So too did Luis reference these strategies personally, in his affect and his body—its scars, its fashion, its relations of desire. Luis was dating a girl who was "too good for him." Headed for a high school diploma, she spoke schoolhouse Spanish and "proper" Kaqchikel, not mixed street *lengua* like Luis. It was a friendly member of her family (the rest of whom hated him) who sent him to me in 2008 to help with an odd job. He arrived attired in a look that Jason de León describes as "urban Latin fabulousness"—skinny jeans with a tight Abercrombie T-shirt and brand-name tennis shoes, the latter two both undoubtedly counterfeit *chafa* from the *paca*.[45] His travels had endowed his Spanish with urban slang that one heard more and more in the highlands but that still—especially coming out of the mouth of a Kaqchikel-speaking San Andrés Semetabaj neocampesino—had a cosmopolitan and slightly foreign ring to it: lots of *nel* for *no* and *simón* for *sí* and *va vos* for *sabes* or *verdad* (meaning "y'know" and also "cheeky" language to use with a gringo señor and another example of the subtle but real diminution of servility as a cultural form). Luis showed me *fotos* of *"la afortunada"*—Ms. Lucky, who got to date him—on his cell phone; it had a camera! And it was full of her *selfis*, in form-fitting traje. It was also full of urban *reggaetón*, with tracks from Wisin y Yandel and Daddy Yankee. It even had some Guatemalan rap. As we got to know each other, he shared about the hostility of his girlfriend's family. He had no promise, and they wanted him gone. "So why does she keep dating you?" I asked. *"Es que soy buenísma onda,"* he answered, really good vibe. Then he swiped to the next picture, a *selfi* of his own, wearing shades, posing by somebody else's shiny car, and looking as thuggish as a skinny sixteen-year-old can. *Pero sí que soy chulo, ¿va vos?* I'm cute, right *vos!* DJ, in his late twenties, made a similar comment at around this same time. We were by the food carts on the street, and he was describing the fare as *"shuca pero rica,"* dirty but delicious. Two *gringa* tourists passed by, and one held his gaze and shot him a wink. "Just like us chapines," he said, cracking up. *"Shucos pero ricos!"* Had this same scenario occurred in New York, DJ would have been less likely to get a reverse *piropo* from a *gringa* than he would have been to get stopped and frisked, more or less how castas of his ilk had been traditionally treated in his own society.

But *gringa* tourists found guys like him *chulo!* Castas had always seen the *chulo* and *rico* in one another. But in a country where "beauty," the kind that got mediatized, that got to be represented, had always been white, or "whiter than you" (perhaps best summed up by a classic old Rubios [Blondes] cigarette ads with Euro-looking Guatemalans puffing away under the slogan *"Sabor del Ganador"* [Taste of the Winner]), *barrio* sexy and barrio authenticity were gaining cultural clout—so too were *callejero* KY slang and popular-class chapinismo.[46] Youth used new technology to share and spread these idioms. This technology was on one hand literal, found on cell phones, in *selfis,* and on the internet, especially on brand-new Facebook, soon to be known as "Face" *(¿tenés Face, vos?).* But it was also "literary," involving creative deployment of cultural forms drawn from the archive of such bottom-up expressions flowering on la KY.[47] These culturally assertive discourses went viral in dialogue with a commercial universe hungry to capitalize on them. The representation of identity changed. With it, cultural power—and, bit by bit, caste relations—changed as well.

The wholesale changes in how class and caste were represented in discourse and media were rooted in lower-class creativity, but they unfolded in dialogue with official youth policies and programs that promoted street art, in part as a prosthetic to cover up the absence of programs that substantively addressed the poverty and lack of opportunity that faced the nation's young. When Luis ended his childhood stint with the feria and came home to the lake in 2008, he returned to a community that exemplified the ways in which the weave of poverty, official youth programs, and street culture were playing out in real life. Subjectivities were changing, both autonomously and in dialogue with the institutions of power. His hometown of San Andrés Semetabaj, itself desperately poor, still sheltered Nueva Esperanza (New Hope), a homeless community displaced by Stan, and was turning to youth programs for its own *nueva esperanza.* Diaz Negros—hard rockers that not long before, despite being Kaqchikel and having placed second in a national competition, would have been looked down on by officials as degenerate scum—was slated to headline a municipal youth talent show that *Ati* helped to sponsor. Art and youth countercultures were taking on new valences, even in small towns, as culturally assertive young people rejected codes of silence, subservience, and servility historically imposed on lower-class, lower-caste Guatemalans. Another local Panajachel hard-rock band, Ezquizoide (Schizoid), participated in local festivals and in a new youth project, the Centro Cultural Ajchel. *Ati* covered them in a piece declaring that *rock chapín*—"a movement involving urban youth (not just from the capital but from all the country's nuclei" [i.e., agro-urban centers])—despite the end of its heyday, was not yet dead.⁴⁸ It was also not yet domesticated. *"Quiero dar, quiero dar, quiero dar!"* screamed the chorus of Diaz Negros's "Corazón de motor" (Motor heart); the lyric had the sense of wanting to rev the engine, to give it gas, with "no fear."⁴⁹ That screaming desire—here given voice by culturally assertive Kaqchikel youth in a heavy-metal band—resided in a space of reaction to agro-urban Guatemala's dangers, its evolving tejido social, and its brutal economy.

Agro-urban metal bands like Diaz Negros iterated a barrio-based identity through their music, joining other genres to provide bottom-up inputs to a grassroots nationalism that was going viral in the new media landscape. Rap music was particularly influential in this regard. Once detested as the closest possible cousin to the tattoo and the street gang, rap was becoming one of the most vibrant genres of rock nacional. In Guatemala City, the Alioto Lokos had remade themselves as Bacteria Soundsystem Crew and were gaining fame around Mesoamerica, as well as in communities of memory in the United States.⁵⁰ Their music was featured in a 2008 short film, *Barrio,* about the murder of an internal migrant, a provincial Maya boy working in a *tienda* in Villa Nueva's Mario Alioto settlement. When it was posted on YouTube, conversation threads broke out that went on for years, in a cacophony that showed migrants' barrio-based memories, on-the-ground interclass rivalries, and anti-Maya racism, along with the willingness of de a pie Maya to tell the racist comment posters what to do with themselves. Other comments evinced the locally based pride of gang members, who posted from cities in El Salvador and towns in Huehuetenango. In one thread, Mexican youth insulted the backward, think-they're-so-bad Guatemalans, eliciting a chorus of responses that bore evidence to grassroots "street nationalism." "Antonio Silva4" wrote, "Mexicanos hijos de la gran puta me caen komo patada en los huevos × presumidos los cerotes de mierda viva guate" (Stuck-up shitty pieces of shit Mexicans *hijos de la gran puta* I like them like a kick in the nuts viva Guate."⁵¹

In a related iteration of barrio nationalism—agro-urban barrio nationalism—Diaz Negros wrote hard-rock songs like "Despierta Guatemala" (Wake up, Guatemala); the accompanying video showed the lake's natural grandeur juxtaposed to its society: fishermen in dugout canoes, a sad-looking woman in traje selling cotton candy, a drunk passed out on the sidewalk, people hauling firewood and furniture on their backs, tourism posters, the label on a bottle of cheap Quetzalteca rum, the Guatemalan flag.⁵² Gemeinshaft/Gesellschaft; Madre Tierra/La Gran Puta. The band's leader married a Spanish woman and moved abroad. "I'm coming back to the land / that saw me born," he sang in "Indio poder" on a return visit. "I was planted

and watered with the blood / of *Indio poder*. . . . I miss the drunk on the corner
. . . / The fine police searching my stuff."⁵³ "Barrio" life was everywhere.
Overlaid with layers of economic hardship and desire and violence and grassroots nationalism, represented through films and music but also through *selfis*
and changing senses of self, the now-national barrio was the seat of the nation-
alizing KY.

Guatemalan barrios now encompassed far more than just Guatemala City
slums. Agro-urban Chiantla, a part of the Huehuetenango city-region,
according to a 2007 architecture thesis, showed "a series of political, cultural,
and social changes [that] have transformed this sector into an urban collage,
between the past and the present—an area where time and space enter into
conflict."⁵⁴ A city embroiled in the nation's escalating mining conflicts and its
ongoing NTA revolution, broccoli-growing Chiantla's center had been converted by "spontaneous urban growth" into a vast informal market choked by
vendors, traffic jams, and visual pollution.⁵⁵ By 2011 the development apparatus had recognized that municipalities were growing out of control; even
Chiantla's supposedly rural areas were urbanizing as settlements swelled on
arable land, continuing a decades-long process, as indicated in the map of
Chiantla in chapter 3. Intermuncipal training plans—in and of themselves,
like the *mancomunidades,* an implicit critique of decentralization and its
administrative atomization—aimed to redraw and rationalize the chaotic
landscape. The Chiantla plan estimated the population at around 85,000 (it
is roughly 105,000 today) and featured maps tracing how the urban area had
doubled since 1954.⁵⁶ What maps could not represent, however, were the
social and cultural changes wrapped up in that process.

As barrios spread, so did barrio culture, which expanded and took on local
idioms and color along with *shuco-pero-rico,* dirty-but-delicious aesthetics as
it did. Middle-class and elite reaction was predictably allergic. Class and caste
divisions, on one hand breaking down in the age of "inclusion," paradoxically
continued to sharpen as KY culture became more assertive. In a biting piece
on the nation's social structure titled "Subspecies," by which he meant those
who benefited from the systems of exploitation, a newspaper columnist wrote
that middle-class *"normales"* like him were an absolute minority, outnumbered by the poor and malnourished in "a country now as poor as Africa." In
the gated rich neighborhoods in Guatemala City and around the country,
better-off youth began early in the decade to refer to *"losers,"* in English (with
a thumb-and-forefinger *L* sign in front of the forehead), and *"rechas,"*
for *rechazados,* or "rejects," in a mass wave of class-and-race-based youthful

bullying.⁵⁷ Status-based youth-on-youth violence remained a constant in Guatemalan society and was at once evidence of "sticky" caste-based distinctions as well as of challenges to such categories from below, as assertive youth from the barrios refused to accept or stay in their "place." A from-above, self-conscious trope of what might be dubbed "third-world shame," seen in the use of the term "third world" over and over again in literature and journalism, collided with a self-conscious "third-world pride," related on a metalevel to brown-skinned barrio beauty, barrio cultural assertiveness, and barrio nationalism. There was an intense consciousness of Guatemala as a so-called third-world country that on one hand redounded on its poor majority in disdainful ways and that on the other—sometimes begrudgingly and sometimes admiringly—recognized that poor majority as the "real," authentic face of the nation.⁵⁸

Private and public programs to "heal" the "losers" and "corrupted" youth in general did little to help them but did a great deal to popularize their image in the mid-aughts. An extreme example was a 2006 reality show called *Desafío 10* that plucked gang members off the street, put them in teams, and had them compete by forming businesses (a shoe-shine and shoe-repair shop and a car wash). They also shared their feelings and process of transformation with the TV audience. At the show's beginning the gang members wore masks to hide their identity—a reminder of Guinea Diez's remarks on a *país de enmascarados*—but shed them as the show progressed. Within a few years all the magically transformed participants were either dead or doing very poorly.⁵⁹ Top-down programs to "save" youth by remaking them proliferated in an age when programs to address structural poverty were completely absent. In another example Huehuetenango gang members met with a Proyecto Rescate Juvenil "youth rescue" team to negotiate their participation in sanitizing spectacles, but the adults soon suffered from an unspecified "abuse of trust on the part of the young *mareros*" (who probably robbed them, a scenario that a young helper on my book project described in Spanglish as *un gran efokiu,* admiring the far-from-servile defiance). The project fell apart.⁶⁰ Programs to house underage deportees and to provide advice on drugs, domestic abuse, suicide prevention, family planning and sexuality proliferated.⁶¹ Often they provided much-needed help, but they could not mitigate the realities of what Michael Denning has dubbed "wageless life."⁶²

In the absence of economic programs and opportunities to help the country's vast poor majority, identity took on outsized importance in ways that showed a back-and-forth tension between the traditional and the new. A

Caracol Producciones film, *El cuento de la democracia* (The story of democracy), made with Iqui Balam's participation and Sobrevivencia's music, depicted a teenage girl "healing" from consumer-culture modernity and youthful apathy through a mix of tradition and leftist resistance, as her Mam grandmother told tales of older ways and the struggle for justice.[63] Cultural revitalization that embedded older discourses of resistance was in fact underway in youth culture, and the efforts of progressive groups like Caracol Producciones and others both had an effect on and reflected changes in popular consciousness. Songs like Diaz Negros's "Indio poder," however, show a cultural revitalization rooted in tradition but voiced to power chords on electric guitars with lyrics that sang of gritty life in the barrio. Full of slippages and ambiguities, discourses of identity became swept up in overlapping spheres of cultural production, as hydraulic changes in self-representation unfolded on la KY in dialogue with mass media, the development apparatus, and the extractive political economy.

Corporate media began picking up on barrio chapinismo in ways analogous to how the banks were picking up on remesas and even to how "officialdom" was embracing youth countercultures. In 2008 the advertising agency BBDO Guatemala debuted a new campaign for snack foods—potato chips and the like—for the Tortrix brand. Tortrix is owned by Pepsico (which also owns Frito Lay North America and Quaker Foods). In the ad "Perrito," a fresa couple is walking down the street in Antigua when they see a curly-haired boy sitting on a doorstep with his dog, too adorable for the woman to resist. The uptight man drones on about "what a pretty little dog" and "how beautiful is your pet." *"A este chapín le faltan Tortrix,"* booms a voice: This chapín needs Tortrix! The bags of chips fall on him from the sky, surround him, and transform him from stodgy Guatemalteco to hip chapín. *"Que chulo tu chucho colocho"* (cute mutt, curly!), he bellows in KY-chapinismo slang. *Chilero, ¿va vos?* the boy replies: cool, right *vos?*[64]

Colocho in this ad, the kid, is fairly light-skinned and of course curly-haired. He still looks more like Guatemala's "10 percent" than like its vast *moreno* majority. In the end the fresa was saved by Tortrix and chapinismo, not by casta authenticity. Yet at the same time, Tortrix itself (as a cheap, downmarket snack food) and chapinismo as a popular idiom and identity were inexorably associated with the pueblo. The ad may have iterated this chapinsmo in semielite ladino strains, but, as was happening with music and youth culture in general, many poor Maya and brown-skinned ladinos were also making it their own and thus expanding its boundaries and scope. "Que chulo tu chucho colocho" was evidence of the cultural force that from-below, barrio-based chapinismo had amassed in the Guatemalan agrotropolis.

CHAPINISMO AND THE ARCHIVAL KY

To say that "que chulo tu chucho colocho" went viral would be to underestimate its popularity. BBDO's creative team kept rolling out spots in the years ahead, but "chulo tu chucho" entered the vernacular. A decade later it was still all over Facebook and a simple search would turn up scores of related websites. I wrote these words in 2018 on a terrace overlooking a construction site and heard the workers, who dress "urban Latin fabulous" and speak a goulash of Kaqchikel and KY-chapín Spanish, use the phrase over and over in bawdy jokes. Back in 2008, right after the campaign aired, Javier Payeras started a *Chulo chucho colocho* blog, posting poems, stories, and thoughts on literature. One early entry, "Buena suerte" (Good luck), dealt with popular class woes: It's payday, but the boss doesn't pay you (a common phenomenon—I noticed that the assistants didn't usually make it more than two weeks, probably because they never got the wage owed to them). There's no food, the electricity gets turned off, and there's no medicine in the social security hospital for your sick kid. You get on the bus, and then it gets robbed. When the thieves find only five quetzales in your wallet you hope they might shoot you and end your misery. Instead they just pistol-whip you. It's your lucky day.[65] Indignity, danger, and poverty were common denominators in *la vida chapina*, and, inevitably, no matter how commercialized it became, the language of chapinismo represented and rerepresented these pains.

Chapinismos proliferated on websites and in widely circulated memes. One early site, "Al buen chapín," overdubbed U.S. cartoons in vulgar and funny but certainly not "politically correct" chapín.[66] Imitators soon sprouted up online. No venue had a greater impact on the tejido social, the imagined KY, and youth identity, however, than Facebook, home to scores of pages such as "Soy chapín y qué putas" and "Al Estilo chapín 502" (502 is Guatemala's telephone country code).[67] By 2010, stated one report, more than six hundred thousand Guatemalans were Facebukiando, a number that surely grew exponentially in the years ahead.[68] Facebook and its stream of self-published jokes and memes and *selfis* were one means by which expressions of KY chapinismo became national *selfis*. Online posts and shares served as a kind of interactive mirror in which youth could see themselves and their experiences reflected on a national scale and add their voices (and jokes and pictures) to the dialogue—a process that helped give shape to an "imagined community" built from the bottom-up.[69]

YouTube was another grassroots self-publishing platform of inestimable impact. In 2009 a comedic send-up of agro-urban indigenous culture appeared called Radio Nahualá. It began with the dedication [*sic* to everything], "Con mucho k-riño y respeto para toda la comunidad indijena de Guatemala" (with much fondness [k as in KY, *cariño*] and respect for the indigenous community). A comic radio DJ from Nahualá ("it's five minutes to five after seven," he says), with an exaggerated version of highlanders' accent and grammatical errors, takes a call from a listener who wants to hear a marimba song about a *chucha* in la KY. From there the video cuts to coverage of the feria of Almolonga, where a football match against Zunil is underway. With agro-urban street scenes in the background, the reporter unleashes a lengthy description of each team's uniforms ("¡ay hijueputa que chulada los colores de los equipos!"). Then (saying, in loose translation, "tune in your radios well, people, because this is just another pirate station"), he announces the game, making fun of Maya last names: "Salanik se la pasa a Poc; Poc se la pasa a Toc; Toc troc troc-toc-toc ¡puta!"[70]

Comic self-reflection, chapinismo sites, and Facebook selfies and posts expressed a popular consciousness and barrio-based "cool" that was not always welcomed by earlier counterculture participants, who viewed themselves as a kind of cultural vanguard. Uniting on discussion sites like *Rock Republik,* they belittled the masses' participation in their once "exclusive" genres and bemoaned rock's commercialization through corporate-sponsored concerts and corporate-produced fan magazines.[71] The *Rock Republik* contributor Alhazred—remember him?—posted to Chingui's thread on the "History of the Underground in Guatemala," asking for a "little respect for what the underground has been . . . and the blood that has flowed to keep it going."[72] He was also posting in the blog's thread on the history of rock in the *guerra interna,* debating whether or not the army used heavy metal as a weapon. "When the age of piracy and the MP3 came," he pontificated, "youth from the lower-middle and lower classes finally got access to the coveted world of rock in Guatemala." This "generated an amalgam of fans dressed in black with Heroes del Silencio [a Spanish band], Viernes Verde, Dimmu Borgay [here he ranks on Norway's Dimmu Borgir], or Santamuerte [Ecuador] tees, woven *típica* bags, and All Star sneakers, who really have no clear concept of what's metal and what's rock. They're just simply happy to feel part of something that makes them forget their need and their family problems." Thus, he concluded, "from on high we can say that the Fuerzas Armadas achieved their goal. There wasn't a rock revolution in Guatemala. There wasn't a new awareness. There were just a lot of sneakers, tee-shirts, jeans, and bottles of booze sold by the groups in power whom in earlier times, by night, *el rock* dreamed of exposing. We [older metaleros] have been like wolves lost among the sheep."[73]

Rock Republik threads covered "black metal, post-black metal, *metal-prehispánico, ska-hispanoamericana, música electronica,* grindcore, and *Krautrock*."[74] The kind of cool its participants embraced was exclusive; it paradoxically formed part of a unifying national, grassroots set of youth cultures and countercultures, even as it rejected what was happening in other genres at the grassroots. There was nothing on the *reggaetón* and *bachata* and *música urbana* heard thumping from every other loudspeaker in the country in the age of artists like Prince Royce and Romeo Santos and Pitbull. Missing too was *rap,* which was having its day as the barrios' beat, and whose practitioners might well have also counted themselves as "wolves . . . among the sheep."

Rap, hip-hop, break dancing, and the B-boy phenomenon had transited from the bloody street wars of the late 1980s and early 1990s (Safiroth: "there were lotsa dead breaks ha ha ha").[75] It joined the "unity of disunities" in the field of youth culture, becoming a national craze among Maya and ladino youth alike, already popular by 2007, when the U.S. documentary *Planet B-boy* came out, noting the spread of the art around the globe.[76] In late 2009 a spin-off video clip of a song from Bacteria Soundsystem's *El Mixtape* album went viral. "La Virula," which means "bicycle" in KY chapín, raps the story of pedaling (because "I don't have a car") around the city, hooking up with friends, and going to Correos—the cultural center in the old post office started with Caja Lúdica early in the decade—to rap and dance. Lyrics like the chorus ("Yo no tengo carro / Pero sí virula") resonated with youngsters on the country's KY. It celebrated the lived and sometimes joyous experience of being young and poor and cool: "la cadena se me zafa . . . que chafa" (the chain fell off . . . what junk); "mi bici es mi nave / despegamos y empieza el viaje / [ffft] espacial" (my bike's my ship / we take off and start the space / [ffft of taking a hit off a joint] trip). Singing about going to the park to drink *"atol"* and eat *"frijol"* or rapping that "por cada avenida / hay una historia negativa y una historia positiva / son las anécdotas en mi virula" (on every avenue / there's a negative story and a positive story / these are the tales of my bike) wasn't only "Guatemala City" any more. It was national.[77]

FIGURE 17. B-boy Chino of Ijatz Crew break-dances in San Pedro La Laguna, Sololá, 2016 (see the conclusion for his story). Photo by Hugo Pablo de León.

The spread of rap and hip-hop bears evidence to the force of street culture in shaping popular consciousness. A hip-hop school called Trasciende had spun off from the Correos cultural center by 2009, promoting the art in the years ahead. Directed by the rapper "Mr. Fer," Trasciende even promoted B-girling, though this was never as visible (if visible at all) on the streets as its male equivalent. B-boying, however, was increasingly visible; Antigua, for example, with its neighboring city-town of Jocotenango, became a major national center for the art.[78] Crews from Guatemala flew to France to compete in the global "Battle of the Year" (BOTY) hip-hop competitions, soon to dream of winning the Red Bull BC One championship.[79]

BOTY and Red Bull competitions represented the from-above, commercialized inspirations behind street art, but that art arose from below, rooted in very real conditions. "Officialdom" indeed promoted, and attempted to domesticate, youth cultures, but these same cultures were born as authentic cultural expressions on la KY. Bacteria's Ángel Cañas captured this dialectic when he poked fun at the NGOs' discourse, saying, "so, it was us who began to take over space and literally 'empower ourselves,' and all those terms that the *ONGs pisadas* use. But it was real, not just for the *informe* [institutional report]."⁸⁰ Rap had become a major commercial genre in Guatemala City by the 2010s, and, thanks to programs like Trasciende and bands like Bacteria Soundsystem Crew, it was spreading all around the agrotropolis.⁸¹ A haunting video titled "Rap en Mam Cajolá" appeared online in late 2011. The singer, "Shat Juárez," raps in Mam wearing a hoodie in front of a mud-brick hut in the countryside; the visuals cut back and forth between that setting and an empty, concrete city at night. One of the several versions available on YouTube translates the Mam lyrics. "Don't make fun of my wife for her *traje,*" the song begins. "She's not with you, she's with me, she loves me and I love her." Near the end it says, "Don't criticize my wife if she can't read, if she can't write. It's not her fault. It was hard to make a living [earn money]."⁸² Comments on YouTube in pure chapín KY slang gave evidence to the commons that street culture had become and to the nationalism from below that it engendered. Jorge Mario Aguilar posted, "*Mano,* sorry I'm writing in Spanish because I don't know MAM, but I'm telling you that I've heard rap in English and in Spanish and I can tell you that this song kicks ass *[le echa riata]* over all those ones that sometimes don't make sense anyway. For real *[a lo macho],* this tune moves me so much *[me llega tanto]* that I almost scream.... It's the shit *[que de al pelo]*."⁸³ "Ismael Juarez" posted, *"Claro esta chido man ... echale gana ... 100% CHAPIN"* (yeah, it's cool [in Mexican slang], man ... go for it). "N3k069" wrote, *"Que buena onda* [good vibe]*, puro Underground chapín"*; "Undeath Core": *Esto sí es rap, no mamada* [this is really rap, no bullshit]"; and "megamalditoXD": *"Viva el Rap Nacional!!!"* A few of the hundreds of comments asked for a translation or suggested singing in both Mam and Spanish, but they read more as requests for music the writers could understand than they did as a lack of respect for the singer's language.⁸⁴

Shat Juárez was born in the late 1980s (1987 or 1988) as Roberto Juárez Lucas. His hometown was San Juan Ostuncalco. This municipality in the greater Quetzaltenango city-region was one of two towns where in the 2010s USAID would interview indigenous youth bent on having careers as "professionals" and who spoke of their "barefoot" and "illiterate" grandparents (we met these youth in the introduction to this book).⁸⁵ Juárez had gotten into music when he was just eleven, in the late 1990s, in the remembered heyday of rock nacional. He produced his own album, *La Espina,* in 2010 and, according to his song, fell deeply in love and married. Two years later he ended up migrating to Washington, DC, where he worked as a carpenter and gigged part-time.[86] He soon released a video of himself rapping on a tour boat in front of the Statue of Liberty.[87] It is unclear whether or not his wife has been able to join him.

Life in the barrio and on its KY served as the referent, the archive, of agrotropolis and the new chapinismo. Hip-hop had come a long way since its practitioners were made to "eat cement" in the capital's street wars of the early 1990s—so too, in terms of cultural power and authenticity, had the *"clases populares"*: the cholos and choleros and shumos and everyone else on the bottom of the system of castas. The social classes evoked in the 1996 *Hasta Atrás* essay, where the kid went to the beach with his bourgeois parents and decried the barrio boys' "I'm poor but it's all good" attitude, were gaining the upper hand in Guatemala's tejido social and the tejido of imaginaries that mapped over it.[88] "Yo no tengo carro / Pero sí virula" captures a pride of self and place, as do phrases like *chulo tu chucho* and *chilero, ¿va vos?*, along with bottom-up cultural expressions such as "Rap en Mam Cajolá." Those at the bottom asserted themselves culturally and represented their life experiences in the public sphere, even as their representations were appropriated from above, both by the development apparatus and corporate advertisers, and rerepresented back at them.[89] As their multiple identities and styles, long in the making, matured and went viral, however, so too did the violence, exclusion, and poverty that underpinned them in the first place.

"IN THE JAWS OF THESE GRAY CITIES"

The government launched a year-long Somos Juventud campaign to promote its new youth policy in the United Nations' 2010–11 Año de la Juventud, and President Colom went on tour around the country to show how he was "Governing with Youth."[90] The campaign had slogans like "Being Young Is Not a Crime" and "We're Different; It's What We Have in Common." Bacteria Soundsystem Crew wrote and performed the title song for the entire campaign. Besides including the "being young is not a crime" lyric, the song had a hard-to-believe "you-can-be-anything" tone to it. "What are you going to be, an athlete, doctor, or singer?" it asked. "You can achieve anything with courage and commitment." The third verse said, "I'm positive, animated, with an active mind / A little stubborn, a dreamer, extroverted / A rebel full of reasons, a good friend / I've always been here, so hear the voice / Of the youth that is change in the pueblos."[91]

FIGURE 18. I caught this image of a pauper *en la pepena* crossing the street in Cuatro Caminos while en route to Huehuetenango in 2016.

The Crew's 2011 track, "Lo que veo" (What I see), captured change in the pueblos better. "Colom, on tour, while the streets of Guatemala / keep getting painted red / blood color, nothing ever changes," they rapped. The song touched on corruption: "I wouldn't give any of these candidates my fingerprint [vote] for anything... thieves with uniforms and badges." And then it opened up: "Shit, the days are hard here / There just aren't limits / They open wounds over scars / Stories here don't have a happy ending / *In the jaws of these gray cities* / Where the gray walls hide crises / And the sad, poor, unhappy men and women / Who are never reached by justice / Because here it's deaf and dumb / And not just blind." The emphasis here is added, but first: "What I see / I see oppression, repression, exclusion / I see marginalization and exploitation / I see some in pain *[en la pena]* and others in total beggary *[en la pepena]* / Because that's the scheme *[la esquema]* of how this fucking system works."[92]

Guatemala had moved "from an era of changes to a change of eras," said a Huehuetenango report in 2010. "The development that capitalism has postulated for the countries of the South has a double standard: on one hand, they ask us to copy the GDP growth of the so-called 'Asian tigers' [in fact, a condition of the Peace Accords] ... but on the other, they hide that those soaring indicators [come at] the cost of greater exploitation of labor, of ongoing miserable salaries, and an almost absolute control of profits on the part of the local and transnational elites," held the analysis. "There is a global ... imperial block under U.S. hegemony [and a system] that intervenes in everything, in work, in the street, in the home, in the life of natural resources, in electoral processes, and even in consumption."[93] *"They open wounds over scars."*

Life was precarious and violent in Guatemala at the turn of the decade. A chilling government report on conflict in the country released a few years later noted a spike in violence and lynchings in 2010; it also stressed that in neoliberal, globalized Guatemala most citizens could barely survive and that in the wake of the global financial crisis, debates were opening about increasing the role of the state in the economy and development, as of yet to no avail. There was a "generalized fragmentation of society at all levels." Violent interest groups thrived as political parties failed to represent the people, corruption was everywhere, and a false binary between "state" and "market" eroded the common good. There were "constant social convulsions," a breakdown in law and order, and a culture of violence and crime. "An analysis of the causes or factors that have unchained social conflict in Guatemala would produce an endless list," claimed the report.[94] Violence, sexual abuse, lynchings, family disintegration, migration, and crime had all increased near the turn of the decade and into the 2010s.[95]

K'atun, the development plan released in 2014, also earmarked the end of the first decade of the 2000s as a watershed, dating the maturation of the nation's long-existing networks of cabeceras and aldeas from fundamentally rural to fundamentally urban in 2009–10. All the aspects it highlighted had already emerged by the end of the 1990s, but K'atun correctly grounded the transformation in a process of development that had been underway since the middle of the twentieth century.[96] Growing up in the jaws of Guatemala's new, gray cities was a generation just born at or after the transition from military to civilian rule, followed by youngsters just through puberty born at the signing of peace. Lucky to have a *virula* to transit through the labyrinths of *callejones* and dusty streets on which the chuchos panted and bred, on which petty thieves went up in flames, they were heirs not only to the history of brutal war but to the fights over "power's destiny" that saw all wealth transferred up and out and relegated the municipality to a battlefield in which locals could tear one another up as they warred among themselves over the scraps. They were "like *duendes*," whether or not they were street waifs, relegated almost inescapably to "loser" status and trapped in a *ni pez ni iguana* space that fomented and dashed dreams all at once—an "if-only-you-could-live-here" mix of rootedness and color and concrete prison walls.

Nene, born in 1981 in Panajachel, did a stint as a delivery driver, and upon return from his routes he would speak in throttled tones of places so horrible as to be indescribable, villages where *"los más pisados"* (the most downtrodden) lived, pinched with hunger and unemployment, lining the sides of the roads. Adonay, born in 1986 in a land invasion outside Antigua, soliloquized, gesturing at the stunning landscape, "you gringos think this place is paradise, but it's *mierda, pura mierrrrda vos.*"[97] He remembered the very urban slum where he grew up, starving, bathing *a guacalazos* (dipping a little plastic bowl into a barrel full of water), filching raspberries from the neighboring finca, as a once-sylvan place, a vision of country-turned-city shared by other twenty-somethings from his barrio. He and his best friend—who call each other *vos cerote* and *vos talega* and *vos maje* (piece of shit, dick, dumbass)—went on and on about how it was horrible but beautiful, not like now, all paved over and hazed with diesel fumes with crack houses and *ladrones* on every corner. Once these *cuates* (buddies) visited an old auntie in Escuintla, and she gave them chickens . . . ¡live chickens! How are you supposed to handle them? Any older person from the barrio would know. *¡Ay diosito!* they joke, putting on an old-folks voice: "Oh Lordy!" This cracks them up. As they told this story, in early 2010, Luis from San Andrés Semetabaj found himself, almost against his own will, in a lynch mob that burned bus robbers alive in the town cemetery. It was Valentine's Day, and he had been out for a *paseo*. "I just watched," he told me, his face half-vacant, half-pained. "I didn't help kill them."[98]

Childhood took on whole new valences for this generation. They had never had one, they say, though Adonay and his *cuate* shared fond memories of having shoplifted from *tiendas* and having fled the *guardianes* in the raspberry fields. Mostly, Adonay remembered Christmas, with "half a dozen eggs for the lot of us," a family of thirteen children. Young women and men all over Guatemala killed themselves working, scraping together pennies any way they could, to give their own children or their younger siblings a kind of childhood they never had—a childhood in which they made it all the way through high school, got to be in school marching bands and sports teams, a childhood in which they got to eat and play. Adonay's little brother Bryan benefited from this, graduating from vocational high school in computer science and ending up working in a bakery. He fell in love, and all looked like it was going well. Then came a call that he could find his *novia* dead under a bridge in Chimaltenango. She had fallen victim to a Facebook scam and, thinking she had won a contest, went off to days of gang rape. She lived and they married, but many others were not so "lucky."

Allí te matan vos (They'll kill you there). Given the litany of horror and violence woven through this history from its beginning in 1983—and that could have been woven in earlier if its starting date were earlier—it is difficult to capture the new register of violence in the first decade of the 2000s and the 2010s. But it got worse. "Femicide" entered the vocabulary.[99] The debate over unregulated foreign adoption of Guatemalan babies, which ultimately led to a moratorium, was full of stories of "fattening houses," where babies for sale made their way to foreign homes.[100] Agro-urban girls headed abroad with coyotes, thinking they were going to work in Los Angeles jewelry stores and restaurants; upon arrival, they had their eyebrows tattooed and their hair dyed as a prelude to being enslaved in brothels.[101] Decapitation became a new hallmark of street crime—as in the case of a gang-raped six-year-old girl whose murderers left her head just hanging on by a sinew—and a terror tactic of the spreading narcotraffic rings, one of which beheaded and dismembered twenty-eight campesinos in the Petén in 2011.[102] Kidnapping rings proliferated, and the security forces that were supposed to stop them, such as, in many cases, the COCODES, turned into what Guatemalans sardonically dubbed *talibanes*—local Talibans that enforced a puritanical morality and conducted social-cleansing campaigns against anyone who did not conform to it—generating a new chapter in the history of terror.[103]

The agrotropolis that comprised both greater Guatemala City and agro-urban municipalities around the country was ground zero in this new chapter. Commenting quite accurately that "violence affects all Guatemalans at a psychological, physical, and economic level," a 2009 think tank reported that the number-one risk factor for death in the nation was being young and "living in poor urban or peri-urban areas."[104] Lynching and mob violence continued to escalate in the provinces, and several communities rejected the state altogether, driving the police and government offices out of town. "Non-state justice" became the norm. Consider this incident from a USAID report titled "Legacies of Exclusion": "In San Juan Cotzal, Quiché Department the ex-mayor constituted a virtual army in link with the . . . police, private security guards, and members of the local juntas with the pretext of protecting the community from gangs and delinquents. The group used physical punishment, forced labor, illegal detention, torture, and other repressive actions to control the local population. In November 2009, the group lynched and killed two people, including an agent of the national police who had come to ask them to release his son who had been detained for having long hair and for looking like a gang member."[105] With the state gone, overlapping realms of authority—the alcaldía, the alcaldía indígena, the COCODES, the security patrols, and the like—often resulted in deadly conflict.[106] Decentralization had come into effect. Under vastly different political, economic, and social circumstances, this policy—one that looked so much like organic, grassroots, participatory democracy on paper—might have worked out differently.

I have had many conversations about COCODES, and none has produced a positive remark. Surely, somewhere, there are or have been honest, productive committees. Often, however, they got caught up in webs of embezzlement. The mayor would be the "robber in chief," falsifying contracts with private-sector actors (who either did not exist or gave kickbacks); he then paid off the COCODES (whose members were supposedly volunteers) in return for organizing their neighborhoods to support him.[107] Outright wars often erupted. COPREDEH documented numerous such cases; in one village COCODE–versus–indigenous authority wars simmered for seven years, involving cutting off water to parts of town, before resulting in mass violence in 2010. In other towns the people themselves rose up against the COCODE for abuse of power. Meanwhile, local security committees—self-appointed vigilante posses—proliferated; there were over three hundred, USAID reported, by 2013.[108]

Such groups did not arise just for no reason in the jaws of these gray cities. Kidnapping and extortion rings made daily life insecure and unbearable from the mid-aughts forward. In Sololá, for example, angry town meetings and threats to burn down the police station circulated constantly; residents kept capturing supposed perpetrators of these crimes, who would bribe their way out of prison and be back on the streets in a day or two. The town's first lynchings, though, broke out over common crime. In 2008 a mob captured a man for robbing pants in the market; known as "El Manía," he belonged to a gang of thieves led by "El Tosh." The townspeople stripped them both to their underwear, made them march through town, and then beat and burned them alive.[109] A year later extortionists went after a bus driver as he piloted the vehicle up the mountain to Sololá from Panajachel; the driver resisted when they tried to pass him a cell phone to receive instructions on where and how to pay protection money, and the criminals shot him. The bus full of passengers nearly plunged over the mountainside, which would have killed everyone. The police arrested the suspects, but the Sololá townspeople forced their release and beat them and burned them alive. They also torched the office of the Ministry of the Interior (Gobernación) and police station and jail, where forty-six entrapped prisoners were saved only by a last-minute rescue. Such incidents continued. In a huge town meeting in 2011, the residents and authorities from Sololá's Barrio San Antonio decided to evict two women for criminal activities, but a crowd of two thousand felt that exile was insufficient and burned their house; the police barely managed to save them from going up in flames themselves.[110]

Down the mountain, in creative, bohemian Panajachel, *Ati* was reporting on youthful creativity, and its editors were helping to organize community cultural projects. But touristed Pana was not immune to problems seen elsewhere. A local bank manager, a dentist, and a drugstore owner all fled town after getting threats from kidnappers. An informal security committee began to congeal in late 2008 that would be registered with the Ministry of the Interior as the Comisión Municipal de Seguridad the following year.[111] It did little to stop crime. In December 2009, the documents state, a group of three women and one man were extorting a local businessman. A lynch mob brutally murdered the man, and the police rescued the women by holding the crowd at bay with tear gas. The enraged mob then burned four police cars, as the locals and tourists shot videos with their cell phones.[112]

Some six months later Tropical Storm Agatha knocked out bridges and houses near the river and on mountainous slopes in highlands. As had happened after Stan, Panajachel residents formed security patrols, this time through their COCODES, which joined and expanded the central security committee. At first this joint effort was a positive force, informants remembered; even Nene was a member. After the storm, led by local businesspeople and supported financially by the mayor, this group became a puritantical band of thugs—the kind of patrol Guatemalans called a *talibán*. In a town famous for drinking and drugging, its members took on a severely moralistic tone. They started carrying baseball bats and wearing hoods *(capuchas)* and became known as Los Encapuchados. On their night patrols Los Encapuchados searched whomever they pleased and beat up anyone who looked drunk or high. Panajachel turned from a town in which, however seedy it was, people could walk around in safety at all hours, to a place of fear and violence.[113]

The national magazine *Plaza Pública* later covered the history of Los Encapuchados. Its first article on the subject accused the "paramilitary" group of being "responsible for dozens of beatings, illegal detentions, and tortures," saying that they carried not only bats but also "pipes, sticks, and tasers."[114] The reporter interviewed members of the patrol, including its adviser and secretary, a soft-spoken Mexican anthropologist who had first arrived in Guatemala with MINUGUA. Like the business owners who headed up Los Encapuchados, she blamed not just the growing web of extortions and kidnappings but also "hippies," drugs, and downmarket tourism for the town's deterioration. "JM," one of the group's founder's, identified major culprits in this regard, accusing them of being "narcos." One was the owner of a bar disco called Aleph that had been originally founded by a member of Bohemia Suburbana. The other was Lucía Escobar of *Revista Ati*.[115]

Los Encapuchados enforced an eleven o'clock curfew in this nightlife town, and, among other offenses, threw victims they found wandering after this hour in a stagnant, sewage-filled pool in the river they called the "Jacuzzi." Locals remember that over the course of 2011 they burned down a "*barra show*" (strip bar) and drove its owner out of town and that they tried to rape a U.S. citizen (a *puertorriqueña,* who got away). They also beat up three young Tz'utujil gay men from Santiago Atitlán who came to enjoy Panajachel's feria.[116] It was during this same feria that they murdered a twenty-three-year-old, Luis Gilberto Tian Senté, popularly known as "Pixica" (pr. pee-*shee*-ca). A well-liked guy and the father of a four-year-old, with another on the way, Pixica had worked since he was fifteen taking care of the boats at the local marina. Accounts of exactly how he fell afoul of Los Encapuchados vary, but all agree that that after he ran into them at night on October 4, 2011, he was never seen again. His bloody clothes were found by the shore. One eyewitness recounted having heard the crack when Pixica's head hit the retaining wall as the patrollers threw him into the river.[117]

The ensuing scandals and accusations about this murder ultimately marked the end of Los Encapuchados, but not before they managed to threaten their detractors with death, Lucía Escobar among them. She denounced them in a stunning, short piece published in *El Periódico*. "If I am the next person with stones tied to his or her body to rest on the bed of the most beautiful lake in the world, you'll know who to blame," she wrote.[118] Still, she had to flee the lake area and start over someplace else.

There are a few points to be made here. First is that most people did not have the option of writing a public denunciation in a major newspaper. Silent, repressed vengeances and vendettas festered throughout the tejido social. Second is that reconstructing the reality of these events is nearly impossible; the 2014 USAID report on "Legacies of Exclusion" included a very different version of the events in Panajachel, one in which the accused perpetrators were innocent and had been framed by local drug dealers, who sold dope to children, bribed the judges, and duped the press.[119] Third is that the absence of the state is in fact a horror, even when we are talking about a state a rotten as Guatemala's. People living through these events around the nation did not just start patrols for no reason, and even those who opposed them as barbarous sometimes admitted to feeling a guilty sense of relief: *if it weren't for these lynchings, there wouldn't be any law at all.* Fourth is that, beyond more tangible social effects (such as fleeing the country to seek asylum in the north) that are easier to document, there were (and are) emotional, psychological, and cultural ramifications of this generalized violence that history will take time to register. These interweave with the temporal flows of history: with the terrains of rich and poor, of Left and Right, and of empowered and disempowered that riddled the landscape with conflict and so-called *talibanes* in the wake of war. They are what Guinea Diez evokes in "Máscaras": the hidden, wounded, fearful inner worlds related in untraceable but real ways to the productive, generative, chulo tu chucho outer worlds, to *"chilero, ¿va vos?"* and display and performativity and "celebration" on la KY.[120]

The emotional and psychological effects of this violent world—this world that wipes out its fictitious middle classes as fast as it generates them—lurk and manifest as well in webs of memory and routines of survival. I was living between Antigua and Panajachel as Los Encapuchados events unfolded, and years later, as I reworked the history of the lynchings with my friends in Sololá and Panajachel, I was surprised that none of us could quite reconstruct them on a timeline. Everyone remembers the "big ones," but there were other incidents: a time when a shopkeeper ran screaming "extortionist!" into the street and almost had a legitimate debt collector burned alive; a time when a cop who didn't know how to drive arrested a criminal and put him behind the wheel to pilot himself to jail, with the predictable result, and a running shootout and spontaneous roadblocks followed; the time when they tied a guy to the back of a pickup truck by his feet and dragged him through the streets, and then someone bashed his head in with a cinderblock. Oh, right. That was the "big one," the one where the three women got away behind clouds of tear gas.

Perhaps most illustrative of the personal dimension of all this, of the webs of memory and community and vengeance behind the violence that erupted in the age of the COCODES and the security committees all around the highlands—far worse in many places than in touristed Panajachel or even than in Sololá, where it was bloodcurdling—is a remark that Los Encapuchados leader JM made, before he was arrested and when he was still trying to defend himself, to the *Plaza Pública* reporter who arrived after Lucía Escobar's public *denuncia*. "Did Los Encapuchados disappear Luis Gilberto Tian?" the reporter asked. "I don't know," JM answered. He then accused "Pixica" of "having tattoos" and having been involved in kidnappings, extortion, and drug dealing. "He was a member of the mara Los Pokemones," JM said, as if that explained everything—Los Pokemones, the gang of adolescents who "stole the schoolhouse bell," the gang that had broken up eight years before, when Pixica was in the middle of his teens.[121]

Conclusion

"MI PAÍS": AGROTROPOLIS AT 13 BAKTUN

"GUATEMORFOSIS," PEPSI'S DEBUT VIDEO in a massive ad and public relations campaign aimed at inspiring productive nationalism among youth, aired right after New Year in 2012. It centered on Ricardo Arjona's song "Mi País," a país in which the once-underappreciated global pop star had not lived since the 1980s. The video's finale was filmed in Panajachel at the end of 2011, when Lucía Escobar was fleeing the town for her life. Framed by volcanoes, Arjona leaped into the lake off a dock. We see only azure waters and stunning nature, but the dock is located between the river and Los Encapuchados' "Jacuzzi" to the left and sewer pipes dumping untreated waste into the water on the right.

The music-video ad was a road trip of national attractions, with clips that captured Guatemala's beauty in places like the Tikal ruins. *"Igual que vos"* (just like you)," it began, "I am my barrio, the *tienda* on the corner, doña Marci, don Beto.... The afternoon *chamusca* soccer game with my *amigos*. I'm my old man teaching me to fly on a bicycle, and the heat of the *comal de las tortillas*.... This is our *tierra*.... To divide among ourselves is to open the door to disgrace.... There's a change awaiting us, and this change will begin only if *you* change *[si vos cambiás]*. I want to change, to change what I don't like, and not wait for somebody else to start. When you're tempted to let Guatemala down, remember that it's yours, and that it would be letting down yourself. *Igual que vos,* this is *mi tierra, mi gente, mi país.*"[1]

"Guatemorfosis isn't just a campaign; it's something more profound," Pepsi publicity stated. "It's about us understanding that we're all agents of change."[2] Critics noted that the implication that youth were what was wrong with the nation was offensive, as was the idea that if they just behaved themselves, everything would somehow transform. Not to blame were years of war, state terror, a genocide, an entrenched oligarchy, a brutally extractive world system, criminal rings, or a gaping hole that a Keynesian state might have helped to fill. An anonymous author lambasted the campaign's "positivist, conservative, and neoliberal discourse" and its "depiction of *pueblos indígenas* as folkloric merchandise.... What we see here is the political, ideological, economic, cultural, and military project of the Right, its business wing, and its rancid oligarchy."[3]

This critique is on point, but at the same time it joins "Guatemorfosis" in overlooking the ways in which young Guatemalans—and in particular poor, de a pie youth—have been and are productive agents of change. Youthful cultural productivity has unfolded in dialogue with globalized, capitalist commercial culture, as well as in dialogue with the violence wrapped up in capital and urban expansion and Guatemala's ongoing legacies of war (Guerramorfosis, perhaps?). It has *also* evolved, however, in dialogue with local life, traditions, history, militancy, and pride. Like so much contemporary discourse, "Guatemorfosis" arrays an invisibilizing assemblage of nationalistic tropes against youth: a productive citizenship that their behavior betrays; an authenticity (the corner store, *chamuscas*, tortillas, *abuelos* like don Beto and doña Marci) of which they need to be reminded; and a rurality that is at the heart of a national identity that they have forgotten (a landscape untainted by the urban: Lake Atitlán, winding coastal roads, indigenous people playing marimba).

The "Guatemorfosis" campaign both captured and at the same time completely missed what was happening at the grassroots in terms of nationalism and self-identifications. The stunning beauty it showed was real, but the top-down, disciplinary nationalism it promoted (what's not beautiful can change only *si vos cambiás*) obliterated a bottom-up history in which Guatemala's vast, de a pie majority had amalgamated the local and the global in a contested but vibrant vernacular idiom of nationalism and national identity under terrible conditions. The BBDO street-nationalism campaign for Pepsico-owned Tortrix that had debuted years before with "chulo tu chucho" captured chapínismo and its related spirit of national identity (and sense of humor) better, as would ads in the 2010s for the used-clothes store chain Megapaca, which featured characters like Maikol Yaxón, Marilyn Monroy, Esvin Disel, and Miguel Tay Son—Michael Jackson, Marilyn Monroe, Vin Diesel, and Mike Tyson—the first and last with Mayan last names.[4] Yet even these celebratory campaigns manage, in a way, to erase the de a pie people who, since the war-torn, state-without-a-nation days of the early 1980s, have taken an unseen and leading role in creating both this vernacular nationalism and the agro-urban built environment in which it took root. They give the viewer a taste of the *clase popular,* but we never see either a person with dark skin and straight black hair *or* a rickety dwelling with a leaky metal roof on an alley full of stray dogs. In these ads, in short, we hear a mediated strain of the voice of the pueblo, but we still don't *see* either the pueblo as a people or the pueblos in the sense of population centers, in which the people live.

More than anything these advertising campaigns bear evidence of the wave of expansion of capital and markets for consumer goods that was wrapped up in the process of what David Harvey terms a "global process of capitalist urbanization" and Álvaro Sevilla-Buitrago analyzes through the lens of "original extended urbanization." The "urban patterns of sociospatial structuration," in Sevilla-Buitrago's words, condensed in Guatemala in the contemporary chapter of an already-ongoing process of capital expansion in which from-below and from-above economic activity collided to give rise to an all-but-unseen constellation of city-regions that are just as much an aspect of "planetary urbanization" as any megacity is.[5] This latest phase of capital expansion and sociospatial structuration began with the reconfigured battles over "power's destiny" that unfolded in the wake of genocide, when counterinsurgent violence made cabeceras grow and brought the ethnic question to the fore, even as the dominance of the capitalist elite and militarism were woven into the body politic of a new and not-very-democratic democracy. Through the changing geopolitics of the global Cold War's end, in dialogue both with capital-city cultural producers and with a neoliberalizing political economy, young, de a pie Guatemalans in agro-urbanizing towns and villages played an underappreciated role in the "Americamorfosis" of social space that not only stressed "this new land called identity" but also instantiated bottom-up, contested, "not fish, not iguana" idioms of self-identification and national belonging.

Youthful cultural creativity and the ways in which casta youth challenged and rejected servility as a cultural form in the capital city and agro-urban centers alike—that is, in agrotropolis—played a central role in creating what is arguably the first hegemonic nationalism, however protean, fragile, and contested it may be, in Guatemala's history. Together these young people gave rise to a KY that was, as Sobrevivencia phrased it, a space of "every possible celebration" but that manifested in ways that made them feel "if only you could live here" and trapped "in the jaws of these gray cities." The extractive, exploitative economy and nuevas pobrezas pushed millions abroad. Crime, "warlordism," and vigilantism spread as the state decentralized. Guatemala's agrotropolis, however, is not just violent, and its colorful, culture-rich pueblos are not just "gray cities." Full of color and life, they have beauty, but, as

George Lovell put it in 1995, in a phrase that was as true at 13 Baktun in 2012 as it is today, it is a "beauty that hurts."[6]

ROAD TRIPS THROUGH AGROTROPOLIS AT THE END OF THE WORLD

I opened this book on Lake Atitlán and with the memory of a road trip not just to introduce the agro-urban landscape and connect to Los Encapuchados and the "Guatemorfosis" video, where the book ends, but also because road trips cut through the kaleidoscopic and contrasting physical and affective terrains of agrotropolis that butt up against and relationally define one another. Before I moved back to the United States in mid-2012, friends from an agro-urban land invasion—Adonay and his brothers—staged weekend road trips with me to say good-bye and *"enamorarte de nuevo de nuestro país,"* make me fall in love again with their country. In one we took a dirt road near El Rodeo and forded a river to get to wellsprings in a finca on the flanks of Volcán de Fuego. We rolled up like a bunch of city thugs *(más un gringo)*, with Spanish DJ Sak Noel's "Loca People" blaring on a boom box. We spent the next few hours hanging out with resident laborers—illiterate farmworkers, *"los más pisados,"* the *"mozos"*—and splashing around with their children in the pools by the riverhead. On the way out we swarmed a mango tree and filled the truck with stolen fruit. Then we stopped at Cerro Mirandilla, a mystical hill topped with a rocky outcropping that looks like a face in silhouette. People sell their souls to the devil for wealth here; a legendary relative of my friends wandered in to work black magic but vanished for ten years, seduced by a young woman who turned out to have the body of a snake (no, a horse; no, a mule, *vos!*). The area was dotted with old campfires, perhaps where people worked *brujería,* but there were plenty of empty bottles and used condoms around as well. Our last stop was an auto-parts store in the city of Escuintla, where the stories changed to ones of gangs and murders. Then we took off through the sugarcane fields and wound our way up mountains back to an agro-urban barrio.[7]

Experiences like these played a formative role in shaping my ideas about class, caste, and "authenticity," as well as about how endlessly relative and intertwined "identities" articulate in geographic urban and agro-urban space as well as in the tilled fields and nature around them. The *agricultores* of El Rodeo were authentic for the brothers in a way related to how working-class people like them were authentic to others from the middle and upper classes (and how they were authentic to me). This imperfect parallel repeats in the ways that Maya people, and especially women—like "folkloric merchandise," in the "Guatemorfosis" critic's words, or as a prosthetic, in Diane Nelson's analysis—were authentic to the nation. All these parallels and levels of meaning and representation could just as easily be phrased in terms of space: the wellspring on the finca, the agro-urban land invasion, the sylvan village, the mall, the gated community, and the like.

I talked with the guys about such ideas. They agreed that "the urban" was sweeping across "the rural" and rewriting it, in ways that changed the way we look at wellsprings and tiny hamlets and the people in those places. We also talked about "servility," which, though a difficult concept for foreigners to grasp, is a commonplace in Guatemala, a country of "bowed heads" and deeply ingrained, hierarchical codes of caste and class and status. At first we talked about servility in terms of the Maya; this family self-identifies as "we're ladino, but *la abuela* wasn't." Like the many indigenous people with whom I have discussed servility, these ladinos agreed that the Maya, especially the young ones, weren't having it any more. They also agreed when I said I thought the same applied to them vis-à-vis the more moneyed sectors. I had noticed the changed attitude of ownership this family of friends had over the país; they would walk into any restaurant or business with a right-to-be-there air they hadn't had when I first met them, back when they were more respectful of the invisible boundaries around spaces where their *"clase de gente"* was unwelcome. Along these lines, I asked Adonay what he thought about the word *shumo*, the "brown-trash" slur, since the people who used the word meant it for him. "I'm not shumo," he said. "I'm *naco"*—a Mexican and macho-coded word for, well, shumo, maybe a tough shumo. And he was proud to be it.[8]

We were talking about shumos in 2012 because a spate of antishumo hate videos was coming out of Guatemala City. They focused on the swank Miraflores Mall, which the so-called shumos had adopted as a hangout spot. The first video that appeared on YouTube, "Los Shumos de Guate" linked the Elmo T-shirt–wearing, tacky, don't-know-their-place, brown-skinned youth in the mall to the growing gay movement in the greater capital-city region. "Hey, in this video we're going to show you people who are in *la pura mierda,"* the video began, showing pictures of youngsters' erotic selfies and running the guys down as *maricas* and *huecos* (bad words for "gay"). Young women weren't spared either; in one shot they were "ridiculous" for flipping the bird in photos; in another a girl's *selfi* appears next to a chat that shouts *"me gusta el sexo."* Indicative of this group's response was the comment that "Alejandra Castellanos6" posted: "si somos shumos q putas les importa serote mamones de vergas" (if we're shumos what the fuck do you care piece of shit cocksuckers).[9] Another hate video soon appeared, declaring that the first hadn't been rough enough. "They're not people; let's call them animals," it says, later modifying that to *"cucarachas."* The classist, racist, sexist, homophobic screed went on and on: "I shit in the graves of their mothers."[10] This was followed by a third video, in which the narrator wore a Guy Fawkes mask, saying the shumos "weren't even worth spitting on."[11]

This Guatemala City variant of youthful national debates about the ethnic question and caste status was grounded, just like the earlier break wars, in the capital's web of private and public schools. The anthropologist Jorge Ramón González Ponciano brilliantly charts how youth defined their status and belonging in his work on "anti-shumo racism" in Guatemala City. He breaks down binary ladino-versus-Maya readings of Guatemalan racism, focusing instead on a battle over "imperial whiteness" and the associated right to be cosmopolitan. At the heart of this battle, he notes, was the fact that lower-caste youngsters, by enacting "cosmopolitanism from below," threatened age-old cultural codes of servility.[12] While González-Ponciano focuses, rightly, on the from-above persistence of such codes among middle- and upper-class Guatemalans, for whom "anti-shumo, anti-muco and anti-cholero sentiment is an important part of the reproduction of the ideological values of whiteness," my goal here is to stress the breaking down of those codes from below.[13] People who once seemed to know their place rejected servility in a historic way.

By the 2010s the "I'm from the ghetto, but it's all okay" and "I'm Maya and the hell with you" kinds of cool had arguably won out over its "I'm light-skinned with some money in my pocket and better than you" counterpart. Battles over class and caste and race had evolved. They still raged, but they raged in a way that put the vocal minority of would-be elitists on the margin. Cultural power in the system of castas was tipping toward *"los de abajo,"* those at the bottom, without either erasing the very real and significant differences among them or erasing the reality of economic domination from above by a tiny national elite and a huge world system that kept them eternally disadvantaged. I spent a great deal of time with these people, both Maya and ladino, and witnessed this happen firsthand. At the lake, countless Kaqchikel and Tz'utujil youth made comments that, similar to a Consejo de Juventudes Indígenas Facebook post, made fun of *"capitalinos"* and *"cultos"* (that is, "cultivated people") for being apolitical and boring. "Their 'cultivated and educated' mind is the most easy to manipulate," the post said.¹⁴ I had heard this kind of critique, usually in more ribald variations, for years, but I remember it becoming particularly common in 2012, when the end of the Maya calendar, and with it issues of Maya culture and identity, became a mass-media and popular-culture event in Guatemala.

The apocalypse was scheduled for the twenty-first of December 2012, when 13 Baktun, the last long count in the ancient Mayan calendar, expired. No counted days remained. In anticipation of the event around Lake Atitlán, it was in vogue to say that *nel vos,* the world wasn't going to end. Instead, the "third eye" would open, heralding a spiritual awakening. "We are children of a millenarian civilization," the Consejo de Juventudes Indígenas posted in more serious language on Facebook. "We want to tell the world that we aren't extraterrestrials, that they couldn't wipe us out, and that on the contrary with this celebration of Oxlajuj Baktun (13 Baktun), we are beginning to wake up and to renovate our spirituality, our culture, and the struggle for the reassertion *[reinvindicación]* of our values and rights."¹⁵

In the circular Mayan calendar, time starts over again once it ends, and 13 Baktun had this feel. Everything seemed both different and the same old story. A "resurgence" was underway, said a late 2011 national *juventud* poll, in the "voice of Guatemalan youth," demanding "fundamental change," including addressing environmental issues, "reforming the political system," ending poverty, and achieving "ethnic and gender equity."¹⁶ This resurgence joined a global chorus; the Arab Spring was in full bloom, and Occupy Wall Street was just a few months old. Through 2011 Guatemalans had been following the antiausterity demonstrations of Spain's Indignados, and "hacktivists" started "Anonymous Guatemala." Guy Fawkes masks were appearing on la KY while Pepsi was producing its paean to productive nationalism; they were soon satired in the antishumo hate videos as well.¹⁷

Meanwhile, Guatemala—as ever, contradictory—indicted one general and elected another. The attorney general charged Efraín Ríos Montt with genocide and crimes against humanity in January 2012, and President Otto Pérez Molina (2012–15) of the Partido Patriota, whose symbol was a clenched fist and whose slogan was *"mano dura"* (iron fist), took office. A general in the highlands during the time of the genocide, Pérez Molina rode the wave of fear and insecurity to victory. In October, state forces killed activists who were protesting electric prices, gold mines, and hydroelectric dams, in what was called the Massacre of Totonicapán.¹⁸ The "fundamental change" that youth demanded was not unfolding in the political economy, nor would it in the years ahead. The historic 2013 conviction of Ríos Montt was a hopeful step, but the verdict was fast overturned, and he died before the matter was resolved.[19] In 2015, massive demonstrations drove first the vice president, and then Pérez Molina, out of office for corruption.[20] Guatemalans, however, then elected another right-wing president (Jimmy Morales, 2016–20) in his place; Anonymous Guatemala invited chapines to participate in the global *"marcha de un millión de mascaras."*[21] Events in 2012 foreshadowed those in 2015. In 13 Baktun, as later, the powerful won and the people lost. The state belonged to the elites and *los corruptos*. Pepsi stepped in to promote neoliberal citizenship with "Guatemorfosis," but in dialogue with such discourses, in the grassroots "million mask march" of everyday life in this *país de enmascarados,* questions of identity and nation remained alive. Whose país was Guatemala going to be?

CODA: "IN MY SMALL CITY"

Sometime around 13 Baktun, Diaz Negros put out an acoustic track called "Sueños muertos" (Dead dreams). A line in the chorus suggests that the song is about lost love, but its lyric on "illusions that give you life and then give you death" speaks to the creation and destruction, the hope and rage, that characterize youth cultures and youthful dreams in Guatemala.[22] In my years of living in Guatemala, I have met many young dreamers—students, nurses, teachers, informal business owners, artisans, tuc-tuc drivers enrolled in night school, and people hoping to migrate. In researching this book, I also came to meet many aspiring musicians who were gigging locally and hoping to make it big. One is the lead singer and guitarist in the Huehuetenango-based band Frenesí Rock, which complements its original compositions with covers of the rock nacional classics. Another, who calls himself Joseph Guath, has a *reggaetón* band called Nota Fa. In the late 2000s, as a teenager in Escuintla, he had begun his career under the nationalistic stage name "Guatelito."[23]

A new generation of Maya musicians was just coming up at 13 Baktun. A nineteen-year-old Kaqchikel vocalist named Sara Curruchich briefly joined Sobrevivencia in 2012. Already on her way to a stunning solo career, Curruchich performed with the Dresden Philharmonic in the same year. Her later hits would include the lyrical "Ch'uti' xtän (Niña)."[24] Most of the notable Maya popular musicians at the time of this writing gained a national stage after 13 Baktun. They included Sololá's Raquel Pajoc, who in 2014 softly

FIGURE 19. Ijatz Crew's self-painted banner hangs inside their studio in San Pedro La Laguna. Photo by Hugo Pablo de León, 2016.

rapped in Kaqchikel over an electromarimba backbeat about the excitement of moving to the capital to study in "Pa' capital," produced with Fernando Scheel.[25] Soft rap and electromarimba also characterized the sound of Kaqchikel-speaking Marcielita Chubay, from Santo Domingo Xenacoj, Sacatepéquez.[26]

Young artists like Curruchich, Pajoc, and Chubay helped to put not just Maya culture but also new "creative cities" on the map. Places known for their creativity had been found around Guatemala for years, including Panajachel and Antigua, where Lucía Escobar ended up, working in a progressive publishing house and cultural center with Yolanda Colom. Creative centers like Panajachel and Antigua have been joined by Comalapa, San Pedro, Sololá, and other places in the Mayan highlands. Curruchich was raised in San Juan Comalapa, Chimaltenango, which had long been notable for its Kaqchikel activists, intellectuals, artists, and musicians and today is a veritable creative city.[27] Notably, indigenous creative cities were gaining attention in many places, in Guatemala as in Latin America as a whole.[28] Javier Payeras wrote of moderating a panel on the arts in the altiplano at a conference in San José, Costa Rica, with Maya artists including Edgar Calel, from Comalapa, and Antonio Pichillá, from San Pedro La Laguna. The multimedia artist Benvenuto Chavajay said to one of the Comalapa panelists,

FIGURE 20. B-boys Sanick, Chino, and Lokillo pose with their street art in San Pedro La Laguna, 2016. Photo by Hugo Pablo de León.

"You have art; we from San Pedro have culture." By 2012, one of San Pedro's rising hip-hoppers was René Dionisio, better know as MC Tz'utu Kan. Years later, when he founded a crew called Balam Ajpu in 2015, MC Tz'utu Kan would prompt Payeras to write of "the cosmopolitan dream to imitate what's happening in great [urban] centers in small provinces," which "has meant going to the great capitals of the world to steal Prometheus's fire and to come back again to light up local spaces."[29] But it was not just imitation. Local artists, like the fusion they produced, were rooted in and drawing on local culture and history.

Guatemala's KY cultures were grounded in lived experiences in agrotropolis. The Ijatz Crew youth of San Pedro, whom we met in the introduction to this work, were still boys at 13 Baktun in 2012. Israel Nicolás "Nico" Chavajay Coché, later to become the crew's B-boy Chino, was away from San Pedro;

his parents had moved to the Antigua area in search of better work than being tenant onion farmers and selling macramé, and he was living in San Juan del Obispo on Volcán de Agua above the old colonial capital. He was falling in love with B-boying, studying break dancing with his mentor, "B-Boy Taz," and practicing "power moves" in Jocotenango, San Bartolo, Santa Ana, Ciudad Vieja, and other towns in the Antigua city-region. Despite the fact that many of these events were sanctioned by the government and NGOs (such as on the Día de la Juventud), he still got regularly chased by the cops. Back in his hometown the youngest of the three future Ijatz B-boys whom I met, Jhonny Ventura "Lokillo" Escún Peneleu, was just ten years old, but he started to practice break dancing and came to the park every day to watch the moves. One of dancers was his uncle and future crewmate Ventura González Flores (called Sanick, meaning "ant"), who was in his early teens. Sanick, whose older brother (*ya muerto,* "already dead," when I met Sanick in 2016) had turned him on to the art, was getting involved with a crew called "Los Jabberwockies" but had to stop dancing after he cracked his spine on a power move. By the time Nico "Chino" came back to the lake, looking for a crew, Sanick had switched from dancing to painting graffiti and writing, performing, and recording rap.[30]

Four years later these young men would share their history with me. Lokillo was still too young to know what he wanted to do; his goal was to finish junior high. Chino was still selling his mom's macramé handcrafts. "Now people want to be professionals," he said, "but I went to la Universidad de la KY." Sanick said he'd like to be a teacher but was working in a restaurant. When we broke for lunch, our server joked with the guys about how many tortillas they were wolfing down. They stopped their animated conversation in Tz'utujil and looked up at her. *"Somos chapines!"* Sanik and Chino chimed in unison.[31]

Ijatz Crew makes recordings in a second-floor studio in a humble concrete-block house near the *parque central*. The walls of the *callejón* beside it are painted with their graffiti, and its small upstairs is lined with egg cartons to keep the noise of the tuc-tucs and the barking chuchos out. Sanick rapped for me in that space, lyricizing about being an indígena who worships not in churches but in nature, the proud child of Tz'utujil campesinos. He chanted of being called a *delincuente,* of the pleasure of performing in the square, of the joy of a kiss with a chapina with whom he ducked into an alley and who didn't tell him no. He sang about life in a place he described with the rap's one and only lyric in English: "in my small city." It was in such small cities, and on their KY, that over decades new generations of Guatemalans became more urban and more urbane. They reconfigured national identity and rejected the terms of a caste system. Whether or not the new Baktun would answer their creative force with economic opportunity or social justice, however, remained an open question.

NOTES

INTRODUCTION

1. Hugo asked me to use his real name (pseudonyms appear in quotation marks at first mention). *Vos,* an informal "you" pronoun (*tú* or *usted* in standard Spanish), is widely used in Guatemala. The common vulgarity *a la gran puta,* often euphemized as *a la gran,* is used where an English speaker might say "damn," "hell/to hell," or "Jeez/Jesus." *Gran puta* literally translates as "great whore."
2. Craib, *Cartographic Mexico.* The Mayan languages are joined by Afro-Caribbean Garífuna; Xinca, a non-Mayan indigenous tongue; and Spanish. Even if Hugo and Tono were fluent Kaqchikel speakers, it is likely that they would find it hard to understand each other's dialects and would use Spanish as a lingua franca.
3. The government conducted censuses in 2002 and again in 2018, but the methodology and results are dubious. Sources differ widely in population counts and other vital statistics.
4. A ring road has opened since I wrote this text; it saves time, but I miss passing through Chimaltenango.
5. Specifically, this work is a historical study of what Lefebvre, *Production of Space,* calls "social space," or space as perceived, conceived, and lived.
6. As is detailed in the text, many of Guatemala's municipal seats, or cabeceras, are nucleated settlements that date back to the 1500s. As centers where markets and local government were found, they were always to some extent "urban" in relation to their surrounding villages and hamlets.
7. This discourse reached a fever pitch in the middle of the Trump administration, when I wrote these words.
8. See Nelson, *Finger in the Wound,* for an in-depth discussion. The generalized use of *indígena* to refer to indigenous people also dates to the late twentieth century, replacing *indio* (Indian), today a racial slur. The project of giving the term "Maya" political meaning dated to the 1970s. Grandin, *Blood of Guatemala,* 238.
9. Bastos, *Multiculturalismo y futuro,* 15. See also Bastos and Brett, *Movimiento maya. De a pie* literally means "on foot."

10. For a history of common Guatemalans, everyday life, and the construction of social space in Guatemala City's marginal neighborhoods and municipal and street markets from 1920 to early in the new millennium, see Way, *Mayan in the Mall*.

11. Brenner, *Implosions/Explosions*, 16. *Agrotropolis* joins this literature in analyzing what Lefebvre, *Production of Space*, calls "social space." See also Lefebvre, *Urban Revolution*.

12. See Gobierno de Guatemala, "Plan Nacional de Desarrollo K'atun: Nuestra Guatemala 2032," 2014, Consejo Nacional de Desarrollo Urbano y Rural/SEGEPLAN, especially pages 3, 95, and 106. I argue that significant urbanization was notable in the provinces by the late 1990s. "K'atun" can also mean a general time period.

13. Florida, *Creative Class;* Florida, *New Urban Crisis;* Davis, *Planet of Slums*. Sassen, *World Economy*, provides an entry into the author's numerous publications; for an entry into the work of the urban theorist Manuel Castells, see *Informational City*. For an overview of policy, see B. H. Roberts, *Managing Systems*.

14. For Guatemala City, see Camus, *Colonia Primero de Julio;* Levenson, *Adiós Niño;* Levenson, *Hacer la juventud;* Levenson, *Trade Unionists against Terror;* Offit, *Conquistadores de la Calle;* O'Neill, *Secure the Soul;* O'Neill, *City of God;* O'Neill and Thomas, *Securing the City;* Vrana, *City Belongs to You;* and Way, *Mayan in the Mall*. For an entry into urbanization in Latin America, see B. Fischer, *Poverty of Rights;* Fischer, McCann, and Auyero, *Cities from Scratch;* McCann, *Hard Times;* and B. R. Roberts, *Making of Citizens*.

15. Pradilla Cobos, "Presente y futuro," 154. Pradilla Cobos's Latin American analysis builds on the concept developed by Allen J. Scott in "Globalization." Similarly, I am building on Pradilla Cobos's concept. His work focuses on the Latin American megacity and its environs; Guatemala's case is different inasmuch as it entailed the rapid urbanization of smaller and more agrarian population centers. Making the same correction for the proximity of megacities, Guatemala's agro-urban cities also resemble Asia's dense *"desakota"* regions, documented by Terry G. McGee, where areas "between large city cores" have come to show "an intense mixture of agricultural and non-agricultural activities." "Emergence of *Desakota* Regions," 124.

16. Most notable was the genocide trial against Efraín Ríos Montt, who had been the military head of state from March 1982 to August 1983. He was declared guilty on 10 May 1983, but the verdict was reversed ten days later. The trial was still underway when he died in April 2018. Ríos Montt was the first head of state in history to be tried for genocide by his home country's courts.

17. Scholars in the volumes Little and Smith, *Mayas in Postwar Guatemala*, as well as McAllister and Nelson, *War by Other Means*, chart the ongoing articulations of counterinsurgent violence. A regional perspective is found in Santamaría and Carey, *Violence and Crime*. An extensive anthropological literature on Maya cultures and politics also takes up the legacy of war and genocide. As an entry, see Burrell, *Maya after War;* Cojtí, *Ri Maya' Moloj pa Iximulew;* Montejo, *Maya Intellectual Renaissance;* Nelson, *Finger in the Wound;* Nelson, *Reckoning*, and Nelson, *Who Counts?* See also Konefal's fine-grained history, *Every Indio Who Falls*.

18. On nontraditional agro-exports, see Fischer and Benson, *Broccoli and Desire*.
19. Maya-run knockoff apparel manufacturing is covered in Thomas, *Regulating Style*. A close reading of how local actors interact with NGOs is found in Beck, *How Development Projects Persist*. For a regional perspective, see DeHart, *Ethnic Entrepreneurs*.
20. Peck, *Constructions of Neoliberal Reason*, 7.
21. Hale, *Más Que un Indio*.
22. These terms are discussed in virtually every work on Guatemala. An essential starting point is McCreery, *Rural Guatemala*. This work charts changes in a long period over which the lines between nonindigenous castas and indigenous people, while remaining distinct categories, began to blur. See also Grandin, *Blood of Guatemala*, a study of Quetzaltenango's K'iche' elite from the late 1700s to 1954. Grandin reminds us that "to understand republican Guatemala as a nation defined *primarily* along ethnic lines is to buy into the racialist assumptions that sought to reduce Guatemala's complex colonial legacy into two competing camps" (148).
23. González Ponciano, *"Patria del Shumo,"* 137. This is an important work on interethnic and interclass relationships. *Shumo* is a class-based insult, but it began its life as an anti-Maya slur and has a racialized, anti-indigenous overlay; for this reason it is heard more frequently in the capital than in the provinces. The term *castas* has also evolved to be race-neutral, referring to the brown-skinned poor in general, both Maya and mestizo.
24. González Ponciano, "*Shumo* Challenge," 309.
25. Carolina Escobar Sartí, "Shumos en un país de castas," *Prensa Libre*, 27 January 2000, cited in González Ponciano, "*Shumo* Challenge," 315.
26. On the "'middle clases'" as a "protean group of people who have been both idealized and reviled," see Walker, *Waking from the Dream*. The quotation is from page 3.
27. McAllister and Nelson, *War by Other Means*.
28. Menchú and Burgos-Debray, *Yo me llamo Rigoberta*. I summarize a complex landscape. While not *every single* person was a seasonal agricultural worker, it was still the norm in the second half of the twentieth century. Seasonal migration has significantly diminished but has not disappeared. On rural Guatemala, see Carey, *I Ask for Justice;* Carey, *Our Elders Teach Us;* Handy, *Revolution in the Countryside;* and McCreery, *Rural Guatemala*.
29. USAID, "Legacies of Exclusion: Social Conflict and Violence in Communities and Homes in Guatemala's Western Highlands," Guatemala Conflict Vulnerability Assessment, Final Report, Public Version, October 2015, prepared by Tani Adams, www.usaid.gov/sites/default/files/documents/1862/Guatemala_Conflict_Vulnerability_Assessment.pdf, 10.
30. USAID, "Legacies of Exclusion," 10.
31. Mbembe, *On the Postcolony*, 115.
32. Hjarvard, *Mediatization of Culture*, 17. The author is specifically analyzing mediatization in "highly industrialized societies" and notes that it articulates differently outside the Global North (18). As an entry to the vast literature on everyday

life, see de Certeau, *Practice of Everyday Life;* and Bordieu, *Distinction.* On capital expansion, see Harvey, *Rebel Cities* (with urban themes); and Harvey, *Brief History of Neoliberalism.* See also Sassen, *Expulsions.*

33. This work thus uses rock nacional and related musical genres and styles as a means to trace greater changes in popular culture that cannot be accessed through available sources. Beyond "provincial cosmopolitanism," Chattopadhyay's reconception of "infra-structure" is also an influence (*Unlearning the City,* 248–49); on "provincial cosmopolitanism," see pages 63–92. For a nuanced reading of style, see Thomas, *Regulating Style.*

34. Williams, *Marxism and Literature;* Cooper, *Colonialism in Question,* 59–90 (quotations on 67, 71). See Nelson, *Reckoning,* on Guatemala's relational identities.

35. Zolov writes that "through the influence of transnational images, music, and actors Mexican youth came to challenge a totalizing discourse of national identity, one that stressed the stasis of an indigenous present and the 'correctness' of patriarchally defined hierarchies. Transnationalism," he adds, "introduced the possibility of selecting among multiple reference points in the reconstruction of one's national as well as individual identity. [As such it was] intimately linked with postmodern identity-formation strategies and the forging of a popular nationalism from below" (*Refried Elvis,* 139).

The alternative popular nationalism discussed in *Agrotropolis* embeds other important idioms of national self-identification. On "indigenous nationalism" and the nationalization of ethnicity, see Grandin, *Blood of Guatemala,* 109, 139–40, 220–21, 229. For an examination of ethnicity and national identity in the mid-1990s, see Nelson, *Finger in the Wound.* On "student nationalism" coming out of the state university, see Vrana, *City Belongs to You.*

36. This work owes an intellectual debt to scholarship on state formation in communities and everyday settings, including Joseph and Nugent, *Everyday Forms;* Lancaster, *Life Is Hard;* and Mallon, *Peasant and Nation.* While it focuses on everyday popular culture and not on revolutionary politics, *Agrotropolis* joins new scholarship that "charts the untold history of how ordinary people challenged the existing social order" (Schlotterbeck, *Beyond the Vanguard,* 3). Like Schlotterbeck, I trace how "change took the form of quotidian transformations in people's everyday lives," leading to "a challenge to the status quo: not in the ideological sense, but in the very real, material remaking of lives." *Agrotropolis* joins *Beyond the Vanguard* in unearthing everyday "efforts to redefine the terms of inclusion and overturn social hierarchies" (6).

37. Government ministries stopped sending their paperwork to the central archive in roughly 1963. Municipalities, meanwhile, often sell their paperwork to be pulped and recycled; almost none archive it properly or in a way that is accessible to researchers.

38. I read hundreds of individual Facebook pages, which helped to lead me to my conclusions. Ultimately, I decided that it was unethical to cite them. This is an issue that remains to be addressed as historians make use of the digital archive.

39. Weld, *Paper Cadavers* (quotations from 5, 13, 253). The clandestine archive of the police force was discovered in 2005.

40. Callaci, *Street Archives*, 11–13.

41. A thorough analysis of Guatemalan youth policies is found in AVANCSO, *Jóvenes en Guatemala*. On Protestantism, see Garrard, *Terror in the Land;* and Garrard, *Protestantism in Guatemala*. The literature on human rights is extensive. As an entry, see Green, *Fear as a Way;* Sanford, *Buried Secrets;* and Weld, *Paper Cadavers*. Social movements are covered in the anthropological literature; see, for example, Bastos and Brett, *Movimiento maya;* McAllister and Nelson, *War by Other Means;* and Yagenova, *Protesta social en Guatemala*. For political history, see Jonas, *Of Centaurs and Doves*.

42. As an entry to this literature, see C. Smith, *Guatemalan Indians;* Grandin, *Blood of Guatemala,* Grandin, *Last Colonial Massacre;* McCreery, *Rural Guatemala;* Taracena Arriola, *Invención criolla;* and Taracena Arriola, Gordillo, and Sagastume, *Etnicidad, estado y nación*. Essential on the 1944–54 revolution is Handy, *Revolution in the Countryside*.

43. Brenner, *Implosions/Explosions;* Lefebvre, *Production of Space;* Sevilla-Buitrago, *"Urbs in Rure."*

44. The department of Guatemala consists of seventeen municipalities, many of them agro-urban, which form a metropolitan area. See Way, *Mayan in the Mall,* for their history. Place-names often repeat; for example, the city of Huehuetenango is the cabecera of both the department and the municipality of the same name.

45. The translations of these centers vary. Technically, an aldea (here translated as village) has between 5,000 and 9,999 inhabitants, among other bureaucratic requirements; a *caserío* (hamlet) has a population of 2,000 to 4,999. Readers familiar with colonial and early national territorial division will note that the category of *pueblo* is no longer deployed. See "Municipio," WikiGuate, accessed 4 June 2020, https://wikiguate.com.gt/municipio/; "Aldea," WikiGuate, accessed 4 June 2020, https://wikiguate.com.gt/aldea/; and "Caserío," WikiGuate, accessed 4 June 2020, https://wikiguate.com.gt/caserio/.

46. Lefebvre, *Production of Space*. To analyze social space as perceived, conceived, and lived, the narrative moves back and forth from the capital city to the provinces. It switches between foregrounding youth cultures, urbanization and sociocultural change, and the political economy, approaching these factors dialectically.

47. Manzano, *Age of Youth*, 2. Manzano frames youth as "the carrier of sociocultural modernization *and* its discontents," a dynamic also explored here, albeit through the analytic lens of spatiality (3). See also Zolov, *Refried Elvis;* Dunn, *Contracultura;* and Pensado and Ochoa, *México beyond 1968*. Pensado, *Rebel Mexico,* explicates the political manipulation of youthful "fun." On the relationship of "youth" to peoples' delayed ability to make a living and start a family (i.e., become adult), see Dixon, "Endless Question." AVANCSO, *Jóvenes en Guatemala,* offers a historical analysis of state discourse on youth in Guatemala. Government documents from Guatemala define "youth" as the years from eighteen to thirty years of age, "adolescence" as thirteen to seventeen, and "childhood" as twelve and under.

48. On the history of the term *chapín* and race, caste, and class relations, see González Ponciano, *"Patria del Shumo,"* 24–26, 44–46, 45n66, 46n67, 63n96.

49. J. Scott, *Domination*. *Servilismo* is a word commonly used in Guatemalan and Latin American political discourse as well; ending national *servilismo* was a commonly stated goal of Guatemala's 1944–54 democratic revolution, for example. In its cultural, ground-level usage in Guatemala, the word tends to refer to deference expressed in body language—bowed heads, averted gazes, and an unwillingness to express disagreement or discontent.

50. Lefebvre, *Production of Space;* Brenner, *Implosions/Explosions;* Dussel, *Twenty Theses on Politics*.

51. For "city-regions," see Pradilla Cobos, "Presente y futuro."

52. Nelson, "Stumped Identities," 314.

CHAPTER 1: "POWER'S DESTINY"

1. Rizzo, *Alternativa*.
2. Levenson, *Adiós Niño*.
3. On the history of "precarious neighborhoods" and grassroots retail, see Way, *Mayan in the Mall*.
4. The song was the B-side of the band's first, 45 rpm release in 1983. The A-side was "Visión satánica" (Satanic vision).
5. Rizzo, *Alternativa;* Camus, *Colonia Primero de Julio*, 204–10; Escobar Urrutia, "Enfrentamientos y violencias juveniles," 39–44.
6. "Sangre Humana: Destino del Poder," 1983 song posted by "Suchitano8," 27 April 2010, YouTube video, www.youtube.com/watch?v = fQio7ZgAVoQ. All links provided for inherently fleeting sources such as this were active at some point between 2016 and 2018.
7. McAllister and Nelson, *War by Other Means;* Camus, Bastos, and López García, *Dinosaurio reloaded*.
8. See Grandin, *Last Colonial Massacre*.
9. A detailed account is found in the memoir of FAR commander, Pablo Monsanto, *Somos los jóvenes rebeldes*.
10. See Barry and Preusch, *Soft War;* Camus, *Colonia Primero de Julio;* Jonas, *Battle for Guatemala;* Berger, *Political and Agrarian Development;* and Way, *Mayan in the Mall*.
11. Dosal, *Power in Transition;* B. R. Roberts, *Making of Citizens;* Way, *Mayan in the Mall*.
12. Way, *Mayan in the Mall*, 72–76.
13. R. Adams, *Crucifixion by Power*.
14. Driscoll, *Absolute Erotic*, xi; Dussel, *Twenty Theses on Politics*, 122–25.
15. Castañeda Maldonado, "Historia del Rock," 48–50; "Historia del rock en Guatemala," *Earth* (blog), *Guaterock*, 28 October 2010, http://guaterock.blogspot.com/2010/10/historia-del-rock-en-guatemala.html; Sierra Marroquín, "Música en Guatemala," 252–65. Other early 1960s bands included Los Fantasmas, Los Marauders, Los Reyes del Ritmo, Los Beatniks, Los Terrícolas, Los Traviesos, and

Los Yakis. Few Guatemalans had televisions in the 1950s; in the capital people watched TV in store windows. National distributors of televisions, record players, and radios in the 1950s included Grundig, Philco, Philips, and Cia-Agro Comercial. Philips had a record store in Guatemala City in the 1950s, but most records were sold at importers' private *tiendas* (shops), from where they spread through grassroots distribution networks. Besides Radio Nacional TGW, radio networks included Radio Panamericana, Radio Faro Aviateca, Radio TGMU, Radio Internacional, and Radio Ciros, with "Club Pepsi Cola." There were also government stations (such as one for the police force). Local stations such as La Voz de Mazatenango were found around the provinces (Sierra Marroquín, "Música en Guatemala," 247–54). Community radio—decades later to follow on the heels of guerrilla radio stations as a battleground between the state and the popular sectors—was born late in 1958 with the foundation of La Voz de Colomba, en Colomba, Costa Cuca, Quetzaltenango. It was staffed by young campesino volunteers (ASIES, *Compendio de historia*, 170). For regional background, see Pacini Hernandez, Fernández L'Hoeste, and Zolov, *Rockin' Las Américas*, 1–21.

16. Castañeda Maldonado, "Historia del Rock," 27–33; Sierra Marroquín, "Música en Guatemala," 260–63.

17. The state operationalized this project through BANVI (Banco Nacional de la Vivienda, or National Housing Bank). See Camus, *Colonia Primero de Julio*.

18. "Polyester" and "urban loneliness" are from Morales, "Cultura y literatura," 5:33–34. *"Modernidad a la chapina"* is from Camus, *Colonia Primero de Julio*, 124–25. A firsthand account of growing up in the city and joining the guerrillas is found in Ramírez, *Guerra;* on university students, see Vrana, *City Belongs to You*.

19. Monsanto, *Somos los jóvenes rebeldes*.

20. Grandin, *Last Colonial Massacre*, 73–104; Way, *Mayan in the Mall*, 72–134. On seasonal migration, see Carey, "Guatemala's Green Revolution." Unequal land distribution and labor exploitation are covered extensively; for an entry, see Berger, *Political and Agrarian Development*.

21. "Historia del rock"; Castañeda Maldonado, "Historia del Rock," 27–33, 39, 44–45, 54, 61–62; Sierra Marroquín, "Música en Guatemala," 247–65. For a regional perspective, see Pacini Hernandez, Fernández L'Hoeste, and Zolov, *Rockin' Las Américas*, 1–21.

22. Mario Payeras, "Latitud de la flor y el granizo: Dialéctica del medio ambiente y la vida social en Guatemala," 1987, annotated manuscript, GT-CIRMA-AH-003 /C08/S1/D319, with introduction written in 1997 by Yolanda Colom (cited), 2–3. (Centro de Investigaciones Regionales de Mesoamérica [CIRMA] citations use *C* for *caja* or *cartapacio* [box or folder], *S* for *serie*, and *D* for *documento*).

23. FLACSO, *Guatemala*, 2:91–95, 131–32.

24. Rizzo, *Alternativa;* AVANCSO, *Jóvenes en Guatemala*, 62–63; Sierra Marroquín, "Música en Guatemala," 270–71.

25. Sierra Marroquín, "Música en Guatemala," 281. Both *la onda* and *fresa* were terms that came from Mexico, where rock and counterculture styles were also suppressed during the 1970s; see Zolov, *Refried Elvis*.

26. Karishnanda's real name was Jorge Ramírez. Castañeda Maldonado, "Historia del Rock," 70; Sierra Marroquín, "Música en Guatemala," 283–84. On San Juan Sacatepéquez, see Way, *Mayan in the Mall,* 113–14.

27. On trova and revolutionary youth, see FLACSO, *Guatemala,* 1:248–49. On the internal divisions in the student movement, see Escobar Urrutia, "Enfrentamientos y violencias juveniles," 39–41.

28. "Poemas, literatura, canciones, chistes, artesanía," mixed documents, ca. November 1985, CIRMA-AH-019/S248/26-01-03, Collection of Song Lyrics, Estudiantina Universitaria, Universidad de San Carlos de Guatemala.

29. Sierra Marroquín, "Música en Guatemala," 304.

30. Flores, *Compañeros.*

31. E. Fischer, *Cultural Logics,* 54–56.

32. Colom, *Mujeres en la alborada.* Colom also stresses machismo in the guerrilla organizations. Social and cultural changes—as well as political alliances—were complex and muddy during the years of the armed conflict. Rural villagers were embedded in systems of what Mallon, *Peasant and Nation,* calls "communal hegemonies" that were often slow to break down, if they did so at all. On the slow, discursive changes by which grassroots historical actors come to challenge systems of power and hegemony, see Gould, *To Lead as Equals.*

33. E. Fischer, *Cultural Logics,* 36–42.

34. Instituto de Ciencia y Tecnología Agrícolas (ICTA), "Investigación y producción de maíz en Guatemala," *CIMMYT Hoy,* no. 14 (1981), University of Florida Digital Collections, http://ufdc.ufl.edu/UF00072041/00001, 3–11, 10. On the military, the state, agricultural commercialization, and the basic grains crisis of the 1970s, see Way, *Mayan in the Mall,* 126–28, 143.

35. Joachim von Braun, David Hotchkiss, and Martin D. C. Immink, "Nontraditional Export Crops in Guatemala: Effects on Production, Consumption, and Nutrition," research report (Washington, DC: International Food Policy Research Institute [IFPRI], 1989), 27–28. In 2016 LAAD shareholders included J. P. Morgan, Monsanto, Cargill, Dole Food, Bank of America and others, and it was on the verge of becoming a US$1 billion enterprise ("Shareholders," Latin American Agribusiness Development Corporation, accessed September 2016, www.laadsa.com/shareholders.html).

36. Von Braun, Hotchkiss, and Immink, "Nontraditional Export Crops," 27–28. See also E. Fischer, *Cultural Logics,* 226–29.

37. On the relation of NTAs to Guatemala's martial green revolution, see Carey, "Guatemala's Green Revolution"; and Way, *Mayan in the Mall,* 124–51. On NTAs in Tecpán, see Fischer and Benson, *Broccoli and Desire.* For global perspective, see Blumi, *Destroying Yemen.*

38. Von Braun, Hotchkiss, and Immink, "Nontraditional Export Crops," 29; E. Fischer, *Cultural Logics,* 228–29.

39. Way, *Mayan in the Mall,* 137–41. On the Panzós massacre, see Grandin, *Last Colonial Massacre.*

40. M. Payeras, *Trueno en la ciudad*. A detailed account is found in a manuscript by Mario Payeras, "La estrategia antiguerrillera del ejército guatemalteco," ca. 1985, CIRMA-AH-003/C08, 37.

41. On the Ríos Montt period, see Garrard, *Terror in the Land;* on the military's campaigns, see Schirmer, *Guatemalan Military Project*.

42. See Schirmer, *Guatemalan Military Project*. On IIC and its precedents, see Way, *Mayan in the Mall*, 132–46. A ground-level description of the military in Patzún and Tecpán is found in E. Fischer, *Cultural Logics*, 57–61. On legacies of militarism, see Little and Smith, *Mayas in Postwar Guatemala;* and McAllister and Nelson, *War by Other Means*.

43. Dussel, *Twenty Theses on Politics*, 122. On legitimacy and the construction of a new hegemony, see pages 104–7.

44. Vrana, *City Belongs to You*, 25; see also 167.

45. Dussel, *Twenty Theses on Politics*, 44.

46. The band started in a Guatemala City high school in 1977, took its name in 1979, and released its first album in 1981. Alvarado, "Guatemala's Alux Nahual," 225 (quotations on 229–30); "Alux Nahual Bio," posted by "AluxNahualTV," 6 November 2014, YouTube video, 5:07, www.youtube.com/watch?v=UDiCsk-3hgk; Sierra Marroquín, "Música en Guatemala," 300.

47. Castañeda Maldonado, "Historia del Rock," 66.

48. Camus, *Colonia Primero de Julio*, 122–23, 206–7 (quotations on 209–11).

49. Mario Efraín Castañeda Maldonado, "El arte desde el rock: Reflexiones," Argenpress Cultural, 11 September 2010, http://cultural.argenpress.info/2010/09/el-arte-desde-el-rock-reflexiones.html; Sierra Marroquín, "Música en Guatemala," 295.

50. Escobar Urrutia, "Enfrentamientos y violencias juveniles," 43; Sierra Marroquín, "Música en Guatemala," 302.

51. "Emiliano: Indígenas y ladinos buscamos lo mismo," in Ejército Guerrillero de los Pobres, *Informador guerrillero* 2, no. 26 (1983): 6–7, CIRMA-AH-019/S147/12-02-01. I have updated the spelling of the name of the ethnic group from the older form, "kanjobal."

52. Konefal, *Every Indio Who Falls*, 73–74 (and in general); Little and Smith, *Mayas in Postwar Guatemala;* Nelson, *Reckoning*. For a firsthand account of the Left's divisions over the ethnic question, see Santa Cruz Mendoza, *Insurgentes*, 19–20, 59.

53. "Carta de los cuadros militares y combatientes que rompen con la Dirección Nacional del EGP, dirigida a la DN y a los compañeros de esa organización, a las organizaciones hermanas de la URNG, al Partido Comunista de Cuba, al Frente Sandinista de Liberación Nacional FSLN, al Frente Farabundo Martí para la Liberación Nacional FMLN y otras fuerzas revolucionarias de nuestro país y el área," 12 February 1984, CIRMA-AH-003/C07/S1/D284.

54. Yolanda Colom, interview with the author, Antigua Guatemala, 5 April 2016.

55. Ejército Guerrillero de los Pobres, "Comunicado interno sobre la maniobra fraccionalista encabezada por Benedicto," February 1984, CIRMA-AH-037/C93/D7, 1–13.

56. Colom, interview; "Carta de los cuadros." On Payeras and Octubre Revolucionario—which worked with a fraction of the Partido Guatemalteco de Trabajo (the communist party) in an alliance called Octubre Revolucionario/PGT-6 de Enero—see also Konefal, *Every Indio Who Falls,* 164–65.

57. Octubre Revolucionario, "Las corrientes político-ideológicas dentro del movimiento indio guatemalteco," internal work material, 1988, CIRMA-AH-003/C08/S3/D09, 2. On Mario Payeras's earlier work for the EGP regarding indigenous issues and on the guerrillas and the "Indian question," see Grandin, *Blood of Guatemala,* 225, 330n21.

58. "Emiliano," 7.

59. FLACSO, *Guatemala,* 3:66–67; Konefal, *Every Indio Who Falls,* 146. For general histories and interpretations, see Cojtí Cuxil, *Ri Maya' Moloj pa Iximulew;* and Bastos and Camus, "Difficult Complementarity," 71–92.

60. "Declaración de Iximché," manifesto, 14 February 1980, Iximché, Guatemala, CIRMA-AH-037/C12/D53. For the finalized version, see "Declaración de Iximché," Albedrio, 14 February 1980, www.albedrio.org/htm/otrosdocs/comunicados/DeclaraciondeIximche1980.pdf, 1080. See also Grandin, *Blood of Guatemala,* 224–25.

61. *Revista del Movimiento Indio,* August 1982, 1–10; October 1982, 1–9; January 1983, 7–8, CIRMA-AH-037/C12/D60–62.

62. The movement went public in 1982. Movimiento Revolucionario del Pueblo Ixim, *Ixim, Órgano de Presencia Internacional,* nos. 1–3 (March–September 1983), CIRMA-AH-003/C09/S03/D78–80.

63. Movimiento Indio de Guatemala, "Guatemala: De la república burguesa centralista a la república popular federal," manifesto, August 1983, CIRMA-AH-037/C12/D59. On the Left's embrace of capitalist narratives of development, see Saldaña-Portillo, *Revolutionary Imagination.*

64. "Guatemala: De la república burguesa."

65. Bastos and Camus, "Difficult Complementarity," 74.

66. Partido Guatemalteco del Trabajo (6 de Enero), "El Partido y las etnias en Guatemala, Parte IV, Tesis 6," internal work document, ca. 1984, CIRMA-AH-003/C09/S3/D112, 1–4.

67. See, for example, "Postura revolucionara, indio nacionalista guatemalteca," manifesto, ca. early mid-1980s, CIRMA-AH-003/C09/S3/D113, 1–4.

68. Movimiento Indio de Guatemala, *Revista Ch'olnoj maya,* February 1984, CIRMA-AH-003/C09/S3/D82, 24.

69. Movimiento Indio, Nacionalista y Revolucionario, manifesto, April 1985, Mayalán, CIRMA-AH-003/C09/S3/D87, 1.

70. Liga de Resistencia Popular Awesh, "Los nuevos movimientos indios," document, ca. 1985–86, CIRMA-AH-003/C09/S3/D88, 12; Octubre Revolucionario, "Corrientes político-ideológicas," 26.

71. Liga de Resistencia Popular Awesh, "Nuevos movimientos indios," 21–26.

72. Octubre Revolucionario, Colectivo para Trabajo Étnico, "La cuestión étnico-nacional, Definiciones y perspectiva política," internal work material, ca. 1989–90, CIRMA-AH-003/C08/S3/D31, 14–16 (quotation on 14).

73. *Prensa Libre*, 13 November 2002, 12.

74. See Solano, "Development and/as Dispossession."

75. Camus, *Colonia Primero de Julio*, 208–9. In the weeks just after the USAC raid, the URNG guerrillas conducted armed actions on fincas in major agro-exporting areas and attacked a Guatemala City police station with fragmentation grenades; soon the military would accuse *them* of being involved in narcotraffic. URNG, "La situación actual y las perspectivas en Guatemala: Visión de la Unidad Revolucionaria Nacional Guatemalteca," booklet, 1 October 1985, CIRMA AH-037/C1/D76, 32–33; URNG, "Hechos y políticas en Guatemala, abril–junio 1987," CIRMA-AH-037/C2/D72, 11.

76. Levenson, *Adiós Niño*, 56, 3; see also Bruey, *Bread, Justice, and Liberty*, 89–94; and Way, *Mayan in the Mall*, 94–96.

77. E. Fischer, *Cultural Logics*, 231. USAID promoted NTAs in places like Uganda and Malawi, claiming that they lessened families' need to migrate seasonally to big plantations for extra income, helped employ women, and generated economic linkages. Terrance J. Brown, assistant to the administrator, U.S. Agency for International Development, to the House Subcommittee on Foreign Agriculture and Hunger, statement, 9 June 1994, CIRMA-AH-019/S108/10-01-02, 1–5.

78. E. Fischer, *Cultural Logics*, 231; Von Braun, Hotchkiss, and Immink, *Nontraditional Export Crops*, 23–25, 29–32, 43–44, 48, 54, 60–80, 85–86. Through the 1970s and most especially in the decades that followed, urbanizing nodes in the countryside would see higher rates of growth than the capital city (ASIES, *Compendio de historia*, 286).

79. On kinship, development, and barrio construction, see E. Fischer, *Cultural Logics*, 174–79.

80. "Explican alcances de proyecto de desarrollo de cooperativas agrícolas del altiplano," Instituto Nacional de Cooperativas, Departamento de Relaciones Públicas, *Boletín Informativo*, no. 103 (12 January 1984), CIRMA-AH-019/S111/10-01-04; "El Plan de Acción Gubernamental incorporá Cooperativismo en la educación," Instituto Nacional de Cooperativas, Departamento de Relaciones Públicas, *Boletín Informativo*, no. 105 (16 January 1984), CIRMA-AH-019/S111/10-01-04; Von Braun, Hotchkiss, and Immink, *Nontraditional Export Crops*; "Tomas de tierra 1995/recortes de prensa/chistes," mixed documents, 1984, CIRMA-AH-019/S111/10-01-04.

81. Although Guatemala avoided the debt crisis seen elsewhere in Latin America in the 1980s, growth was stagnant and formal-sector unemployment was staggering. The government floated "stability bonds," and introduced a regressive value-added sales tax in 1982. The quetzal had fallen from par with the U.S. dollar by 1984, and the state freed banks to trade in foreign currency. It also created three exchange rates—an official one-to-one rate, a regulated parallel rate, and a rate for bids and contracts. This benefited NTA exporters, who were forced to change only half their

dollars at the one-to-one rate, unlike the 75 percent mandated of coffee exporters. Meanwhile, private-sector elites began to clamor for the privatization of the electric company, the telecommunications sector, and the ports. Both the privatization debate and a weak economy continued throughout the decade; a falling quetzal and inflation reduced real wages, a problem compounded by Cerezo's removal of price controls on essential foods. Opposition to plans for redistributive tax and other fiscal policies was led by CACIF, the Coordinating Committee of Agricultural, Commercial, Industrial and Financial Associations. See also Bulmer-Thomas, *Economic History*, 364–83; Dosal, *Power in Transition*, 159; Inter-American Development Bank, "Industrial Policy in Guatemala: A Case of Policy Inertia under Changing Paradigms," IDB Working Paper Series, No. IDB-WP-169, prepared by Mario Cuevas, Sigfrido Lee, and Bismarck Pineda, www.econstor.eu/handle/10419/89177, vi; Von Braun, Hotchkiss, and Immink, *Nontraditional Export Crops*, 23; URNG, "Las condiciones de vida en Guatemala," report, April 1990, Centro de Documentación de la URNG, CIRMA-AH-037/C1/D1, 49–50, 52–53.

82. URNG, "Hechos y políticas," 11. In the early 1990s, although without success, the CUC aided Huehuetenango campesinos in suing the DEA for damages caused by these fumigations. *El Regional* (Jacaltenango, Huehuetenango), no. 15 (February 1992): 4.

83. Levenson, *Adiós Niño*, 56.

84. Thomas, *Regulating Style*.

85. "Alhazred," "Música en Guatemala: Rock en la guerra interna de Guatemala," *Rock Republik* (blog), 29 March 2011, http://rockrepublik.net/topic/11988/.

86. See Levenson, "Life That Makes Us."

87. "Alhazred," "Música en Guatemala."

88. "Ramses," "Música en Guatemala: Rock en la guerra interna de Guatemala," *Rock Republik* (blog), 29 March 2011, http://rockrepublik.net/topic/11988/.

89. "Mike1701," "Música en Guatemala: Rock en la guerra interna de Guatemala," *Rock Republik* (blog), 19 April 2011, http://rockrepublik.net/topic/11988/; "Gerardo Perez," "Música en Guatemala: Rock en la guerra interna de Guatemala," *Rock Republik* (blog), 19 April 2011, http://rockrepublik.net/topic/11988/.

90. "Gerardo Perez," "Música en Guatemala."

91. See Nelson, *Reckoning*, 86–114, on horror and horror films in the Guatemalan body politic as a whole.

92. These examples of de a pie historical memory are from real conversations. The first comment referred to the military government's embrace of cooperatives under Kjell Eugenio Laugerud García (1974–78). The phrasing *el cerote de Kjell* (pr. "shell") is syntactically common. *Cerote* functions in a way akin to "motherfucker" in U.S. street English; it can be insulting or appreciative.

93. Camus, *Colonia Primero de Julio*, 204n3; Escobar Urrutia, "Enfrentamientos y violencias juveniles," 66; Sierra Marroquín, "Música en Guatemala," 321; *Siglo Veintiuno*, 17 July 1993, 16.

94. Camus, *Colonia Primero de Julio*, 210, 210n11.

95. Levenson argues that the street gangs became more violent over time, as "necroliving" became a way of life. She makes a "plea to pay heed to the historical agency of horror and trauma" even though it is impossible to "prove" the direct connection between state terror and phenomena on the street (*Adiós Niño*, 6–7, 17).

CHAPTER 2: "AMERICAMORFOIS"

1. QP stands for *¿qué putas?*
2. J. Scott, *Domination*. On humor and violence, see Nelson, *Finger in the Wound*. On the "aesthetics of vulgarity," see Mbembe, *On the Postcolony*.
3. Serrano Elías, *Guayaba tiene dueño*.
4. The album was released on the DIDECA label in 1987. Song by Paulo Alvarado, with kind permission; see Alvarado, "Alto al fuego Alux Nahual original," posted by AluxNahualTV, 9 April 2013, YouTube video, 3:34, www.youtube.com /watch?v=4maslpo5zw4.
5. Alux Nahual, "500 Años"; song by Alvaro Rodrigo Aguilar, used with kind permission.
6. Sevilla-Buitrago, *"Urbs in Rure."* The author uses a Lefebvrian notion of space as perceived, conceived, and lived. In dialogue with the works of David Harvey, he applies the ongoing moment of Marxian primitive accumulation to the phenomenon of planetary urbanization. The "process of original extended urbanization" is an "ongoing dynamic" that is "characterized by the continuous reworking and creative destruction of already capitalist realms of social life, as the subsumption of labor is deepened and new aspects of sociality are commodified and recommodified" (241).
7. Among the military elite, old-school developmentalists opposed probusiness neoliberals; see FLACSO, *Guatemala,* 4:326. Of particular importance during this early period of what Schirmer, *Guatemalan Military Project,* calls the "civilian-military pact" was the Thesis of National Stability, promulgated by the minister of defense, Col. Alejandro Gramajo. Building on earlier programs, it wove together military issues and development. Meanwhile, the URNG espoused "neoliberal" measures such as bringing in transnational mining companies and promoting NTA-like agricultural commercialization. URNG, "Posición de la URNG sobre la operación de empresas de carácter transnacional dedicadas a la explotación de recursos naturales en todo el territorio de Guatemala," corrected draft of communiqué, July 1986, CIRMA-AH-037/C1/D68, 1; URNG, "Carta política por la salvación nacional," communiqué, 1 October 1987, CIRMA-AH-037/C1/D53, 4–5.
8. Inter-American Development Bank, "Industrial Policy in Guatemala: A Case of Policy Inertia under Changing Paradigms," IDB Working Paper Series, No. IDB-WP-169, prepared by Mario Cuevas, Sigfrido Lee, and Bismarck Pineda, www .econstor.eu/handle/10419/89177, i.
9. Governments of Costa Rica, El Salvador, Guatemala, Honduras, and Nicaragua, "Acuerdo de Esquipulas II," (7 August 1987), www.acnur.org/fileadmin/Documentos

/BDL/2004/2530.pdf; URNG, "Declaración de la Comandancia General de la URNG acerca de la Reunión de Esquipulas II," communiqué, August 1987, CIRMA-AH-037/C1/D54, 2; URNG, "Guatemala, la democracia negada," propaganda, 1988, CIRMA-AH-037/C1/D43.

10. FLACSO, *Guatemala*, 1:326.

11. Comité de Unidad Campesina, "Hoy el CUC crece y se desarrolla para aportar en el fortalecimiento de la lucha popular," September 1986, CIRMA-AH-003/C09/S3/D90, 3; Domingo Hernández and Francisca Álvarez, "Algunos elementos de aproximación a la situación de la población india guatemalteca," OR internal work material, July 1986, Mexico, CIRMA-AH-003/C08/S3/D01, 1–3; Cooperación Voluntaria/Octubre Revolucionario, *Opinión Política*, no. 10 (January 1987): 4–5, CIRMA-AH-003/C07/S1/D285; URNG, *Boletín Internacional*, no. 1 (November 1986): 5–6, CIRMA-AH-037/C1-60, 5–6; URNG, "Hechos y políticas en Guatemala, abril–junio 1987," CIRMA-AH-037/C2/D72, 49–50. Major labor confederations included the Coordinadora de Sindicatos de Trabajadores del Estado; the Sindicato de Trabajadores de la Educación de Guatemala; the Federación de Sindicatos de Trabajadores del Estado; and local groups. On social movement webs, see Bruey, *Bread, Justice, and Liberty*.

12. FAR, "Tesis de organización de las Fuerzas Armadas Rebeldes (FAR): Contenido y forma; estructura y funcionamiento," internal work material, February 1987, CIRMA-AH-037/C93/D13; OR/PGT (6 de Enero), "Comunicado de Octubre Revolucionario OR-PGT: Las delegaciones de Dirección de OR y PGT acordaron la resolución en contra de las acciones realizadas por la URNG," 10 September 1989, CIRMA-AH-003/C07/S1/D295, 1–2; URNG, "Panorama básico sobre la situación militar actual en Guatemala desde 1986 a 1989," communiqué, ca. late 1989–early 1990, CIRMA-AH-037/C1/D36, 2–5.

13. FLACSO, *Guatemala*, 4:30, 195–96; URNG, "Siete años de lucha: Mensaje de la Comandancia General de la URNG," flyer, 7 February 1989, CIRMA-AH-037/C1/D37, 2–8; URNG, "Propuesta para una reunión con la participación del Gobierno, Ejército, los Partidos Políticos, sectores religiosos, los sectores populares y la Comandancia General de la URNG para encontrar la solución al conflicto armado interno," open letter, communiqué, August 1989, CIRMA-AH-037/C1/D21, 2.

14. Zapata, *Proceso de formación*, 80–81. The author discusses "veto players" throughout the work.

15. World Bank, "Social Investment in Guatemala, El Salvador and Honduras: Paper prepared for the Technical Consultation on Poverty Alleviation, Basic Social Services and Social Investment Funds, Paris, June 29 and 30, 1990," CIRMA-AH-019/S96/09-01-06, 16. This internal report was released in 2012 and is available online: http://elibrary.worldbank.org/doi/abs/10.1596/0-8213-3025-X. Summaries of Bolivia's crisis and shock-therapy measures are found in Klein, *Shock Doctrine*, 188–96; and Horton, "Labour Markets."

16. Glaessner et al., *Poverty Alleviation*, v–vii, xii–xiii, 4, 23–24, 31, 55–56; World Bank, "Social Investment in Guatemala."

17. Aid came from donor nations, the World Bank, and the IDB. Social funds active by the end of 1994 included not only FONAPAZ and FIS but also one devoted to community development (the Development Ministry's FDRC, Regional Fund for Community Development, later transferred to the Executive Secretariat of the Presidency and renamed as FSDC, the Solidarity Fund for Community Development) and another, FODIGUA (Fund for Guatemalan Indigenous Development), specifically for the indigenous population. Ibarraran et al., "Welfare Impacts," 4–5.

18. Schirmer, *Guatemalan Military Project*, 101.

19. Beck, *How Development Projects Persist*, 44–47.

20. Thomas, *Regulating Style*, 52–55.

21. Nordstrom, *Global Outlaws*.

22. FLACSO, *Guatemala*, 4:84–85.

23. Alexander, *New Jim Crow*; Briggs, *Somebody's Children*.

24. Camus, *Colonia Primero de Julio*, 213, 213n15; Escobar Urrutia, "Enfrentamientos y violencias juveniles," 53–54. Youth policies are detailed in AVANCSO, *Jóvenes en Guatemala*.

25. The song was rereleased on the 1993 *Americamorfosis* album (Sony Music). The band published 2010 concert footage: "Como un duende: Alux Nahual sinfónico," posted by AluxNahualTV, 4 May 2013, YouTube video, 6:10, www.youtube.com/watch?v=Y4uYa-10vTc.

26. URNG, "Hechos y políticas," 87. For examples of press coverage, see *El Gráfico*, 29 October 1988, 7; and *Prensa Libre*, 2 March 1988, 17; 2 August 1988, 12; 10 November 1988, 4; and 18 July 1989, 8. Collected clippings may be found in CIRMA, GT-CIRMA-AH-038, CIEPRODH, *código* 29, on "niños." On moral panic over *robaniños* and adoption in 1994, see Rothenberg, "Panic of the Robaniños" (see 11–14 on the 1980s). See Briggs, *Somebody's Children*, on adoption; on moral panic and capitalistic change, see Derby and Werner, "Devil Wears Dockers."

27. Rothenberg, "Panic of the Robaniños," 188–89; see also Nelson, *Finger in the Wound*, 64–67.

28. See Frankfurter, *Evil Incarnate*. From the United Kingdom, the panic spread to Kenya and Nigeria (3).

29. Rothenberg, "Panic of the Robaniños," 13. I was present at a 1992 demonstration of street children *("desechables")* in Bogotá who were protesting illegal organ harvesting.

30. Sevilla-Buitrago, *"Urbs in Rure,"* 240.

31. URNG, "Las condiciones de vida en Guatemala," report, April 1990, Centro de Documentación de la URNG, CIRMA-AI I-037/C1/D1, 3–7, 48–50 (quotation on 3).

32. Santa Cruz Mendoza, *Insurgentes*, 71–73. While guerrilla field commanders were overwhelmingly ladino, educated Maya insurgents did occasionally achieve command ranks. See Grandin, *Blood of Guatemala*, 234.

33. See Thomas, *Regulating Style*; E. Fischer, *Cultural Logics*; and Fischer and Benson, *Broccoli and Desire*.

34. Schirmer, *Guatemalan Military Project*, 103–24.

35. Santa Cruz Mendoza, *Insurgentes*, 165, 183, 199–200; URNG, "Partes de Guerra, 21–26 de mayo 1989," communiqué, May 1989, CIRMA-AH-037/C1/D28, 1–4; URNG, "Partes de Guerra, 20–22 de julio 1989," communiqué, July 1989, CIRMA-AH-037/C1/D25, 2; URNG, "Entrevista al Comandante Gaspar Ilom, miembro de la comandancia general de la URNG, en exclusiva para el semanario Crónica," transcript of interview, 1 August 1989, CIRMA-AH-037/C1/D23, 1, 5.

36. Santa Cruz Mendoza, *Insurgentes*, 212–13; Schirmer, *Guatemalan Military Project*, 119.

37. Early in 1991, as part of its change in strategy, the URNG began to distribute comic book–style leaflets in rural areas explaining why they would negotiate with the *ricachones* (rich fat cats). Santa Cruz Mendoza, *Insurgentes*, 213; URNG, booklet on negotiations, January 1991, CIRMA-AH-037/C2/D66.

38. Santa Cruz Mendoza, *Insurgentes*, 210, 213–14; URNG, "El proceso de negociación, situación y perspectivas," Declaración de la Comandancia General de la URNG, 9 October 1991, CIRMA-AH-037/C8/D61.

39. Santa Cruz Mendoza, *Insurgentes*, 2006, 225–27 (quotation on 227).

40. *Central America Report* 18, no. 41 (1991): 315, and 19, no. 36 (1992): 283; Santa Cruz Mendoza, *Insurgentes*, 231–33; URNG, "Verdadera situación de las negociaciones en el tema de los derechos humanos," Declaración de la Comandancia General de la URNG, 5 November 1991, CIRMA-AH-037/C8/D60, 2. For the story of a September 1992 army attack on Volcán de Agua on a Frente Unitario unit led by Sergio Aguilar, a commander born to an elite K'iche' family from Quetzaltenango, see Grandin, *Blood of Guatemala*, 234.

41. "Time to Be Born," *El Regional*, no. 1 (April 1991): 4. *El Regional* is housed at CIRMA (GT-CIRMA-AH-039, Colección Eulalia Camposeco sobre la publicación El Regional). Its numeration was highly idiomatic, consisting (after the first few issues) of *años* (years), sometimes divided by *semanas* (weeks) or *quincenas* (two-week periods) and sometimes into exact date ranges. During some phases of publication, *años* corresponded to *épocas* (epochs). This numbering system was further complicated by the addition of topical and regional supplements in the mid-1990s. Citations are provided exactly as they appear in the printed versions.

42. "Crisis and Identity," *El Regional*, no. 1 (April 1991): 5.

43. On development and counterinsurgency, see Schirmer, *Guatemalan Military Project;* and Way, *Mayan in the Mall*. On Protestantism, see Garrard, *Terror in the Land;* Garrard, *Protestantism in Guatemala*. *El Regional*, no. 3 (June 1991): 2, 4; no. 15 (2a Quincena February 1992): 4, 9.

44. Santos A. García Domingo, letter, *El Regional*, no. 16 (1a Quincena March 1992): 7.

45. *El Regional*, época 3, año 3, no. 91 (12–18 November 1993): 22–23 (quotation on 22).

46. *El Regional*, época 3, año 2, no. 28 (12–18 July 1992): 1–2 (quotation on 16); no. 60 (7–13 March 1993): 1–3; época 3, año 3, no. 87 (15–21 October 1993): 3; año 4,

no. 114 (20–26 May 1994): 19. See also *La Hora,* 19 September 1992, 2; 20 September 1992, 5; and 3 October 1992, 5.

47. This observation is based on a reading of the paper over the period. See, for example, *El Regional,* año 2, no. 28 (12–18 July 1992); and año 2, no. 24 (3a Semana June 1992): 14; año 4, no. 110 (22–28 April 1994): 17.

48. *El Regional,* año 2, no. 28 (12–18 July 1992): 1–2.

49. This observation comes from interviews; the Led Zeppelin memory was provided by an academic who was in Huehuetenango in 1970. On the habitus, see Bordieu, *Distinction.*

50. Sierra Marroquín, "Música en Guatemala," 309–19. On new regional marimba and *son huasteco* (western Guatemalan/Mexican traditional music) bands, see *El Regional,* no. 14 (1a Quincena February 1992): 17, 19.

51. The population of over eighty thousand sustained itself by small-scale agriculture and seasonal migration to Pacific-coast plantations. They also had an expanding network of *tiendas* (package stores), where many contraband goods from Mexico were sold, as well as clothing cottage industries, where garments were produced using contraband Mexican cloth. OR, Colectivo para Trabajo Étnico, "El poder local en San Miguel Acatán," internal work material, ca. late 1980s–early 1990s, CIRMA-AH-003/C09/S3/D110, 1–12, quotation on 6.

52. Consejo de Comunidades Étnicas Runujel Junam, "Por una sociedad justa y humana, porque todos somos Runujel Junam (Todos Iguales), y por qué en nuestra tierra 'haya paz, mucha paz,'" ca. 31 July 1988, Santa Cruz del Quiché, CIRMA-AH-037/C12/D44. The CERJ was a member of the UASP (Unidad de Acción Sindical y Popular; Union and Popular Action Unity).

53. FLACSO, *Guatemala,* 3:68. These groups also worked with the Academia de las Lenguas Mayas de Guatemala, founded in 1984.

54. Coordinación Maya Majawil Q'ij (El Nuevo Amanecer), boletín no. 1, leaflet, 17 September 1991, CIRMA-AH-037/C12/D74; Coordinación Maya Majawil Q'ij, "Tecún Umán, símbolo de resistencia de nuestros pueblos," comunicado, 20 February 1992, Olintepeque, CIRMA-AH-037/C12/D73, 2–3; Coordinación Maya Majawil Q'ij, "Vida, resistencia y futuro," booklet, 12 October 1992, CIRMA-AH-037/C12/D72, 8, 15; Coordinación Maya Majawil Q'ij, "Que es Majawil Q'ij," booklet, ca. early 1993, CIRMA-AH-037/C12/D69.

55. Coordinación Maya Majawil Q'ij, "Tecún Umám y Rigoberta Menchú Tum: Conmemoramos el día de Tecún Umám recordando las grandes batallas de nuestros pueblos por conquistar nuestra libertad," comunicado, 20 February 1993, Santa Cruz del Quiché, CIRMA-AH-037/C12/D68, 1–5; "Petición pública de participación del Pueblo Maya en el proceso diálogo-negociación por la paz," master copy of *campo pagado* by Organizaciones y Agrupaciones del Pueblo Maya, January 1992, CIRMA-AH-037/C8/D59, 1.

56. *El Regional,* época 3, año 3, no. 88 (22–28 October 1993): 21.

57. Coordinación de Organizaciones del Pueblo Maya de Guatemala, "Identidad y derechos de los pueblos indígenas: Propuesta para las negociaciones de paz," 1994,

CIRMA-AH-003/C09/S3/D107; Bastos and Camus, "Difficult Complementarity," 79; Konefal, *Every Indio Who Falls,* 174. On these groups' role in the body politic, see Nelson, *Finger in the Wound.*

58. Municipalidad de Sololá, "Plan Comunitario de Desarrollo de la Cabecera Municipal, Años 2002–2010," 6, courtesy of the Municipalidad de Sololá; Barrios, *Tras las huellas;* Ochoa, *Alcaldías indígenas;* T. Smith, "Democracy Is Dissent." A study of the K'iche' elite of Quetzaltenango is found in Grandin, *Blood of Guatemala.*

59. Alcaldía Indígena de Sololá, "Asociación Guatemalteca de Alcaldes y Autoridades Indígenas–AGAAI-[2]," flyer, 9 March 1996, CIRMA-AH-037/C12/D7, 4; Way, "Movement." On the Mayan movement and indigenous leaders in municipal politics from 1970 forward, see E. Fischer, *Cultural Logics,* 98–107.

60. Sololá's crops are destined primarily for local and national markets, making the area an excellent example of agrarian commercialization associated with but not directly attributable to the NTA boom. This summary is based on numerous visits to and interviews in Sololá from 1991 to 2018, as well as on a reading of its neighborhood-development documents.

61. Unattributed transcript of *cabildo abierto,* 27 July 1992, Sololá, CIRMA-AH-019/S110/10-01-03, 6–8.

62. *Levantamiento de Santiago Atitlán,* posted by Xelani Luz, 7 August 2017, YouTube video, www.youtube.com/watch?v=gioVMa2Kpao.

63. Navarro García, Pérez-Sales, and Fernández-Liria, "Exhumation Processes," 48–83, 50.

64. Ajcalón Choy, "Municipalidad"; T. Smith, "Tale of Two Governments."

65. More districts in the Sololá municipality were winning official representation in the early 1990s; *caserío* Pancá, for example, gained an *alcalde auxiliar* in 1992 who represented the hamlet as a "community mayor" in the Sololá alcaldía. Municipalidad de Sololá, "Plan Comunitario de Desarrollo del Caserío Pancá, Cabecera Municipal de Sololá (2011–2018)," 3, courtesy of la Municipalidad de Sololá.

66. Ajcalón Choy, "Municipalidad," 9n11, 65, 84, 84n104, 85; Barrios, *Tras las huellas,* 378; T. Smith, "Democracy Is Dissent," 19; *Prensa Libre,* 27 March 1990, 27. The group to aid the alcaldía indígena was called the Comité de Apoyo a la Municipalidad Indígena. Other active groups included CONAVIGUA (Coordinadora Nacional de Viudas de Guatemala, the national widows' organization), Usaquil Tinamit, and the CERJ (Consejo de Comunidades Étnicas "Runujel Junam").

67. In Chichicastenango in 1991, for example, the PAC leaders and the mayor got into a violent conflict. *Siglo Veintiuno,* 5 February 1991.

68. See Konefal, *Every Indio Who Falls.*

69. Bastos, *Multiculturalismo y futuro.*

70. I have known "Estuardo" since 2002 and have visited the house to which I refer. It should remembered that "tradition" is a social construction. See Hobsbawm and Ranger, *Invention of Tradition.*

71. The author uses this phrase in explaining his conceptualization of "inner-city street culture," a phrase that is at once apt and a bit of a stretch for rustic and rural-

looking Sololá in the early 1990s. Bourgeois, *Search of Respect,* 8. García Canclini's classic work on "hybrid cultures," *Culturas híbridas,* came out as these changes were underway in agro-urban and urban Guatemala.

72. Brenner, *Implosions/Explosions.*

73. In a radically different context, Guatemalan "bad boy" cultural expressions show what Medovoi, *Rebels,* describes among midcentury U.S. youth in "the new, politicized category of the teenager, a subject occupying a space of autonomous identity, in which free play became an alternative pedagogy, a means of achieving self-determination for a democratic future through a transitional period of independence" (134). Like Medovoi's subjects, agro-urban highland youth were arguably engaging in a "psychopolitics of identity" that began "not with a wounded attachment to one's victimization, but rather with a proud declaration of emergence into power" (5).

74. In 1992, after three years of negotiation with the Permanent Commission of Refugees in Mexico, an agreement for the refugees' return was reached. The camps had been the last place where new guerrillas could be recruited. *Central America Report* 19, no. 26 (1992): 203–4; Santa Cruz Mendoza, *Insurgentes,* 241–24, 255–56.

75. *El Regional,* año 2, no. 32 (9–15 August 1992): 1, 3; Santa Cruz Mendoza, *Insurgentes,* 256; URNG, "La voluntad política se muestra con hechos: La paz es viable si tiene contenido; Declaración de la Comandancia General de URNG," 10 January 1993, CIRMA-AH-019/S139/12-01-04, 1–2.

76. OR and PGT (6 de Enero), "Comunicado de Octubre Revolucionario OR-PGT: Disolución de OR y PGT," October 1992, CIRMA-AH-003/C07/S1/D298, 1; Ciudadanos por la Democracia, "Declaración básica, principios y objetivos de Ciudadanos por la Democracia, ex miembros de OR y PGT," 31 October 1992, CIRMA-AH-003/C07/S1/D299, 1–3; Yolanda Colom, interview with the author, Antigua Guatemala, 5 April 2016; "Insurgencia, pasaron a mejor vida," *Crónica* 6, no. 252 (1992): 27–28, CIRMA-AH-003/C07/S1/D300, 27–28; Mario Payeras, "Carta fraternal de Mario Payeras sobre reflexiones de la experiencia de OR en la hora de reagrupamiento," original copy of letter published in *Momento,* special supplement to *Siglo Veinituno,* 24 January 1993, CIRMA-AH-003/C07/S1/D301, 1–14. After OR's dissolution, still in exile, Payeras founded *Jaguar-Venado,* a literary and cultural magazine, but he never lost his desire for revolutionary change, Yolanda Colom says. *Jaguar-Venado: Revista guatemalteca de cultura y política* 1, no. 4 (1995): 1–48, Mexico City, CIRMA-AII-054/C1/01-02.

77. Santa Cruz Mendoza, *Insurgentes,* 269, 274, 283.

78. *El Regional,* año 2, no. 32 (9–15 August 1992): 10.

79. J. Payeras, *Ruido de fondo,* 22. The novel was first published in 2003.

80. Saldaña-Portillo, *Revolutionary Imagination.*

81. J. Payeras, *Ruido de fondo,* 15–17 (quotations on 13, 29).

82. Castañeda Maldonado dates the origin of *valeverguismo* to the 1970s ("Historia del Rock," 66–67). See also Camus, *Colonia Primero de Julio,* 122–23, 204–11.

83. Sierra Marroquín, "Música en Guatemala," 305, 312. On the Spanish rock explosion, see Pacini Hernandez, Fernández L'Hoeste, and Zolov, *Rockin' Las Américas*, 220–40.

84. Sierra Marroquín, "Música en Guatemala," 302, 322. A more complete list includes "Tzantoid, Extasis, Psycho, Abbadon, Denial, Scars, Yttrium ... Slayer, Carcass, King Diamond, Halloween and Bathory" (302).

85. Camus, *Colonia Primero de Julio*, 213, 213n15; Castañeda Maldonado, "Historia del Rock," 8, 8n11.

86. Sierra Marroquín, "Música en Guatemala," 315; "Giácomo Buonafina Aguilar," WikiGuate, updated 28 September 2018, https://wikiguate.com.gt/giacomo-buonafina-aguilar/.

87. The October 1993 confrontation is covered in Sierra Marroquín, "Música en Guatemala," 322.

88. Camus, *Colonia Primero de Julio*, 212–13; Escobar Urrutia, "Enfrentamientos y violencias juveniles," 7, 73. Private schools mapped onto and helped to create class and caste categories. While anxiety over class and caste status was important, Camus and Escobar also note the role of *gender* anxiety, as young men from the middle and lower-middle sectors banded together to show their bravery and valor.

89. Camus, *Colonia Primero de Julio*, 208; Escobar Urrutia, "Enfrentamientos y violencias juveniles," 65, 65n112; Levenson, *Adiós Niño*, 21, 77; Sierra Marroquín, "Música en Guatemala," 321–22.

90. Antibreaks met one another in their high schools, at school fund-raisers, and in nightclubs. Escobar Urrutia, "Enfrentamientos y violencias juveniles," 66–69. One of Escobar's informants, a "break," described the differences in style: a break was *"caquero"*—of pretentious style—wearing bracelets and high-top sneakers, usually knockoffs, and Mexican- or chicano-style shorts. "Cholebreaks" (where cholero meets *break*) donned U.S. football T-shirts, though any U.S. T-shirt would do, along with moccasins and white socks. "Cholos," who evolved out of the first two groups, had oversized jeans held up with leather belts, white T-shirts, and tattoos (67).

91. Escobar Urrutia, "Enfrentamientos y violencias juveniles," 69.

92. Camus, *Colonia Primero de Julio*, 211–12, 211n13; Escobar Urrutia, "Enfrentamientos y violencias juveniles," 69. I also heard the same claims about wanton violence in Guatemala City in conversations and interviews in the 1990s and early 2000s.

93. Escobar Urrutia, "Enfrentamientos y violencias juveniles," 69–73.

94. Escobar Urrutia, 52, 52n87; URNG, "La Comisión de Derechos Humanos de la ONU pide la abolición de las PAC el SIPROCI," Comunicado del Equipo Político Diplomático, 5 March 1992, CIRMA-AH-037/C2/D60. Schirmer writes that SIPROCI, the Sistema de Protección Ciudadana, an initiative of the Presidential General Staff, "integrated 26,000 agents" from multiple branches of the military and the state and was active from 1988 to 1991 (*Guatemalan Military Project*, 197).

95. Schirmer, *Guatemalan Military Project*, 199.

96. "Ill Treatment of Street Children," Amnesty International, 27 January 1992, www.amnesty.org/en/documents/amr34/005/1992/en/.

97. *Prensa Libre*, 18 February 1991, 6.
98. J. Payeras, *Ruido de fondo*, 12, 17–18. For another reading of the same scene, see Escobar Urrutia, "Enfrentamientos y violencias juveniles," 70.
99. Escobar Urrutia, "Enfrentamientos y violencias juveniles," 72–74.
100. Escobar Urrutia, 74.
101. "Safiroth," "Música en Guatemala: Historia del underground en Guatemala; Sus bandas de ayer y de hoy," *Rock Republik* (blog), 17 June 2010, http://rockrepublik.net/topic/9103/s120/.
102. For another reading of *Ruido de fondo* and other novels from the new generation, see Bentley, "Peripheral Network City."
103. This observation comes from conversations in 1991, 1992, and 1994. A friend from Barrio El Gallito, a Guatemala City slum, made me change out of my black jeans and T-shirt lest I be taken for an antibreak.
104. It should be remembered that Guatemala's historically mobile population had always moved between agrarian areas, large cabeceras, and the capital city, although such transmigration increased from the 1980s forward.
105. José Chamalé, "Una isla en la ciudad: Apuntes de un cantautor," *Noticias de Guatemala*, August 1994.

CHAPTER 3: "NOT FISH, NOT IGUANA"

1. Néstor Galicia, "A 21 años de Libertad de Expresión ¡Ya!," *Prensa Libre*, 17 December 2015, www.prensalibre.com/hemeroteca/a-21-aos-de-libertad-de-expresion-ya. Quotation from José Chamalé, "Una isla en la ciudad: Apuntes de un cantautor," *Noticias de Guatemala*, August 1994.
2. Galicia, "21 años"; Rizzo, *Alternativa;* Galicia, "21 años."
3. Pinzón, quoted in Rizzo, *Alternativa.*
4. "Paz en Iximulew!," *El Regional,* special ed., 29 December 1996, 1.
5. See Pradilla Cobos, "Presente y futuro"; and A. Scott, "Globalization."
6. The literal translation of "neither fish nor iguana" loses the lyric's spirit. I added the definite article to the phrase "not the water" to make the translation fit the rhythm.
7. For information on the band, the album, and downloads, see "Bohemia Suburbana," accessed 7 June 2020, www.bohemiasuburbana.net/. The official video can be accessed on "Bohemia Suburbana: Peces e Iguanas (en Vivo); Lyric Video," posted by Bohemia Suburbana, 6 July 2018, YouTube video, 7:11. www.youtube.com/watch?v = 423AoyJSG9g.
8. *El Regional*, época 3: año 4, no. 130 (9–15 September 1994): 12, 16; no. 133 (30 September–6 October 1994): 11; no. 134 (7–13 October 1994): 19; no. 142 (2–8 December 1994): 4; no. 149 (17–23 February 1995): 14; URNG, *Servicio de información y análisis*, no. 43 (10–15 January 1995), newsletter, 8, CIRMA-AH-019/S139/12-01-07. On scams and pyramid schemes, see Nelson, *Reckoning*. The United Nations changed MINUGUA's official title on various occasions over the

course of its existence, but it was consistently referred to as the "Misión de las Naciones Unidas en Guatemala."

9. See Jonas, *Centaurs and Doves*.

10. MINUGUA, "First Report of the Director of the United Nations Mission for the Verification of Human Rights and of Compliance with the Commitments of the Comprehensive Agreement on Human Rights in Guatemala," 1 March 1995, UN General Assembly, 49th Session, Agenda Item 42, "The Situation in Central America: Procedures for the Establishment of a Firm and Lasting Peace and Progress in Fashioning a Region of Peace, Freedom, Democracy and Development," Annex, undocs.org/A/49/856, pp. 9–12, paras. 27–45.

11. MINUGUA, "First Report of Director," p. 6, para. 15; p. 7, para. 18; pp. 13–14, paras. 50–54; quotation on p. 26, para. 106. On repatriated refugees, see North and Simmons, *Journeys of Fear*; and Taylor, *Return of Guatemala's Refugees*.

12. MINUGUA, "First Report of Director," pp. 31–32, paras. 131–37; *El Regional*, época 3, año 6, no. 212 (28 June–4 July 1996): 2–3.

13. Asamblea de la Sociedad Civil, "Fortalecimiento del poder civil y función del ejército en una sociedad democrática," September 1994, CIRMA-AH-037/C9/D21, 1.

14. Asamblea de la Sociedad Civil, "Aspectos socioeconómicos y situación agraria: Propuesta de consenso," 8 September 1994, CIRMA-AH-037/C9/D22, 1.

15. The 1994 agreements were Comprehensive Agreement on Human Rights (March); Agreement on a Timetable for the Negotiation of a Firm and Lasting Peace (March); Agreement on Resettlement of the Population Groups Uprooted by the Armed Conflict (June); Agreement on the Establishment of the Commission to Clarify Past Human Rights Violations and Acts of Violence (June). A full history is found in Jonas, *Centaurs and Doves*; see especially pages 43–45 and 95.

16. COPMAGUA, "Propuesta para las negociaciones de paz gobierno-URNG, 'Identidad y Derechos de los Pueblos Indigenas,'" 30 May 1994, CIRMA-AH-037/C12/D14, 3–4, 6–8.

17. "Acuerdo sobre identidad y derechos de los pueblos indígenas" (Mexico City: Gobierno de Guatemala y URNG, 31 March 1995) 1; FLACSO, *Guatemala*, 3:75; Bastos and Brett, *Movimiento maya*, 9.

18. URNG, "Guatemala, propuesta a la sociedad: Cuatro objetivos, nueve cambios, cuatro prioridades," flyer, April 1995, CIRMA-AH-037/C2/D40. On "differentiated citizenship," see Sieder, "Customary Law," 97–115, especially 103–5.

19. See, for example, *Identidad*, no. 16, supplement to *Prensa Libre*, 26 August 1995. A thorough treatment is found in Nelson, *Finger in the Wound*.

20. *El Regional*, época 3, año 6, no. 218 (9–15 August 1996): 7.

21. Bastos, *Multiculturalismo y futuro*; Bastos and Brett, *Movimiento maya*; Hale, *Más Que un Indio*; Little, "Outside of Social Movements."

22. Coordinación Maya Majawil Q'ij, *Voz y pensamiento Maya: Periódico de Majawil Q'ij*, November 1995, CIRMA-AH-037/C12, 2; "Declaración pública del Frente Democrática Nueva Guatemala," as emailed to international cooperation groups, 1 July 1995, CIRMA-AH-019/S161/14–01–03; Frente Democrática Nueva Guatemala, "Plan de gobierno, 1996–1999," (October 1995), CIRMA-AH-019

/S161/14-01-03, 22; *El Regional,* época 3, año 5, no. 168 (7–13 July 1995): 2–3; MINUGUA, "Second Report of the Director of the United Nations Mission for the Verification of Human Rights and of Compliance with the Commitments of the Comprehensive Agreement on Human Rights in Guatemala," 29 June 1995, UN General Assembly, 49th Session, Agenda Item 42, "Situation in Central America," Annex, undocs.org/A/49/929, p. 4, para. 9; MINUGUA, "Third Report of the Director of the United Nations Mission for the Verification of Human Rights and of Compliance with the Commitments of the Comprehensive Agreement on Human Rights in Guatemala," 12 October 1995, UN General Assembly, 50th Session, Agenda Item 45, "Situation in Central America," Annex, undocs.org/A/50/482, pp. 28–29, paras. 139–44; Santa Cruz Mendoza, *Insurgentes,* 290–91.

23. Rolando Morán, Comandante en Jefe del EGP, "Comunicado del CEJ en el XXIV aniversario del Ejército Guerrillero de los Pobres -EGP," 25 January 1996, CIRMA-AH-019/S142/12-01-10, 1; Santa Cruz Mendoza, *Insurgentes,* 300–301.

24. Asamblea de la Sociedad Civil, "Aspectos socioeconómicos." See Jonas, *Centaurs and Doves,* 78–81, on debates about the accord.

25. Santa Cruz Mendoza, *Insurgentes,* 316.

26. Santa Cruz Mendoza, *Insurgentes,* 287, 308–11, 316–17; Raúl Molina, "Información sobre el FDNG," memorandum to international community, 25 September 1995, CIRMA-AH-019/S139/12-01-07, 1–5; *El Regional,* época 3, año 5, no. 178 (15–21 September 1995): 6; *La República,* 19 October 1995, 2.

27. Beltranena, quoted in Mario Roberto Morales, "La Guatemala de la posguerra," interview, Politólogo, *Crónica,* 1 July 1994, 22–23, CIRMA-AH-037/C8 /D7, 23. On "Maya hackers," see Nelson, *Finger in the Wound.*

28. The peace process was nearly thrown off course when some renegade ORPA militants kidnapped Olga de Novella, a matriarch of a wealthy, elite family who was in her eighties. In the end Gaspar Ilom resigned from the negotiations in a gesture of repentance and the march to peace went on. URNG, "Declaración de la Comandancia General de la URNG," caso Olga de Novella, 30 October 1996, CIRMA-AH-037/C9/D4, 1–3; Santa Cruz Mendoza, *Insurgentes,* 331–32.

29. *El Regional,* época 3, año 6, no. 212 (28 June–4 July 1996): 2–3.

30. *El Regional,* época 3, año 5, no. 206 (17–23 May 1996): 1, 12; año 6, no. 220 (23–29 August 1996): 2, 6; MINUGUA, "Fifth Report of the Director of the United Nations Mission for the Verification of Human Rights and of Compliance with the Commitments of the Comprehensive Agreement on Human Rights in Guatemala," 19 July 1996, UN General Assembly, 50th Session, Agenda Item 45, "Situation in Central America," Annex, undocs.org/A/50/1006, pp. 6–7, para. 23.

31. "FDNG a partir de 1995," mixed documents, CIRMA-AH-019/S160/14-01-03; "FDNG demanda detener los linchamientos," FDNG press release, 10 April 1996, CIRMA-AH-019/S160/14-01-03; "FDNG a partir de 1995," mixed documents, 13 April 1996, InterPress Service, CIRMA-AH-019/S160/14-01-03; *El Regional,* época, año 5, no. 210 (14–20 June 1996): 9. On similar dynamics in Bolivia, see Goldstein, *Outlawed;* and Goldstein, *Spectacular City.*

32. *El Regional,* época 3, año 5, no. 202 (19–25 April 1996): 7; MINUGUA, "Fifth Report of Director," 19 July 1996, p. 22, para. 117; MINUGUA, "Seventh Report on Human Rights of the United Nations Verification Mission in Guatemala," 10 September 1997, UN General Assembly, 52nd Session, Item 45 of the Provisional Agenda, "Situation in Central America," Annex, undocs.org/A/52/330, p. 14, paras. 77–78.

33. MINUGUA, "Fifth Report of Director" 19 July 1996, p. 4, para. 10; pp. 12–13, paras. 59–60; p. 14, para. 71; p. 17, paras. 83–84; González-Izás, "Labor Contractors."

34. The translation is figurative: "La dimensión de la política de terror en Guatemala es tal y tan prolongada, que difícilmente la misma historia futura pueda registrar su magnitud." URNG, "Guatemala la democracia plena: Meta revolucionaria en el fin del milenio; Orientaciones sobre el momento actual," booklet, June 1996, Ediciones URNG, CIRMA-AH-019/S142/12–01–10, 16.

35. At the time of this writing (ca. 2019), official tracks and lyrics were available on the Bohemia Suburbana website, www.bohemiasuburbana.net/.

36. See Bordieu, *Distinction.*

37. J. Payeras, *Ruido de fondo,* 55–57.

38. Rizzo, *Alternativa.* It should be noted that Andrade himself never finished school and that he was hardly a fresa; born in the San Marcos department, he moved to the capital in childhood and had a rough upbringing that differentiated him from the other members of the rock scene. Fernández, *Si aquí se pudiera vivir,* 18, 35–38.

39. Rizzo, *Alternativa.*

40. On 5 October 1995 soldiers killed eleven and wounded thirty more in the Aurora 8 de Octubre returnee community located in Xamán, Alta Verapaz. MINUGUA, "Fourth Report of the Director of the United Nations Mission for the Verification of Human Rights and of Compliance with the Commitments of the Comprehensive Agreement on Human Rights in Guatemala," 24 February 1996, UN General Assembly, 50th Session, Agenda Item 45, "Situation in Central America," Annex, undocs.org/A/50/878, pp. 6–7, paras. 25–32; URNG, "Partes de guerra, 1995," CIRMA-AH-037/C2/D37, 1.

41. From the *Hasta Atrás* masthead: "Hasta Atrás están: Pablo Gordillo, Lucía Escobar, Kurt Zierlein, Edgar Calderón, Igor Castillo, Germánico Barrios, Giacomo Buonafina, Ricardo Miranda, Liza Flores, Luis Urrutia, Luís Villacinda, Jessica Lagunas, Ana Carpio, Estuardo "Jaras" Jaramillo." *Hasta Atrás,* no. 1 (31 October 1995): 2, GT-CIRMA-AH-098/paquete no. 1; Sierra Marroquín, "Música en Guatemala," 315. For the lively afterlife of *Hasta Atrás* on the internet, see "Primera Generación Records: 1997; Fragmentos de conciencia," *El Blog de Topo,* 22 August 2008, http://elblogdeltopo.blogspot.com/2008/08/primera-generacin-records-1997.html; Pablo Bromo, "111 Minutos de flashback: Anotaciones dispersas sobre Bohemia Suburbana," esQuisses, 8 March 2013, www.esquisses.net/2013/03/111-minutos-de-flashback-anotaciones-dispersas-sobre-bohemia-suburbana/; Rockchapin.com Facebook fan page, photo of *Prensa Libre* insert *Aula 2000* cover from 27 January 1998, with coverline "Extinción en serie," featuring *Hasta Atrás,* www.facebook.com/rockchapinfanpage

/photos/pb.162845527095240.-2207520000.1457789669./1057981580914959/?type = 3; and "Música en Guatemala: Q-sha," *Rock Republik* (blog), 15 August 2006, http:// rockrepublik.net/topic/1101/so/.

42. *Hasta Atrás,* no. 1 (31 October 1995): 1, 3.

43. Judy Cantor, "The Next Wave," *Miami New Times,* 10 August 1995, www .miaminewtimes.com/news/the-next-wave-6363605; Sierra Marroquín, "Música en Guatemala," 313. An academic overview of the Latin rock phenomenon may be found in Pacini Hernandez, Fernández L'Hoeste, and Zolov, *Rockin' Las Américas;* a journalist account is found in Lechner, *Rock en Español.*

44. *Hasta Atrás,* no. 4 (ca. January 1996): 6.

45. The Foeticide song appears in web searches as "Putrefact Corpse." In *Hasta Atrás* it was called "Putrefact Cunt." Advertisement, Primera Generación Records, in *Hasta Atrás,* no. 1 (31 October 1995): 4.

46. Camus, *Colonia Primero de Julio,* 224, 224n19; *Hasta Atrás,* no. 5 (ca. February 1996): 5; Sierra Marroquín, "Música en Guatemala," 312.

47. Fernández, *Si aquí se pudiera vivir,* 19, 20-24; Sierra Marroquín, "Música en Guatemala," 320. A brief history of Yttrium, as well as a diatribe against DIDECA's lack of support for its artists, may be found in Alejandro Campo, "Yttrium Rock de Guatemala de los años 90," 9 December 2008, http://alexcampocultura.blogspot. com/2008/12/yttrium-rock-de-guatemala-de-los-aos.html.

48. *El Regional,* época 4, año 7, no. 247 (2-8 May 1997): 10.

49. *El Regional*'s "Conctacto juvenil" section was a new venue for pop news. For a Quetzaltenango FM radio "Xela stereo" playlist including Luis Miguel, Juan Gabriel, and John Secada, among others, see *El Regional,* regional supplement, *El Regional de los Huista,* año 4, no. 5 (17-23 March 1995): 14. On Fernando Scheel, see *El Regional,* época 3, año 5, no. 160 (12-18 May 1995): 14; and "Fernando Scheel," Deguate, 14 August 2008, www.deguate.com/artman/publish/personajes_musicos /fernando-scheel.shtml#.WIY6eFMrLX4. See also "Canción de la Firma de la Paz," posted by Álvaro Arzú, 22 March 2011, YouTube video, www.youtube.com/watch?v = Du1f4Pzo4jo.

50. Rizzo, *Alternativa.*

51. MTV was commercialized "KK" (*caca,* crap) for kids with Nintendo and skateboards, *Hasta Atrás* held, as was reality television ("Who cares about the life of some random loser, anyway?"). *Hasta Atrás,* no. 6 (ca. March 1996): 7.

52. These topics are covered in detail in Way, *Mayan in the Mall.*

53. *Hasta Atrás,* no. 1 (31 October 1995): 6-7.

54. *Hasta Atrás,* 6-7.

55. The observations on interclass tensions come from multiple interviews and decades of living and researching in Guatemala. On skateboarding, see *Hasta Atrás,* no. 3 (ca. December 1995): 4-5.

56. *Hasta Atrás,* no. 6 (ca. March 1996): 8.

57. A land invasion refers to a settlement started by squatters on empty land.

58. Sources differ on when the group named itself Alioto Lokos. The bandmates were in and out of Iqui Balam; the histories of the two organizations are intertwined

but not one and the same. Desobedientes, "Alioto Lokos-Sobre la faz de la tierra (2010)," *Desobedece* (blog), 13 November 2011, https://desobedientes.noblogs.org/post/tag/mario-alioto-lopez-sanchez/; Carolina Gamazo, "Iqui Balam: De cómo el teatro le dobló el brazo a la violencia en Guatemala," *Fronterad* (Madrid), 9 October 2015, www.fronterad.com/?q = iqui-balam-como-teatro-le-doblo-brazo-a-violencia-en-guatemala; "Aborigen Salvaje, hip hop crudo y salvaje," *La Hora*, 11 December 2015, http://lahora.gt/aborigen-salvaje-hip-hop-crudo-y-salvaje/; Sierra Marroquín, "Música en Guatemala," 322–27.

59. Alioto Lokos and Bacteria Soundsystem Crew, "Qué Pasó?," song and music video, dir. Pepe Orozo, 2010, YouTube video, uploaded by Zanate Mojado, 19 November 2010, www.youtube.com/watch?v = Vvujl7Ht6Z8.

60. Carolina Gamazo, "De la pandilla al arte," *Plaza Pública*, 31 July 2015, www.plazapublica.com.gt/content/de-la-pandilla-al-arte.

61. Zamora Mejía, *San Miguel Totonicapán*; ASIES, *Compendio de historia*, 157.

62. UN General Assembly, 51st Session, Agenda Item 40, "Situation in Central America," 30 June 1997, undocs.org/A/51/936, p. 14, para. 66; *El Regional*, época 4, año 6, no. 240 (8–14 March 1997): 10. On *desmadre*, a Mexican loanword, see Zolov, *Refried Elvis*, 27, 269n53.

63. Pradilla Cobos, "Presente y futuro."

64. "Metrópolis 2010: Plan de desarrollo metropolitano," 1995, Municipalidad de Guatemala. On Guatemala City's growth, see Way, *Mayan in the Mall*.

65. Raúl Cuellar Betancourt and Josué Samayoa Herrera, *Niñez de la calle y opinión pública*, (Guatemala: Programa de Atención, Movilización e Incidencia por la Niñez y la Adolescencia [PAMI], November 1996), CIRMA-AH-054/C5/103; María Eugenia Villarreal and Carlos Peralta Chapetón, *Menores trabajadores en labores de alto riesgo*, tomo 2, *Sectores productivos de la construcción y cohetería* (Guatemala: PAMI, January 1996), CIRMA-AH-054/C5/104, 13–14, 18–20, 37–43.

66. "Minimercado La Democracia," advertisement insert, *El Regional*, época 4, año 7, no. 260 (1–7 August 1997): 1–5.

67. *El Regional*, época 4, año 7, no. 272 (24–30 October 1997): sección *El Regional de Xela*, no. 38, p. 3.

68. Graphic details of the Quetzaltenango death squads may be found in *El Regional*, época 4, año 7, no. 274 (7–13 November 1997): sección *El Regional de Xela*, no. 39, pp. 1–2; época 4, año 7, no. 275 (14–20 November 1997): sección *El Regional de Xela*, no. 41, pp. 1–2. The transvestite prostitution scare is covered in *El Regional*, época 4, año 8, no. 316 (18–24 September 1998): sección *El Regional de Xela*, no. 82, pp. 1–2. For details on the phenomenon around the nation, see *El Regional*, época 4, año 8, no. 302 (12–18 June 1998): 1–3; MINUGUA, "Ninth Report on Human Rights of the United Nations Verification Mission in Guatemala," 10 March 1999, UN General Assembly, 53rd Session, Agenda Item 44, "The Situation in Central America: Procedures for the Establishment of a Firm and Lasting Peace and Progress in Fashioning a Region of Peace, Freedom, Democracy and Development," Annex, undocs.org/A/53/853, p. 5, para. 17; MINUGUA, "Eighth Report on

Human Rights of the United Nations Verification Mission in Guatemala," 15 June 1998, UN General Assembly, 52nd Session, Agenda Item 45, "Situation in Central America," Annex, undocs.org/A/52/946, pp. 4–5, paras. 14–22.

69. *El Regional* opined that perhaps the cult members had come from Costa Rica, from where they had recently been ejected, and noted that they were also proselytizing in El Salvador and Honduras. By October the government had ordered the expulsion of eight Japanese and one Brazilian Moonies at their visas' expiration. *El Regional,* época 4, año 7, no. 263 (22–28 August 1997): 3; *El Regional,* época 4, año 7, no. 270 (10–16 October 1997): sección *El Regional de Xela,* no. 36, p. 5.

70. *El Regional,* época 4, año 8, no. 295 (24–30 April 1998): sección *El Regional de Huehue,* no. 61, p. 2. Huehuetenango's Centro Comercial El Triángulo was constructed between 1996 and 1998. *El Regional,* época 4, año 8, no. 321 (23–29 October 1998): sección *El Regional de Xela,* no. 87, pp. 13–15.

71. *Controversia: Revista Huehueteca,* año 1, no. 5 (December 1997): 28. In CED-FOG vertical archive.

72. "Reflexiones y propuestas iniciales para un plan de seguridad ciudadana en el departamento de Huehuetenango," unattributed draft report, ca. early 1997, CEDFOG HA/363/R4/005615, 1–5, 10–12.

73. *Controversia,* año 1, no. 3 (June–July 1997): 5, 12–13.

74. "Reflexiones y propuestas," 5.

75. *El Regional,* época 4, año 8, no. 299 (22–28 May 1998): 1–3.

76. *Controversia,* año 1, no. 3 (June–July 1997): 5.

77. *El Regional,* época 4, año 7, no. 252 (6–12 June 1997): 2, 5. All of this socioeconomic change was happening in advance of the "telecommunications revolution." Barillas, for example, touted the addition of four pay phones (it already had one) as late as 1998. *El Regional,* época 4, año 8, no. 295 (24–30 April 1998): sección *El Regional de Huehue,* no. 61, p. 6.

78. Barillas, with a population of just over eighty-one thousand, classified over 90 percent of its population as rural in 1999. "Plan estratégico municipal, Municipio de Barillas, departamento de Huehuehtenango" (Barillas: Cooperación Española and Unidad Técnica de Planificación Municipal, Barillas, 1999), CEDFOG H/338.9/B3/004940, 3, 16, 18, 67.

79. *Ye' Qatanum: El Aguacateco* (Aguacatán), regional newspaper, housed in CEDFOG vertical archive, año 1, no. 1 (January–February 1998): 4. Aguacatán is multilingual; besides Awakateko, Chalchiteko, K'iche', and Mam are also spoken in the municipality. Spelling of these languages varies; they are sometimes seen as Awakateco and Chalchiteco.

80. *Ye'Qatanum: El Aguacateco,* año 1, no. 1 (January–February 1998): 1–2; año 1, no. 2 (March–April 1998): 4.

81. *Ye'Qatanum: El Aguacateco,* año 1, no. 3 (June 1998): 3, 4, 14. Aguacatán, like many highland communities, had been undergoing a process of modernization that dated to the 1944 revolution and accelerated in the developmentalist 1960s. See Brintnall, *Revolt against the Dead.*

82. Fink, *Maya of Morganton*.

83. Coordinación de ONG y Cooperativas CONGCOOP, "El impacto de las migraciones de guatemaltecos al exterior, reflexiones y datos iniciales: Memoria de un Taller," 1997, (Mixco), CEDFOG HF/304.82/I4/003070, 13. Male migration also caused gender imbalance and changes in gender roles (25–28).

84. Unlike their parents, the new generation of youth was getting basic schooling; the number of preschools and primary schools doubled or more over the period. Ramírez Raymundo, "Financiamiento de la producción," 7–31, 50.

85. *El Regional,* época 4, año 8, no. 307 (17–23 July 1998): 1–2.

86. I have argued elsewhere that, in some instances, the grassroots agro-urban gangs of the 1990s could be read as expressing an inchoate and ludic, but discernable, social commentary (Way, "City Streets"). My analysis follows Guha, *Elementary Aspects,* in seeing the grassroots gangs as generally being a protopolitical popular reaction to a criminalizing body politic and lack of economic opportunity at a time of rapid financialization and commercialization. I also see the agro-urban gangs—like other globalized, youthful cultural expressions in the provinces—as evidence of the new generations' rejection of what Guatemalans call "servility" as a cultural form.

87. *El Regional,* época 3, año 3, no. 95 (10–16 December 1993): 8; Way, "City Streets."

88. *El Regional,* época 4, año 7, no. 256 (4–10 July 1997): 8.

89. *El Regional,* época 4, año 7, no. 261 (8–14 August 1997): sección *El Regional de Huehue* (insert), no. 27, pp. 5, 10, 3.

90. *El Regional,* época 4, año 7, no. 272 (24–30 October 1997): sección *El Regional de Huehue,* no. 38, p. 3; no. 43, p. 3.

91. *El Regional,* época 4, año 8, no. 326 (27 November–3 December 1998): 12.

92. URNG, "URNG: El partido político que Guatemala necesita," 21 March 1997, CIRMA-AH-037/C2/D26, 6.

93. MINUGUA, "Seventh Report on Human Rights," 10 September 1997, pp. 3–4, para. 14; UN General Assembly, 52nd Session, Agenda Item 45, "The Situation in Central America: Procedures for the Establishment of a Firm and Lasting Peace and Progress in Fashioning a Region of Peace, Freedom, Democracy and Development: United Nations Verification Mission in Guatemala [MINUGUA], Report of the Secretary-General," 4 February 1998, undocs.org/A/52/757, p. 12, para. 64. On the police, see Weld, *Paper Cadavers*.

94. Comisión Especial de Incorporación, "Incorporación: Acuerdo sobre bases para la Incorporación de la Unidad Revolucionaria Nacional Guatemalteca a la Legalidad," November 1998, CIRMA-AH-037/C9/D2, 4–14; "Fundación Guillermo Toriello," flyer, January 1999, CIRMA-AH-037/C2/D16; UN General Assembly, "Situation in Central America," p. 14, para 79–81.

95. Luz Méndez, Equipo de Trabajo Internacional, URNG, "El papel de las mujeres en la URNG," October 1997, internal work document, CIRMA-AH-037/C2/D19, 1–3.

96. *El Regional,* supplement, *Yejonel, Cooperación en la Acción, Iximulew, Organo divulgativo para el Decenio del Pueblo Maya,* no. 1 (November 1995): 5; *El Regional,* época 3, año 5, no. 188 (24–30 November 1995): 13.

97. See Grandin, *Blood of Guatemala,* 227.

98. Coordinación Maya Majawil Q'ij, "Elecciones 1995: El voto Maya," flyer, 1995, CIRMA-AH-037/C12/D63, 7–8; Coordinación Maya Majawil Q'ij, *Voz y pensamiento Maya,* 2; Nukuj Ajpop, "Declaración de creación del Nukuj Ajpop," 10 July 1995, CIRMA-AH-037/C12/D10; Nukuj Ajpop, "¡Por nuestro derecho a la participación política a todos los niveles!" ca. mid-July to early November 1995, CIRMA-AH-037/C12/D8, 3; Nukuj Ajpop, "Por una Guatemala democrática, pluricultural y multilingüe," manifesto, 18 July 1995, CIRMA-AH-037/C12/D9.

99. Nukuj Ajpop, "Por una Guatemala democrática," 1.

100. For more on this election, see Ajcalón Choy, "Municipalidad"; T. Smith, "Tale of Two Governments"; and Way, "Movement."

101. MINUGUA, "Suplemento regional del tercer informe (A/53/421), Oficina Regional de Sololá y Oficina Subregional de Chimaltenango," 28 September 1998, Wikisource, https://es.wikisource.org/wiki/MINUGUA,_Oficina_regional_de _Solol%C3%A1_-_Suplemento_del_Tercer_Informe, pp. 1–2, para. 5.

102. Ajcalón Choy, "Municipalidad"; Barrios, *Tras las huellas,* 376–77; T. Smith, "Democracy Is Dissent," 20.

103. T. Smith, "Democracy Is Dissent," 20.

104. Ajcalón Choy, "Municipalidad," 126–29. Researchers interested in the zotz' should note that the spelling of the word varies.

105. "La cueva de los murciélagos de Sololá," Facebook, accessed 27 December 2017, www.facebook.com/Aza202/ (site discontinued).

106. *Ye'Qatanum: El Aguacateco,* año 1, no. 3 (June 1998): 3, 4, 14.

107. "Someone Made Lotería for Millennials and It's for Sure Gonna Sell Out Fast," *Vívala,* 27 July 2017, www.vivala.com/identity/loteria-for-millennials/7199.

108. *El Regional,* época 4, año 8, no. 296 (1–7 May 1998): sección *El Regional de Huehue,* no. 62, sección *Poder Local,* año 1, no. 5 (May 1998): 2; no. 318 (2–8 October 1998): sección *El Regional de Xela,* no. 82, sección *Poder Local,* año 1, no. 10 (October 1998): 2–3.

109. Advertising supplement, Centro Comercial El Triángulo TRI, *El Regional,* época 4, año 8, no. 321 (23–29 October 1998): sección *El Regional de Xela,* no. 87, pp. 13–15; *El Regional,* época 4, año 8, no. 307 (17–23 July 1998): 9.

110. Barrios, *Tras las huellas,* 376; *Escúchennos... Qué significa ser niño/a o joven en Guatemala* (Guatemala: PAMI, June 1998), CIRMA-AH-054/C4/101, 9, 22–23, 26–27.

CHAPTER 4: "IF ONLY YOU COULD LIVE HERE"

1. Fernández, *Si aquí se pudiera vivir;* Guinea Diez, *Gramática,* 55. This essay, from a book of the author's collected works, appeared in the September 2002 *Revista Magna Terra,* a publication of Magna Terra, which Guinea founded in 1994.

2. Mario Sosa, "De la incompetencia y los retos de la izquierda en Guatemala," Centro de Medios Independientes, 17 July 2015, https://cmiguate.org/de-la-incompetencia-y-los-retos-de-la-izquierda-en-guatemala/.

3. Guinea Diez, *Gramática,* 201, 202–3 (emphasis added).
4. Dussel, *Twenty Theses on Politics,* 78–79.
5. This had been true of cultural forms for centuries, explaining Guatemala's remarkable cultural retention—a retention that, far from being timeless "tradition" had evolved over the years. Processions, devil burnings, and holidays marked by specific costumes and rituals have diversified but not disappeared since the widescale entry of globalized music, films, television, and web-based content. See Díaz Castillo, *Cultura popular.*
6. *Encarnar(se)* captures the Sein-to-Dasein transition in a way no English verb can match. The phrase *el mundo al revés,* meanwhile, appears in dozens of Spanish-language songs.
7. Rizzo, *Alternativa,* scene change at 1:09:35.
8. Ixtahuacán's miners had led a historic protest march to the capital in 1977; its residents later became protagonists in the antimining movement of the 2000s. Marcelo Colussi, "Entrevista al grupo 'Sobrevivencia,' de Guatemala: No deben existir barreras culturales," *Argenpress Cultural,* 29 November 2008, http://cultural.argenpress.info/2008/11/entrevista-al-grupo-musical.html; Rock Chapin Retro, "Sobrevivencia: B'itzma," 8 December 2009, https://rockchapinretro.blogspot.com/2009/12/sobrevivencia-bitzma.html; "Sobrevivencia-Guatemala," *Centroamericanto,* 10 January 2009, https://centroamericanto.net/2009/01/10/sobrevivencia-guatemala/ (quotation). A literary critic later called Sobrevivencia a "space of resistance and accommodation"; Valle Escalante, "Discursive Economy," 33.
9. An earlier instance of privatization was Aviateca, the state-owned airline, which became a part of TACA (Transportes Áeros del Continente Americano) in 1989. The IDB and the World Bank promoted privatization and bank reforms, in particular through a Financial Sector Modernization Program that dated to 1993. According to Guerra-Borges, 1994 banking laws had "privatized the financing of the state" by reducing the role of the central bank, the Banco de Guatemala (Banguat), and opening the door to private finance. Instead of selling bonds to Banguat at 2 percent, the government sold them to private institutions and investors at 8 percent, a move that Guerra-Borges says in part necessitated the state's selling off its productive resources. *Guatemala,* 193, 203, 207; "Country Program Evaluation: Guatemala, 1993–2003," Office of Evaluation and Oversight, Inter-American Development Bank, 10 December 2004, annex 5, pp. 1, 12. Inter-American Development Bank (IDB) papers are available through the organization's online archive: https://publications.iadb.org/en.
10. The privatization of GUATEL (TELGUA by 1998) involved various auctions and name changes. Thanks to a concession from the Cerezo administration, Comcel (Tigo) had offered service in Guatemala since 1989. In 1998 the phone company came under the control of América Móvil, owned by the Mexican billionaire Carlos Slim, whose Claro brand was soon joined by competitors; cell phone penetration grew from half a million users in 1995 to 13.3 million in 2007. Kara Andrade, "Androids Land in Guatemala," *Americas Quarterly,* 18 May 2010, www.americasquarterly.org/node/1557; "La historia de las telecomunicaciones en Guatemala," Jdguillen's Weblog, 15 October 2008, https://jdguillen.wordpress.com

/2008/10/15/hello-world/; "Venta obscura de la telefónica Guatel por Álvaro Arzú," *Prensa Libre,* 9 June 2000, www.prensalibre.com/hemeroteca/venta-obscura-de-la-empresa-telefonica-estatal-guatel-por-el-gobierno-del-pan.

11. See Hudson, *Killing the Host*. As with telecommunications, electricity's privatization had a back-story of transnational and national initiatives, including an IDB loan with a "specific rural expansion objective" begun in 1997 for infrastructure reform in "power, telecommunications, civil aviation and hydrocarbons." Iberdrola of Spain purchased Guatemala's electricity-generating company, and Spanish Unión Fenosa bought the privatized regional distribution companies, DEOCSA and DEORSA. Prices skyrocketed despite a "social tariff" mandating the sale of the first few kilowatt hours at a discount. "Country Program Evaluation," annex 5, pp. 3–4.

12. Banrural was formed in 1998 from BANDESA, the state-owned Banco Nacional de Desarrollo Agrícola (National Agricultural Development Bank), a 1971 creation of the military government. See Way, *Mayan in the Mall,* 126–28; "Banco de Desarrollo Rural S.A. (Banrural)," Instituto de Estudios Peruanos, ca. 2012, http://web.bancosdesarrollo.org/fp_cont_871_ESP.html; Guerra-Borges, *Guatemala,* 207; UN General Assembly, 55th Session, Agenda Item 43, "The Situation in Central America: Procedures for the Establishment of a Firm and Lasting Peace and Progress in Fashioning a Region of Peace, Freedom, Democracy and Development; United Nations Verification Mission in Guatemala [MINUGUA], Report of the Secretary-General," 1 June 2001, undocs.org/A/55/973, pp. 9–10, para. 53.

13. The financial world, in politically incorrect language, dubbed the financial crises of 1997 and 1998 the "Asian Contagion" and the "Russian Flu." ASIES, *Compendio de historia,* 237; IDB, "Financial Sector Reform Program II: Loan Proposal," 1 May 2002, project nos. 1400/OC-GU, GU0119, 4, 7; IDB/OVE, Annex 5, p. 2; "Country Program Evaluation," annex 5; Santo Urías, "Exclusión de activos," 11; Banco de Guatemala, Documentos de Trabajo, No. 102, "Consolidación, concentración y clima de competencia en la industria bancaria de Guatemala durante 1999–2006," 2007, Carlos Gerardo Acevedo Flores, 2007, 3, 6–7, 15–16. Papers from the Banco de Guatemala are available on the organization's online archive. See www.banguat.gob.gt/inc/ver.asp?id=/publica/Investigaciones_Ec/index.htm&e=141231.

14. This investment began in 1993. IDB, "Financial Sector Modernization Program: Loan Proposal," 24 November 1993, project nos. 783/OC-GU, 784/OC-GU, 917/SF-GU, GU0018. Significant advances in education—and particularly in offering bilingual education in Maya-majority areas—are not covered in this work. For an entry, see Maxwell, "Bilingual Bicultural Education."

15. Sosa, "De la incompetencia."

16. *Guatemala.* See also Goldman, *Art of Political Murder.*

17. Comité para el Esclarecimiento Histórico, *Guatemala.* The 1999 referendum would have mandated the use of Mayan languages in the justice, health, and education systems; indigenous issues were one of four areas addressed. FLACSO, *Guatemala,* 3:138; Nelson, *Reckoning,* 49–50.

18. FLACSO, *Guatemala,* 3:79.

19. Dussel, *Twenty Theses on Politics*, 27, 32, 13–19, 23, 24–35. Dussel discusses the pueblo at great length; the term is translated as "the people." Of course, the Guatemalan government had not reflected *potentia* since the 1944–54 democratic revolution; most scholars would locate it in the resistance and the social movements.

20. USAID, "Legacies of Exclusion: Social Conflict and Violence in Communities and Homes in Guatemala's Western Highlands," Guatemala Conflict Vulnerability Assessment, Final Report, Public Version, October 2015, prepared by Tani Adams, www.usaid.gov/sites/default/files/documents/1862/Guatemala_Conflict_Vulnerability_Assessment.pdf, 22. Dussel locates a functioning legal system at the center of a legitimate state. Guatemala lacks this. Dussel, *Twenty Theses on Politics*, 52, 50–55.

21. MINUGUA, "Ninth Report on Human Rights of the United Nations Verification Mission in Guatemala," 10 March 1999, UN General Assembly, 53rd Session, Agenda Item 44, "The Situation in Central America: Procedures for the Establishment of a Firm and Lasting Peace and Progress in Fashioning a Region of Peace, Freedom, Democracy and Development," Annex, undocs.org/A/53/853, p. 16, para. 68.

22. MINUGUA, "Ninth Report on Human Rights," 10 March 1999, pp. 4–5, paras. 13, 15, 17. An example of how varied such groups could be is found in Santiago Atitlán. Its Comité Pro-Seguridad y Desarrollo (Pro-Security and Development Committee) was involved in legal battles with the mayor in 1998–99 but was not the typical antidelinquency sort of group seen elsewhere, having been formed after a December 1990 army massacre to provide security and administer funds from NGOs and foreign organizations. Comité Pro-Seguridad y Desarrollo de Santiago Atitlán, Coordinadora Nacional Indígena y Campesina, "Informe sobre la problemática de Santiago Atitlán y el Comité Pro-Seguridad y Desarrollo (junio 98 a febrero 99)," internal document, 3 March 1999, in CIRMA-AH-019/S143/12–01–10. See also Carlsen, *War for the Heart*.

23. Cooperación Española and Unidad Técnica de Planificación Municipal, "Plan estratégico municipal, Municipio de Barillas, Huehuehtenango," 1999, CEDFOG H/338.9/B3/004940, 3, 16.

24. Thus, on one hand Guatemala had Spanish money pumping into municipal government; on the other it had Spain's "second conquest" of the electric company. Canada (with IDB support) spearheaded DECOPAZ (Desarrollo Comunitario para la Paz), a Community Development for Peace program that promoted local democracy in war-torn departments, even as Canadian gold-industry firms were paving the way for the major conflicts of the first decade of the 2000s. DECOPAZ and Centro Canadiense de Estudios y Cooperación Internacional, microregion final reports, 2001, CEDFOG HF/307.1/D49; Dougherty, "Global Gold Mining Industry," 403–18. See also Solano, *Guatemala*; Solano, "Development and/as Dispossession"; and Way, "Movement."

25. MINUGUA, "Suplemento regional del tercer informe (A/53/421), Oficina Regional de Sololá y Oficina Subregional de Chimaltenango," 28 September 1998, Wikisource, https://es.wikisource.org/wiki/MINUGUA,_Oficina_regional_de_Solol%C3%A1_-_Suplemento_del_Tercer_Informe, pp. 3–4, paras. 19–20.

26. The categories they used in these meetings were economic development, health and housing, education, urbanism and infrastructure, community organization, and the environment. On-the-ground efforts involved not only the drive to create consensus-forging development councils but also huge initiatives in literacy, education, and public health. National roundtables are covered in Zapata, *Proceso de formación*. MINUGUA, "Suplemento regional del tercer informe (A/53/421), Oficina Regional de Quetzaltenango y Oficina Subregional de San Marcos," 28 September 1998, Wikisource, https://es.wikisource.org/wiki/MINUGUA,_Oficina_ regional_de_Quetzaltenango_-_Suplemento_del_Tercer_Informe, p. 1, para. 9–16.

27. The procedures are described in Municipalidad de Sololá, Guatemala, "Plan de desarrollo integral del Municipio de Sololá," September 2002. The various Sololá development plans cited in this chapter are courtesy of the Muncipalidad de Sololá.

28. Municipalidad de Sololá, Guatemala, "Plan Comunitario de Desarrollo [PCD] de la Cabecera Municipal, años 2002–2010," 51, 53, 57, 63, 67, 82–84, 87.

29. Municipalidad de Sololá, "PCD del Centro Poblado Pancá, Periferia Urbana, años 2002–2010," 11–16; "PCD del Caserío Monte Mercedes, Cantón Sacsiguán, anos 2002–2010," 13.

30. Mbembe, *On the Postcolony*, 115; Dussel, *Twenty Theses on Politics*, 15.

31. Radiolatina Sacmixit, Facebook, accessed 24 March 2019, www.facebook .com/Radiolatina-Sacmixit-758327647592866/.

32. Fernández, *Si aquí se pudiera vivir*, 72.

33. La Tona, "Interna/Externa," BMG, recording from Atmósfera Omplug (4–5 November 1999), posted by La Tona-Topic (provided by TuneCore), 13 July 2016, YouTube video, www.youtube.com/watch?v=qO83GuaeNrI.

34. Martín-Barbero, "From Latin America," 43.

35. The dismissal of the new generation typifies discourse in the period. Guinea Diez, *Gramática*, 46–47.

36. "A 20 años de la Casa Bizarra," GT Cultura, ca. 2016, https://gtcultura .com/a-20-anos-de-la-casa-bizarra/; Josseline Pinto, "Metamorfosis de una leyenda: E/X," esQuisses, 7 July 2014, www.esquisses.net/2014/07/metamorfosis-de-una-leyenda-ex/.

37. *La Chalupa*, 2000, CIRMA-AH-098/paquete-1/LE30, 1. This was a single-issue magazine produced with support from the government program ADESCA.

38. Burrell, *Maya after War*, 143–44; see also Burrell, "Intergenerational Conflict."

39. *La Chalupa*, 1, 3, 7–8, 11, 16–17. The cited poem, called "Encargo" in Spanish, is on page 17.

40. See J. Payeras, *Región más invisible*, 49–51.

41. Morales, "Cultura y literatura," 5:50–51.

42. Morales, *Articulación de las diferencias*, 313–22 (quotation on 313), 316–17. For a critique, see Warren, "Indigenous Movements," 165–95, esp. 175–77.

43. Maurice Echeverría, untitled poem, *La Chalupa*, 12.

44. Guinea Diez, *Gramática*, 49–54; originally published in *Magnaterra* 10 (July 2001).

45. Maurice Echeverría, "De uniformes y uniformados," *La Chalupa*, 9–10.

46. *Merriam-Webster*, s.v. "adscription," accessed August 9, 2020, www.merriam-webster.com/dictionary/adscription.

47. On masks and identifications, see Nelson, *Reckoning*, 1–30.

48. ADESCA also paid to publish *La Chalupa*. Ministerio de Cultura y Deportes de Guatemala, "III Informe de ADESCA al Congreso de la República," 2000, https://adesca.org.gt/wp-content/uploads/2016/07/Memoria-de-Labores-ADESCA-2000.pdf, 4.

49. J. Payeras, *Región más invisible*, 59–61; Memoria Virtual Guatemala, "Caja Lúdica," accessed June 2018, www.memoriavirtualguatemala.org/es/caja-l%C3%BAdica; Joselline Pinto, "Sobre la importancia de la eternidad: Generación, encuentro profesional/diagnóstico," esQuisses, 4 May 2015, www.esquisses.net/2015/05/sobre-la-importancia-de-la-eternidad-generacion-encuentro-profesionaldiagnostico/.

50. Ten years later Javier Payeras reflected on this legacy: "The movement of contemporary artists started by the *bizarros* [of the Casa Bizarra] and our counter-culture, far from fracturing, has grown and renovated itself. Festivals in Sololá, San Juan Comalapa, and Quetzaltenango show that something is really happening." (J. Payeras, *Región más invisible*, 67).

51. Barrera Ortiz, *Portillo*, 49. See Televisiete, "Himno Nacional de Guatemala: Varias lenguas," video from "Buenos días nuestro mundo," posted by "Teberodx7 Videos," 20 September 2012, YouTube video, www.youtube.com/watch?v=36TXSh7UXkI.

52. Mago de Oz, "Wizard of Oz," is a Spanish folk-metal band formed in 1988.

53. MINUGUA, "Eleventh Report on Human Rights of the United Nations Verification Mission in Guatemala," 26 July 2000, UN General Assembly, 55th Session, Agenda Item 43, "The Situation in Central America: Procedures for the Establishment of a Firm and Lasting Peace and Progress in Fashioning a Region of Peace, Freedom, Democracy and Development," Annex, undocs.org/A/55/174, p. 14, paras. 68–70; Daniel Valencia Caravantes, "La comunidad que lincha," El Faro, 17 July 2011, www.salanegra.elfaro.net/es/201107/cronicas/4764/La-comunidad-que-lincha.htm. An in-depth analysis is found in Burrell, *Maya after War*, 115–37.

54. Nelson, "Stumped Identities," 314. "I argue that for the Guatemalan nation-state the mujer Maya overcomes the missing Mayan representation in the recent peace process and, like a peg leg, supports the nation's limping political economy," Nelson adds. "For the Mayan cultural rights movement, which must prove itself appropriate to modernity while retaining the tradition that legitimates it, 'she' fills in this impossible divide" (314).

55. Nelson, *Reckoning*, 318–19, 332–33.

56. MINUGUA, "Los linchamientos: Un flagelo que persiste," July 2002, Wikisource, https://es.wikisource.org/wiki/Los_linchamientos:_un_flagelo_que_persiste, paras. 72–74.

57. MINUGUA, "Thirteenth Report on Human Rights of the United Nations Verification Mission in Guatemala," 22 August 2002, UN General Assembly, 57th

Session, Item 38 of the Provisional Agenda, "The Situation in Central America: Procedures for the Establishment of a Firm and Lasting Peace and Progress in Fashioning a Region of Peace, Freedom, Democracy and Development," Annex, undocs.org/A/57/336, p. 5, para. 18. The anthropologist Stener Ekern observed that in Totonicapán "the local Maya authority ... [had] profoundly modernized and democratized" and that people saw themselves more and more as "residents and fellow citizens" rather than as groups of "relatives and in-laws." Still, lynchings in the area were up, and people were rejecting state authority. In August 2001 the government declared a state of siege in Totonicapán during massive demonstrations over tax laws and corruption. Ekern, "Comunidad maya," 202–3.

58. Gobierno de Guatemala, "Plan Nacional de Desarrollo K'atun: Nuestra Guatemala 2032," 2014, Consejo Nacional de Desarrollo Urbano y Rural/SEGEPLAN, 36; Carolina Gamazo, "El ascenso y la caída," *Plaza Pública*, 6 August 2015, www.plazapublica.com.gt/content/el-ascenso-y-la-caida-0; Carolina Gamazo, "Iqui Balam: De cómo el teatro le dobló el brazo a la violencia en Guatemala," *Fronterad* (Madrid), 9 October 2015, www.fronterad.com/?q = iqui-balam-como-teatro-ledoblo-brazo-a-violencia-en-guatemala.

59. Nelson, "Stumped Identities," 314.

60. Viernes Verde, *Remedios para el alma*. The verses of "Requiem en E" speak of national pride and reject the idea that it's better to migrate. See "Requiem en E," provided by TuneCore, posted by "viernesverdeTV," 28 July 2018, YouTube video, www.youtube.com/watch?v = 4_6F3S7DfCo.

61. Hermenegildo Pérez Feliciano, "Letras y acordes de canciones emblemáticas de Sobrevivencia: Grupo rock indígena de Huehuetenango," EDoc, accessed 16 June 2018, https://edoc.site/letras-y-acordes-sobrevivencia-pdf-free.html; Discogs, "Sobrevivencia: Twi' Witz," accessed 29 June 2018, www.discogs.com/Sobrevivencia-Twi-Witz-En-La-Cima-Del-Cerro/release/8998859; Sobrevivencia, "El Grito," posted by Movimiento de Artistas Mayas Ruk'u'x, 19 May 2012, YouTube video, www.youtube.com/watch?v = TxA-2TrHbYc; Sobrevivencia, "La Juventud," posted (with the tagline "este es mayan pride 100% 4 life," by "c4jol4boy,") 12 March 2010, YouTube video, www.youtube.com/watch?v=PaRHRnKw7Xg.

62. Perry, "Love Parade 1996."

63. A. Adams, "Reviving Our Spirits"; Hale, "Does Multiculturalism Menace?"

64. Yagenova, *Protesta social en Guatemala*, 44.

65. Information in this section is based on interviews and conversations in the Lake Atitlán region, mostly between 2003 and 2018. I have changed people's names. I was invited to the full-moon parties but never attended. "Las marimbas del infierno: La película guatemalteca," *Go Revolt!* (blog), 17 December 2010, https://gorevolt.wordpress.com/2010/12/17/las-marimbas-del-infierno-la-pelicula-guatemalteca/.

66. Pamela Saravia, "Vuelve el Rave del Castillo," *Prensa Libre*, 16 January 2013, www.prensalibre.com/espectaculos/vuelve-encanto-castillo_0_848315251.html. The techno scene commercialized quickly; by 2002 a DJ named "Lennyman" was promoting events for Red Bull. Mercedes Vaides, "Lennyman: De los pioneros en la

escena electrónica," *Siglo Veintiuno*, 26 August 2016, http://s21.gt/2016/08/26/lennyman-los-pioneros-en-la-escena-electronica/.

67. *Supositorio*, no. 14, *Fiesta* (La Fosa Común) 26, 16 February 2002, rave/party magazine, Colección Thelma Porres, CIRMA-GT-AH-040, 3, 13.

68. Antigua's after-parties were also part of this phenomenon, and the organizers of such events in the capital, in Antigua, at the lake, and in Quetzaltenango often moved in the same circles. Many of the city's art and literary elite have memories of Panajachel. Javier Payeras, for example, saw his first rock concert there in 1998, when he was fourteen years old; the headline band was Alux Nahual. J. Payeras, *Región más invisible*, 73.

69. "Alhazred," "Música en Guatemala: Rock en la guerra interna de Guatemala," *Rock Republik* (blog), "29 March 2011, http://rockrepublik.net/topic/11988/.

70. *El Regional*, época 3, año 6, no. 227 (11–16 October 1996): 4.

71. The term "Guatemaya" popularized in the early 2000s. The song, by the Barcelona band Barrio Candela (lead singer Dr. Sativo), dates to the late 2007. "Barrio Candela: Guatemaya," posted by Roberto Andrade, 25 September 2012, YouTube video, www.youtube.com/watch?v = mSkDlXSoGMg. On the reactions of Kaqchikel crafts vendors to the identifier "Maya," see Little, "Outside of Social Movements."

72. Craib, *Cartographic Mexico*.

73. I heard innumerable variations of this "agro-urban legend." In some the unknown men were guerrillas who had never surrendered. Others had the sound of a scary story that parents made up to keep their kids in line.

74. Tabal is held on the eighth of December. See El Tabal Sololá, Facebook, December 2017, www.facebook.com/profile.php?id = 100008448601980; Marvin Romero Santizo, "El Tabal: Patrimono cultural de Sololá," posted by Csd Saprissa de Guatemala, 2013, www.scribd.com/doc/187863210/El-Tabal-Patrimonio-cultural-de-Solola-y-Guatemala. Another example of violence in fiestas is Panajachel's Corpus-Christi Baile de los Negritos, which by the 2010s operated under strict regulation after youth battles resulted in injuries.

75. Interviews, Panajachel and Sololá.

76. The television show was dubbed into Spanish in 1999. I have eliminated the accent in the trademark to follow Spanish-language stress.

77. This information comes from dozens of interviews. Several people used the "schoolhouse bell" expression.

78. Dussel, *Twenty Theses on Politics*, 51–53.

79. Congreso de la República de Guatemala, decreto 11–2002, Ley de los Consejos de Desarrollo Urbano y Rural, 12 March 2002; decreto 12–2002, Código Municipal, 2 April 2002; decreto 14–2002, Ley General de Descentralización, 11 April 2002; Presidente de la República, Acuerdo Gubernativo Numero 312–2002, Reglamento de la Ley General de Descentralización, 6 September 2002. The new municipal code also recognized the alcaldía indígena, but, according to Ochoa, it was a "weak recognition," framing such institutions as "entities representative of communities" but not as a form or part of government. *Alcaldías indígenas*, ix, 8–9.

80. See López Castillo, "Análisis del proceso," especially page 29. See also Barrientos, *Participación ciudadana*, 35.

81. Ajcalón Choy, "Municipalidad," 107–9 (on the burning alive threats); T. Smith, "Tale of Two Governments, 26–28; T. Smith, "Democracy Is Dissent," 16, 18, 22–25.

82. Ekern, "Production of Autonomy," 115.

83. DECOPAZ and Centro Canadiense de Estudios y Cooperación Internacional, "Informe final Microregión III, Asociación de Desarrollo Microregional Santa Cruz-ADEMSAC," October 2001, Barillas, CEDFOG HF/307.1/D49, V. 3/005700, 11, 15.

84. The Comisión Departamental de Atención a Conflictos was created in 2001. "Conflictividad en Huehuetenango 2001," SORHUE/ASERI, November 2001, CEDFOG HF/303.6/C6/004768, 3; *El Periódico*, 12 October 2002, 3; *Prensa Libre*, 12 October 2002, 2, 13 October 2002, 6, 22; *Siglo Veintiuno*, 12 October 2002, 8. On Pop Caal and his funeral, see A. Adams, "Reviving Our Spirits," 30.

85. Fernández, *Si aquí se pudiera vivir*, 6, 9, 91–92, 99–100.

86. Nordstrom, *Global Outlaws*, xvii.

87. Fernández, *Si aquí se pudiera vivir*, 62; Jiménez, *Casa de enfrente*. See "La casa de enfrente," WikiGuate, accessed 14 April 2020, https://wikiguate.com.gt/la-casa-de-enfrente/; and "Mi opinión de 'La casa de enfrente,'" *Guate360* (blog), 6 November 2003, www.guate360.com/blog/2003/11/06/mi-opinion-de-la-casa-de-enfrente/.

88. MINUGUA, "Thirteenth Report on Human Rights," 22 August 2002, p. 9, paras. 52–53.

89. Portillo's immunity was revoked in February 2004, and he fled to Mexico. He was extradited back to Guatemala four years later and freed on the day of his return. His ensuing legal battle ultimately resulted in his acquittal, but the United States had him extradited north in 2013. Portillo spent a year in a U.S. prison, returning to Guatemala in 2015, where he launched an unsuccessful congressional run. See Barrera Ortiz, *Portillo*, 203–14, 303–18.

90. Serrano Elías, *Guayaba tiene dueño*, 294.

91. Barrera Ortiz, *Portillo*, 30, 123–27, 153–54, 175, 175n13. Portillo had other accomplishments. He oversaw a more progressive labor code and reforms to the educational system and had more Maya cabinet members than administrations before or after. For another counternarrative on Portillo, see "Alfonso Portillo," Guatemala.com, 8 November 2016, https://aprende.guatemala.com/historia/personajes/presidente-alfonso-antonio-portillo-cabrera-2000-2004/. This piece holds that the importation of Cemento Cruz Azul from Mexico undercut the Novella family and Cementos Progreso and that Tyson and Hudson chicken from the United States undercut companies such as Avícolas Villalobos. The moves in beer got the most press. Ambev's Brahma-brand beer had to be renamed "Brahva" (brave, vicious) in Guatemala, since in chapín, *brahma* means "heat," as in "a dog in heat." On the beverage wars, see Andrés Zepeda, "Viaje al interior de la guerra entre la Gallo y la Brahva," *Nómada*, 21 August 2014, https://nomada.gt/politica/gallo-brahva/.

92. Gobierno de Guatemala, "Pacto Fiscal: Para un futuro con paz y desarrollo," Portal Transparencia Fiscal, 25 May 2000, http://transparencia.minfin.gob.gt/transparencia/BibliotecaDigital/Documentos/Pacto1.pdf.

93. See Nordstrom, *Global Outlaws;* and Nelson, "Stumped Identities."

94. Besides the IDB, the Consultative Group included donor nations, the IMF, the World Bank, the UN, and watchdog groups such as the International Labour Organization. "Country Program Evaluation," 17. Municipal credit had been handled by the government's Municipal Development Institute (INFOM), which arranged poorly documented loans from commercial banks. IDB, "Municipal Development Program Loan Proposal," 5 October 1999, project nos. 1217/OC-GU, GU0134, quotation from Executive Summary, 3.

95. IDB, "Program for Institutional Strengthening and Policy Development in Support of Microenterprises and Small and Medium-Sized Enterprise (MSME) in Guatemala," Donors Memorandum, 27 April 1999, project nos. ATN/MT-6500-GU, TC9805443, Executive Summary, 1; IDB, "Labor Market Program Loan Proposal," 1 May 2002, project nos. 1401/OC-GU, GU0158; IDB, "Line of Credit for Small and Micro Credit Enterprises," Project Concept Document, 24 July 2002, project no. GU0154, 10; IDB, "Program for Training in Social Policy and Program Design and Management, Plan of Operations," 1 July 2003, project nos. ATN/CF-8364-GU, TC0301021, Executive Summary, 1.

The IDB began working with the government in 1998 to restructure the Ministry of Agriculture and Livestock, and in the years ahead it supported "agro-industrial" development in the central, NTA-producing areas of the Chimaltenango and Sacatepéquez departments, soon expanding around the western highlands in partnership with the Aj Ticonel Trading Company and an associated NGO called OPCION (Organización para la Promoción Comercial y la Investigación). IDB, "Support for Restructuring of Food and Agriculture Production Loan Proposal," 16 November 1998, project nos. 1153/OC-GU, GU0070, Executive Summary, 1; IDB, "Competitiveness of Small-Scale Indigenous Farmers," Social Entrepreneurship Program, Memorandum, 18 April 2002, project nos. SP0105020, TC0105020; IDB, "Guatemala: Production and Marketing of Export Crops Grown by Small-Scale Farmers," Social Entrepreneurship Program, Loan and Technical Cooperation, 10 December 2004, project nos. ATN/SF-9004-GU, GU-S1002, SP/SF-04-36-GU, Executive Summary, 1–2; IDB, Secretary to Board of Executive Directors, "Executive Summary of a Proposal for Financing and Technical-Cooperation Funding for a Project to Boost the Competitiveness of Small Specialty Coffee Growers," memorandum, 19 December 2005, PR-3016, project no. GU-S1006. On Aj Ticonel, see also Fischer and Benson, *Broccoli and Desire,* 62–66.

96. Fischer and Benson, *Broccoli and Desire,* 16, 26–27 (quotations on 3–4, 58, 100–105).

97. Thomas, *Regulating Style,* 1, 16–17. In 2001 Mayor Servicios (MASESA) started importing tuc-tucs to Guatemala from India. Valdés Toledo, "Herramientas financieras," 4.

98. J. Scott, *Moral Economy,* 6–7.

99. Way, *Mayan in the Mall*, 74, 152–80. See also Thomas, *Regulating Style*, 58–59.
100. "Checha y su India Maya: El Tuc Tuc, Música de Guatemala," posted by Difosa Music, 27 May 2010, YouTube video, www.youtube.com/watch?v = Kb-6cPQcApk. See also https://chechaysuindiamaya.com/.
101. See Offit, *Conquistadores de la Calle;* and Offit "Cacique for a Neoliberal Age."
102. It is common for the municipality to simply not pay workers. On selling OmniLife, see Nelson, *Who Counts?;* and Kiyosaki, *Rich Dad, Poor Dad.*

CHAPTER 5: "IN THE JAWS OF THESE GRAY CITIES"

1. Landslides buried the village of Panabaj, near Santiago Atitlán, killing more than a thousand people; the government declared the town a mass grave. See Luna, "Assessment and Modelling."
2. *¿Por qué tanta destrucción?*, 58, 71. The Movimiento Tzuk Kim Pop formed in the wake of the Peace Accords. See *Demandas y propuestas políticas de los pueblos indígenas de Iximulew* (Guatemala City: Coordinación y Convergencia Nacional Maya Waqib' Kej, 2015), www.gt.undp.org/content/dam/guatemala/docs/publications/undp_gt_iximulew.pdf, 23.
3. Diaz Negros, "Fuego a mi favor," posted by "diaznegros," 22 August 2008, YouTube video, www.youtube.com/watch?v = WOtUHdwy3vw.
4. See Hjarvard, *Mediatization of Culture.* Yolanda Colom refused to discuss her brother in our interviews. His administration was fraught with scandal, most notably when Rodrigo Rosenberg, an attorney, paid assassins to have himself shot in 2009, leaving a video blaming the Coloms behind.
5. The 2005 youth policy, created through the roundtable method, resulted in a spate of organizations and programs. It was also linked to decentralization. Besides festivals and an anti-AIDS campaign, CONJUVE's biggest efforts were in creating youth commissions in the municipal development committees, the COCODES. Gobierno de Guatemala/MIDES, "Política nacional de juventud, 2012–2020" (Guatemala City: Ministerio de Desarrollo Social [MIDES], Secretaría de Planificación y Programación de la Presidencia [SEGEPLAN], y Consejo Nacional de la Juventud [CONJUVE], 2012), 42–47.
6. *¿Por qué tanta destrucción?*, 71; Luna, "Assessment and Modelling," iii.
7. The Banco de Guatemala claimed that 90,000 Guatemalans had migrated per year—that is, 250 a day—from 1995 to 2002 and that there were an estimated 1.4 million Guatemalans living abroad in 2006, mostly in the United States. "Remittances are the single most important source of foreign exchange in Guatemala, more important than other traditional sources of foreign exchange, like tourism or coffee and sugar exports.... They represent the second largest foreign-exchange source measured as a share of total foreign exchange; just behind total exports, and more important than net capital flows," the central bank reported. Banco de Guatemala,

Documentos de Trabajo, No. 103, "Emigrant Remittances and the Real Exchange Rate in Guatemala: An Adjustment-Cost Story," Juan Carlos Castañeda Fuentes and Juan Carlos Catalán Herrera (Guatemala, 2007), 4–5, 20 (quotation on 5).

8. IDB, "Public Financial Management Reform Program Loan Proposal," 6 June 2006, project nos. 1747/OC-GU, GU-L1005, 4–5.

9. In the IDB's words, "most banks in Guatemala are members of an economic group. These groups are organized informally around the commercial bank in the group. The financial companies in each group focus their services on the industrial, and commercial companies that are members of the group." IDB, "Financial Sector Reform Program II Loan Proposal," 1 May 2002, project nos. 1400/OC-GU, GU0119, 7.

10. Ultimately, depositors with dollar accounts in offshore banks lost money, while national quetzal-denominated accounts were protected. Banco de Guatemala, Documentos de Trabajo, No. 102, "Consolidación, concentración y clima de competencia en la industria bancaria de Guatemala durante 1999–2006," 2007, Carlos Gerardo Acevedo Flores, 2007, 15; Sara Melini y Julio Lara, "Exdirectivos de Bancafé deben ir a la cárcel," *Prensa Libre,* November 3, 2015, www.prensalibre.com/guatemala/justicia/exdirectivos-de-bancafe-deben-ir-a-la-carcel. IDB, "Financial Sector Reform Program II," 7; Molina Calderón, *Siglo y seis lustros,* 276–77.

11. There were fears of a *corralito,* in which bank accounts are fully or partially frozen or seized, and false rumors were circulating that Banco G&T was about to go under. Molina Calderón, *Siglo y seis lustros,* 274–75, 280–81; "Sigue insuficiencia de billetes en mercado," *Prensa Libre,* 20 December 2006, www.prensalibre.com/2006/12/20/economia/Sigue-insuficiencia-billetes-mercado-0-133188372.

12. Urías Gamarro, "Q5 mil millones perdidos en fraudes bancarios y financieros," *Prensa Libre,* 27 June 2014, www.prensalibre.com/noticias/justicia/Q5-mil-millones-perdidos-fraudes-0-1164483552.

13. Guinea Diez, *Gramática,* 72. Foreign and national investment in construction, textiles, and agro-industry also boomed. One observer compared the situation to the economic growth seen after the formation of the Central American Common Market in the 1960s. Molina Calderón, *Siglo y seis lustros,* 282.

14. From 2002 to 2004 the IDB had started a new round of liberalizing financial reforms and participated in writing Guatemala's new financial-sector laws. IDB, "Project to Strengthen Bank Supervision," donors memorandum, 1 April 2002, project nos. ATN/MT-7827-GU, TC9802449, 7, Executive Summary, 1, 2; IDB, "Financial Sector Reform Program II," 6; "Country Program Evaluation: Guatemala, 1993–2003," Office of Evaluation and Oversight, Inter-American Development Bank, 10 December 2004, annex 5, 2.

15. In 2002 Guatemala was placed on the list of noncooperative countries by the intergovernmental Financial Action Task Force (on money laundering). IDB, "Financial Sector Reform Program II," 4, 9–10.

16. IDB, "Financial Sector Reform Program II," 3; emphasis added.

17. Superintendencia de Bancos de Guatemala, "Boletín anual de estadísticas del sistema financiero 2006," viii; "Memoria de labores, 2008–2009," 16; "Memoria de

labores, 2012–2013," 70. (Superintendencia de Banco documents may be found on www.sib.gob.gt/.) On banks and links with the elite, see Solano, "Development and/as Dispossession."

18. McAllister, "Indigenous Community"; USAID, "Legacies of Exclusion: Social Conflict and Violence in Communities and Homes in Guatemala's Western Highlands," Guatemala Conflict Vulnerability Assessment, Final Report, Public Version, October 2015, prepared by Tani Adams, www.usaid.gov/sites/default/files/documents/1862/Guatemala_Conflict_Vulnerability_Assessment.pdf, 26–27.

19. Malacates Trébol Shop, "Ni un centavo," Barceloneta Music, 1999.

20. See Way, *Mayan in the Mall,* 89–91, 157–58.

21. IDB, "Project to Support the Rural Economic Development Program Loan Proposal," 3 May 2006, project no. GU-L1006, 5.

22. For example, see IDB, "Community Development for Peace Program (DECOPAZ) Loan Proposal," 22 October 1996, project nos. 968/OC-GU, 984/SF-GU, GU0099; DECOPAZ and Centro Canadiense de Estudios y Cooperación Internacional, "Evaluación del desempeño durante el segundo ciclo de proyectos de las Entidades Representativas Microregionales-ERMs-, Paquete de Servicios II, Huehuetenango," March 2000, CEDFOG HF/307.1/D43/005657. The comment on geography and languages is from an anonymous interview.

23. Secretaria de Planificación y Programación, "Guía de seguimiento y evaluación de los PET y PDM" (República de Guatemala, August 2007). Housed in CEDFOG vertical archive.

24. Besides larger "urban" centers (Sololá and Panajachel, for example), Mankatitlán also included areas that were ground-zero targets for "rural" development, such as San Andrés Semetabaj and San Antonio Palopó. Municipalidad de Panajachel, Departamento de Sololá, "Plan de Desarrollo Municipal con enfoque territorial 2008–2022"; Municipalidad de San Andrés Semetabaj, Departamento de Sololá, "PDM con enfoque territorial, 2008–2022"; Municipalidad de San Antonio Palopó, Departamento de Sololá, "PDM con enfoque territorial, 2008–2022." This set of plans can be accessed on the SEGEPLAN website: www.segeplan.gob.gt.

25. Consejo de Desarrollo Departamental, Chimaltenango, "Plan Estratégico Territorial, Territorio Agroproductivo de Chimaltenango, 2008–2023"; CODEDE, Chimaltenango, "PET, Territorio Agroecoturístico de Chimaltenango, 2008–2023"; CODEDE, Chimaltenango, "PET, Territorio Bocacosta de Chimaltenango, 2008–2023"; CODEDE, Chimaltenango, "PET, Territorio Industrial de Chimaltenango, 2008–2023." At the time of my research and writing, the Guatemalan government had not made these documents available online. Interested researchers should consult the SEGEPLAN website for updates (www.segeplan.gob.gt/), remaining aware that any version accessed might be updated from the original. I was able to access the PETs in May 2018 on the Issuu page of the plans' graphic designer, Thelma Palma: https://issuu.com/thelmapalma.

26. The IDB's 2006 finance reform proposal, for example, beyond its macrolevel focus, included support for systems to help collect taxes, systematize municipal contracting systems, and standardize municipal budgeting. IDB, "Public Financial

Management Reform Program Loan Proposal"; IDB, "Social Investment Program to Reduce Rural Poverty Loan Proposal," 10 May 2006, project nos. 1736/OC-GU, GU0166; IDB, "Banco de Desarrollo Rural (Banrural)," project abstract, 25 May 2007, project no GU-L1010; IDB, "Banco de Desarrollo Rural (Banrural)–Environmental and Social Compliance Report," 1 June 2007, project no. GU-L1010, 1; IDB, "Banco Continental Financing Facility," project abstract, 18 November 2008, project no. GU-L1040; IDB, "Support for Modernization of the Ministry of Public Finance Loan Proposal," 12 November 2008, project no. GU-L1031; IDB, "Project to Support," 5; Ministerio de Economía de Guatemala, "Guatemalan National Action Plan: Strategy for Strengthening and Creating Trade Related Capabilities," November 2007, https://ustr.gov/archive/assets/Trade_Agreements/Regional/CAFTA/asset_upload_file320_3360.pdf, 8–9.

27. "Loco," among other informants, remembers paying twenty times what his new stereo was worth. Such Guatemalans joined a global trend; in 2012 Grupo Elektra would buy Advance America, the largest provider of payday loans in the United States. "Loco," interview with the author, Sololá, 2017; Molina Calderón, *Siglo y seis lustros*, 270; "Mexican Billionaire Buys Advance America, Largest Payday Lender in U.S.," *Forbes*, 23 April 2012, www.forbes.com/sites/erincarlyle/2012/04/23/mexican-billionaire-buys-advance-america-largest-payday-lender-in-u-s/#70c090691799.

28. By 2006 PRONACOM (founded in 1990) was working with "the Spanish Agency for International Cooperation, OXFAM Novib, GTZ, USAID, the World Bank, the IDB ... the Friedrich Ebert Foundation, FUNDESA, CACIF, the Guatemalan Chamber of Industry, and others," as well as with the IDB. IDB, "Strengthening of the National Network of Community Promotion Groups, Plan of Operations," 21 February 2007, project no. GU-T1059, 1–2. See also Ministerio de Economía, PRONACOM, www.mineco.gob.gt/programa-nacional-de-competitividad-pronacom.

29. IDB, "Project to Support," 5.

30. *Ati, la Revista del Lago* (Panajachel), no. 0 (February 2006), CIRMA-AH-098/C1. Escobar has also published in many other venues, including a column, "Lucha Libre," in *El Periódico*.

31. *Ati*, no. 0 (February 2006): 6.

32. *Ati*, no. 13 (April–May 2008): 21–23. The effects on Mayan handcrafts vendors, especially the children (many of whom I have seen grow up and know personally), could be tragic, since they typically grew up working on the streets instead of going to school and learning to read and write. Many of the boys in these families became deeply embittered when they were no longer cute little kids who could successfully sell to tourists and suddenly faced a world in which they were completely unqualified for anything but the lowest-level, starvation-wage work. Some gathered rocks from the riverbed for use in construction or otherwise labored in dead-end jobs, some migrated north, and still others got involved in the region's growing cocaine and crack scene and ended up in jail. Girls had a different but related experience. In part because of the mystique of traje (see Nelson, "Stumped Identities"), they were better able to continue selling (or work as weavers) when they became

women. Many, however—given the drugs and the poverty and the nation's *machista* culture—ended up in relationships that could often be extremely abusive; abuse from which some would later seek asylum in the United States. The migration of men trapped at the bottom of the wage scale, meanwhile, occasioned the growth of a social class of single mothers in Guatemala.

33. "Macho Alfa." *Ati*, no. 11 (December 2007): 14–15. There was of course male-on-male and male-on-female sex tourism (including pederasty) as well, but it did not generalize to the extent that female-on-male festivity did. By pointing this out, I in no way intend to demean genuine love affairs or transnational marriages, nor do I mean to imply a puritanical sensibility that sees all sex between adult travelers and hosts as wrong.

34. This "valuation" of casta beauty had a flip side as well. The attractiveness of foreign women to local men was related to their whiteness, and dating them was, for some, a sign of distinction.

35. IDB, "Competitive Development of Cultural Tourism with Indigenous Communities," donors memorandum, 14 December 2005, project no. GU-M1005, 3.

36. *Ati*, no. 14 (July 2008): 12–13; Jennifer A. Devine, "Politics of Post-war Tourism in Guatemala: Contested Identities, Histories, and Futures," *L'espace Politique* 28, no. 1 (2016): https://journals.openedition.org/espacepolitique/3723.

37. See the Río Negro website, www.rio-negro.info/che/.

38. Flynn, *Discovering Dominga*.

39. Estrada, "Ka Tzij," 208.

40. IDB initiatives specifically addressed remesas. Its Hometown Initiatives program drew on diasporic communities of memory, seeking to link U.S.-based "Hispanic philanthropists" from Mexico, the Dominican Republic, Nicaragua, El Salvador, Argentina, and Guatemala with microenterprises in their communities of origin. Meanwhile, its More Than Remittances program supported a cooperative from the Quetzaltenango department that grew into a remesa-processing center that offered credit cards, banking services, bill payments, and the like. IDB, "Promoting Diaspora and Local Support for Productive Initiatives," donors memorandum, 22 March 2006, project no. RG-M1069; IDB, "More than Remittances," donors memorandum, 29 November 2005, project no. GU-M1004, 2.

41. Tagline written by YouTube user "c4jol4boy" on uploaded video version of Sobrevivencia, "La Juventud," titled "grupo-sobvrevivencia la juventud lettras.wmv," 12 March 2010, YouTube video, www.youtube.com/watch?v = PaRHRnKw7Xg.

42. Richard H. Adams, Jr., "Remittances, Household Expenditure and Investment in Guatemala," Policy Research Working Paper; No. 3532. (Washington: World Bank, 2005), 1, 18–20.

43. "Ángel," interviews with the author, Panajachel, 2006, 2015. He remembers that his parents used to leave food for the guerrillas.

44. "Luis," interview with the author, Panajachel, 2012.

45. De León, *Land of Open Graves*, 220. *Chafa* means junk, or counterfeit merchandise; *paca* refers to the sale of used clothes and housewares imported in bulk from the United States.

46. On sexual desire and still-very-much-existing discourses of whiteness and racial improvement, see Arenas, *Sexo y raza*.

47. These cultural forms are an example of what Callaci calls "street archives" (*Street Archives*).

48. *Ati*, no. 14 (July 2008): 16–17, 20; no. 15 (September–October 2008): 14–16; *Centro Artístico Ajachel* (blog), latest entries 2010, http://centroajachel.blogspot.com; "Centro Artístico Ajachel," posted by Canal 5 Sololá, 5 August 2009, YouTube video, www.youtube.com/watch?v=BylArYJ3qxc; Centro Artístico Ajachel, Facebook, 26 July 2020, www.facebook.com/centroartistico.ajachel; "Ezquizoide," posted with the tagline "Grupo de Pana, toke en el Festivalote, para www.ajachel.com," by Freddie Rosales, 21 November 2007, YouTube video, www.youtube.com/watch?v=X-pSdj4S7pA; "Ezquizoide: Hombres Arbol," posted by Freddie Rosales, 17 June 2009, YouTube video, www.youtube.com/watch?v=E8veFYVqvUk; Panajachel Festivalote 2009 blogspot, http://festivalote.blogspot.com/.

49. "Corazón de motor: Diaz Negros," posted by Joseph Producción, 25 June 2009, YouTube video, www.youtube.com/watch?v=BegdDJG_nV8.

50. "Bacteria Sound System Crew," 20 January 2010, Deguate, www.deguate.com/artman/publish/cultura-cultura-guatemala/bacteria-sound-system-crew.shtml; Bacteria Soundsystem Crew, "About," Facebook, www.facebook.com/pg/BacteriaSoundsystemCrew/about/?ref=page_internal.

51. Walter Cruz, dir., *Barrio*, short film, November 2008, YouTube video, www.youtube.com/watch?v=JY-uwa3eICM. Hating Mexicans (who "think they're better than we are") is a theme in working-class Guatemalan youth culture, likely because Mexico is the "giant next door" with a much more advanced culture industry.

52. "Diaz Negros: Despierta Guatemala," 2009 song, posted by Rock Chapín, 6 November 2013, YouTube video, www.youtube.com/watch?v=CpLWbYUKMjo.

53. "Diaz Negros: Indio poder," 2010 live performance, posted by Rock Chapín, 13 November 2013, YouTube video, www.youtube.com/watch?v=f15Z7HExN1c.

54. Villar Herrera, "Renovación de la imagen," 2.

55. The mining conflicts involved not just gold but also new ventures in lead, silver, and zinc. See Palencia Prado, *Huehuetenango*, 58–64, 67; Villar Herrera, "Renovación de la imagen," 38, 45, 78, 85; and Yagenova, Donis, and Castillo, *Industria extractiva*. See also the documentary film by Caracol Producciones: Revenga, *Oro o la vida*.

56. There are not reliable population statistics; the figures are estimates. INFOM and Unión Europea, Proyecto de Desarrollo Rural y Local, "Cursos de formación en temas intermunicipales-PDRL-Huehuetenango, Guatemala, informe final," May 2011, contrato no. PDRL/SERV/22/09, anexo II, "Informe de capacitaciones en la formulación de planes de gestión urbana en los municipios de Huehuetenango, Chiantla, y Malacatancito," apéndice 4, "Plan de gestión urbana para el municipio de Chiantla," April 2011, CEDFOG HP/338.9/P6/22-09/V. 2.3/015087, 12, 18–21.

57. AVANCSO, *Jóvenes en Guatemala*, 210, 210n42; Garcés de Marcilla del Valle, "Hablando del otro"; García Estrada, *Candiles de la calle*, 280–81, 151–52, 175–76; González Ponciano, *"Patria del Shumo,"* 138–39.

58. For literary examples, see, for example, J. Payeras, *Región más invisible;* J. Payeras, *Ruido de fondo;* and Guinea Diez's essay "El país del abandono," in *Gramática,* 41–43.

59. Guinea Diez's essay "Máscaras" is discussed in chapter 4; *Gramática,* 49–54. Desafío 10 is analyzed in O'Neill, *Secure the Soul,* 82–85. See also Harold Sibaja, "Desafío 10, Paz para los EX: Guatemala," Iniciativa de Comunicación, 7 June 2006, www.comminit.com/la/content/desaf%C3%ADo-10-paz-para-los-ex-guatemala; Marcela Sanchez, "Fighting Gangs with Reality TV," *Washington Post,* 23 February 2006, www.washingtonpost.com/wp-dyn/content/article/2006/02/23/AR2006022301252 .html; and "Neoliberal Reality TV Fantasy: USAID Exploits Youth Gang Members in Guatemala," first half of unattributed documentary titled "USAID and the Gang," posted by Countercamera, 5 January 2010, YouTube video, www.youtube.com/watch?v = CgisPfLyCPs.

60. The failed project was supported by CONJUVE, USAID, various government ministries, and other institutions. "Informe Ejecutivo Proyecto Rescate Juvenil, Huehuetenango 2005" (Huehuetanango: Espacio de Coordinación Interinstitucional de Huehuetenango, 2005), CEDFOG HF/323.352/I5/007729, 4.

61. Examples include Quetzaltenango's Casa del Migrante Juvenil Nuestras Raíces, which housed nearly six thousand underage deportees. Like Cuenta Conmigo (Count on Me), a counseling hotline on drugs, sex, abuse, and suicide, and JuvenFami (Fundación para la Juventud y la Familia), a foundation working to prevent sexual abuse of youth, it was supported by a plethora of institutions and foundations. The municipality of Barillas had an "Encuentro Interactivo Juvenil–Unidos por la construcción de un futuro mejor" that dealt with themes including "drugs, alcohol, domestic abuse, family disintegration, gangs, and loss of values"; youthful musical and theater groups from around the area were invited to participate. Municipalidad de Santa Cruz Barillas, "Proyecto Mujeres y Jóvenes por una alternativa sostenible, mayo 2006–agosto 2007," 2007, CEDFOG HF/307.1 /P8/008789, 21–22; *Prensa Libre,* 12 March 2007, 50; *La Hora,* 16 February 2007, 10–11; *Siglo Veintiuno,* 17 March 2007, 10.

62. Denning, "Wageless Life."

63. *Cuento de la democracia.*

64. "Tortrix A este Chapín le faltan Tortrix (Perro)," posted by "sandovalescobedo," 27 May 2008, YouTube video, www.youtube.com/watch?v = KIIgB4u NstM; "TorTrix Celebrates 50 Years of Tradition in Guatemala," Pepsico, 24 May 2012, www.pepsico.com/live/story/tortrix-celebrates-50-years-of-tradition-in-guatemala05242012539.

65. Javier Payeras, "Buena suerte," *Chulo chucho colocho* (blog), 15 July 2008, http://javierpayeras.blogspot.com/2008/.

66. Ronald Mackay, "Al buen chapín,"was still active at the time of this writing. See www.albuenchapin.com/.

67. "Soy chapín y qué putas," Facebook, accessed 3 June 2018, www.facebook .com/chapinyqueputas/; "Al estilo chapín 502 Facebook page," Facebook, accessed 3 June 2018, www.facebook.com/AlEstiloChapin502/timeline.

68. Alfredo Vicente, "Emprendedores en Facebook," *Prensa Libre,* 30 October 2010, www.prensalibre.com/tecnologia/Titulo-articulo-edicion-impresa-0-362963759.

69. "Imagined community" references Anderson, *Imagined Communities.* As this book was going to press, a similar dynamic was unfolding in the United States on the TikTok app among "dreamers" and other migrant youth engaged in a rich and often funny dialogue through which they expressed their own brand of bottom-up U.S. nationalism.

Facebook, of course, also had a serious side, serving as a means for political youth (and other) groups to organize. Some appeared earnest, and others had the distinct tone of "adult supervision," dovetailing with efforts like the 2009 formation of RENOJ, the Red Nacional de Organizaciones de Jóvenes Mayas. By the early 2010s groups such as the Cobán-based Consejo de Juventudes Indígenas were posting on Maya identity and antimining issues, while in the Lake Atitlán area the Iniciativa Juvenil Acción Tz'utujil promoted sexual abstinence. Such messages, however, were swimming against the tide of most of the youthful discourse on Facebook and other social media sites. On the National Maya Youth Organization Network, see Ramos, *Jóvenes urbanos,* 31. Online, see Consejo de Juventudes Indígenas (Indigenous Youths Council), posts on Maya culture, 16 December 2012, and against mining, 22 December 2012, Facebook, www.facebook.com/Consejo-de-Juventudes-Ind%C3%ADgenas-381359348593379/timeline/; Iniciativa Juvenil Acción Tz'utujil, Facebook, 29 October 2011, www.facebook.com/ijatz.atitlan).

70. "Radio Nahualá," posted by Walter Soberanis, 22 December 2009, YouTube video, www.youtube.com/watch?v = xFqsxV8Nl2g. The description of the soccer uniforms translates along the lines of "aw damn what beauties them team colors!" Soberanis wrote a note underscoring his respect and explaining that his intention was to entertain, not to offend. (For Spanish speakers *[sic]* throughout): "Con todo respeto a mi gente indigena de guatemala, este video fue hecho con el puro proposito de diversion y entretenimiento mi intencion no es ofender a nadie espero y lo disfruten." A second version was uploaded in 2010 by another user: "Radio Nahualá: Segunda Parte," posted by "fjuarez88," 24 September 2010, YouTube video, www.youtube.com/watch?v = djaIbm3nbjQ.

71. One such corporate magazine was *Radioguaterock,* founded in 2009, which also had an online site (accessed 27 April 2016, http://radioguaterock.blogspot.com/p/revista-guaterock.html). It covered pop stars like Tavo Bárcenas (*Revista Radioguaterock,* no. 1 [November 2009], 6–7), who did ads and acted in the nation's first and short-lived reality TV show *Bulevar Hotel* in 2004. The idea that "authentic" rock nacional had died was implicit in the "rockumentary" film *Alternativa.* Finished in 2010 and released the year after, it was a sort of a "requiem" for the golden age of the genre.

72. "Alhazred," "Música en Guatemala: Historia del underground en Guatemala; Sus bandas de ayer y de hoy," *Rock Republic* (blog), 23 December 2009, http://rockrepublik.net/topic/9103/s120/.

73. This text is all one sentence in Alhazred's Post. "Alhazred," "Música en Guatemala: Rock en la guerra interna de Guatemala," *Rock Republik* (blog), 29 March 2011, http://rockrepublik.net/topic/11988/.

74. *Rock Republik* (blog), https://rockrepublik.net/forum/styles/.

75. "Safiroth," "Música en Guatemala: Historia del underground en Guatemala; Sus bandas de ayer y de hoy," *Rock Republik* (blog), 17 June 2010, http://rockrepublik.net/topic/9103/s120/.

76. Lee, *Planet B-boy*.

77. The beat was originally popularized in Dr. Dre's "Xxplosive." Bacteria Soundsystem Crew, "La Virula," video clip extracted from Mix Tape BSC 2009 Bacteria, posted by "Ele Dos," 16 January 2010, YouTube video, www.youtube.com/watch?v = sssLrlHZwqY; Bacteria Soundsystem Crew, "About."

78. Alejandro García, "Trasciende. apostando por el arte urbano," Deguate, 18 April 2011, www.deguate.com/artman/publish/cultura-actualidad-guatemala/trasciende-apostando-por-el-arte-urbano.shtml; Selene Mejía, "El breakdance renace en Antigua gracias a los B-Boys de '501 Crew,'" Soy 502, 7 September 2014, www.soy502.com/articulo/breakdance-renace-antigua-guatemala-gracias-video; "Mini Documental Trasciende: Hip Hop de Guatemala," posted by "Ele Dos," 8 October 2010, YouTube video, www.youtube.com/watch?v = HBqfMoOcL-A; "Representantes Hip Hop femenino Guatemala," posted by "Mug Marca," 22 November 2011, YouTube video, www.youtube.com/watch?v = 61cTozG-I18; "Trasciende 2012," posted by Zanate Mojado, 20 January 2012, YouTube video, www.youtube.com/watch?v = N1WaZoQmJ1Q; Trasciende Guatemala, Facebook, accessed 27 July 2018, www.facebook.com/trasciende.guatemala/.

79. Chapín Crew represented Guatemala in 2010; in 2011 it was Guatemaya Crew. "Chapín Crew, Guatemala en Francia BOTY 2010 (ADELANTO)," posted by Zanate Mojado, 1 May 2011, YouTube video, www.youtube.com/watch?v = oS2htwbCkq8; "BOTY 2011: Showcase; Guatemaya Crew (Guatemala)," posted by "Battle of the Year," 6 February 2013, YouTube video, www.youtube.com/watch?v = IAm2_HOaAEI. The Wikipedia BOTY page lists the competition winners; Chapín Crew won the Guatemala category in 2010, and Guatemaya Crew won the Central America category in 2011; see "Battle of the Year," Wikipedia, accessed 29 July 2018, https://en.wikipedia.org/wiki/Battle_of_the_Year; Mejía, "Breakdance renace en Antigua."

80. Ángel Cañas, quoted in Carolina Gamazo, "Iqui Balam: De cómo el teatro le dobló el brazo a la violencia en Guatemala," *Fronterad* (Madrid), 9 October 2015, www.fronterad.com/iqui-balam-de-como-el-teatro-le-doblo-el-brazo-a-la-violencia-en-guatemala/.

81. Lists of crews, bands, clubs, and associations such as GuateUrban and their Da-Radio project were detailed on the Bolígrafos Urbanos Blogspot, accessed 20 December 2017, http://boligrafosurbanos.blogspot.com.

82. Translation from "Talento guatemalteco: Rap en Mam," posted by "Juventud MNR," 4 August 2013, YouTube video, www.youtube.com/watch?v =

PwFXP65oq5s. The video has also been uploaded as "Shat J. Kq'onkje Video Official HD Rap Mam San Juan Ostuncalco," posted by "MCFuneral Juárez," 21 December 2011, YouTube video, www.youtube.com/watch?v = SKZWo_AlwWY; and Shat Juárez (Shat J. Kq'onkje), "Rap en Mam Cajolá 2012," posted by "Djcarlos de Guate," 11 February 2012, YouTube video, www.youtube.com/watch?v = d24AI2swKu4.

83. Jorge Mario Aguilar, 2014, post on "Talento guatemalteco."

84. These comments date to roughly 2012–13. "Rap en Mam Cajolá 2012," posted by "Djcarlos de Guate," 11 February 2012, YouTube video, www.youtube.com/watch?v = d24AI2swKu4.

85. USAID, "Legacies of Exclusion."

86. Leslie de León, "Idioma perdura a través de la música: 'Shat Juárez' produce rap en Mam," *El Quetzalteco,* 17 March 2014, 12; R. Martínez, "Canta en su idioma materno," *Prensa Libre,* 9 September 2013, https://issuu.com/prensalibregt/docs/plmt09092013. The album was on Shat Juárez's website, "MyRecordsFullFuneralShat," accessed 4 August 2018, https://shatjuarez.es.tl/Home.htm.

87. Shat Juárez, "Qa Bana: Rap en Mam Cajolá 2014," posted by "El Rey del Rap en Mam, Shat Juárez," 14 February 2014, YouTube video, www.youtube.com/watch?v = Z6dJycKvVus. For more of this artist's work, see "Rap romántico Shat Juárez," posted by "MCFuneral Juárez," 8 June 2012, YouTube video, www.youtube.com/watch?v = mvgWali3i7A; Shat Juárez, "Rap en Mam #2 2013," live concert footage, posted by "El Rey del Rap en Mam, Shat Juárez," 24 August 2012, YouTube video, www.youtube.com/watch?v = LphKTMNFZh8.

88. *Hasta Atrás,* no. 6 (ca. March 1996), 8.

89. See Latham, *Consuming Youth,* on "a dialectic of exploitation and empowerment rooted in youth's practices of consumption" (2) and how a "consumerist ethos," while capitalist, also "provided opportunities for self-determination and communal exchange . . . mobilizing of teenagers as potentially autonomous social subjects" (96).

90. *La Hora,* 22 July 2010, http://lahora.gt/hemeroteca-lh/colom-participa-en-gobernando-con-la-juventud-en-chimaltenango/. The pop star Tavo Bárcenas also contributed, working with a group called Jóvenes contra la Violencia (Youth against Violence) to make a song and music video. "Jóvenes contra la Violencia," posted by Jóvenes contra la Violencia Guatemala, 23 February 2011, YouTube video, www.youtube.com/watch?v = _i4I4h-5vzE. The campaign "included a media strategy (press conferences, production and promotion of a musical video clip), public activities (panels, art festivals), and a series of visual items (tee-shirts, stickers, posters)" and achieved very little, writes Leslie Lemus in AVANCSO, *Jóvenes en Guatemala,* 216.

91. Bacteria Soundsystem Crew, "Somos juventud," video clip produced for 2010–11 Año de la Juventud, posted by Zanate Mojado, 6 December 2010, YouTube video, www.youtube.com/watch?v = WioiUMUbRvg.

92. Bacteria Soundsystem Crew, "Lo que veo (versión original)," posted by "Bacteria Soundsystem Crew," 29 November 2016, YouTube video, www.youtube.com/watch?v = WL-6g6MsiUE. A *pepenachenka* is someone so poor they scavenge for discarded cigarette butts on the street to get the last puff.

93. Palencia Prado, *Huehuetenango,* 9.

94. COPREDEH, "Sistematización de experiencias en casos de conflictividad social atendidos por COPREDEH" (Guatemala, March 2013), 13–14, 18, 33, 27–28 (quotations on 13).

95. See, for example, Camus, Bastos, and López García, *Dinosaurio reloaded;* Little, "Living and Selling;" Normanns Morales, *Violencia;* Palencia Prado, *Huehuetenango.*

96. Gobierno de Guatemala, "Plan Nacional de Desarrollo K'atun: Nuestra Guatemala 2032," 2014, Consejo Nacional de Desarrollo Urbano y Rural/SEGEPLAN, 93, 95.

97. *Mierda* has been a lasting theme in Guatemala's urban and urbane landscape. See, for example, Ameno Córdova, "Guatemala está en la mierda y sus videoclips," *Barrancópolis* (blog), 22 September 2016, http://barrancopolis.com/guatemala-esta-en-la-mierda-y-sus-videoclips/. *Barrancópolis* refers to the *barrancos,* or ravines where Guatemala City's slums are located. The post makes reference to Bacteria Soundsystem Crew's song, "La Virula."

98. These stories come from interviews and conversations and are but a small sample of similar narratives. The San Andrés Semetabaj lynching of 14 February 2010 is documented in COPREDEH, "Sistematización," 46.

99. An excellent thesis on the persistence of patriarchal struggles reframes this as "feminicide." Ihmoud, "Problematizing Discourses."

100. See Briggs, *Somebody's Children;* and, for example, *Al Día,* 18 August 2007, 3; *La Hora,* 22 August 2007, 11; *Siglo Veintiuno,* 24 August 2007, 10.

101. Federal Bureau of Investigation, United States Department of Justice, "International Human Trafficking," 13 November 2009, 2, https://en.wikisource.org/wiki/International_Human_Trafficking.

102. In the "Caso Evelyn," two members of the "satanic" gang called "Los Rockeros" had been sentenced to stiff prison terms, having narrowly escaped first a lynch mob and then the death penalty, for raping and nearly decapitating Evelyn Karina Isidro Velásquez, a six-year-old girl in Guatemala City. *El Periódico,* 3 January 2007, 5; *Nuestro Diario,* 5 January 2007, 3; 19 January 2007, 6; 7 December 2007, 4; *Al Día,* 21 February 2007. On decapitation, see *Siglo Veintiuno,* 11 January 2006, 9; *Prensa Libre,* 15 October 2007, 56; and *El Periódico,* 26 March 2007, 2–3. In May 2011 the Zetas, a Mexican cartel that was territorializing Guatemala as a result of the drug wars in their own country, decapitated twenty-eight campesinos in the Petén, and also dismembered several of them. *El País,* 16 May 2011, https://elpais.com/internacional/2011/05/16/actualidad/1305496811_850215.html; *La Prensa,* 16 May 2011, www.laprensa.hn/mundo/540701-97/zetas-asesinan-a-unos-28-campesinos-en-guatemala.

103. I have heard numerous Guatemalans refer to the security patrols as "Talibans." An example in the press is Eduardo Blandón, "La destra," *La Hora,* 28 January 2009, http://lahora.gt/hemeroteca-lh/la-destra/.

104. Bismarck Pineda and Lisardo Bolaños, "Diagnóstico de la violencia juvenil en Guatemala: Documento para discusión," unidentified internal work material, July 2009, CIRMA-AH-054/C5/108, 3–4.

105. USAID, "Legacies of Exclusion," E-1.

106. An exploration of these polities and concepts of sovereignty is found in Sieder, "Contested Sovereignties." On the role of indigenous authorities, often as intermediaries and conflict-resolvers, see Alcaldía Maya Mam, Santa Barbara Huehuetenango, "Declaración comunitaria 2010: Normas para la prevención y transformación de conflictos desde la cultura Maya Mam," CEDFOG HF/303.69 /D4/013327; COPREDEH, "Sistematización," 5.

107. This observation is based on dozens of interviews in the Sacatepéquez, Chimaltenango, Sololá, Quiché, and Huehuetenango departments, as well as with social scientists and townspeople from Alta and Baja Verapaz. The payoff to the COCODE could take the form of money or corrupt dealings (such as allowing a for-profit parking lot on a soccer field built with public money for the kids) or of attending to the sector's needs (such as installing running water, for example) at the expense of other neighborhoods.

108. COPREDEH, "Sistematización," 62, 66–69; USAID, "Legacies of Exclusion," 22. On San Pedro Necta, see Copeland, *Democracy Development Machine*.

109. COPREDEH, "Sistematización," 40. At the same time, a local crime ring named "Los Noj" was active in Sololá. Ajcalón Choy, "Municipalidad," 109.

110. COPREDEH, "Sistematización," 42–44.

111. Carolina Gamazo, "Bajo las cenizas de Los Encapuchados, un año después," *Plaza Pública*, 11 November 2012, www.plazapublica.com.gt/content/bajo-las-cenizas-de-los-encapuchados-un-ano-despues.

112. I was in Panajachel when this occurred but did not witness the lynching firsthand. COPREDEH, "Sistematización," 47–48.

113. Alberto Arce, "La impunidad de los encapuchados de Panajachel," *Plaza Pública*, 30 October 2011, www.plazapublica.com.gt/content/la-impunidad-de-los-encapuchados-de-panajachel; Gamazo, "Bajo las cenizas." Lake Atitlán's waters rose significantly after Agatha, putting Panajachel's beach underwater and wiping out dozens of lakeshore homes. Noticias Sololá, Facebook, 21 October 2011, www.facebook.com/NoticiasSolola/timeline.

114. Arce, "Impunidad de los encapuchados." Aleph had been founded by Juan Carlos "Juanca" Barrios, an early lead guitarist of Bohemia Suburbana. *Ati*, no. 6 (February 2007): 26–28.

115. Patrol members' real names can be found in the press reports; I am omitting them here. Arce, "Impunidad de los encapuchados."

116. Inhabitants told these stories to a *Plaza Pública* reporter, but I have added information from my own experience and research. In this period there was a notable population of young, gay, male Tz'utujiles who wore traditional red-and-white striped traje pants, combined with women's or gender-bending blouses on top. The victims were from this population. Gamazo, "Bajo las cenizas." Interestingly, Panajachel's alcaldía indígena had been a part of the security patrol, but, after the events of late 2011, they dropped out. Ochoa, *Alcaldías indígenas*, 41.

117. Arce, "Impunidad de los encapuchados"; Gamazo, "Bajo las cenizas."

118. Lucía Escobar, "De cuervos, ojos y demonios," http://lasotrasluchas.blogspot.com/2011/10/de-cuervos-ojos-y-demonios.html, originally published 18 October 2011 in *El Periódico*.
119. USAID, "Legacies of Exclusion," E-2.
120. Guinea Diez, *Gramática*, 49–54.
121. Arce, "Impunidad de los encapuchados."

CONCLUSION

1. Pepsi Guatemala, "Guatemala Arjona Pepsi: Video Oficial," posted by "Pepsi Guatemala," 28 January 2012, YouTube video, www.youtube.com/watch?v = 95TqWSHqrfU.
2. "Guatemorfosis," PuntoGuate, January 2012, www.puntoguate.com/2012/01/guatemorfosis.html.
3. Nelton Rivera, "'Guatemorfosis' un hijo más de la rancia oligarquía guatemalteca," *Saraguate-selva* (blog), 28 February 2012, http://saraguateselva.blogspot.com/2012/02/guatemorfosisunhijomasdelarancia.html (site discontinued).
4. "La Megapaca y su estilo de buen vestir," Todas por las ideas, 5 September 2016, https://todoporlasideas.wordpress.com/tag/maicol-yaxon/; Herman Díaz, "El efecto Megapaca," *Nómada*, 18 November 2014, https://nomada.gt/cotidianidad/el-efecto-megapaca/. There are numerous take-ups of these campaigns and of Megapaca on YouTube.
5. Harvey, "Cities or Urbanization?," 57; Sevilla-Buitrago, "Urbs in Rure," 240–41.
6. "Sobrevivencia-Guatemala," *Centroamericanto*, 10 January 2009, https://centroamericanto.net/2009/01/10/sobrevivencia-guatemala/; Fernández, *Si aquí se pudiera vivir*; Lovell, *Beauty That Hurts*.
7. In June 2018 Volcán de Fuego erupted and buried many of the places—and probably the people—I remember from that day under a pyroclastic flow. Adonay and his brothers, like others from the barrios, helped to organize aid and rescue brigades.
8. These same brothers helped me move out of my apartment in Antigua. When the light-skinned, ladina landlord showed up, she started giving Adonay orders as if he were a domestic servant. To avoid a scene, he complied, but not before he shot her a look that left no doubt as to exactly what he thought of her.
9. Comment posted on "Los shumos de Guate," posted by "ShumosGuate," 18 February 2012, YouTube video, www.youtube.com/watch?v = so-HTnzDS2c.
10. "Los Shumos de Miraflores 2 Loquendo," posted by "asimeexpresoantetodo," 25 February 2012, YouTube video, www.youtube.com/watch?v = brEDFcZZJHo.
11. "Shumos de Miraflores parte 3," posted by "Shaggyanon buu," 2 June 2012, YouTube video, www.youtube.com/watch?v = sBtT28cgbl4. A less verbally violent video redubbed the Brazilian singer Michel Teló's hit song "Ai se eu te pego," as "Ai, sos un shumo," with new lyrics about seeing *shumitas lindas* but deciding not to flirt

because "nossa, nossa, no salgo con shumos" (I don't date shumos; the "nossa" is from the song's chorus). "Ai sos un shumo (eu si te pego) parodia (shumos)," posted by Antonio Ruiz, 16 February 2012, YouTube video, www.youtube.com/watch?v = xqFkcWmWbXY).

Progressive columnists denounced the antishumo discourse. See Claudia Navas Dangel, "Shumos contra la pobreza," *La Hora,* 6 July 2012, http://lahora.gt/hemeroteca-lh/shumos-contra-la-pobreza/online; and Eduardo Villatoro, "Acerca de licenciados, shumos y cachimbiros," *La Hora,* 17 December 2012, http://lahora.gt/hemeroteca-lh/acerca-de-licenciados-shumos-y-cachimbiros/.

12. González Ponciano, "*Shumo* Challenge." González Ponciano, *"Patria del Shumo,"* traces discourses and rites of servility in Guatemalan culture from the colonial period to the 2000s.

13. González Ponciano, *"Patria del Shumo,"* 109.

14. Post on Consejo de Juventudes Indígenas, Facebook, 23 September 2013, www.facebook.com/Consejo-de-Juventudes-Ind%C3%ADgenas-381359348593379 /timeline/.

15. Consejo de Juventudes Indígenas, Facebook, 16 December 2012.

16. ENJU, as the poll was called, noted a fast-transforming country soon to "have a predominantly urban population structure." It also stated that schools were failing to instill values of "good citizenship" in the vast young population. Secretaria Ejecutiva del Servicio Cívico, Consejo Nacional de Juventud, and Instituto Nacional de Estadística, *Primera encuesta nacional de juventud en Guatemala (ENJU 2011),* 2011, http://conjuve.gob.gt/descargas/enju.pdf, 7, 26, 35, 88. On youth, education, and citizenship, see Bellino, *Youth in Postwar Guatemala.* There were vibrant movements in environmental, gender, and identity politics. The antimining movement has been particularly militant, belying narratives about the end of popular resistance. See Illescas, *Huehuetenango,* 70–87; and "El oro o la vida: Recolonización y resistencia en Centroamérica," documentary film, Caracol Producciones, 2011, www.caracolproducciones.net/en/documentales/2-uncategorised/15-el-oro-o-la-vida.

17. The Guy Fawkes masks had been popularized by the film *V for Vendetta* and were seen globally, including in the Anonymous movement. "Anonymous Guatemala opera desde las sombras, *Prensa Libre,* 14 May 2017, www.prensalibre.com /guatemala/comunitario/la-operacion-20-desde-las-sombras-de-anonymous-guatemala. See "#OpMinera 2.0 de Anonymous Guatemala," posted by "Anonymous Guatemala," 7 January 2012, YouTube video, www.youtube.com/watch?v = bSxBDWK1JBg; "#OpNiñosLibres," posted by "Anonymous Guatemala," 25 April 2012, YouTube video, www.youtube.com/watch?v = 2Xz9KDbmeUE.

18. Consejo de Juventudes Indígenas, Facebook, 4–14 October 2012; Illescas, *Huehuetenango,* 55, 61, and in general on right-wing politics in Huehuetenango.

19. Ríos Montt was convicted and sentenced to eighty years in prison on 10 May 2013, becoming the first head of state to be tried for genocide and crimes against humanity by courts in his own home county, but the Constitutional Court effectively vacated the verdict just over a week later. A retrial began in mid-2015, with

many twists and turns; Ríos died (on 1 April 2018) before the retrial was settled. On the events of 2013, see the documentary series: Yates, *Dictator in the Dock*. See also Oglesby and Nelson, *Guatemala;* and Ross, "Ríos Montt Case." A summary can be found on "Trial Watch: Efraín Ríos Montt," Trial International, 11 June 2012, https://trialinternational.org/latest-post/efrain-rios-montt/.

20. The vice president, Roxana Baldetti, resigned on 8 May 2015; Pérez Molina stepped down on the second of September. The underlying corruption scandal is known as La Línea.

21. Anonymous Guatemala claimed that "the Guy Fawkes mask identifies the Anonymous Collective worldwide and is a symbol of the struggle against corrupt and tyrannical governments.... We are all Anonymous: the schoolteacher in Syria, the Japanese police officer, the Guatemalan student, the Bolivian homemaker, the Mexican nurse; the mask unites us." "Anonymous Guatemala invita a todos a la 'Marcha del Millón de Máscaras,'" Deguate, 4 November 2015, www.deguate.com /artman/publish/seguridad_ciber/anonynous-guatemala-invita-a-todos-a-la-mar-cha-del-millon-de-mascaras.shtml.

22. "Diaz Negros-Sueños muertos," video of undated song, posted by Omar Morales, 8 April 2013, YouTube video, www.youtube.com/watch?v = 76Ala AWgxnA.

23. The Frenesí Rock Facebook page, active at the time of this writing, is no longer online. Nota Fa's page was still active in July 2020; see Nota Fa, Facebook, www.facebook.com/NOTA-FA-Oficial-165326800218342/.

24. "Conferencia de prensa de Sara Curruchich presentado su sencillo 'Resistir,'" posted by "Rock Chapín," 2 March 2016, YouTube video, www.youtube.com /watch?v = XUSRUBdP-VU; Sara Curruchich Gómez, "Ch'uti' xtän (Niña)," posted by "Symphonic Distribution," 13 July 2019, YouTube video, www.youtube .com/watch?v = YfUcU9-YWq4.

25. Fernando Scheel and Raquel Pajoc, "Pa' capital," posted by "Fasmusic," 1 October 2014, YouTube video, www.youtube.com/watch?v = N4evy_IMFKQ; "Entrevista, Pa' capital con Fernando Scheel y Raquel Pajoc," telecast of interview in the studios of CANAL 20, Cable Visión 2000 y BraKvisión, San Juan Sacatepéquez, posted by BraKvisión Canal 20, 10 November 2014, YouTube video, www.youtube.com /watch?v = tuFxGNKpj9k. Scheel has worked extensively with Maya musicians.

26. "Marcielita Chubay: Talento guatemalteca en el idioma Kaqchikel," video of television performance on Guatevisión, posted by Andrés Tambríz, 23 January 2016, YouTube video, www.youtube.com/watch?v = CvMH21bamFc.

27. With "creative city," I reference Florida, *Creative Class*. For more on Sara Curruchich, see "Conferencia de prensa." On Comalapa, see Chirix, *Ru rayb'äl ri qach'akul;* Esquit, *Otros poderes, nuevos desafíos;* and Esquit, "Movilización política indígena." On art, see FLACSO, *Guatemala,* 5:125–29.

28. On the Andes, see Swinehart, "Tupac in the Veins"; and Ypeij, "Cholos, incas y fusionistas."

29. J. Payeras, *Región más invisible,* 11, 15–16. MC Tz'utu Kan is treated in Bell, "This Isn't Underground." See also Dr. Sativo/M.C.H.e. and Tzutu Baktun Kan,

"Lago Negro," posted by "Unheardworld's Channel," 10 November 2012, YouTube video, www.youtube.com/watch?v = I4qzpHd_Ugo.

30. Israel Nicolás Chavajay Coché, Jhonny Ventura Escún Peneleu, and Ventura González Flores, interviews with the author, San Pedro La Laguna, August 2016. In part they were influenced by Bacteria Soundsystem, whose albums just kept coming and who had gigged in Panajachel and San Pedro La Laguna as early as 2009. "Cultura Electrónica," *Cube-Culture* (blog), ca. 2009–13, http://cube-culture.blogspot.com/; "Entrevista a Bacteria Soundsytem," *Cube-Culture* (blog), 25 August 2009, http://cube-culture.blogspot.com/2009/08/; Bacteria Soundsystem Crew, "About," Facebook, www.facebook.com/pg/BacteriaSoundsystemCrew/about/?ref = page_internal.

31. In the mid-2010s chapinismos gained official recognition; national slang words such as *chamusca* for "pickup soccer games" and *chipichipi* for "light rainfall" were first being included in Spain's official *Diccionario de la lengua española* and articles with titles like "Guatemala Dixit" were explicating terms such as *cerote* (piece of shit, turd) and *hueco* (an antigay slur). Haroldo Shetumul, "Chapinismos universales," *PrensaLibre*, 19 October 2014, www.prensalibre.com/cultura/chapinismos-guatemaltiquismos-DRAE-idioma-espanol-o-1232876716; Gabriel Woltke, "Guatemala dixit," *ContraPoder*, 27 April 2015, http://contrapoder.com.gt/2015/04/27/guatemala-dixi/.

WORKS CITED

What follows is a list of secondary works cited, including books, scholarly articles and book chapters, and academic theses. Films and novels are also listed here unless they were self-produced or self-published. Acronyms are used in the citations for organizations that are commonly referred to by their initials, including AVANCSO (Asociación para el Avance de las Ciencias Sociales en Guatemala); CIRMA (Centro de Investigaciones Regionales de Mesoamérica); FLACSO (Facultad Latinoamericana de las Ciencias Sociales); and USAC, the national university (Universidad de San Carlos de Guatemala). FLACSO's *Guatemala: Historia Reciente* is a five-volume, multiauthor set. Only chapters cited multiple times appear in this list of works cited; otherwise, the volume number and pages are provided in the corresponding endnote.

All citations for primary sources and oral history interviews are found in the endnotes. Primary research was conducted in archives in CIRMA (located in Antigua); in CEDFOG (Centro de Estudios y Documentación de la Frontera Occidental de Guatemala) in Huehuetenango; in municipalities (particularly Sololá); and online. Sources consulted include counterculture publications and regional newspapers and magazines, as well as extensive collections from Mayan movement organizations; guerrilla groups, particularly the URNG and Octubre Revolucionaria; Guatemalan government ministries, departmental governments, and municipalities; MINUGUA; the Inter-American Development Bank; the World Bank; Guatemala's central bank (Banco de Guatemala); and the international cooperation agencies of several donor nations, particularly USAID. Other primary periodicals, articles, websites, and blogs—including numerous Facebook pages and YouTube videos—may also be found in the endnotes.

Adams, Abigail E. "Reviving Our Spirits: Revelation, Re-encuentro, and Retroceso in Post-peace Accords Verapaz." In Little and Smith, *Mayas in Postwar Guatemala,* 30–41.

Adams, Richard Newbold. *Crucifixion by Power: Essays on Guatemalan National Social Structure, 1944–1966.* Austin: University of Texas Press, 1970.

Ajcalón Choy, Rigoberto. "Municipalidad, participación indígena y democratización en Sololá a partir de la firma de los acuerdos de paz 1996–2010." Licenciatura thesis, USAC, July 2011.

Alexander, Michelle. *The New Jim Crow: Mass Incarceration in the Age of Colorblindness.* New York: New Press, 2010.

Alvarado, Paulo. "Guatemala's Alux Nahual: A Non-'Latin American' Latin American Rock Group?" In Pacini Hernandez, Fernández L'Hoeste, and Zolov, *Rockin' Las Américas,* 220–40.

Anderson, Benedict. *Imagined Communities.* Rev. ed. London: Verso, 2013.

Arenas, Clara, ed. *Sexo y raza: Analíticas de la blancura, el deseo y la sexualidad en Guatemala.* Guatemala City: AVANCSO, 2015.

ASIES (Asociación de Investigación y Estudios Sociales). *Compendio de historia de Guatemala, 1944–2000.* Guatemala City: ASIES, 2010.

AVANCSO. *Jóvenes en Guatemala: Imágenes, discursos y contextos.* With Instituto de Estudios Humanísticos de la Universidad Rafael Landívar. Guatemala City: AVANCSO/IEH, 2013.

Barrera Ortiz, Byron. *Portillo: La democracia en el espejo.* Guatemala City: F y G, 2014.

Barrientos, Claudia Inés. *Participación ciudadana y construcción de ciudadanía desde los Consejos de Desarrollo: El caso de Chichicastenango.* Guatemala City: FLACSO/Agencia Sueca de Cooperación Internacional, 2007.

Barrios, Lina. *Tras las huellas del poder local: La Alcaldía Indígena en Guatemala, del siglos XVI al siglo XX.* Guatemala City: Universidad Rafael Landívar, Investigaciones Económicas y Sociales, 2001.

Barry, Tom, and Deb Preusch. *The Soft War: Uses and Abuses of U.S. Aid in Central America.* New York: Grove, 1988.

Bastos, Santiago, ed. *Multiculturalismo y futuro en Guatemala.* Guatemala City: FLACSO/Oxfam, 2008.

Bastos, Santiago, and Roderick Leslie Brett, eds. *El movimiento maya en la década después de la paz (1997–2007).* Guatemala City: F y G, 2010.

Bastos, Santiago, and Manuela Camus. "Difficult Complementarity: Relations between the Mayan and Revolutionary Movements" In McAllister and Nelson, *War by Other Means,* 71–92.

Beck, Erin. *How Development Projects Persist: Everyday Negotiations with Guatemalan NGOs.* Durham: Duke University Press, 2017.

Bell, Elizabeth R. "'This Isn't Underground; This Is Highlands': Mayan-Language Hip Hop, Cultural Resilience, and Youth Education in Guatemala." *Journal of Folklore Research* 54, no. 2 (2017): 167–97.

Bellino, Michelle J. *Youth in Postwar Guatemala: Education and Civic Identity.* New Brunswick: Rutgers University Press, 2017.

Bentley, Andrew. "In and Out of the Peripheral Network City: Urban Spaces Written by Violence in Postwar Guatemala." PhD diss., Hispanic Cultural Studies, Michigan State University, 2019.
Berger, Susan A. *Political and Agrarian Development in Guatemala*. Boulder: Westview, 1992.
Blumi, Isa. *Destroying Yemen: What Chaos in Arabia Tells Us about the World*. Berkeley: University of California Press, 2018.
Bordieu, Pierre. *Distinction: A Social Critique of the Judgment of Taste*. Translated by Richard Nice. Cambridge: Harvard University Press, 1984.
Bourgeois, Philippe. *In Search of Respect: Selling Crack in El Barrio*. 2nd ed. Cambridge: Cambridge University Press, 2003.
Brenner, Neil, ed. *Implosions/Explosions: Towards a Study of Planetary Urbanization*. Berlin: Jovis, 2014.
Briggs, Laura. *Somebody's Children: The Politics of Transracial and Transnational Adoption*. Durham: Duke University Press, 2012.
Brintnall, Douglas E. *Revolt against the Dead: The Modernization of a Mayan Community in the Highlands of Guatemala*. New York: Gordon and Breach, 1979.
Bruey, Alison. *Bread, Justice, and Liberty: Grassroots Activism and Human Rights in Pinochet's Chile*. Madison: University of Wisconsin Press, 2018.
Bulmer-Thomas, Victor. *The Economic History of Latin America since Independence*. New York: Cambridge University Press, 1994.
Burrell, Jennifer. "Intergenerational Conflict in the Postwar Era." In Little and Smith, *Mayas in Postwar Guatemala*, 96–109.
———. *Maya after War: Conflict, Power, and Politics in Guatemala*. Austin: University of Texas Press, 2013.
Callaci, Emily. *Street Archives and City Life: Popular Intellectuals in Postcolonial Tanzania*. Durham: Duke University Press, 2017.
Camus, Manuela. *La colonia Primero de Julio y la "clase media emergente."* Guatemala City: FLACSO, 2005.
———. *Ser indígena en la Ciudad de Guatemala*. Guatemala City: FLACSO, 2002.
Camus, Manuela, Santiago Bastos, and Julián López García, eds. *Dinosaurio reloaded: Violencias actuales en Guatemala*. Guatemala City: FLACSO, Fundación Constelación, 2015.
Carey, David, Jr. "Guatemala's Green Revolution: Synthetic Fertilizer, Public Health, and Economic Autonomy in the Mayan Highlands." *Agricultural History* 83, no. 3 (Summer 2009): 283–322.
———. *I Ask for Justice: Maya Women, Dictators, and Crime in Guatemala, 1898–1944*. Austin: University of Texas Press, 2013.
———. *Our Elders Teach Us: Maya-Kaqchikel Historical Perspectives*. Tuscaloosa: University of Alabama Press, 2001.
Carlsen, Robert S. *The War for the Heart and Soul of a Highland Maya Town*. Rev. ed. Austin: University of Texas Press, 2011.

Castañeda Maldonado, Mario Efraín. "Historia del Rock en Guatemala: La Música Rock como expresión social en la ciudad de Guatemala entre 1960 a 1976." Licenciatura thesis, USAC, October 2008.

Castells, Manuel. *The Informational City: Information Technology, Economic Restructuring, and the Urban Regional Process.* Oxford: Blackwell, 1989.

Chattopadhyay, Swati. *Unlearning the City: Infrastructure in a New Optical Field.* Minneapolis: University of Minnesota Press, 2012.

Chirix, Emma. *Ru rayb'äl ri qach'akul: Los deseos de nuestro cuerpo.* Antigua, Guatemala: Pensativo, 2010.

Cojtí Cuxil, Demetrio. *Ri Maya' Moloj pa Iximulew: El Movimiento Maya.* Guatemala City: Colsamaj, 1997.

Colom, Yolanda. *Mujeres en la alborada: Guerrilla y participación femenina en Guatemala, 1973–1978.* 4th ed. Antigua, Guatemala: Pensativo, 2013.

Comité para el Esclarecimiento Histórico. *Guatemala: Memoria del silencio.* Guatemala City: Comité para el Esclarecimiento Histórico, 1999.

Cooper, Frederick. *Colonialism in Question: Theory, Knowledge, History.* Berkeley: University of California Press, 2005.

Copeland, Nicholas. *The Democracy Development Machine: Neoliberalism, Radical Pessimism, and Authoritarian Populism in Mayan Guatemala.* Ithaca: Cornell University Press, 2019.

Craib, Raymond B. *Cartographic Mexico: A History of State Fixations and Fugitive Landscapes.* Durham: Duke University Press, 2004.

El cuento de la democracia: El pueblo mam ante el circo electoral. Film. Guatemala City: Caracol Producciones with Asociación Ceiba, 2007.

Davis, Mike. *Planet of Slums.* London: Verso, 2006.

De Certeau, Michel. *The Practice of Everyday Life.* Translated by Steven Rendall. 3rd ed. Berkeley: University of California Press, 2011.

DeHart, Monica. *Ethnic Entrepreneurs: Identity and Development Politics in Latin America.* Stanford: Stanford University Press, 2010.

De León, Jason. *The Land of Open Graves: Living and Dying on the Migrant Trail.* Berkeley: University of California Press, 2015.

Del Valle Escalante, Emilio. "The Discursive Economy of Maya *Culturales* in Guatemala." *Hispanófila* 157 (December 2009): 25–38.

Denning, Michael. "Wageless Life." *New Left Review* 66 (November–December 2010): 77–94.

Derby, Robin, and Marion Werner. "The Devil Wears Dockers: Devil Pacts, Trade Zones, and Rural-Urban Ties in the Dominican Republic." *New West Indian Guide* 87 (2013): 294–321.

Díaz Castillo, Roberto. *Cultura popular y clases sociales.* 2nd ed. Guatemala City: Centro de Estudios Folklóricos/USAC, 2005.

Dixon, Dwayne Emil. "Endless Question: Youth Becomings and the Anti-crisis of Kids in Global Japan." PhD diss., Duke University, 2014.

Dosal, Paul. *Power in Transition: The Rise of Guatemala's Industrial Oligarchy, 1871–1994.* Westport, CT: Praeger, 1995.

Dougherty, Michael L. "The Global Gold Mining Industry, Junior Firms, and Civil Society Resistance in Guatemala." *Bulletin of Latin American Research* 30, no. 4 (2011): 403–18.

Driscoll, Mark. *Absolute Erotic, Absolute Grotesque: The Living, Dead, and Undead in Japan's Imperialism*. Durham: Duke University Press, 2010.

Dunn, Christopher. *Contracultura: Alternative Arts and Social Transformation in Authoritarian Brazil*. Chapel Hill: University of North Carolina Press, 2016.

Dussel, Enrique. *Twenty Theses on Politics*. Translated by George Ciccariello-Maher. Durham: Duke University Press, 2008.

Ekern, Stener. "La comunidad maya en tiempos de cambio ¿La base del movimiento maya?" In Bastos and Brett, *Movimiento maya*, 201–32.

———. "The Production of Autonomy: Leadership and Community in Mayan Guatemala." *Journal of Latin American Studies* 43, no. 1 (February 2011): 93–119.

Escobar Urrutia, María Gabriela. "Enfrentamientos y violencias juveniles en la Ciudad de Guatemala (1985–1993)." Licenciatura thesis, USAC, July 2005.

Esquit, Edgar. "Movilización política indígena en Comalapa en la era de la paz." In Bastos and Brett, *Movimiento maya*, 233–65.

———. *Otros poderes, nuevos desafíos: Relaciones interétnicas en Tecpán y su etorno departamental*. Guatemala City: Instituto de Estudios Interétnicos, 2002.

Estrada, Alicia Ivonne. "Ka Tzij: The Maya Diasporic Voices from *Contacto Ancestral*." *Latino Studies* 11, no. 2 (2013): 208–27.

Fernández, Sergio. *Si aquí se pudiera vivir: La historia de los últimos adictos*. 3rd ed. Guatemala City: Impresos Cancinos, 2013.

Fink, Leon. *The Maya of Morganton: Work and Community in the Nuevo New South*. Chapel Hill: University of North Carolina Press, 2003.

Fischer, Brodwyn. *A Poverty of Rights: Citizenship and Inequality in Twentieth-Century Rio de Janeiro*. Stanford: Stanford University Press, 2010.

Fischer, Brodwyn, Bryan McCann, and Javier Auyero, eds. *Cities from Scratch: Poverty and Informality in Urban Latin America*. Durham: Duke University Press, 2014.

Fischer, Edward F. *Cultural Logics and Global Economies: Maya Identity in Thought and Practice*. Austin: University of Texas Press, 2001.

Fischer, Edward F., and Peter Benson. *Broccoli and Desire: Global Connections and Maya Struggles in Postwar Guatemala*. Stanford: Stanford University Press, 2006.

FLACSO. *Guatemala: Historia reciente (1954–1996)*. Edited by Virgilio Álvarez Aragón, Carlos Figuero Ibarra, Arturo Taracena Arriola, Sergio Tischler Visquerra, and Edmundo Urrutia García. 5 vols. Guatemala City: FLACSO, 2012.

Flores, Marco Antonio. *Los compañeros*. 3rd ed. 1976. Reprint, Guatemala City: F y G, 2000.

Florida, Richard. *Cities and the Creative Class*. New York: Routledge, 2005.

———. *The New Urban Crisis*. New York: Basic Books, 2017.

———. *The Rise of the Creative Class*. New York: Basic Books, 2002.

Flynn, Patricia, dir. *Discovering Dominga*. Oakland: POV, 2003.

Frankfurter, David. *Evil Incarnate: Rumors of Demonic Conspiracy and Satanic Abuse in History*. Princeton: Princeton University Press, 2008.

Garcés de Marcilla del Valle, María Cecilia. "Hablando del otro: Categorías y estereotipos racistas en Guatemala; El caso de estudiantes de diversificado en cuatro centros educativos en la Ciudad de Guatemala." Licenciatura thesis, USAC, April 2003.

García Canclini, Néstor. *Culturas híbridas: Estrategias para entrar y salir de la modernidad*. Mexico City: Grijalbo, 1990.

García Estrada, César Augusto. *Candiles de la calle*. Guatemala City: Don Quijote, 2005.

Garrard, Virginia. *Protestantism in Guatemala: Living in the New Jerusalem*. Austin: University of Texas Press, 1998.

———. *Terror in the Land of the Holy Spirit: Guatemala under General Efraín Ríos Montt*. Oxford: Oxford University Press, 2010.

Goldman, Francisco. *The Art of Political Murder: Who Killed Archbishop Gerardi?* New York: Atlantic Books, 2010.

Goldstein, Daniel M. *Outlawed: Between Security and Rights in a Bolivian City*. Durham: Duke University Press, 2012.

———. *The Spectacular City: Violence and Performance in Urban Bolivia*. Durham: Duke University Press, 2004.

González-Izás, Matilde. "Labor Contractors to Military Specialists to Development Experts: Marginal Elites and Postwar State Formation." In McAllister and Nelson, *War by Other Means*, 261–82.

González Ponciano, Jorge Ramón. "*De la Patria del Criollo a la Patria del Shumo*: Whiteness and the Criminalization of the Dark Plebeian in Modern Guatemala." PhD diss., University of Texas, Austin, 2005.

———. "The *Shumo* Challenge: White Class Privilege and the Post-race, Postgenocide Alliances of Cosmopolitanism from Below." In McAllister and Nelson, *War by Other Means*, 307–29.

Gould, Jeffrey L. *To Lead as Equals: Rural Protest and Political Consciousness in Chinandega, Nicaragua, 1912–1979*. Chapel Hill: University of California Press, 1990.

Grandin, Greg. *The Blood of Guatemala: A History of Race and Nation*. Durham: Duke University Press, 2000.

———. *The Last Colonial Massacre: Latin America in the Cold War*. 2nd ed. Chicago: University of Chicago Press, 2011.

Green, Linda. *Fear as a Way of Life: Mayan Widows in Rural Guatemala*. New York: Columbia University Press, 1999.

Guatemala: Nunca más. Guatemala City: Oficina de Derechos Humanos del Arzobispado de Guatemala, 1998.

Guerra-Borges, Alfredo. *Guatemala: 60 años de historia económica (1944–2004)*. Guatemala City: Programa de las Naciones Unidas para el Desarrollo, 2006.

Guha, Ranajit. *Elementary Aspects of Peasant Insurgency in Colonial India*. Durham: Duke University Press, 1999.

Guinea Diez, Gerardo. *Gramática de un tiempo congelado: Ensayos y obra periodística (1994–2007)*. Guatemala City: Cultura, 2008.

Hale, Charles R. "Does Multiculturalism Menace? Governance, Cultural Rights and the Politics of Identity in Guatemala." *Journal of Latin American Studies* 34, no. 3 (August 2002): 485–524.

———. *Más Que un Indio (More Than an Indian): Racial Ambivalence and the Paradox of Neoliberal Multiculturalism in Guatemala*. Santa Fe: School of American Research Press, 2006.

Handy, Jim. *Revolution in the Countryside: Rural Conflict and Agrarian Reform in Guatemala, 1944–1954*. Chapel Hill: University of North Carolina Press, 2000.

Harvey, David. *A Brief History of Neoliberalism*. Oxford: Oxford University Press, 2007.

———. "Cities or Urbanization?" In Brenner, *Implosions/Explosions*, 52–66.

———. *Rebel Cities: From the Right to the City to the Urban Revolution*. London: Verso, 2012.

Hjarvard, Stig. *The Mediatization of Culture and Society*. London: Routledge, 2013.

Hobsbawm, Eric, and Terence Ranger, eds. *The Invention of Tradition*. Cambridge: Cambridge University Press, 1983.

Horton, Susan. "Labour Markets and the Shock Treatment in Bolivia." *Canadian Journal of Latin American and Caribbean Studies / Revue canadienne des études latino-américaines et caraïbes* 17, no. 33 (1992): 45–71.

Hudson, Michael. *Killing the Host: How Financial Parasites and Debt Bondage Destroy the Global Economy*. Petrolia, CA: CounterPunch Books, 2015.

Ihmoud, Sarah Emily. "Problematizing Discourses of Feminicide in Guatemala: Feminist Universalism, Neoliberal Subject Formation and Hypervisibility." Master's thesis, University of Texas, Austin, May 2011.

Illescas Arita, Gustavo A. *Huehuetenango, análisis de coyuntura, 2011–12: Huehuetenango desde el plano nacional y viceversa*. Huehuetenango, Guatemala: CEDFOG, 2013.

Jiménez, Elías, dir. *La casa de enfrente*. Guatemala City: Casa Comal, 2003.

Jonas, Susanne. *The Battle for Guatemala: Rebels, Death Squads, and U.S. Power*. Boulder: Westview, 1991.

———. "La democratización por medio de la paz: El difícil caso de Guatemala." In Álvarez Aragón et al., *Guatemala*, 4:25–68.

———. *Of Centaurs and Doves: Guatemala's Peace Process*. Boulder: Westview, 2000.

Joseph, Gilbert M., and Daniel Nugent, eds. *Everyday Forms of State Formation: Revolution and the Negotiation of Rule in Modern Mexico*. Durham: Duke University Press, 1994.

Kiyosaki, Robert T. *Rich Dad, Poor Dad: What the Rich Teach Their Kids about Money That the Poor and the Middle Class Do Not*. New York: Warner Books, 1997.

Klein, Naomi. *The Shock Doctrine: The Rise of Disaster Capitalism*. New York: Picador, 2007.

Konefal, Betsy. *For Every Indio Who Falls: A History of Maya Activism in Guatemala, 1960–1990*. Albuquerque: University of New Mexico Press, 2010.

Lancaster, Roger N. *Life Is Hard: Machismo, Danger, and the Intimacy of Power in Nicaragua*. Berkeley: University of California Press, 1994.
Latham, Rob. *Consuming Youth: Vampires, Cyborgs, and the Culture of Consumption*. Chicago: University of Chicago Press, 2002.
Lechner, Ernesto. *Rock en Español: The Latin Alternative Rock Explosion*. Chicago: Chicago Review Press, 2006.
Lee, Benson, dir. *Planet B-boy*. New York: Mondo Paradiso Films, 2007.
Lefebvre, Henri. *The Production of Space*. Translated by Donald Nicholson-Smith. 1974. Reprint, Oxford: Blackwell, 1991.
———. *The Urban Revolution*. Translated by Robert Bononno. 1970. Reprint, Minneapolis: University of Minnesota Press, 2003.
Levenson, Deborah. *Adiós Niño: The Gangs of Guatemala City and the Politics of Death*. Durham: Duke University Press, 2013.
———. *Hacer la juventud: Tres generaciones de una familia urbana*. Guatemala City: AVANCSO, 2004.
———. "The Life That Makes Us Die/The Death That Makes Us Live: Facing Terrorism in Guatemala City." *Radical History Review* 85 (Winter 2003): 94–104.
———. *Trade Unionists against Terror: Guatemala City, 1954–1985*. Chapel Hill: University of North Carolina Press, 1994.
Little, Walter E. "Living and Selling in the 'New Violence' of Guatemala." In Little and Smith, *Mayas in Postwar Guatemala*, 54–66.
———. "Outside of Social Movements: Dilemmas of Indigenous Handicrafts Vendors in Guatemala." *American Ethnologist* 31, no. 1 (2004): 43–59.
Little, Walter E., and Timothy J. Smith, eds. *Mayas in Postwar Guatemala: Harvest of Violence Revisited*. Tuscaloosa: University of Alabama Press, 2009.
López Castillo, José Marco Vinicio. "Análisis del proceso de descentralización de la administración pública en Guatemala." Licenciatura thesis, Universidad de San Carlos de Guatemala, August 2005.
Lovell, George. *A Beauty That Hurts: Life and Death in Guatemala*. 2nd ed. Austin: University of Texas Press, 2010.
Luna, Byron Quan. "Assessment and Modelling of Two Lahars Caused by 'Hurricane Stan' at Atitlán, Guatemala, October 2005." Master's thesis, University of Oslo, June 2007.
Mallon, Florencia E. *Peasant and Nation: The Making of Postcolonial Mexico and Peru*. Berkeley: University of California Press, 1995.
Manzano, Valeria. *The Age of Youth in Argentina: Culture, Politics, and Sexuality from Perón to Videla*. Chapel Hill: University of North Carolina Press, 2014.
Martín-Barbero, Jesús. "From Latin America: Diversity, Globalization, and Convergence." *Westminster Papers in Communication and Culture* 8, no. 1 (2011): 39–64.
Maxwell, Judith M. "Bilingual Bicultural Education: Best Intentions across a Cultural Divide." In Little and Smith, *Mayas in Postwar Guatemala*, 84–95.
Mbembe, Achille. *On the Postcolony*. Berkeley: University of California Press, 2001.

McAllister, Carlota. "Seeing Like an Indigenous Community: The World Bank's Agriculture for Development Report Read from the Perspective of Postwar Rural Guatemala." *Journal of Peasant Studies* 36 (2009): 645–51.

McAllister, Carlota, and Diane M. Nelson, eds. *War by Other Means: Aftermath in Post-genocide Guatemala*. Durham: Duke University Press, 2013.

McCann, Bryan. *Hard Times in the Marvelous City: From Dictatorship to Democracy in the Favelas of Rio de Janeiro*. Durham: Duke University Press, 2014.

McCreery, David. *Rural Guatemala, 1760–1940*. Stanford: Stanford University Press, 1994.

McGee, Terry G. "The Emergence of *Desakota* Regions in Asia: Expanding a Hypothesis." In Brenner, *Implosions/Explosions*, 121–37.

Medovoi, Leerom. *Rebels: Youth and the Cold War Origins of Identity*. Durham: Duke University Press, 2005.

Menchú, Rigoberta, and Elisabeth Burgos-Debray. *Yo me llamo Rigoberta Menchú y así me nació la conciencia*. Havana: Casa de las Américas, 1983.

Molina Calderón, José. *Guatemala: Un siglo y seis lustros de banca, bancos, y banqueros (1877–2007)*. Guatemala City: Banco Industrial, 2007.

Monsanto, Pablo. *Somos los jóvenes rebeldes: Guatemala insurgente*. Guatemala City: F y G, 2013.

Montejo, Víctor. *Maya Intellectual Renaissance: Identity, Representation, and Leadership*. Austin: University of Texas Press, 2005.

Morales, Mario Roberto. *La articulación de las diferencias, o el síndrome de Maximón: Los discursos literarios y políticos del debate interétnico en Guatemala*. 2nd ed. Guatemala City: Palo de Hormigo, 2002.

———. "Cultura y literatura en Guatemala (1955–2010)." In FLACSO, *Guatemala*, 5:25–54.

Navarro García, Susana, Pau Pérez-Sales, and Alberto Fernández-Liria. "Exhumation Processes in Fourteen Countries in Latin America." *Journal for Social Action in Counseling and Psychology* 2, no. 2 (2010): 48–83.

Nelson, Diane M. *A Finger in the Wound: Body Politics in Quincentennial Guatemala*. Berkeley: University of California Press, 1999.

———. *Reckoning: The Ends of War in Guatemala*. Durham: Duke University Press, 2009.

———. "Stumped Identities: Body Image, Bodies Politic, and the Mujer Maya as Prosthetic." *Cultural Anthropology* 16, no. 3 (2001): 314–53.

———. *Who Counts? The Mathematics of Death and Life after Genocide*. Durham: Duke University Press, 2015.

Nordstrom, Carolyn. *Global Outlaws: Crime, Money, and Power in the Contemporary World*. Berkeley: University of California Press, 2007.

Normanns Morales, Gustavo Adolfo. *La violencia: Señales y respuestas sociales. Estudio comparativo de los perfiles de violencias en cuatro municipios de Jutiapa y Sololá*. Guatemala City: Instituto de Transformación de Conflictos para la Construcción de la Paz en Guatemala/Universidad Rafael Landívar, 2012.

North, Liisa L., and Alan B. Simmons, eds. *Journeys of Fear: Refugee Return and National Transformation in Guatemala*. Montreal: McGill-Queens University Press, 1999.

Ochoa, Carlos Fredy. *Alcaldías indígenas: Diez años después de su reconocimiento por el estado*. Vol. 2. Guatemala City: Asociación de Investigación y Estudios Sociales, 2013.

Offit, Thomas. "Cacique for a Neoliberal Age: A Maya Retail Empire on the Streets of Guatemala City." In O'Neill and Thomas, *Securing the City*, 67–82.

———. *Conquistadores de la Calle: Child Street Labor in Guatemala City*. Austin: University of Texas Press, 2008.

Oglesby, Elizabeth, and Diane M. Nelson, eds. *Guatemala: The Question of Genocide*. London: Routledge, 2016.

O'Neill, Kevin Lewis. *City of God: Christian Citizenship in Postwar Guatemala*. Berkeley: University of California Press, 2010.

———. *Secure the Soul: Christian Piety and Gang Prevention in Guatemala*. Berkeley: University of California Press, 2015.

O'Neill, Kevin Lewis, and Kedron Thomas, eds. *Securing the City: Neoliberalism, Space, and Insecurity in Postwar Guatemala*. Durham: Duke University Press, 2011.

Pacini Hernandez, Deborah, Héctor Fernández L'Hoeste, and Eric Zolov, eds. *Rockin' Las Américas: The Global Politics of Rock in Latin/o America*. Pittsburgh: University of Pittsburgh Press, 2004.

Palencia Prado, Tania. *Huehuetenango: Análisis de coyuntura, 2009–2010*. Huehuetenango, Guatemala: CEDFOG, 2010.

Payeras, Javier. *La región más invisible*. Guatemala City: Ministerio de Cultura y Deportes/Editorial Cultura, 2017.

———. *Ruido de fondo*. Guatemala City: Piedra Santa, 2006.

Payeras, Mario. *El trueno en la ciudad: Episodios de la lucha armada urbana de 1981 en Guatemala*. 4th ed. Antigua, Guatemala: Pensativo, 2014.

Peck, Jamie. *Constructions of Neoliberal Reason*. Oxford: Oxford University Press, 2010.

Pensado, Jaime. *Rebel Mexico: Student Unrest and Authoritarian Political Culture during the Long Sixties*. Stanford: Stanford University Press, 2013.

Pensado, Jaime, and Enrique C. Ochoa, eds. *México beyond 1968: Revolutionaries, Radicals, and Repression during the Global Sixties and Subversive Seventies*. Tucson: University of Arizona Press, 2018.

Perry, Joe. "Love Parade 1996: Techno Playworlds and the Neoliberalization of Postwall Berlin." *German Studies Review* 42, no. 3 (2019): 561–79.

¿Por qué tanta destrucción? Las amenazas naturales y estructurales: Sistematización de la vulnerabilidad, la negligencia y la exclusión regional del altiplano occidental en la tormenta asociada Stan. Guatemala City: Editorial Ciencias Sociales, 2006.

Pradilla Cobos, Emilio. "Presente y futuro de las metrópolis de América Latina." With Lisett Márquez López. *Territorios* 18–19 (2008): 147–81.

Ramírez, Chiqui. *La guerra de los 36 años: Vista de ojos de mujer de izquierda*. Guatemala City: León Palacios, 2001.

Ramírez Raymundo, William Tomás. "Financiamiento de la producción de unidades pecuarias (engorde de ganado ovino) y proyecto producción de huevos de gallina: Municipio de Santa Eulalia, Departamento de Huehuetenango." Licenciatura thesis, USAC, March 2007.
Ramos, Carlos Guillerrmo, ed. *Jóvenes urbanos: Cultura política y democracia de posconflicto en Centroamérica: Guatemala*. San Salvador, El Salvador: FLACSO, 2013.
Revenga, Álvaro, dir. *El oro o la vida: Recolonización y resistencia en Centroamérica*. Guatemala City: Caracol Producciones, 2011.
Rizzo, Vinizzio, dir. *Alternativa: La historia del rock en Guatemala*. Guatemala City: Rizzo Producciones/Jam Producciones, 2010.
Roberts, Brian H. *Managing Systems of Secondary Cities: Policy Responses in International Development*. Brussels: Cities Alliance/United Nations Office for Project Services, 2014.
Roberts, Bryan R. *The Making of Citizens: Cities of Peasants Revisited*. 2nd ed. London: Routledge, 1995.
Ross, Amy. "The Ríos Montt Case and Universal Jurisdiction." *Journal of Genocide Research* 18, nos. 2–3 (2016): 361–76.
Rothenberg, Daniel. "Panic of the Robaniños: Gringo Organ Stealers, Narratives of Mistrust, and the Guatemalan Political Imagination." PhD diss., University of Chicago, 2018.
Saldaña-Portillo, María Josefina. *The Revolutionary Imagination in the Americas and the Age of Development*. Durham: Duke University Press, 2003.
Sanford, Victoria. *Buried Secrets: Truth and Human Rights in Guatemala*. London: Palgrave Macmillan, 2003.
Santa Cruz Mendoza, Santiago. *Insurgentes: Guatemala, la paz arrancada*. Mexico City: Era, 2006.
Santamaría, Gema, and David Carey Jr., eds. *Violence and Crime in Latin America: Representations and Politics*. Norman: University of Oklahoma Press, 2017.
Santo Urías, José Fernando. "La exclusión de activos y pasivos aplicada a una entidad bancaria privada guatemalteca." Licenciatura thesis, USAC, November 2006.
Sassen, Saskia. *Cities in a World Economy*. 5th ed. Thousand Oaks: Sage, 2018.
———. *Expulsions: Brutality and Complexity in the Global Economy*. Cambridge: Harvard University Press, 2014.
Schirmer, Jennifer. *The Guatemalan Military Project: A Violence Called Democracy*. Philadelphia: University of Pennsylvania Press, 1999.
Schlotterbeck, Marian E. *Beyond the Vanguard: Everyday Revolutionaries in Allende's Chile*. Berkeley: University of California Press, 2018.
Scott, Allen J. "Globalization and the Rise of City-Regions." *European Planning Studies* 9, no. 7 (2001): 813–26.
Scott, James C. *Domination and the Arts of Resistance: Hidden Transcripts*. New Haven: Yale University Press, 1992.
———. *The Moral Economy of the Peasant: Rebellion and Subsistence in Southeast Asia*. New Haven: Yale University Press, 1976.

Serrano Elías, Jorge. *La guayaba tiene dueño: El secuestro del Estado en Guatemala.* 4th ed. Guatemala City: F y G, 2012.

Sevilla-Buitrago, Álvaro. "*Urbs in Rure:* Historical Enclosure and the Extended Urbanization of the Countryside." In Brenner, *Implosions/Explosions,* 236–59.

Sieder, Rachel. "Contested Sovereignties: Indigenous Law, Violence and State Effects in Postwar Guatemala." *Critique of Anthropology* 31, no. 3 (2011): 161–34.

———. "Customary Law and Local Power in Guatemala." In Sieder, *Peace Accords,* 97–115.

———. *Guatemala after the Peace Accords.* London: Institute of Latin American Studies, 1998.

Sierra Marroquín, Jorge R. "La música en Guatemala desde la contrarevolución (1954–1996)." In FLACSO, *Guatemala,* 5:243–332.

Smith, Carol A., ed. *Guatemalan Indians and the State: 1540 to 1988.* Austin: University of Texas Press, 1992.

Smith, Timothy J. "Democracy Is Dissent: Political Confrontations and Indigenous Mobilization in Sololá." In Little and Smith, *Mayas in Postwar Guatemala,* 16–29.

———. "A Tale of Two Governments: Rural Maya Politics and Competing Democracies in Sololá, Guatemala." PhD diss., State University of New York, Albany, 2003.

Solano, Luis. "Development and/as Dispossession." In McAllister and Nelson, *War by Other Means,* 119–42.

———. *Guatemala: Petróleo y minería en las entrañas del poder.* Guatemala City: Inforpress Centroamericana, 2005.

Swinehart, Karl. "Tupac in the Veins: Hip Hop Alteño and the Semiotics of Urban Indigeneity." *Arizona Journal of Hispanic Cultural Studies* 16 (2012): 79–96.

Taracena Arriola, Arturo. *Invención criolla, sueño ladino, pesadilla indígena: Los Altos de Guatemala; De región a estado, 1750–1850.* Antigua, Guatemala: CIRMA, 1997.

Taracena Arriola, Arturo, Enrique Gordillo, and Tania Sagastume. *Etnicidad, estado y nación en Guatemala, 1808–1944.* Vol. 2, *¿Por qué estamos como estamos?* Antigua, Guatemala: CIRMA, 2004.

Taylor, Clark. *Return of Guatemala's Refugees: Reweaving the Torn.* Philadelphia: Temple University Press, 1998.

Thomas, Kedron. *Regulating Style: Intellectual Property Law and the Business of Fashion in Guatemala.* Berkeley: University of California Press, 2016.

Valdés Toledo, Karla Fernanda. "Herramientas financieras para la evaluación de opciones en la adquisición y reemplazo de vehículos en una empresa de servicio de taxis rotativos de tres ruedas." Licenciatura thesis, USAC, November 2014.

Villar Herrera, Ana Maerylin. "Renovación de la imagen urbana del Municipio de Chiantla, Huehuetenango." Thesis, USAC, September 2007.

Vrana, Heather. *This City Belongs to You: A History of Student Activism in Guatemala, 1944–1996.* Berkeley: University of California Press, 2017.

Walker, Louise E. *Waking from the Dream: Mexico's Middle Classes after 1968.* Stanford: Stanford University Press, 2013.

Warren, Kay B. "Indigenous Movements as a Challenge to the Unified Social Movement Paradigm for Guatemala." In *Cultures of Politics, Politics of Cultures: Revisioning Latin American Social Movements,* edited by Sonia E. Alvarez, Evelyn Dagnino, and Arturo Escobar, 165–95. Boulder: Westview, 1998.
Way, J. T. "City Streets in Rural Places: Emerging Cities, Youth Cultures, and the Neoliberalization of Guatemala." *Journal of Social History* 53, no. 1 (2019): 76–106.
———. *The Mayan in the Mall: Globalization, Development, and the Making of Modern Guatemala.* Durham: Duke University Press, 2012.
———. "The Movement, the Mine and the Lake: New Forms of Maya Activism in Neoliberal Guatemala." In *Global Indigeneities and the Environment,* edited by Karen L. Thorber and Tom Havens, 86–106. Basel, Switzerland: MDPI, 2016.
Weld, Kirsten. *Paper Cadavers: The Archives of Dictatorship in Guatemala.* Durham: Duke University Press, 2014.
Williams, Raymond. *Marxism and Literature.* Oxford: Oxford University Press, 1978.
Yagenova, Simona Violetta. *La protesta social en Guatemala: Una aproximación a los actores, demandas, formas, despliegue territorial, límites y alcances, Octubre 2004–Septiembre 2006.* Guatemala City: FLACSO, 2007.
Yagenova, Simona Violetta, Claudia Donis, and Patricio Castillo, eds. *La industria extractiva en Guatemala: Políticas públicas, derechos humanos, y procesos de resistencia popular en el período 2003–2011.* Guatemala City: FLACSO, 2012.
Yates, Pamela, dir. *Dictator in the Dock.* New York: Skylight Films, 2013.
Ypeij, Annelou. "Cholos, incas y fusionistas: El nuevo Perú y la globalización de lo andino." *Revista Europea de Estudios Latinoamericanos y del Caribe* 94 (April 2013): 67–82.
Zamora Mejía, Fabián Marcelo. *Ser "moderno" en San Miguel Totonicapán: El baile del convite y la globalización cultural.* Guatemala City: FLACSO, 2007.
Zapata, Adrián. *El proceso de formación de la política pública de desarrollo rural en Guatemala: Período 1996–2006.* Guatemala City: FLACSO/Agencia Sueca para el Desarrollo Internacional, 2009.
Zolov, Eric. *Refried Elvis: The Rise of Mexican Counterculture.* Berkeley: University of California Press, 1999.

INDEX

Adams, Richard, 32
"Adonay," 192–93, 202–203, 261nn7,8
advertising, 33, 89fig., 179; BBDO/Tortrix, "chulo tu chucho," 183–84, 189, 200; Megapaca, 200–201; Pepsi, Guatemorfosis, 199–200; and corporate sponsorship, 139
agriculture: in agro-urban landscape, 3–5, 9–10, 19, 57, 96map, 165–66, 202, 212n15; coffee, 133, 151, 221n81, 248n95; and cooperatives, 40; crop commercialization, 75; and development, 31–32, 38–39, 52–53, 125, 159, 169–70, 248n95; and generational change, 14, 43, 52, 59, 116, 119–22, 144, 161, 176–81, 209–10; and labor, 14, 34, 39–40, 114–16, 188–89, 213n28, 227n51; maize, 39, 52, 169. See also nontraditional agro-exports
agrotropolis: as concept, 4–7, 15, 131; emergence of, 24–26, 96map, 131, 165, 167; as global/local, 4, 7, 25, 162, 167, 173, 188, 208; and interclass dialogue, 173; and memory, 175; and nationalisms, 131, 201; road trips through, 1–4, 202–203; and strategic territorial planning, 171; and street/barrio life, 7, 131, 175, 183–84, 188–89, 208; and urban studies, 9–10, 19–20; and violence, 25, 131 193. See also agro-urbanization; barrio, the; calle/KY; city-regions; urbanization
agro-urbanization: and already-existing urban-rural networks, 19–20, 69, 95, 119, 191, 211n6; as cultural, economic,

social, physical: 4–7, 9, 12–13, 19–20, 21–26, 52–53, 114–15, 131; and cultural cosmopolitanism, 5, 9–10, 12–13, 15, 25, 80, 84, 131, 166–67, 169, 178, 204, 208, 214n33; and *desakota* regions, 212n15; described visually, 2–4, 96map, 97–98, 120fig., 192, 202–3; earthquake of 1976 and, 38; ENJU on, 262n16; and epidemiological discourse, *see* disease; and foreign aid, 64–66, 115, 145–56, 156–57 (*see also* development, Inter-American development bank); and foreign media and consumer culture, 62, 72–77, 84, 104, 114, 121, 137, 142–43; and global urbanization, 9–10, 19, 62–63, 68, 127, 167, 201, 212n15, 223n6; and guerrilla's move to central areas, 1986 forward, 70–72, 85–86, 101, 103; and industrialization of Guatemala City in 1950s-60s, 31–32; and infrastructure development and communications technology, 14, 44–45, 69, 73, 75, 109, 115, 119, 125, 134, 166–67, 179, 216–17n15; invisibility of, 69–70, 93, 128, 130–31, 201; K'atun development plan on, 9, 191; and labor regimes, 14, 34, 52, 69, 71, 114–16, 122, 133, 144, 161–65, 176–78, 182, 213n28, 252n32; and land invasions and poor neighborhoods, 59, 75–76, 83–84, 99, 116, 192, 202 (*see also barrios marginales*); and *mancomunidades,* 171, 181; and Mayan movement, see Mayan movement; and multigenerational

279

agro-urbanization *(continued)*
guerrilla families, 72; and moral economy of the tuc-tuc, see tuc-tuc; and multisector negotiation model, 64, 136–37, 156–57, 170–71; and *mundo al revés*, 131–35, 176*fig.*; and *mundo en libertad*, 149–53, 157–58, 160; and narcotraffic and drug trade, 53, 118, 152, 161; and nationalism, see nationalism; and "NGO-ification," 53, 66, 104, 115, 125; and nontraditional agro-exports, 39–40, 52–53, 75, 156, 161, 169; pace of, accelerated, 114–5; and population growth, 1, 5, 20, 22, 39, 52, 69, 95, 96*map*, 115–6, 121, 134, 181; and privatization, banking, economic reforms, and capital expansion, late 1990s forward, 132–34, 156, 160–61, 165–67, 169–76; and price of land, process of *lotificación*, 52, 134; and provincial city-regions, 10, 23, 95–97, 114–22, 131–32, 167, 171, 181, 188, 201, 209; and real and imagined street, see *calle*/KY, barrio; remapping and "territorial interventions," 169–72; and remittances (remesas) 11, 57, 75, 115, 119–21, 253n40; and retail, commercial, and banking services, 52–53, 116–19, 134, 171; and returned refugees, 85, 99, 158; and "rural-to-less-rural" migration, 52, 69, 71, 83–84, 176–77; and schools and educational services, 52–53, 116, 125, 137, 163–64; and servility, see servility; and sex, sexual attractiveness, sexualized discourses, 75, 80, 117–18, 150, 155, 173–74, 178–79, 182, 260n116; and social investment funds, 64–66; and tourism, see tourism; and Vamos Guatemala program, 170; and violence of militarism and counterinsurgency, 10–11, 40–42, 53, 57–58, 65–66, 71, 77–78, 83, 98–100, 104 *(see also* military); and violence of vigilantism, crime, and "warlordism," 5, 97, 99, 104–5, 118–19, 121–22, 135–36, 155–56, 191–98, *(see also* gangs, vigilantism); and youth, cultural assertiveness, 7, 23–24, 62, 76–77, 118, 131–32, 138, 144, 166–67, 178–82, 189, 203–5, 238n86 *(see also*

servility); and youth culture, 13, 53–54, 56, 62, 76, 92–93, 114–15, 119, 126, 138, 144, 150, 206–10 *(see also* panic); and youth culture, global, see *calle*/KY, musical genres, youth; and youth culture, hippie styles, 80, 152–53, 164, 173; and youth culture, "oppositional styles," 84–85, 228n71, 229n73; and youth culture, touring bands, 102*fig.*, 109–10, 115, 131–32, 138, 158; and youth, *de a pie* Maya pride, 22–4, 49, 76–77, 81, 83–6, 100, 110, 123, 126, 130–32, 144, 164, 204–5 *(see also* Mayan movement); and youth, differing experiences of, 102–3*figs.*, 154*fig.*; and youth, generational change 4–5, 52, 62, 76–77, 81, 95, 103–4, 128, 138–40, 173, 177–78, 191–92; and youth, identities, 4–6, 8, 15–17, 20–25, 43, 68, 73, 76–77, 83–86, 96–97, 127, 139–41, 147, 152–53, 176, 182–83, 201, 203–5; and youth, Maya musicians and artists, 5, 13, 20, 25, 98, 132, 148–49, 162, 166, 179–81, 188–89, 206–10; and youth programs, 4, 18, 67, 97, 132, 145–46, 148, 166–67, 179, 182, 187, 189–90, 244n50, 256n69; and youth, rivalry and street wars, 127, 155, 182. *See also* agro-urbanization, regional; *alcaldía indígena*; *barrio; calle*/KY; Consejos de Desarrollo; development; Mayan movement; municipal government and politics; urbanization; youth
agro-urbanization, regional: Aguacatán, 119–20, 120*fig.*, 126–27, 237n81; Antigua and environs, 1, 72, 109, 187, 192–93, 207–9; Barillas, 118–19, 136–37, 157–58, 255n61; Chiantla, 96*map*, 181; Chimaltenango, 2–3, 71, 76, 115, 117, 171, 193; Coatepeque, 122, 127; Escuintla, 72, 101, 102*fig.*, 115, 117, 202; Guatemala City outskirts and environs, 32, 36, 39, 103–4, 143, 115–16, 152; Huehuetenango, 3–4, 19, 75–76, 85–86, 97, 109, 115, 117–18, 122, 127, 158, 180, 182, 191, 206; Jacaltenango and elsewhere in Huista region, 72–77, 97–99, 118, 121–22, 132, 153; Lake Atitlán area, 1–2, 13, 80–81; 102*fig.*, 151–57, 162–64–66, 171–73,

176–81, 195–98, 206–10, 251n24; Nahualá, 3, 185; Quetzaltenango and environs, 3, 73, 115–17, 188, 255n61; San Andrés Semetabaj, 177–79, 192, 251n24; San Idelfonso Ixtahuacán, 132, 134; San Juan Ostuncalco, 188–89; San Miguel Acatán, 77–78; San Miguel Petapa, 116; Santa Cruz del Quiché, 3, 76, 82, 98, 136; Santa Eulalia, 120–21; Sololá, 80–82, 83–84, 124–8, 137, 157, 194–95; Tecpán, 3, 161; Todos Santos Cuchumatán, 142, 146–47
Aguacatán, 119–20, 120*fig*.;description of, 4; diversity in, 126; languages in, 237n79; modernization of, 237n81
AIDS: anxiety regarding, 75–76; CONJUVE campaign, 249n5; foreigners linked with, 80
Ajcalón Choy, Rigoberto, 82; on zotz', 125–26
alcaldes auxiliares (auxiliary mayors), 83. *See also* military; municipal government and politics
alcaldía indígena (indigenous municipality), 78–80, 101, 124–26, 194, 246n79, 260n116. *See also* municipal government and politics
Alhazred. *See* internet/social media blogs, posts, and pages
Alioto Lokos, 112–14, 116; and Bacteria Soundsytem Crew, 145, 180; and Octubreazul, 145. *See also* Bacteria Soundsytem Crew; rap
Alternativa (film), 109, 131–32, 139, 256n71
Alux Nahual, 22; Alvarado, Paulo on, 44, 219n46; "Alto al fuego" and *Americamorfosis*, 61 (*see* Americamorfosis); and *duendes*, "Como un duende," song and idea, 67–68, 92, 148, 192; and Javier Payeras, 246n68
Alvarado, Paulo, 44, 219n46, 223n4
Ambev, 159, 247n91
Americamorfosis: Alux Nahual album, 61; concept introduced, 22–23; and discourses of identity and identity politics, complicated, 61–62, 83, 201; emotions of, 93; and urbanization of physical and social space, 61–63, 68–70, 76–77, 201

Andrade, Ricardo, 106, 129; childhood of, 234n38; death of, 129, 151, 158
Anonymous Guatemala: beginning of, 205; demonstrations, 206; postings by, 262n17
antibreaks. *See* break dancing; break wars
Antigua Guatemala: in advertising, 183; in city-region of, 1, 71–72, 192, 209; in city-region of, Jocotenango, 187, 209; creative center, 187, 207; parties in, 246n68; residence in, 17, 197, 261n8; tour stop, 109. *See also* urbanization
antishumo discourse. *See* shumo
Aporte para la Descentralización de la Cultura (ADESCA, Support for Cultural Decentralization): arts sponsorship, 145; and centralization, 149; publishing, 243n37, 244n48
Arana Osorio, Carlos, 36
archives (cultural forms as, "living"), 176, 179–81, 189; community, 175; concepts of, 16–17; of the street, 17, 24, 254n47
Área Metropolitana de Guatemala (AMG, Guatemala Metropolitan Area), 116
Arjona, Ricardo, 87; Pepsi campaign, 25, 199
army. *See* military
arts, artists: from above and below, 145–46; Calel, Edgar, 207; and chapín, 141–43; Chavajay, Benvenuto, 207–208; and creative cities, 207–8; Galindo, Regina José, 145; and inner-city youth, 113; and Maya nationalism, 48; and national image, 166; Osorio, José, 145; and Panajachel, 80; Pichillá, Antonio, 207; and "power grids," 158–59; and rock nacional, 107; San Juan Comalapa and San Pedro La Laguna as centers of, 207–8. *See also* musical artists; musical genres
Arzú, Álvaro, 111; and crime, 105; election of, 124; and peace process, 101
Asamblea de la Sociedad Civil (ASC), 78, 99, 101
Asociación Guatemalteca de Alcaldes y Autoridades Indígenas (AGAAI, Guatemalan Association of Indigenous Mayors and Authorities), 80

Ati: La Revista del Lago, 172–74, 196; Arrillaga, Juan Miguel, 172; community cultural projects, 179, 195; ethnotourism, 174; on youth, 179, 195. *See* Escobar, Lucía

baby boom, 1, 28, 164; and gangs, 121
bachata, 76, 109, 186
Bacteria Soundsystem Crew, 259n97, 264n30; and Alioto Lokos, 145; "Lo que veo," "in the jaws of these gray cities," lyric and idea, 190, 190–98, 201; popularity, 180; popularizing rap, 186, 188; youth campaign, 189–90
banks, 221n81, 249n7, 253n40; archives of, 16; Bancafé, 168; Banco Azteca, 171; Banco de Guatemala (Banguat), 240n9, 244n13, 249n7, 250n10; Banco Nacional de Desarrollo Agrícola (BANDESA, National Agricultural Development Bank), 39, 241n12; Banco Nacional de la Vivienda (BANVI, National Housing Bank), 217n17; Banrural, 133, 241n12; and "CAFTA effect," 167–69, 250n9; and crime, 116; and decentralization, 171; and laws, 150, 250n14; and neoliberalization, 160; offshore banks, 11, 66, 77, 129, 150, 168–69, 250n10; and privatization, 132–34; and "rural-to-less-rural" migration, 52; spread of, 11; structure of, in Guatemala, 250n9. *See also* financialization; Inter-American Development Bank; World Bank
Barillas. *See* Santa Cruz Barillas
Barrera Ortiz, Byron: on Portillo, Alfonso, 159, 247n91
Barrio (film), 180, 254n51
barrios marginales (poor, "marginal" neighborhoods): agro-urban, described, 5, 192; and CAFTA effect, 169; in Chiantla, 181; in Guatemala City, 28, 32, 57, 110, 259n97; in Guatemala City, El Gallito, 51, 231n103; in Guatemala City, Mario Alioto López Sanchez settlement, 112–13, 145, 180; in Guatemala City, *repasos* in 33–34; and *lotificación* of farmland, 52–53; and marketing of poor youth, 144–46; and rural-urban and inter-ethnic encounters, 38, 76, 144; in San Miguel Petapa, 116; in Santa Eulalia, 121

barrio, the, as social space, 7 (global, cf hood), 128; and authenticity of popular class, 111, 128, 144, 173–75, 179; *Barrio* (film), 180; "barrio cool," 25; "barrio gangs," 121, 161 (*see also* gangs); 192, 203; "barrio nationalism," 25, 43, 176–84, 186, 189, 199; and urban youth territories in Guatemala City, 34–35, 88–92; and moral panic about youth, 76–77, 83–85, 137. *See also calle*/KY; gangs; informal economy
Bastos, Santiago, 48
Battle of the Year (BOTY), 187, 257n79. *See also* break dancing
BBDO Guatemala, 183–84, 200
B-boys, B-boying, 4, 145, 166, 187, 208*fig.,* 208–209; B-girling, 187; Ijatz Crew, 5, 13, 20–21, 145
Beck, Erin, 66, 213n19
Beltranena, Francisco, 103–4
Benson, Peter, 161
Berger, Óscar, 151, 159, 166; and neoliberalization, 160
Bethania, 112
being and becoming, 45, 143
Blandón de Cerezo, Raquel, 27
Bohemia Suburbana: "Aire," 105–6; band introduced, 94–95; formation of, 106; in *Hasta Atrás,* 107; Javier Payeras on 106; global fame, 108; inspiring local bands, 114; in Panajachel, 196, 102*fig.,* 260n114; "Peces e iguanas" ("ni pez ni iguana, ni tierra ni agua"), song and idea, 23, 94–97; 105–6; 115, 126, 128–29, 148, 192, 201; in soundtrack, *La casa de enfrente,* 159. *See also* Pinzón, Giovani
Bordieu, Pierre, 76
Bourgeois, Philippe, 84, 228n71
Brahva beer, 159, 247n91
break dancing, 57, 145, 186–7, 230n90. *See also* break wars
break wars, 88–93, 97, 113, 204, 230n88, 230n90, 231n103
Brenner, Neil, 9, 22

282 · INDEX

Buonafina, Giácomo: Primera Generación Records, 88, 89*fig.*, 95–96, 107. See also *Hasta Atrás;* Primera Generación Records

CAFTA-DR. *See* Central American-Dominican Republic Free Trade Agreement
Caja Lúdica, 145, 186
Callaci, Emily, 16–17, 254n47
calle/KY, 7, 13–14, 17, 131; as archive of cultural forms, 17, 24, 147, 176, 179, 189; and development apparatus, 148, 187–88; and dialogical relationship with political economy, 57–58, 131, 133–36, 144, 149, 160, 183; as global/local imaginary, 13, 54, 175; KY-based history of agro urban towns, 153; KY chapinismo, 147–49, 172–73, 176, 179, 183–88; KY, emergence of, as contested national commons, 24, 131–35, 140, 143–44, 147, 149, 167, 186; and Maya identities, 132, 138, 153, 173–74, 184, 188, 208–10; mix of festivity and violence on, 135, 140, 149–50, 201; and popular nationalism, 24, 131, 140, 147–48, 181, 184–85, 209–210; and public/private involutions, 24, 138, 147, 154–55, 167, 197; relation to elite culture, 142, 144; Sobrevivencia on, 132; 210; and social self, 131. *See also barrio,* the, as social space; internet/ social media blogs, posts, and pages; nationalism; tuc-tuc
Camus, Manuela, 44, 48, 230n88
Cañas, Ángel. *See* Alioto Lokos; Bacteria Soundsystem Crew; Iqui Balam
Caracol Producciones, 183
Casa Bizarra, 141–42, 145, 244n50
Casa de enfrente (film), 159–60
Castañeda Maldonado, Mario, 33, 34, 216n15
caste, *castas,* 6, 12, 21–26, 164, 201–5, 210, 213nn22,23; in 1980s: 29–30; and client-patron relations, 114–15; and cultural authenticity, 110–13, 182, 189, 202–203; cultural assertiveness and self-esteem, 7, 23, 60, 62, 166–67, 175, 178–79, 182–84, 210, 253n34 (*see also* servility, as cultural form); importance of popular youth culture in analyzing, 32–33; intercaste dialogue, 12–13, 143–45, 172–79; Guatemala City break wars and, 87–93; guerrilla camps and, 37–38; and the "ethnic question", 43, 49 (*see also* "ethnic question"); and ladino worldview, 109–10; "oppositional styles" and, 83–85; in polyvalent chapín identity, 140–41; and reconfigured national image, 166; youth contestation over, 54, 57, 87–93, 106, 116, 180–82, 203–5, 230n88. *See also* break wars; musical genres; nationalism; servility as a cultural form; style; youth
Castillo, Rodolfo, 108
cell phones. *See* telephones
Central American-Dominican Republic Free Trade Agreement (CAFTA-DR), 11, 25; "CAFTA effect," 166–69, 172, 175, 178
Cerezo, Vinicio, 28, 80, 240n10; and business elite, 63; CONJUVE, 67; and guerrilla organizations, 60, 64; price control, 69, 221n81; Sistema de Protección Ciudadana (SIPROCI), 91; social protest, 60, 69; and World Bank, 65
CERJ. *See* Consejo de Comunidades Étnicas Runujel Junam
cerote, 56, 180, 192, 222n92, 264n31
chapinismo, chapinismos: chapín defined and discussed, 2, 8, 13, 21, 215n48, 264n31; *"chapines locales;"* and ladino worldview, 23–24, 109–11; "Chapinlandia," 95; chapín modernity of 1960s, 33; Ijatz Crew and, 13, 209, and la KY, 131 (*see also calle*/KY); "Luis," chapín slang, 178; Mayan movement on chapín national identity, 48; and Megapaca ad campaign, 200–201; and Pepsi ad campaign, 199–200; polyvalent chapín identity, 140–41; and popular nationalism 24–25, 95, 140, 147–49, 166, 176; popular class influence on, 14–15, 92–93, 166, 173, 176, 179, 189; and popular youth culture, 15, 18, 24–25, 84, 88, 107, 139, 148–49, 188; "Soy chapín de sangre," 148, 164; and Tortrix ad

INDEX · 283

chapinismo, chapinismos *(continued)* campaign, 183–84, 200–201; undermining caste system 92–93 *(see also* caste, castas*)*; as unifying discourse and articulation, 147; villaging-up *(aldeando)* of, 144, 172–73; "La Virula," 186, 189; websites, 184–85, 259n97, 264n31

Chattopadhyay, Swati, 15, 214n33

Chavajay, Benvenuto, 207

Checha y Su India Maya Caballero, 138, 162

Chiantla, 3–4, 96*map*, 181

Chichicastenango, 4, 228n67

childhood, children, 154*fig.*, 163*fig.*, and agriculture, 52; changed conception of in new generation, 192–93; child labor, 46, 95, 116, 153, 163–64, 176–80, 252n32; and counterinsurgency, militarism, 50, 55–57, 71–72; in diaspora, 172; as defined by Guatemalan state, 215n47; and education, 116, 137; and foreigners, 82; and inner-city, 112–13; of "Luis," 176–79; and Maya, 153; and *robaniños*, 67–68, 147; "second childhood," 164; and social cleansing, 91–93; and state propaganda, 146; and tourism, 174; and USAID, 14. *See also* Caja Lúdica; Iqui Balam; panic, moral panic; street children; youth

Chimaltenango, 19, 71, 101, 248n95

cholera, 75–76

cholo, cholero, 12, 57, 91, 189; anti-cholero sentiment, 204; and break dancing, 90; cholebreaks, 90, 230n90; Los Cholos (Todos Santos), 142; and hip hop, 29; as identification, 147; style, 84, 230n90

"Chulo tu chucho colocho," 176, 183–84, 189, 197, 200

Círculo Experimental de Cantautores de Guatemala (Experimental Circle of Guatemalan Singer-Songwriters), 36

city-regions, 10, 114–23, 131, 167, 191–92, 201, 212n15; of Antigua, 71–72, 187, 192–93, 202, 209; of Chimaltenango, 171; emergence of, 23, 95, 115; Guatemala City Metropolitan Area (AMG, Área Metropolitana de Guatemala), 116; Huehuetenango, 117–18; Huehuetenango-Chiantla, 3–4, 96*map*, 181; in Huehuetenango department, 118–19; and political decentralization, 170–71, 181; Quetzaltenango, 116–17, 188. *See also* agro-urbanization

Civil Affairs, military, 83. *See also* military

Civilian Self-Defense Patrol. *See* PAC

Claro. *See* telephone

class, 1, 7–8, 12, 17, 22, 31–33, 179, 202–3; and agro-urban/urban geography, 3, 5, 28–29, 32–35, 52, 69–70, 73, 89, 113, 115–16, 161, 181–82, 193, 201; and authenticity, 23–25, 110–13, 128, 144, 146, 173–74, 179, 182–83, 189, 202–3; class in Maya society, 37, 83–84, 178 *(see also* Mayan movement*)*; classism, 6, 12, 21, 99, 109–10, 185–86, 199–201; creative class, 107; and emergent cultural commons, 12, 20, 25, 62, 113–14, 143–49, 166, 172–73, 205; fictitious middle classes, 197; interclass rivalry, 23, 29–30, 44–45, 53–54, 57, 88–93, 94, 116, 180, 203–5, 213n23; interelite battles, 28; landless agricultural laborers, 39; middle-class antihero, 86–87, 189; middle-class creation, 6, 31, 44; middle classes, 6, 28, 44, 55, 110–12; mobility, 14, 24, 115, 121, 161; solidarity, 47, 51–52, 63–64, 68; and street culture, see *calle*/KY; upper- and middle-class "lost generation," 23, 86–87, 91; versus ethnicity, in guerrilla organizations, 46–47, 49; working-class cultural assertiveness, *see* servility. *See also* barrio; *calle*/KY; de a pie; caste, castas; "ethnic question"; servility; youth

Coatepeque, 122, 127

Cobán, 158; Consejo de Juventudes Indígenas, 256n69

Coffee, *See under* agriculture

cofradías, 77, 80, 83

Cold War: coming of age in, 92; counterinsurgency against, 31; displacements of, 61, 66; end of, 6, 70; impact on Guatemala, 10; and Maya activism, 77; and neoliberalism, 6, 9; public and private, 65; subverting the narrative of, 59–60; and violence, 11

colegios, see education

Colom, Álvaro, 166, 249n4; critique of, 190; youth campaign, 189
Colom, Yolanda: and Colom, Álvaro, 166, 249n4; and creative centers, 207; and ladino-Maya encounters, 37–38; on machismo, 218n32; on Maya complexities, 77; and the Mayan highlands, 35, 70; on negotiated peace, 85; on Octubre Revolucionario (OR), 46, 85; and social movement webs, 63. *See also* Octubre Revolucionario (OR); Payeras, Mario
Comalapa. *See* San Juan Comalapa
Comcel (Tigo). *See* telephone
comisionados (military commissioners): as auxiliary mayors, 41, 83; demobilization of, 101; and Misión de las Naciones Unidas en Guatemala (MINUGUA), 98; and violence, 41, 99, 104, 105. *See* military
Comisión Presidencial Coordinadora de la Política del Ejecutivo en Materia de Derechos Humanos (COPREDEH, Presidential Commission Coordinating Executive Policy on Human Rights), 194
Comité Coordinador de Asociaciones Agrícolas, Comerciales, Industriales y Financieras (CACIF, Coordinating Committee of Agricultural, Commercial, Industrial and Financial Associations), 221n81, 252n28
Comité de Unidad Campesina (CUC): actions, 40, 222n82; Committee to Support the Maya Municipality, 82; expansion of, 63; and Maya, 47; and violence, 98
Comité Voluntario de Defensa Civil (CVDC, Civilian Volunteer Defense Committee), 98, 104–5. *See also* Patrulla de Autodefensa Civil (PAC)
Communist Party, 48, 220n56
community development plans. *See* municipal and community development plans
competitiveness, economic, 160, 171–75, 248n95, 252n28. *See also* PRONACOM
Consejo Nacional de la Juventud (CONJUVE). *See* youth programs
Consejos de Desarrollo Comunitarios, Municipales, Departamentales (COC-

ODEs, COMUDEs, CODEDEs), 157, 170, 193–95, 198, 249n5, 259n107
Controversia, 117–118
Consejo de Comunidades Étnicas Runujel Junam (CERJ, Runujel Junam Ethnic Communities Council), 78, 227n52, 228n66
Consejo de Juventudes Indígenas (Council of Indigenous Youths). *See* youth programs
Consejo Supremo de Metal, 88
Consultative Group on Guatemala, 160, 248n94
Contra War, 50, 63, 66
convites, 114
cooperatives: and Banrural, 133; Cuatro Pinos, 39; linked to/rooted in counterinsurgency, 53, 56; and nontraditional agro-exports, 39–40; and Sololatecos United for Development (SUD), 125; and IDB More than Remittances program, 253n40
Cooper, Frederick, 15
Coordinación de Organizaciones del Pueblo Maya de Guatemala (COPMAGUA). *See* Mayan movement
Coordinación de Organizaciones Mayas de Guatemala (COMG). *See* Mayan movement
corruption (political), 244n57, 260n107, 263n20; and alternative popular nationalism, 15, 24; in art, 129–30, 159, 190–91; and banks, 168–70; and decentralization, 159–62; force against, 148; "from below" meeting "from above," 160, 206; in Huehuetenango, 158; and identity, 155; and *libertad*, 150–51; and grassroots organizing, 125; and "organized bands," 132; and security posse, 136; of youth and lifeworld (discursively), 23, 72–76, 182
counterculture, 5, 8, 22, access to, 14; in body politic, 13; chapín "underground," 27, 36, 87–88, 92, 107, 139, 142, 185–6, 188; commercialization of, 108; and evolution of, 6, 33, 217n25; and highlands, 80; and struggles for power, 54–57; and Maya pride, 84; national spotlight on, 27, 87; ondero, 36; and police, 35–36; and

INDEX · 285

counterculture *(continued)*
politics, 36–37, 43–45; proliferation of, 87–88, 104, 107–8; and social change, 28–29; use of counterculture work, 16, 18, 23; and terror, 34. *See also* musical genres
Craib, Raymond, 1, 154, 211n2
credit, 11, 100, 129, 133–34, 160, 168, 171–72, 248n95; Banco Azteca in Elektra stores in, 171, 252n27; global markets and, 133; municipal, 160, 248n94; and remittances *(remesas)*, 253n40. *See also* microcredit/microfinance
crime, 5–6, 23–24, 75, 89, 128, 191, 193–98; attributed to, 104–5; and commercialization, 139; criminality and the body politic, 6, 158–59, 201, 238n86; criminality and youth discourse, 7–8, 62, 75, 104, 189 *(see also* delinquency); and decentralization, 130; and gangs, 121–22; and moral panic, 67; organized, 11, 105, 136, 157, 260n109; and "power grids," 158–59; and security patrols, 2, 99; and social cleansing, 117–19; and technology, 115; and vigilantism, 97
crimes against humanity, human rights violations, 10, 18, 135, 205, 262n19
CUC. *See* Comité de Unidad Campesina

Davis, Mike, 10
death squads, 10, 27, 34, 91, 117. *See also* military
de a pie: defined, 8, 211n9; and categories of identity, 8, 20, 22–26, 30, 43, 57, 93; *de a pie* people and Maya culture and Maya pride movement, 8, 20, 23–24, 84–85, 109–10, 146; as focus of work, 8–9, 12, 17, 22–25; as invisibilized majority, 15, 32, 42–43, 200–201; and popular nationalism, 25, 200–201; and rejection of caste status and servility as cultural form, 12–13, 15, 30, 32, 110, 180 *(see also:* caste, *castas;* servility, as cultural form); sources on, 9; styles, slang, and humor, 15, 49, 56–57, 59–60, 84, 222n92; and subaltern history, 9, 12, 15, 17, 45. See also *calle*/KY; youth
decentralization, 24–5, 63, 124, 149–51, 156–60, 166, 192; and CAFTA effect,

169, 175; and "centralization" of grassroots culture, 140–41, 148–9; and cultural decentralization programs, 145, 249n5; and *poder local* movement, 77–83, 99–101, 124–25, 127, 135; and creation of regions and microregions, 170–72, 181, 242n24, 251n22; and lawlessness, 136, 194, 201; and neoliberal multiculturalism, 129–30. *See also* Consejos de Desarrollo Comunitarios, Municipales, Departamentales; development; municipal government and politics; social investment funds
de León Carpio, Ramiro, 60, 65, 80
de León, Jason, 178
de León López, Ramiro, 116
delinquency, discourses of, 6–7, 137, 150, 153, 209; and "antibreaks," 90–92; as national problem, 67; and security, 194; and social cleansing, 51; and tradition, 119
Denning, Michael, 182
DEOCSA, DEORSA. *See* electricity
derecho maya, 105
Desafío 10, 182, 255n59
desmadre: definition of, 115; and tourism, 173–75
development: and agro-urbanization, 69, 71, 248n95; analysis of, 165–66, 191; apparatus of, 11; archives of, 16; and Canada, 242n24; committees, 105, 127, 136; Community Development Plans (PCDs), 137, 243n26; cooperatives, 39; and counterinsurgency, 39, 41–42, 53, 61–62, 71, 73; and decentralization, 169–72; Desarrollo Comunitario para la Paz (DECOPAZ, Community Development for Peace), 242n24; development zones and poles, 31, 39, 41–42, 43, 53, 61–66; discourse, displacement of, 22–23, 61–62; and "ethnic question," 42; and ethnotourism, 174; and highland communities, 237n81; and identity, 183, 189; Integrated Community Development (ICD), 31; InterInstitutional Coordination (IIC), 41–42, 53; and local power, 11, 77, 101, 156, 170; and the Left, 220n63; and

military, 223n7; and moral panic, 68–69; and movements, political and ethnic, 139; "multiculturalized," 133; narratives of, 86; and nationalism, 43; and peace accords, 115; and social investment funds, 64–66, 69, 133, 225n17; Sololatecos United for Development (SUD), 125, 157; streamlining of, 160; systemization of, 150; *territorial interventions*, 170–72; types of, continuities of, 65–66, 130; urban, 5–6, 9, 115–16, 171, 181, 191; and youth culture, 148. *See also* agro-urbanization; Consejos de Desarrollo Comunitarios, Municipales; Departamentales (COCODES, COMUDES, CODEDES); Inter-American Development Bank; international cooperation; K'atun; military; municipal and community development plans; municipal government; nontraditional agro-exports; social investment funds; Urban and Rural Development Committees; World Bank

Development Poles, 41, 65. *See also* military

Diaz Negros, 166, 173, 179–80, 183, 206

DIDECA. *See* Discos de Centroamérica

Dionisio, René. *See* MC Tz'utu Kan

Discos de Centroamérica (DIDECA), 44, 107, 108, 223n4; critique of, 235n47

Discovering Dominga (film), 174–75

disease 15, 75–76, 80, 249n5; discourse of, 91

"DJ," 164–65, 169, 178

Dole Food, 218n35

Driscoll, Mark, 32, 43

drug use, drugs, 2, 87, 90, 142, 146, 156, 160, 182, 195–98, 255n61; addiction to, 97, 137; and anxiety around youth, 75, 80, 118, 121–22; cocaine/crack, 51, 66, 90, 192, 252–53n32; ecstasy/MDMA, 151–52; heroin poppies, 53; and music, 34, 36–37, 44, 148; and Panajachel, 173; and "playworlds," 150; trafficking, 50–53, 118; "war on drugs," 61–62, 66, 151. *See also* narcotraffic

duendes. *See* street children

Dussel, Enrique, 22, 33, 135; intersection of cultural, economic, and political fields, 43–44, 50; and law, 156, 242n20; on the people, 242n19; and popular culture, 138; on top-down power, 130

Echeverría, Maurice, 141, 147; in film, 159; on masks, 144; on uniforms, 143

Editorial X, 141

education, 164, 178, 192–93, 204, 206, 238n84, 243n26, 247n91, 252n32, 262n16; and activism, 125; art, dance schools, 48, 145, 179, 186–87 (*see also* Iqui Balam); bilingual, 48, 173, 241n14; and cabeceras, 118; campaigns, 31, funding of, 52–53, 63, 101, 134; and guerillas, 37–38; literacy, 9, 13, 14, 31, 37, 70, 95, 116, 137, 138, 143, 177, 188, 202, 243n26, 252n32; and outcomes, 116; policies and programs, 18; private schools (*colegios*), 44, 87, 89–91, 94, 106, 121, 204, 230n88, 230n90; reform, 100; trade schools, 163, 193. *See also* schools; universities

Ejército Guerrillero de los Pobres (EGP): and the army, 40; and Colom, Yolanda, 37; critiques of, 46, 219n53; formation of, 35; on interethnic relations, 46

Ekern, Stener, 157, 244n57

electricity: electric games and rides in *feria*, 177; electrification and National Electrification Institute (INDE), 69, 71, 73, 121, 125; electromarimba, 207; "El INDE" street gang, 122; insurgent and criminal sabotage of, 98–99, 122; poor service satirized, 184; post-privatization protests, 133, 158, 205, 242n24; privatization, 11, 63–64, 129, 132, 221–2n81, 241n11; Spanish transnationals (Iberdrola, Unión Fenosa, DEOCSA, DEORSA), 241n11; and SUD, 125

Elektra, 171, 252n27

El Mezquital, 112

El Salvador: "dollarization," 133; export to, 122; and gangs, 180; and Moonies, 237n69; and remittances 253n40; revolution, 38; and *robaniños*, 68

Encapuchados, Los, 195–98

environment, environmentalism, pollution: anti-mining movement, 166, 181, 205, 262n16; deforestation, 167; hydroelectric protests, 205; Paraquat, 53; pesticides and fertilizers, 39; sewage, 75–76, 199; visual pollution, 181

Escobar, Lucía: in *Hasta Atrás* and CIRMA Historical Archive, 107; in *Chalupa, La*, 142; in *Supositorio*, 152; in *Ati*, 172–73; and Encapuchados, Los, 196–99, 207, 234n41

Escobar Urrutia, María, 90, 45, 230nn88,90

Escuintla, 192, 202; attacks in, 101; FJT shutdown, 72; and gangs, 117; and "Guath, Joseph," 206; and Organización Revolucionaria del Pueblo en Armas (ORPA), 71; soldier in, 102*fig.*; urbanization, 115, 117

Esquipulas II Accord: and "democratization," 66; and the National Reconciliation Commission (CNR), 64; and neoliberalization, 63; and youth campaigns, 67

Estudiantina, La, 36

"ethnic question," 22, 42–49, 201; debated in left-wing politics and guerrilla movement, 37–38, 42–49, 70–71; in peace negotiations, 99–100; in youth culture, 57, 86, 148, 204. *See also* nationalism

ethnotourism. *See* tourism

Evangelical churches, 75, 118–19, 153, 164; and youth gangs, 122

extortion, 104, 118, 194–98

Fábulas Áticas, 107, 110–11

Facebook: and chapinismo, 25, 184–85; and "*chulo tu chucho*," 184; and "imagined community" and popular consciousness 184–85, 256n69; and legacies of war, 138; Maya youth on, 204–5, 256n69; rapists on, 192; use of, as source, 16, 214n38; and zotz', 126

fashion. *See* style

feria, 4, 185; as business, 177–79, 177*fig.*; murder at a, 196; new and old commerce, 119; "traditional" and "global," 126–27

Fernández, Sergio ("Taz"): on Atmósfera Omplog, 138; *Si aquí se pudiera vivir*, 129; on touring indigenous-majority towns, 131–32, 137–38, 162; on Los Últimos Adictos, 106, 129. *See also* Andrade, Ricardo; Los Últimos Adictos

film, foreign films, 112, 240n5; animé, 156; *Dictator in the Dock*, 262–63n19; *Discovering Dominga*, 174–75; futurist-punk, compared to a, 111; hip-hop, 57; horror, 222n91; *Planet B-boy*, 186; *V for Vendetta*, 262n17; violence in, 118, 137

film, Guatemalan films, 107, 145, 159, 181; *Alternativa*, 109, 131–32, 139, 256n71; *Barrio*, 180; Caracol Producciones, 183, 254n55; Casa Comal, 158; *La casa de enfrente*, 158–59; *El cuento de la democracia*, 183; *El oro o la vida*, 254n55, 262n16

financial crises: in 1980s, 221n81; Asian and Russian, 1997–1998, 241n13; and culture, 141; Guatemala, 1998, 133; Guatemala, 2006, 168–70, 250n10, 250n11, 250n14; global, of 2007–2009, 191

financialization, 7, 11, 15, 175; and crisis, 133, 168–71; and "mediatization," 25; social commentary on, 238n86

Financial Sector Modernization Program. *See* Inter-American Development Bank

Fink, Leon, 120

Fiscal Pact. *See* Pacto Fiscal

Fischer, Edward, 161

Flores, Marco Antonio, 36–37

Florida, Richard, 10, 212n13, 263n27

FODA. *See* SWOT

Fondo de Desarrollo Indígena Guatemalteco (FODIGUA, Fund for Guatemalan Indigenous Development), 225n17

Fondo de Inversión Social (FIS, Social Investment Fund), 65–66, 225n17. *See also* Social Investment Funds (SIF)

forced recruitment, 41–42, 73, 102*fig.*; and memory, youth bloggers, 55; protest against, 82

Fosa Común, 151–52

Franco, Leonardo, 98

Franja Transversal del Norte (FTN, Northern Transversal Strip), 51

free trade. *See* trade

Frente Democrática Nueva Guatemala (FDNG): and army, 104; elections, 124–25; and Mayan movement, 100–101
Frente Republicano Guatemalteco (FRG), 135, 161
Frente Unitario (Unitary Front) of URNG, 226n40
fresa, 159, 183; definition of, 36, 106, 217n25; interclass rivalry, 111; as street identity, 57, 147
Frito Lay North America, 183
Fuerzas Armadas Rebeldes (FAR): and EGP, 35; and youth, 34
Fundación Guillermo Toriello, 124

Gallo beer, 144, 159–60
gangs, 17, 110, 113, 202; and agro-urbanization, 114, 116; appearance in mid-1980s, 28, 50–52, 57, 89–90; *delincuentes,* 67; discourse on youth, 7, 14, 118, 123; grassroots/local, 117–18, 121–22, 127, 132, 137, 142; grassroots and global commerce, 161; grassroots and neoliberalization, 144, 150, 155–57; grassroots, as protopolitical, 238n86; and interclass rivalries, 88–92; Levenson, on "necroliving," 52, 223n95; *mara,* as "in crowd," 28, 108, 111–12; *marero,* 7, 28, 90, 112, 182; and militarism, 50, 55; *muco,* 12, 57; and music, 180; Los Pokemones, 156, 198; and rape, 193, 259n102; and reality television, 182, 255n59; Los Simpson, 121–22, 132, 137, 156; and "street nationalism," 180; and security, 2, 104, 194; and social cleansing, 91, 117–18. *See also* break wars
García, Romeo Lucas, 40
Garra Chapina, 139, 140 *fig.2*
gender: bending, 260n116; and B-girling, 187; divide, 18, 147, 162; feminist discourses and politics, 142, 205, 262n16; and guerrillas, 37, 40, 103*fig.,* 124; and identity crisis, 147; and "informal" economy, 32; machismo, macho, 37, 87, 111–2, 160, 174, 203, 218; male-coded cultural forms, 18; and male anxiety, in break wars, 230n88; and male migration, 238n83; Mayan movement on, 100,

183; *"mujer Maya,"* Diane Nelson on, 147, 244n54; need for further study, 18–19; *naco,* 164, 203; norms, 33, 84; and tuc-tucs, 162; and tourism, 174, 253n33; women's traje, discourse on, 124, 144, 147, 188, 203, 252–3n32; Yolanda Colom on, 37, 218n32
genocide, 5, 13, 28–30, 40, 42, 46, 57, 212n17; and activism, 43, 81; displaced anxieties from, 62, 76; legacy in living archives, 17; and migration, 28; popular memory of, 55, 59, 122, 138; sites of, 2; trials regarding, 10–11, 18, 205, 212n16; 262n19; and truth commission, 135
Gerardi Conedera, Juan José, 135
Global South, 162, 191; versus Global North, 213n32
González, Roberto "Blacko," 27, 45
González-Ponciano, Jorge Ramón, 12, 204, 213n23, 215n48, 262n12
graffiti, 1, 122, 156, 209; as "urban text," 16–17
Grupo de Apoyo Mutuo (GAM, the Mutual Support Group), 63
Grupo Elektra. *See* Elektra
GUATEL, TELGUA. *See* telephone
Guatemala City, 2, 212n10; agro-urban outskirts of, 39, 116, 152; Barrio El Gallito, 51; antibreaks in, 88–93 *(see also* break wars); antishumos in, 203–5 *(see also* shumo); bottom-up economy and geography, 32; linked with provincial centers in national commons, 7, 56, 62, 69–70, 167, 181, 186, 193; bus fare protests, 1985, 51–52; *casta* authenticity in, 23, 111–12, 181–82 *(see also* caste, *castas; cholo;* break wars; shumo); described as "futurist punk film," 111; drugs in, 44, 51; elite literati and artists in, 24, 104, 107, 141–45 *(see also* arts); gangs in, *see* gangs; guerrillas in, 35, 40, 71, 107, 221n75; Javier Payeras on, 86–87; malls and franchises, spreading, 110–11, 203; Maya/ladino and urban/rural binaries in, blurred, 12, 32; metro area, 115–16; migration/transmigration to, *see* migration; "new middle class" project, 31, 33; "Pa' capital," 207; *robaniños* panic in,

Guatemala City *(continued)*
67–68; rock concerts in, *see* musical concerts; and urban studies, 10; shantytowns, land invasions, and poor neighborhoods, 28–29, 38, 51, 112–15, 181, 259n97; similitude with urbanizing provincial centers, 2–3, 70; youth cultures in, anticonformist, late 1970s-late 1980s, 13, 22, 28–29, 44–45 *(see also* musical genres); youth cultures in, anticonformist, late 1980s-mid1990s, 87–93; youth cultures in, new rock nacional of mid-1990s forward, 94–95, 106–9 (see also musical genres, Primera Generación Records); youth cultures in, rap and hip-hop, *see* Alioto Lokos, Bacteria Soundsystem Crew, break wars, musical genres, youth; youth cultures in, raves and techno, 151–52; youth cultures in, *repasos*, 33–34; youth, street children, *see* street children; war orphans in, 50. *See also* break wars; gangs; González Ponciano, Ramón; migration: internal; musical genres; shumo; social cleansing; street children
Guatemorfosis, 202, 203; and identity, 200, 206; role of youth, 25, 199–200
guerrillas, 2, 6, 10, 17, 18, 253; actions, 221n75; and alcaldía indígena, 82; in Antigua, 72; archives of, 16; and bands, 97, 109; into cities and centers, 70–71; and civilian rule, 60; at Concert for Peace, 27, 30; as costume, 114; disarmament, 115, 124; disguised as, 99; and "ethnic question," 46–49, 148, 225n32; first phase, 31; fronts, 33; and gender norms, 37–38, 102*fig.*, 124; on joining, 217n18; in literature, 86; and local power, 127; as Mayan cause, 42; Maya encounters, 110; and media, 72; Morán, Rolando, 233n23; as political party, 130, 150; in peace negotiations, 61, 98; perception of, 56, 61, 266n73; problems of, 71–72; radio station, 216n15; recruitment, 229n74; reintegration, 124, and reviving tradition, 124; on *robaniños*, 67; on rurality, 69; and Sistema de Protección Ciudadana (SIPROCI), 91;

on social movements, 64; takeover, 107; as third revolutionary generation, 30; and tourism, 174; as youth rebellion, 34. *See also* Colom, Yolanda; Ejército Guerrillero de los Pobres (EGP); Octubre Revolucionario; Organización Revolucionaria del Pueblo en Armas (ORPA); Payeras, Mario; peace process; Santa Cruz Mendoza, Santiago
Guinea Diez, Gerardo, 239n1; and "death of everything" trope, 130; on importance of culture in neoliberalizing world, 141, 148; on internalization and externalization, 130, 138; on masks, 143, 147, 182, 197; on MINUGUA, 130; on neoliberalism, 129, 138, 149, 168

hackers, hactivists: Anonymous Guatemala, 205–6, 262n17. *See also* Nelson, Diane
Hale, Charles, 151
Harvey, David, 201, 223n6
Hasta Atrás, 89*fig.*, 112, 142; on class, 111, 189; and commoditization, 110; masthead, 234n41; on MTV, reality television, 235n51; and postmodernity, 113; on *trasheros*, 108; on tribes and territories, 110–111; underground counterculture, 107. *See also* Buonafina, Giácomo; Escobar, Lucía; Primera Generación Records
heavy metal. *See* musical genres
hippies, *jipis*, 36, 80, 164; and identity, role playing, 147, 153, 173; globalism, 152; and music, 27, 34
HIV. *See* AIDS
Hjarvard, Stig, 15, 166, 213n32
homosexuality: homophobia, *hueco*, 203–4, 264n31; LGBT movement, 203; in media, 75, 142; and style, 113, 203; and violence, 196, 260n116
Hudson, Michael: on neoliberalism, 133; on privatization, 241n11
human rights violations, 98–99, 134, 159. *See also* crimes against humanity; genocide
Huehuetenango (department), 74*map;* case studies in, 19; counterinsurgency in,

77–78, 85, 123fig.; crime in, 97, 118–19, 222n82; "Emiliano" in, 46; gangs in, 118, 121–22, 142, 182; guerrillas in, 35, 38, 46, 77; infrastructure development and urbanization in, 73, 75, 118–19, 237n77; internet in, 115; political conflict in, 136, 157–58, 247n84, 254n55; *Sobrevivencia* in, 132, 149 (*see also* Sobrevivencia); social change in, 97–98, 118–22, 191, 237n77; youth culture and discourse in, 98, 109, 118–22, 131–32, 180, 182, 255n61. *See also* agro-urbanization; development; *El Regional;* Huista region
Huehuetenango (municipality and cabecera), 3–4, 5; radio in, 109; urbanization of, 19–20, 75–76, 115, 117–18, 127, 237n70; youth in, 97, 118, 182, 206; cholera in, 75, 76; city-region with Chiantla, 4, 96 map 3, 181
Huista region, 19, 73–77, 74*map*, 97–98; crime and gangs in, 104; 118, 121–22; Manuel Santos Montejo Camposeco in, 98; rock concerts in, 131–32; See also *El Regional*
Hurricane Mitch, 145, 153

Iboy Chiroy, Pedro, 124–25
identity, identifications, 4–6, 22–25, 201; and cultural hybridization, 152–53; defined as multiple and relational, 8, 15–16, 20–21; discourse of identity politics, 61–62, 68; representation and discourses of, changes in, 173, 183, 189. *See* agro-urbanization; barrio; break wars; *calle*/KY; caste, *castas;* "ethnic question"; Maya; musical genres; servility; shumo; youth
Ijatz Crew, 1, 13, 145, 187fig., 207fig., 208. *See also* B-Boys
Ilom, Gaspar, peace process, 72, 233n28
Impuesto de Valor Agregado (IVA, Value Added Tax), 221n81
Indignados, 205
informal economy, 34, 206; and agro-urban space, 11, 181; and children, 116; discourse of, 32, 66, 133–34; "gig," 24, 127, 161–164, growth of, 69; history of, 6; and privatization, 134; small and medium sized business (PYME, pequeña y mediana empresa), 133; *tiendas,* 80; and tuc-tucs, 24, 161–64; and women, 32
infrastructure, 241n11, 243n26; and agro-urbanization, 69; and counterinsurgency, 31; and Iboy Chiroy, Pedro, 125; Inter-American Development Bank (IDB), 134; and municipalities, 150; state role in, 157. *See also* development; electricity; radio; television; telephone
Integrated Community Development (ICD), 31
Inter-American Development Bank (IDB), 11; in the Consultative Group, 248n94; and crisis, 168; Financial Sector Modernization Program, 134, 160, 175, 240n9, 241n14, 250nn14,15, 251n26; and gangs, 156a; and *calle*/KY, 132–34, 160; and microcredit, 160, 171; and nontraditional agro-exports (NTAs), 248n95; and peace accords, 63, 115; as "private operator," 136; "territorial interventions," 25; Vamos Guatemala program, 170. *See also* banks; credit; microcredit/microfinance; financialization
Inter-Institutional Coordination (IIC), 41–42, 53, 219n42
international cooperation, 98, 116, 159, 252n28, Agencia Española de Cooperación Internacional para el Desarrollo (AECID), 136; Centro Canadiense de Estudios y Cooperación Internacional (CECI), 241n24; and "donor nations," 133, 136, 144, 157, 225n17, 248n94. *See also* Inter-American Development Bank (IDB)
International Monetary Fund (IMF), 150, 157, 168, 248n94
internet/social media blogs, posts, and pages, 18, 25, 126, 138, 166, 179, 184–85, 256n59; by "Alhazred," 54–55, 152–53, 185; re Anonymous Guatemala, 263n21; on Barrancópolis site, re *mierda,* 259n97; Al buen chapín site, 184; re chapinismos, 264n31; on Facebook, Consejo de Juventudes Indígenas, 204–205; on Facebook, "Al estilo

internet/social media blogs *(continued)* chapín 502," 184; Facebook pages, personal, 214n38; on Facebook, "Soy chapín y qué putas," 184; by "Gerardo Perez," 55–58, 73, 98; re Guatemorfosis, 200; nationalistic, re *Barrio,* 180; nationalistic, re "Rap en Mam Cajolá," 188; nationalistic, re Sobrevivencia, 175; as national *selfis,* 184–86; on Rock Republik, re heavy metal and war, 54–58, 73, 98; on Rock Republik, re break wars, 92; on Rock Republic, re Panajachel, 152–53; on Rock Republik, re underground, 185–86; by "Safiroth," 91, 186; on YouTube, Radio Nahualá, 185; on YouTube, Shat Juárez, 188–89; on YouTube, shumo videos and reactions, 203–205. *See also* Facebook

Iqui Balam, 112, 113, 145; and Alioto Lokos, 235n58; and UNICEF, 148. *See also* Alioto Lokos; Bacteria Soundsystem Crew

Iximuleu, 95, 123

Ixtahuacán. *See* San Idelfonso Ixtahuacán

Jacaltenango, 73; crime in, 97, 118; music in, 98, 132; goods and services in, 118

jipis. See hippies

Job Sis, Alex: touring indigenous-majority towns, 137; on youth, celebration, 132. *See also* Sobrevivencia

Jocotenango. *See* Antigua city-region

jóvenes, juventud. See youth

Juárez Lucas, Roberto "Shat," 188–89

JuvenFami (Fundación para la Juventud y la Familia), 255n61

Kaibiles, Los, 55, 122, 138

Karishnanda (Jorge Ramírez), 36, 218n26

K'atun, Plan Nacional de Desarrollo K'atun, 9, 191, 212n12

kidnapping (for ransom), 11, 67, 104–105, 118, 168–69, 193–96, 198. *See also* panic: *robaniños*

KY, la. *See calle*/KY

ladino: and "antibreaks," 91; and chapinismo, 147, 173, 183; definition of, 12 ; as everyday people, 17; and fincas, 40, 54; further study of, 19, 45; and guerillas, 31, 42, 46–49; and *calle*/KY, 144–45, 173; in "lost generation," 23; and Mayan movement, 100, 103–104; and military, 55; and *municipalidad mixta,* 79; and national commons, 166; Payeras, Mario, 35; and popular culture, 138; ladino-Maya divide, 12–13, 32, 52, 77, 186, 203–4; ladino-Maya "encounters," 35, 37–38, 46–49, 70–71, 84–85, 109–110, 172. *See also* break wars; caste, *castas;* "ethnic question"; guerrillas; Mayan movement; municipal government; social movements

Lake Atitlán, lake basin, 152*map,* 164; 256n69, 260n113; artists in, 206–10; identities in, 154–56; municipal and ethnic politics in, 80–81; music in, 179–81; and national identity, 199–200; and Organización Revolucionaria del Pueblo en Armas (ORPA), 71; parties in, 151–53, 205, 246n68; road trip to, 1–2, 4, 202; and security, 194–98; "territorial interventions" in, 171–74; and zotz', 126; *See also* Panajachel; San Pedro La Laguna; Santiago Atitlán; Sololá

Lámpara de Acuario, 36

Latin American Agribusiness Development Corporation (LAAD), 39; shareholders, 218n35

Laugerud García, Kjell Eugenio, 56, 222n92

laws: and banking, 150, 168, 240n9, 250n14; breakdown of, 191; and Citizens for Democracy, 85; *derecho maya* (traditional Maya law), 105; Fondo de Inversión Social (FIS), 65; international, 40; lawlessness, 97, 99, 135, 156, 168; and lynching, 197; and municipalities, 151, 156–57; outside of, 161; tax, 244n57

Lefebvre, Henri, 22, 211n5, 212n11, 215n46

Levenson, Deborah: on trauma and violence, 223n95; on urban demonstrations, 51; on urban youth, 52–53

Libertad de Expresión ¡Ya!, 94, 97, 106, 108

Liga de Resistencia Popular Awesh (LRP-

Awesh, Awesh Popular Resistance League), 49
Línea, La, 263n20
literature, 231n102; blog on, 184; and *Chalupa, La,* 141–44; on commercialization, 106–7; the "lost generation," 92–93; onderos in, 36–37; on souless youth, 86–87; "third world" in, 182. *See also* Casa Bizarra; *Chalupa, La;* Echeverría, Maurice; Editorial X; Flores, Marco Antonio; Morales, Mario Roberto; Payeras, Javier
lotería, 126–27, 142, 177
lotificación, 52, 134. *See also* agro-urbanization
Lovell, George, 202
"Luis," 177–78, 192
lynching. *See* vigilantism

machismo, macho. *See* gender
Majawil Q'ij, 78, 79*fig.*, 82, 124–125
Malacates Trébol Shop, 169
mancomunidades, 171, 181; Sistema Urbano Mancomunidad Mankatitlán, 171. *See also* municipal government and politics
Manzano, Valeria, 20, 215n47
maquiladoras, 3, 112, 143
maras. See gangs
marimba: Checha y Su India Maya Caballero, 138, 162, 185; in Guatemorfosis campaign, 200; in Mayan fusion music, 132, 207; new regional forms, 227n50; in Radio Nahualá, 185
Mario Alioto López Sánchez (settlement), 112, 180. *See also* Alioto Lokos; Bacteria Soundsystem Crew; *Barrio* (film); Iqui Balam
Martín-Barbero, Jesús, 141; culture as "direct productive force," 141, 144, 147–48
masks: discourse on, 24, 139–40, 143–44, 147, 182; in *Desafío 10,* 182; Guy Fawkes, 205, 262n17; in Tabal, 155
Massacre of Totonicapán, 205
Maya, as cultural/ethnic identifier, 7–8, 11–12, 37, 100, 147, 203–5; and articulations, complex, 32, 151–53, 172–76; cosmovision, values, and traditions, 37, 39, 44, 46, 77–80, 83, 105, 125, 205 (*see also* Mayan movement); and cultural assertiveness, 62, 76–77, 81, 83–85, 180, 110, 203–210; *derecho maya,* 105; in diaspora, 174–75; and everyday people, 17 (*see also* de a pie); and ladino, 12; "Guatemaya," 95, 153, 164, 172, 246n71, 257n79; ladino-Mayan encounters, 35, 37–38, 70–71, 172–73, 203–210; and local power, see decentralization; and intersectionality, 13, 20, 127, 172–76; "Mayanization," 8, 83, 100, 125, 127; *mayences,* 48–49; Nelson, on *"mujer Maya,"* 147; and neoliberal multiculturalism, 101, 130, 144–46, 150–51, 171; and other identifiers, 37, 127; and "Paz en Iximuleu!," 95; renaissance, 105, 122, 125, 144. *See also* de a pie; caste, *castas;* "ethnic question"; genocide; ladino; musical genres: Maya folk, rock, fusion, and rap; nationalism; tourism; youth
Mayan movement, 21–26, 62, 76–83; deradicalization of, 151; Defensoría Maya, 78; diversity in, 8, 153; and Esquipulas II, 63–64, 95; height of, 11; and Central American-Dominican Republic Free Trade Agreement (CAFTA-DR), 11, 129; Campesino Unity Committee (CUC), 40; *clasistas/culturalistas,* 46; Coordinación de Organizaciones del Pueblo Maya de Guatemala (COPMAGUA), 78, 99–100, 129, 150; Coordinación de Organizaciones Mayas de Guatemala (COMG), 78; and "death of everything," 150; *derecho maya* (traditional Maya law), 105; and guerilla movement, 42, 46–47; and kidnapping, 158; militancy, 28; Maya revolutionary nationalism, 22, 47–49; Movimiento de Acción y Ayuda Solidaria (MAYAS, Movement for Action and Aid in Solidarity), 47; Movimiento Indio de Guatemala, 48; Movimiento Indio, Nacionalista y Revolucionario, 48; Movimiento Indio Tojil, 47; Movimiento Revolucionario del Pueblo Ixim (MRP-Ixim), 47; Movimiento Tzuk Kim Pop, 165, 249n2; and music, 27;

Mayan movement *(continued)*
Maya nationalism, 49; Misión de las Naciones Unidas en Guatemala (MINUGUA), 97—100; and *poder local*, 77, 101, 157, 170–71; and power movement, 43; pride, 123–28, 130, 144; and *Regional, El*, 73, 76–77, 95; visibility of, 135. See also *alcaldía indígena; COPMAGUA*; decentralization; municipal government and politics; nationalism: neoliberal multiculturalism; peace process
Mbembe, Achille, 15, 138
McAllister, Carlota, 29, 212n17
McDonald's, 59–60, 92, 110
Megapaca, 200
Mejía Víctores, Óscar Humberto, 41, 45
Menchú, Rigoberta: CUC, 40; on labor regime, 14; Nobel Peace Prize, 82; *Regional, El*, 73
Menéndez, Gustavo, 108
mediatization, 7, 11, 15, 24, 134, 166–67, 179; defined, 15, 213n32
microcredit/microfinance, 129, 133, 171, 248n95
microenterprise, 66, 133–4, 160, 248n95, 253n40
microfincas, 121, 166
migration: cultural expressions of, 59, 129; diaspora, 172, 174–75; and generational change, 14; internal, and child labor, 176–77; internal, migration and transmigration to Guatemala City, 28, 31–32, 38, 180; internal, long history of, 231n104; internal, provincial, 31, 52, 69, 71, 83–84, 119, 176–77; internal, seasonal, to fincas, 34, 39, 52, 150, 213n28, 217n20, 227n51; male migration, 238n83, 252n32; minidiasporas, 176; outmigration, as destructive force, 139, 191; to the United States, 75, 97, 99, 115, 119–21, 166, 176, 188–89. See also remittances *(remesas)*
military, 102*fig.*, 103*fig.*; and agriculture, 39, 53; campaigns, 31, 40, 70, 71; Civil Affairs, 71, 83; and civilians, 40; and crime, 23, 50–51, 55, 67, 90–91, 104–105, 135, 205, 212n16, , 262n19 *(see also* crimes against humanity); critique of, 29,

199–200; connectivity of, 55–57 and counterinsurgency, 41–42, 90–91, 135, 199–200; and death squads, 10, 27, 34, 90; and development, 31–32, 39–42, 53, 65–66, 223n7, 241n12; as elected officials, 205, 212n16, , 262n19; end of occupation, 81; foreign support of, 47; in Franja Transversal del Norte (FTN), 51; genocide, 1, 5, 41–42, 103, 212n16; in highlands, 62, 76; and indigenous leadership, 77, 82; martial "return to democracy," 28; mass graves, 10–11, 82; militarization of society and body politic, 23, 29–30, 39, 42, 50, 55, 83, 99, 136, 138, 193–94; military occupation of countryside, 2, 4, 22, 69, 71, 73, 76, 77, 80–82, 85, 98–99, 123, 125, 127, 131–32, 156; military rule, 10, 17; and music, 45, 54; and peace process, 98–105; paramilitary structures, 23, 35, 50, 90–91, 104; and "return to democracy," 28, 50; and security, 85; and Serrano Elías constitutional crisis, 60; in Sololá, 2; and violence, infective, 29; and youth consciousness, 54–58, 83, 92, 138, 185. *See also* listings for individual heads of state; *comisionados;* Comité Voluntario de Defensa Civil (CVDC, Civilian Volunteer Defense Committee); crimes against humanity; forced recruitment; genocide; human rights violations; Patrullas de Autodefensa Civil (PACs); sexual violence; Sistema de Protección Ciudadana (SIPROCI); Task Force Hunapú
Miraflores Mall, 203, 261n11
Misión de las Naciones Unidas en Guatemala (MINUGUA, Mission of the United Nations in Guatemala), 101, 123*fig.*, 196, 231n8; arrival of, 97–99; on corruption and clandestine groups, 159; departure of, 130; on *derecho maya*, 105; influence of, 98; on lynching, security patrols, and lawlessness, 104–5, 136, 147; on organized crime, 104–5; on Portillo, 159; on social cleansing, 117; on rejecting state authority, 148; on state's human rights abuses, 98–99, 159, 234n40; on

Sololá municipal politics and development, 125, 137
Monsanto, Pablo, 34
Montejo Camposeco, Manuel Santos, 98
Moonies, 117, 237n16; and Unification Church, 117
moral economy: "immoral economy," 163; James Scott on, 161; of the tuc-tuc, 24, 161–64
Morales, Evo, 151
Morales, Jimmy, 206
Morales, Mario Roberto, 142, 233n27
moral panic. *See* panic
moreno (brown-skinned), 174, 183
Morganton, North Carolina, 119–20
mosh pits, moshing, 94–5, 138
motor rickshaw, moto-taxi. *See* tuc-tuc
movements, *movimientos*. *See* Mayan movement, social movements
mozo, 12, 34, 109, 144, 202
MTV, 87, 108, 235n51; and authenticity, 110; and class, 44, 57
muco, 12, 57, 204
mundo al revés, 131, 134–35, 240n6; and changing political economy, 131–39
mundo en libertad, 149–52, 155–57, 160; and changing culture and political economy, 149–58; and "playworlds," 151–53
municipal and community development plans: Planes Comunitarios de Desarrollo, (PCDs, Community Development Plans), 137; Planes de Desarrollo Municipal (PDMs, Municipal Development Plans), 170–71; Planes Estratégicas Territoriales (PETs, Strategic Territorial Plans), 171; Strategic Municipal Plans (of 1999-early 2000s), 136–37, 243n26; of Barillas, 136, 170–71; of Sololá, 136–37, 243n27
municipal government and politics, 19, 251nn24,26; in Barillas, 136, 157–58, 255n6; decentralization of, 135, 151, 156–58, 160, 170–71; and the Maya 77–83, 100–101, 123–27, 135; and the military, 42, 83, 135; municipal code reforms of 2002, 156, 246n79; municipal credit, 160, 248n94; reconfiguration of, 72; revolt in 1962, 33; in Quetzaltenango, 124; in Quiché, 136; in San Miguel Acatán, 77; and security, 136; in Sololá, 80–84, 124–26, 136–37, 157, 228n65, 228n66, 243n26; Strategic Municipal Plans (of 1999-early 2000s), 136–137; as urban collage, 181; vibrancy of, 30; and workers, 249n102; in Zacapa, 136. *See also* Inter-American Development Bank; Financial Sector Modernization Program
music: and alternative popular nationalism, 15, 24, 25–26, 109, 114, 148–49, 214n35, 245n60 (*see* nationalism: alternative popular); and alternative popular nationalism, agro-urban barrio, 180–81; and analysis of identity as fluid, relational, 20–21; and antirhetorical yet cohesive identities, 95–97, 176; and "*chapines locales*," 109–10; and CAFTA effect, 169; and calls for peace, 94–95; and *Chalupa, La*, 142; commercialization of, 61, 106–10, 130, 139–40, 151, 185–87, 235n51, 245n66, 256n71; for diaspora, audible archive, 176; and elite schools, 106; and the "ethnic question," 57, 70, 175; and "Guatemaya," 153, 164; and *Hasta Atrás*, 107–8, 110–12; and identities, 36–37, 68, 73, 153, 164, 178, 185–86 (*see also* break dance, break wars); and identities, *rastafarismo*, 173; and *libertad*, 23–24, 91, 128, 149–53, 155–57, 160; as means of tracing popular culture, 8, 13, 15–18; and Mayan movement, 23, 29; and Maya highlands, 76, 84, 126, 128; and militarism, 29, 34, 54–58, 98, 185; on national stage, 27, 29, 87–88, 109–10, 114, 186; "organized bands," 97–105, 118–119, 122, 127; and overlapping spheres of cultural production, 183; and political meaning, 45, 54, 61; and popularization of street culture, 185–89; and public/private space, 24, 110, 147; "Sing with me, joven," 75; and social conformity, rock and roll, 33; and social space, overview, 22–25, 128; and urban space, 33–35, 57, 89–90, 110–15, 118–9, 132, 134, 137–8, 188–9; and youth campaigns, Guatemorfosis, 199–201;

music *(continued)*
and youth programs, 27, 112–13, 145–46, 148, 179–80, 258n90; and youth programs, Año de la Juventud, 189–90. *See also* musical band; musical concerts; musical genres; youth

musical bands, musicians: Bárcenas, Tavo, 256n71, 258n90; Chubay, Marcielita, 207; Curruchich, Sara, 206–7; DJ Chronic, 151; DJ Megadose, 152; Frenesí Rock, 206; generations of, 20; generations, 1950s-mid 1960s 33, 216–17n15; generations, mid-1960s-late 1970s 35–37 *(see also* musical genres); generations, late 1970s-early 1990s, 44–45 *(see also* musical genres); generations, early-mid 1990s, 94–95 *(see also* musical genres: *rock nacional)*; generations, circa 2012, 206–10; ladino, in "deep Guatemala," 109–11, 132; local, garage bands of early 1990s, 106; local, Maya heavy metal, Ezquizoide, 179 *(see also* Diaz Negros); MC Tz'utu Kan, 208, 263n29; Megadeth, 56, 73, 98; Miguel, Luis, 109, 235n49; Nota Fa, 206; Pitbull, 186; SOS, Rony de León, 35, 94; Viento en Contra, 138. *See also* music; musical concerts; musical genres; listings for individual bands and artists

musical concerts: of Alux Nahual, 225n25, 246n68; Atmósfera Omplug, 138–9; Concerts for Peace, 27–30; and CONJUVE, 67, 88; Fábulas Áticas reviewed in *Hasta Atrás*, 110–11; and foreign artists, 108–109; Garra Chapina, 139, 140*fig.*; Lámpara de Acuario, 36; Libertad de Expresión ¡Ya!, 94, 106, 108; Últimos Adictos, final, 151, 158; Woodstockito, 35–6

musical genres: *bachata, música tropical, música urbana,* and *reggaetón,* 76, 109, 178, 186, 206; Central American rock/grunge, 88; heavy metal, 27, 45, 54–58, 87–88, 108, 185–86, 230n84 *(see also* Diaz Negros); marimba, 138, 162, 185, 206–7, 227n50; Maya folk, rock, fusion, and rap, 98, 132, 148–49, 175, 188–89, 206–10, 246n71, 264n30 *(see also* Diaz Negros);

nueva canción, 36; *la onda, onderos,* (of 1970s), 35–37; *ranchera,* 76, 109; rap/hip hop, 57, 88–93, 112–14, 145, 180, 186–90, 208–10 *(see also* break dance; break wars); rock (of mid-1960s-1980s), 34–35, 44, 61, 67; rock and roll (1950s and 1960s), 33, 216–17n15; *rock en español,* 87; *rock nacional* (1990s-2010s), 94–7, 105–112, 129, 131–2, 139–40, 148–9, 151, 158–59, 169, 179–80, 206; *rock pesado/pesados,* 37, 45; *son huasteco,* 227n50; techno/house, 151–2, 245n66, 246n68; thrash/trash, 87, 108; trova, 36, 93

naco, 164, 203
nahual, 44
Nahualá, 3; discourse of, 50–51, 221n75; narcotraffic, 11, 28, 66; Radio Nahualá, 185, 256n70; and violence, 118, 193
narcotraffic, 66, 129; and addiction, 118; and agriculture, 161; arrests, 105; and beheadings, 193, 259n102; discourse of, 50–53; and military, 55, 221n75; newness of, 11, 28
National Agricultural Development Bank. *See* banks
National Civil Police. *See* police
National Fund for Peace (FONAPAZ), 65, 225n17. *See also* Social Investment Funds (SIFs)
National Police. *See* police
nationalisms, 214n35; alternative popular, and agro-urbanization, *see* agro-urbanization, *calle*/KY, barrio, youth; alternative popular, as analytical category, 6, 12–13, 15–17, 43, 131, 214n35; alternative popular, and antithetical yet cohesive identities, 15, 97, 109–110, 114, 128, 140–41; alternative popular, and archive of cultural forms, 176 *(see also* archives); alternative popular, and chapinismo, 24–25, 95, 131, 140, 147–49, 166, 176, 209; alternative popular, and *de a pie* Maya pride, 49, 81, 84–85, 110, 123, 126, 144, 164, 204–5; alternative popular, and decentralization, 140–41, 149; alternative popular, dialogical relationship with official discourse, 43,

146–47, 199–202, 205; alternative popular, overview, 22–26, 201; alternative popular, and *potentia,* 130–31, 147; alternative popular, and servility, 6, 15–16, 21, 167 (*see also* servility); anticommunist, 33; "barrio nationalism," 25, 43, 176–84, 186–89, 199; evolving and emerging discourses of, 22–26, 97; and *forma de ser,* 5, 15–16, 21; Grandin on, 214n35; "Guatemaya," 95, 153, 164, 172, 246n71, 257n79; hegemonic, 43, 99, 156, 201, 218n32, 219n43; Iximuleu, 95, 123; Maya national anthem, 146; Maya revolutionary nationalism, 22, 47–49; kaleidoscopic strands of, 43, 214n35; Nelson on, 147; and neoliberalization, 139, 175–76, 200–202; protean and contested, 201; and racism, 6, 99, 100, 103–4, 180, 204 (*see also* shumo); and rap in Mam, commentary on, 188; stateless, 43; street culture and, 24, 131, 140, 147–48, 181, 184–85, 209–210 (*see also calle*/KY); vernacular idiom of, 13, 15, 24, 131, 140, 148, 200; Viernes Verde, "Requiem en E," "*soy chapín de sangre,*" 148–49, 164, 245n60; Vrana on, 43, 214n35; Zolov on, 214n35. See also agro-urbanization; caste, *castas;* "ethnic question"; identities; internet/social media; youth

Nelson, Diane: on "mujer Maya" as "prosthetic," and "stumped identities," 24, 147, 203, 244n54, 252n32; on horror, 222n91; on referendum of 1999, 241n17; on Maya as ethnic identifier, 211n8; on postpeace violence, 29

"Nene," 156, 169, 192; "moral economy of tuc-tucs," 163–164; on parties, 151–53; in security patrols, 195

neoliberalism, 11, 65, 151: and alternative popular nationalism, 84–85 (*see also* nationalisms); Asamblea de la Sociedad Civil on, 99; and cultural creativity, 140; dichotomized with past, 8; and discourses of youth as consumeristic, apathetic, 15, 22, 26, 29, 59–62, 76–77, 84–85, 130–31; Hudson on, 133; neoliberal multiculturalism, 6, 11–12, 68, 77,

129, 135, 144, 151; and "pink tide," 151; and social space, overview, 22–26 neoliberalization, 9–11, 22, 26, 95, 139–40, 144, 160, 200–202; as contested and stepwise process, 23, 28, 39, 61–63, 66, 150–51, 159–60, 223n7; and decentralization, community-driven development, *see* decentralization, development municipal government and politics; and identity politics, 61, 68; and despair and "death of everything," 129–30, 140, 150–51; and free trade, "CAFTA effect," 166–69, 172, 175, 178; Guatemorfosis, as expression of, 199–201, 206; Guinea Diez on, 129, 141; and intensified class antagonisms, 44; and moral economy of the tuc-tuc, 161–64; and multisector forums, 64, 136–37, 171; and militarism, 42, 130; and "new poverties" (*nuevas pobrezas*), 166–67, 169, 172, 176–78, 201; and NTAs, *see* nontraditional agro-exports; Peck on, 9; and *potestas,* 130; presidencies of Portillo and Berger and, 150–51, 159–60; and relationship to emergent KY, 131 (*see also* agro-urbanization; *calle*/KY); Serrano Elías on, 60; and urbanization of social space, 8–9, 22–26, 69–70, 131, 134, 149, 160–61, 191–92, 202–3 (see also agro-urbanization; *calle*/KY); and violence, 191 (*see also* crime, vigilantism). *See also* banks; Central American-Dominican Republic Free Trade Agreement (CAFTA-DR); development; financialization; financial crises; microcredit/microfinance; microenterprise; panic, moral panic; *mundo al revés; mundo en libertad;* privatization; social investment funds; trade

nongovernmental organizations (NGOs): and "agro-industry," 248n95; and Barillas Plan, 136; and base closure, 125; and cooperatives, 53; and culture, 145–46; and decentralization, 65, 77; and *derecho maya* (traditional Maya law), 105; and development committees, 242n22; and ethnotourism, 174; and Maya entrepreneurship, 213n19; and Misión

nongovernmental organizations *(continued)* de las Naciones Unidas en Guatemala (MINUGUA), 98, 105; "NGO-ification," 66, 95, 105; and Peace Accords, 115; perceptions of, 122, 137; profusion of, 11; Programa de Atención, Movilización e Incidencia por la Niñez y la Adolescencia (PAMI), on rural-urban divide, 116; and Urban and Rural Development Committees (COCODEs, CODEDEs, and COMUDEs), 157; and youth, 112–14, 116, 127, 146, 187–88, 209
nontraditional agro-exports (NTAs), 218nn35,37, 221nn77,81, 223n7, 228n60, 248n95; Aj Ticonel Trading Company, 248n95; Alimentos Congelados, SA (ALCOSA), 39–40; introduction of, 39–40, 75; and microcredit, 160–61; and money flow, 115; and Organización Revolucionaria del Pueblo en Armas (ORPA), 71; popular memory of, 59; as "reversal of truth," 52–3; and urban growth, 181
Nordstrom, Carolyn, 66, 158, 161
Nukuj Ajpop, 124–25

Octubreazul, 145
Octubre Revolucionario (OR), 46–47, 49; dissolution, 85, 229n76; on Maya Guatemala's complexities, 77–78; PGT-6 de Enero, 48; on social movements, 63. *See also* Colom, Yolanda; Payeras, Mario
offshore banks. *See* banks
onda, onderos, 36–37, 178, 188, 217n25
Operation Cleanup, 34
Organización Revolucionaria del Pueblo en Armas (ORPA), 35, 40; Frente Javier Tambriz (FJT, Javier Tambriz Front), 70–72, 85; in important agro-urbanizing areas, 71–72; and indigenous issues, 46; and peace process, 72, 233n28. *See also* Frente Unitario of URNG; Santa Cruz Mendoza, SantiagoOsorio, José, 145
Oxlajuj Baktun. *See* Trece Baktun

PACs. *See* Patrullas de Autodefensa Civil, Civilian Self-Defense Patrols

Pacto Fiscal, 160
Pajoc, Raquel, 206–7
Panajachel, 102*fig.*, 151–56, 154*fig.*, 173, 246n74, 251n24; area introduced, 4, 17, 80; "DJ" in, 164–65, 169, 178–79; Los Encapuchados in, 195–98, 199, 207; ethnotourism in, 172–73; Lucía Escobar on, 173; gangs in, 155–56; and hippy styles, 153, 164; lynching and vigilantism in, 195–98, 260nn113,116; "Nene" in, 151–53, 156, 163–64, 169, 192, 195; Pana Rock, 151, 155, 158; rave culture in and around, 151, 246n68; relations and rivalry with Sololá, 126, 155, 246n74; as rock center, 80, 102*fig.*, 109, 166, 179–80, 264n30; sex tourism in, 155, 173–74, 178, 253n33; street culture in, 180–81; tourism in, 2, 80, 153, 172–74, 180, 195–96, 252n32; tropical storms in, 165–66, 195; and tuc-tucs, 162–64, 176; Últimos Adictos in, 151, 158. *See also Ati: La Revista del Lago;* Diaz Negros; musical artists; tourism
Pana Rock, 151, 155, 158
panic, moral panic: and child pornography, 67–8, 75, 92; and exposure to pornography, 75, 118, 137, 161; and gangs, 90, 122, 155; globally, 66–68, 225n28, 225n29; and lynching, 147; *robaniños* and adoption, 23, 67–68, 193, 225n26; and transvestite prostitution, 117; youth culture and behaviors, 23, 62–68, 70, 75–77, 84, 88, 92, 118. *See also* gangs; youth; vigilantism
Partido de Avanzada Nacional (PAN), 124
Patrullas de Autodefensa Civil (PAC, Civilian Self-Defense Patrols) 41*fig.*, 66, 73; creation of, 40; Comités Voluntarios de Defensa Civil (CVDC, Civilian Volunteer Defense Committee), 98, 104, 105; disbanding of, 99, 123*fig.;* and ethnotourism, 174; leaders, 41–42, 77, 83; movement against, 81–82; and security, 85; and violence, terror, 83, 104–5, 174, 228n67
Payeras, Javier, 92, 112; blog, 184; on legacy, 244n50; and new creative cities, 207–8;

Octubreazul, 145; and parties, 246n68; *Ruido de fondo*, 86–87, 106
Payeras, Mario, 35, 37, 70; and Colom, Yolanda, 35, 37, 46–47, 63, 85, 217n22, 229n76; death of, 98; and Ejército Guerrillero de los Pobres (EGP) 35, 46, 220n57; and *Jaguar-Venado*, 229n76; and Octubre Revolucionario, 46–47, 63, 77–78, 85, 219n56, 229n76; on genocidal campaigns, 40, 219n40; on negotiated peace, 85; on social movement activism, 63–64; and Payeras, Javier, 86. *See also* Colom, Yolanda; guerillas; Octubre Revolucionario (OR)
Peace Accords, 23, 95, 232n15; and activism, 43, Acuerdo sobre aspectos socioeconómicos y situación agraria (Accord on Socioeconomic Aspects and the Agrarian Situation), 99; Acuerdo sobre identidad y derechos de los pueblos indígenas (AIDPI, Accord on the Identity and Rights of the Indigenous Peoples), 99–100; conditions of, 191, and Frente Javier Tambriz (FJT), 70; and Maya, 100; theme song for, 109
peace process, 10, 60, 70; activism during, 81–83, 97 (*see also* Mayan movement), 123–26; and Asamblea de la Sociedad Civil (ASC), 78, 99–100 (*see also* Mayan movement); concerts for, 27–30; and counterinsurgency forces, 65–66, 73, 85–86, 98–99, 105; and crime, violence, 23–24, 29, 93, 104–5, 157; and cynicism, 129–30, 138; and gender, 102*fig.*; guerrilla actions relating to, 61, 71–72, 85, 98, 100, 101, 103, 103*fig.*; and inner spheres, 24; and media, 73, 101, 103; National Fund for Peace, FONAPAZ, 65–66; National Reconciliation Commission (CNR, Comisión Nacional de Reconciliación), 64; Nobel Peace Prize, 14, 40, 82; Novella, Olga de, 233n28, 247n91; "peace generation," 93–97, 102*fig.*, 103, 111–14, 119, 148, 191–92; post peace disappointment, 59, 111, 135, 154, 156–57, 244n54, 244n57; Path of Peace development plan, 148; and *robaniños* panic, 68; Youth for Peace

program, 67. *See also* Misión de las Naciones Unidas en Guatemala (MINUGUA)
Peck, Jamie, 9
Pepsi, Pepsico: and adscription, 144; advertising, 25, 183, 199–200; and neoliberalism, 206; radio, 216n15; satire of, 205
Pérez Molina, Otto, 205–6; 263n20
photography, 107. *See also* arts
Pinzón, Giovanni, 94, 96
Plan de Reorganización Social, 63
plans, development and municipal. *See* municipal and community development plans
Plan Puebla Panamá, 158
poder local. *See* decentralization
Pokemones, Los, 156, 198. *See also* gangs; grassroots/local
police, 46, 87, 101, 127, 157, 163; corruption, 98, 136; and decentralization, 193; and fear, 92; harassment, 35–36, 181; National Police Archives, 16, 214n39; organized crime, 105; Policía Nacional (PN, National Police) 122, 194; Policía Nacional Civil (PNC, National Civil Police), 122; protest involving, 81*fig.*; at public gatherings, 17; radio station, 217n15; rejection of, 148; resistance to, 158; retaliation against, 4, 67–68, 161, 194–95, 221n75; and rockeros, 44; secret, 82; Spanish Embassy Massacre, 40; Sistema de Protección Ciudadana (SIPROCI), 91; Task Force Hunapú, 91; torture, 91; violence, 112
Pop Caal, Antonio, 150, 158, 247n84
Portillo, Alfonso, 135, 247n91; corruption, 159, 247n89; Pacto Fiscal, 160; versus neoliberal elite, 150–52
Pradilla Cobos, Emilio, 10, 212n15
Primera Generación Records, 89*fig.*; artist space, 107; founding and closing of, 88, 151; *Hasta Atrás*, 107; Libertad de Expresión, ¡Ya!, 108
private schools. *See* education
privatization, 129, 146; banks, electricity, and telecommunications, 11, 64, 122, 221n81, 240nn9,10, 241n11; and *calle/KY*, 24, 131–34; as contested process, 62;

privatization *(continued)*
  as a global process, 156; in peace process, 99; public private alliances, 60; semiprivatized, 69. *See also* neoliberalization
Programa Nacional de Competitividad (PRONACOM, National Competitiveness Program), 172–73, 252n28

Quemé Chay, Rigoberto, 124
Quetzaltenango (department), 19; gangs in, 122, 127; guerrillas in, 101, 226n40; *Regional, El* in, 73; and remittances *(remesas)*, 253n40; Unification Church (Moonies) in, 117; USAID interviews in, 188. *See also* agro-urbanization, regional
Quetzaltenango (municipality/cabecera), 3, 5, 188; art in, 244n50; death squads in, 236n68; leaders in, 124; parties in, 76, 246n68; peace march in, 97l radio in, 235n49; *Regional, El* in, 73; Segundo Encuentro Continental de Pueblos Indígenas in, 78; as tour destination, 109; urbanization in, 3, 73, 115–17, 188, 255n61; youth program in, 255n61. *See also* agro-urbanization; gangs; urbanization
Quiché (department) 4, 193–94; counterinsurgency in, 82, 98; guerillas in, 38; exhumations in, 82. *See also* agro-urbanization, regional; Santa Cruz del Quiché

racism: 6–7, 12, 100, 103–4, 180; antishumo, 12, 57, 87, 91, 203–5; Asamblea de la Sociedad Civil (ASC) on, 99; González Ponciano on, 12, 204, 213n23; mestizaje/mestizo, 7; "reverse," 70; structural, 100. See also *break wars;* caste, *castas;* "ethnic question"
radio: AM-to-FM transition, 45, 87, 115; bloggers on 54–55; community radio, guerrilla radio, 216n15; and early hiphop, 57; Contacto Ancestral, in Los Angeles, 175; and corporate sponsorship, 130, 139; and early rock and roll, 33, 216–17n15; *Hasta Atrás* on, 107–8; and heavy metal, 45, 87–88; and guerrilla publicity, 72–73; Metro Stereo, 88; and *onderos*, 36; Radio Cuba, 36; *Radioguaterock,* 256n71; Radio Juventud, 36; Radio Nahualá (comedy video), 185; Radio Sacmixit, 138; in provinces, 109, 115, 119, 134; La Voz de Huehue and Stereo Mam, 109; and youth discourse, 73
Radio Nahualá, 185, 256n70
RadioVox, 108
ranchera. See musical genres
rap, *raperos. See* musical genres
rape. *See* sexual violence
raves, 2, 151–52, 153*fig.*, 245n66; and after parties, 246n68; as background noise, 156; del Castillo, 152; DJ Chronic, 151; DJ Megadose, 152; as playworlds, 150; ecstasy, MDMA, 151–52
referendum of 1999, 135, 241n17
refugees/returnees in/from Mexico, 85, 99, 158; camps, 50; disputes, land conflicts, 99, 158; and guerrilla recruitment, 85, 229n74; and human rights, 234n40; reintegration, 124; remittances, 119; role in agro-urbanization, 85
Regional, El, 132; on crime, lynching, 104; diffusion of mass media, 73; on gangs, 117, 122; and Mayan movement, 76; on Moonies, 237n69; numbering system, 226n41; on *poder local,* 127; on youth, 73, 75
reggaetón, See musical genres
remittances *(remesas),* 168, 177, 249n7; and agro-urbanization, 11, 57–58, 75, 115, 119–21, 253n40; and banks, 183; and "Hispanic philanthropists," 253n40; and local economies, 5, 120–21
repasos, 33–34
República de Indios, 78
Revista del Movimiento Indio, 47
Río Negro, Alta Verapaz, 174–75; Centro Histórico y Educativo Riij Ib'ooy, 174. *See also* tourism
Ríos Montt, Efraín, 46, 135, 161, 205, 262n19
robaniños, 23, 67–68, 225n26
rock, *rock nacional. See* musical genres
Rothenberg, Daniel, 68, 225n26
Ruido de fondo, 86–87, 91–92, 106, 231n98, 231n102

sacerdotes mayas, 78, 83
Sac Mixit, Totonicapán, 138, 162
San Andrés Semetabaj, 177–79, 192, 251n24
Sangre Humana, 27–29; "Destino del poder" (Power's destiny), song and idea, 28–30, 42, 50; formation of, 45. See also González, Roberto "Blacko"
San Idelfonso Ixtahuacán, 40, 132, 134, 240n8
San Juan Comalapa, 207, 244n50
San Juan Sacatepéquez, 263n25; concert in, 36; maquiladoras in, 143
San Miguel Acatán, 77–78, 227n51
San Miguel Petapa, 161
San Pedro La Laguna, 1–2, 13, 145, 151, 207*fig*., 208*fig*.; B-boys in, 187*fig*., 208–10; creative center, 207–10, 208*fig*., interviews in, 264n30. *See also* Ijatz Crew
San Pedro Sacatepéquez, 103
Santa Cruz Barillas: agrarian modality of city-region, 118–19; crime in, 118; local politics, 157–58; Strategic Municipal Plan, 136, 237n78; telephones arrive, 237n77; United Nations Mission, 98; youth programs, 255n61
Santa Cruz del Quiché (municipality/cabecera of Quiché department), 4; earthquake 38; exhuming graves, 82; murders in, 98, 136; and music, 76; "non-state justice" in, 193. *See also* agro-urbanization, regional
Santa Cruz Mendoza, Santiago: and economic centers, 71, 101, on "ethnic question," 70, on guerrilla recruitment, 72, 85, 229n74; and "hearts and minds," 103; leaflets, 226n37; Maya command ranks, 225n32; on peace process, 233n28; retirement of, 85, 150; return of, 101
Santa Eulalia, 121
Santiago Atitlán, 196; and the army, 2, 80–82; landslides near, 249n1; and security, 2, 242n22
Santos, Romeo, 186
Sassen, Saskia, 10, 212n13
Scheel, Fernando, 207; and Maya musicians, 263n25; Peace Accords song, 109
schools: and agro-urbanization, 116; as an analytical factor, 45; and Anonymous

Guatemala, 263n21; and "antibreaks," 90–92, 230n90; anxiety about youth, 118, 262n16; buses, 166; and caste/class distinctions, 87, 89, 144, 178, 204, 230n88; and childhood, 192–93, 252n32; in fiction, 90–92, 112; and gangs, 90–92, 121, 156, 198; hip hop, 187; increase in education, 238n84; and Maya, 52, 146; and music, 84, 106, 139, 219n46, 234n38; and protests, 51; and *repasos*, 33; schoolhouse bell, 156, 198, 246n77; school kids, 2; teachers, 173; and tuc-tuc drivers, 163, 206; vocational, 164. *See also* education, universities
Schirmer, Jennifer: on FIS, FONAPAZ, 65–66; linking military and development, 223n7; on Sistema de Protección Ciudadana (SIPROCI), 230n94; on "social cleansing," torture, 91
Scott, James, 21, 60, 161, 216n49
security patrols, 8, 99, 260n116; crisis, 166; counterinsurgency and the security state, 9–10, 23, 66, 68, 85–86, 88, 90–91, 105, 122; and decentralization, 157; described as, 259n103; and Encapuchados, Los, 196–98; and growth of, 194–95; and kidnapping, 193; and *calle*/KY, 147; and migrants, 97; and military, 23, 242n22; protection from crime, gangs, 2, 8, 118; securitization, 135–36; and social cleansing, 104–5, 118
Segundo Encuentro Continental de Pueblos Indígenas, 78, 79*fig*.
Serrano Elías, Jorge, 60, 135
servility, as cultural form: as analytical category and concept, 6–7, 12, 21, 262n12; challenging, Maya musicians and artists, 131–32, 166, 173, 179–83, 206–210; challenging, rap music, 113, 206–210; challenging, youth satire 119; 203–205; cultural assertiveness as challenge to, 23–26, 60, 76–77, 92–93, 109, 118–19, 128, 176, 201; as cultural performance, 21, 167, 216n49; erosion of, 88–89, 91–92 (*see also* break wars); and generative cultural production, 62, 130, 167, 176, 238n86; lack of deference, 165, 261n8; and masks, 143–44; and

servility, as cultural form *(continued)* "shumo" resistance, 203–205; and street aesthetics, 178–82, 203–205; and Viernes Verde, "Requiem en E," 148–49; Yolanda Colom on, 37–38; *See also* barrio; *calle/*KY; musical genres

sexual violence: domestic violence, 182, 252–52n32, 255n61; femicide, 193; forced prostitution, 67, 193; rape and gang-rape, 90, 118, 193, 196; rape as tool of war, 41, 174; sexual abuse, 191, 255n61

Sevilla-Buitrago, Álvaro: on urbanization, 19, 62, 201, 223n6; on violence of condensation, 68

shumo: antishumo discourse, 203–5, 261n11; and assertiveness, 91, 189, 203–5; and Maya-ladino binary, 12; and pride, 164; and race, 213n23; and servility, 21; spread of, 57, 87

SIFs. *See* Social Investment Funds

Simpson, Los, 121–22, 132, 137, 156. *See also* gangs: grassroots/local

Sistema de Protección Ciudadana (SIPROCI, System of Citizen Protection), 91, 230n94

slang, 1, 15, 28, 37, 87, 92, 131, 139, 179, 188, 264n31; *agricultor,* 14; and binaries, 12; *chamusca,* 132; *chapín, chapina, chapinismo,* 15, 21, 33, 40, 107, 139, 178, 183, 188; *cerote,* 56, 192; *chilero, ¡va vos?* 183; *chiquitiar,* 59; *cholo, cholero,* 12; *chulo, chucho, colocho,* 183; *cuate,* 192; *"este es mayan pride100%4life"* 175; *estupideces, muladas,* 15; *flex,* 59; *forma de ser,* 15, 21; *fresas,* 57; *hasta atrás,* 107; *hueco,* 203; *la KY,* 131; *metaleros,* 57; *mozo,* 12; *muco,* 12, 57; *nel, simón, va vos,* 178; *onderos,* 57; *pedo,* 2; *pepena,* 190, 190*fig.; pesados,* 37, 40; *pura paja,* 15; *puta, gran puta,* 1, 153*fig.; que trance, ¡va?,* 56; *QP,* 223n1, *rapero,* 87; *shumos,* 12, 21, 57, 87; and style, 214n33; *valeverguismo, me vale verga, me pela la verga,* 40, 87; *virula,* 186; *vos,* 1; *vos cerote, vos talega, vos maje,* 192. *See also cerote;* chapinismos

slums. See *barrios marginales*

Smith, Timothy: on Iboy, 125; on Sololá, 82, 125

Sobrevivencia: as archive, 175–76; celebration, 132; and foreign media and technology, 134; and hope, 149, 154; and identity, 175, 183; Maya rock-fusion 132; rejection of servility, 148, 201; resistance and accommodation, 240n8; and Sara Curruchich, 207; touring indigenous-majority towns, 137. *See also* Job Sis, Alex

social cleansing, 51, 146; "antibreaks," 90–92; and anxiety, 91–92, 117; security, 88, 90–92, 104, 117; and undesired people, 117, 136, 166, 193

social fabric/*tejido social,* changes to, 165–69, 180, 184, 189, 197; and adscriptions, 144; and activism, 125; built from below, 32; and communities of memory, 175; corruption of, 159; integrating youth into, 146; and internal versus external, 139

social investment funds (SIFs), 64–66, 69, 133, 225n17; Fondo de Inversión Social (FIS, Social Investment Fund), 65–66, 225n17; National Fund for Peace (FONAPAZ), 65, 225n17

social movements, 18, 262n16; and bus fare protests of 1985, 50–51; by period, 1970s-early 1980s, 37–38, 40, 42, 240n8; by period, from return to democracy (1986) to peace (late 1996), 28, 30, 60, 63–64, 69; Grupo de Apoyo Mutuo (GAM), 63; oppressed during war, 34, 91; postpeace, 130, 166, 203, 205–6; postpeace, antiglobalization protests of 2002, 158; postpeace, antimining, 20, 166, 181, 240n8, 242n24, 254n55, 256n69, 262n16; and *potentia,* 242n19; social movement webs, 63, 224n11; and strike of 2003, 151; unions, 31, 34, 40, 63, 91, 120, 136. *See also* Mayan movement

Sololá (department), 19; guerrillas in, 71, 85. *See also* Lake Atitlán; Panajachel; San Pedro La Laguna; Santiago Atitlán

Sololá (municipality and cabecera), 206; counterinsurgency in, 2, 82–84; description of, 4; and feria, 176–78, 177*fig.;* and gangs, 155–56; and lynchings, 194–95, 197–98; Maya and municipal politics in, 80–84, 81*fig.,* 124–27, 136–37, 157, 194–95; municipal planning, 136–37,

243n27; Tabal, 155; and tradition, 84; and tuc-tucs, 162–63, 163*fig*.; zotz' symbol, 125–26, 126*fig*. See also agro-urbanization, regional; municipal government and politics
Somos Juventud campaign, 189
SOS. See musical bands, musicians
Strategic Plans, Municipal and Territorial: Barillas Plan, 136, 237n78; Chiantla plan, 181; Guatemala City, *Metrópolis 2010*, 116–117, 236n64; Plan Comunitario de Desarrollo (PCD), 137, 157, 228n65; Plan de Desarrollo Municipal (PDM), 170–171; Plan Estratégico Territorial (PET), 171, 251n25
street children, 57, 110, 116, 192; called *duendes*, 67, 92, 148, 192; and robaniños, 67–68 (see also panic; *robaniños*); and social cleansing, 91–93; war orphans, 50
style, 213n33, 229n73, 230n90; and "aesthetic effervescence," 161; and anxiety, 119; from below, 32, 142–44, 189; and class, 90, 106–108; contours of, 8; foreign, 12, 73, 76, 87, 106–8; global and local, 49, 53–54; hip-hop, 29; and identity, 20–21; mainstreaming of, 139; and Maya identity, 153; street, 15, 83–85, 131, 176; and technology, 178–79; and tradition, 126
Supositorio, 152, 153*fig*., 172. See also raves
SWOT (FODA), 137, 150, 170–71

tabal, 155, 246n74
Task Force Hunapú, 91
Taz. See Fernández, Sergio
Tecpán, 161, 219n42
Tecún Umán, 97, 121
tejido social. See social fabric/*tejido social*, changes to
telephones, telephone service: cell phones, 3, 115, 178, 179, 195; Claro, 240n10; Comcel (Tigo), 240n10; country code, 184; democracy, modernization, 69, 74; GUATEL, TELGUA, 240n10; privatization, 129; rural-urban divide, 119
television, 45, 73, 121, 137, 216n15; cable, 44, 69, 87, 90, 119; MTV, 44, 57, 87, 108, 110, 235n51; nonthreatening to cultural retention, 240n5; Pokemones, Los, 156, 246n76
territory: territorial division of space, 19–20; "territorial interventions," 25, 170–78
Thomas, Kedron, 66, 161
Tian Senté, Luis Gilberto ("Pixica"), 196, 198
Todos Santos Cuchumatán, 142, 146–47
La Tona: formation of 106; inspiring new bands, 114; "Interna Externa," song and idea, 24, 138–39, 147, 154
Tortrix, 183, 200; "chulo tu chucho colocho," 176, 183–84, 189, 197, 200
Totonicapán: department of, 19, 112, 117, 157; local authority, 244n57; massacre of, 205; Sac Mixit, 138
tourism 47, 71–72, 80, 115, 180, 196, 249n7; and diasporic memory, 25, 174–76; ethnotourism/ecotourism, 146–47, 172–76; sex tourism, 155, 173–74, 253n33
trade, trade agreements: Asamblea de la Sociedad Civil (ASC) on, 99; in babies and bodily organs, 68; in children, through adoption, 67, 193; Central American Common Market (CACM), 32, 250n13; in drugs, internal, 50–51 (see also narcotraffic); in foreign currency, 221n81; Plan Puebla Panamá, protests, 158; World Trade Organization, 98. See Central American-Dominican Republic Free Trade Agreement (CAFTA-DR)
traje, 2, 142, 144, 188, 260n116; mystique of, 252n32; on zotz', 126
Trasciende, 187–88
13 Baktun. See Trece Baktun
Trece Baktun, 2, 5, 25, 202, 205–6, 208, 210
tropical storms : Agatha, 195; Stan, 165, 167
trova, 36, 93
tuc-tuc, 3, 206, 209, 248n97; moral economy of, 24, 161–64, 163*fig*.

Los Últimos Adictos: and Atmósfera Omplog, 138; formation of 106; and highland gigs, 131–32, 137–38; last concert 151, 158; "si aquí se pudiera vivir" (If only you could live here), book title, song lyric and idea, 24, 129,

INDEX · 303

Los Últimos Adictos *(continued)* 131, 158, 164, 201; in soundtrack, *Casa de enfrente,* 159. See also Andrade, Ricardo; Fernández, Sergio "Taz"
Unidad Revolucionaria Nacional Guatemalteca (URNG), 47–49, 85, 105, 122; actions, 72, 98–99, 101; activism and popular culture, 72, 101, 226n37; on Cerezo, 63–64; and invisibility of agro-urbanization, 69–70; as political party, 134, 150, 157; political program, 100
Unification Church, Moonies, 117, 237n16
United Nations: as archival source, 16; monitoring, 128; on police, 122; truth commission, 10, 135; UNICEF, 148; youth campaign, 189. See also Misión de las Naciones Unidas en Guatemala (MINUGUA)
United States Agency for International Development (USAID): and agriculture, 39, 52; and NTAs, 221n77; on violence, 193–94, 197; on youth, 14, 188; youth rescue, 182, 255n60
universities: discourse about, portrayals of, 86, 87, 144, 209; Karl Marx University, 35; students, 27, 111; Universidad del Valle, 125; Universidad de San Carlos de Guatemala (USAC), 36, 43; Universidad Rafael Landívar, 106, 142. See also education
Urban and Rural Development Committees, 136. See municipal government and politics
urbanization: of Antigua, 192–93, 209; of Chiantla, 4, 96*map,* 181; concepts and theories of, 9–10, 15, 61, 201, 223n6; global, "planetary," 5, 7–10, 15, 26, 62, 68, 167, 201, 223n6; of Guatemala City and environs, 27–29, 32–34, 38, 110–16, 215n44; of Huehuetenango (cabecera), 4, 117–18, 127; of Quetzaltenango (cabecera), 3, 116–17; and rural, 19, 84; and subcultures, 22. See also agro-urbanization; city-regions
URNG. See Unidad Revolucionaria Nacional Guatemalteca
USAID. See United States Agency for International Development

valeverguismo, 44, 87, 229n82
Vamos Guatemala, 170
Viernes Verde: in Atmósfera Omplog, 138; formation of 106; inspiring new bands, 114; international tours, 108; highland gigs, 132; street nationalism, "Requiem en E," "soy chapín de sangre," 148, 164, 245n60
vigilantism: and decentralization, 201; lynching, 23, 150, 166, 197, 259n102; lynching, and panic, 104–5; lynching, growth of, 117–18, 158, 191–95, 244n57; lynching, into vernacular, 97; lynching, psychological effects of, 25; lynching tourist, 147; and military/paramilitary structures, 98–99, 105, 212n17; and peace, 23, 97; rejection of state, 148, 161; and security, 8, 194; "unknown men," 155. See also break wars; security patrols
virula, 186, 189, 191, 259n97
Vrana, Heather, 43, 214n35, 217n18

Weld, Kirsten, 16, 214n39, 238n93
Williams, Raymond, 15
Woodstock, Woodstockito, 35, 94
World Bank, 11, 160, 226n17, 248n94; and Maya, 77; and privatization, 132–34, 136, 157, 160, 240n9; social investment funds, 64–66
World Trade Organization, 98

Ye'Qatanum: El Aguacateco, 119
youth: as analytical category, 20, 215n47, 258n89; and agriculture, 38; baby boom, 1, 5; baroque character of youth cultures, 13, 15, 138, 144, 150, 161–63, 176; from-below, 14–15, 130, 137, 142–43; and body politic, 13–16; and commercialization, 106–114; discourse about, changes in, 51–54, 59–62, 189, 199–200; discourse about, lost, 67–68, 72–73, 75–77, 80, 83–92, 118–22; discourse about, Maya, 100, 103–104, 109–110; generational change, 5–7, 11, 40, 138–45, 173, 175–93, 206; and national cultural commons, 62; and national cultural commons, and *aldeando* (villaging up) of culture, 144, 172; and national cultural commons,

and archives, 16–17, 175, 188–89; and national cultural commons, and decentralization, 24; and national cultural commons, definition of, 12–13; and national cultural commons, expansion of, 166–67, 169, 180–81, 186; and national cultural commons, globally inflected, 7; and national cultural commons, la KY, 131–32, 140–41 (see also *calle*/KY); and national cultural commons, masks, 143–46; and national cultural commons, rejecting servility, 200–203, 210 (*see also* servility); and "NGO-ification," 94–98; and peace, 128; and power 30–31, 43–45; and revolution, 49–50; and servility, 6–7, 21; and technology, 103. *See also* break wars; casta; *castas; calle*/KY; childhood; de a pie; barrio, the, as social space; internet/social media blogs, posts, and pages; musical genres; nationalism; servility, as cultural form; shumo; slang; style

youth programs, 18, 179; Año de la Juventud, 189; Consejo de Juventudes Indígenas (Council of Indigenous Youths), 204, 256n69; Consejo Nacional de la Juventud (CONJUVE), 67, 167, 255n60; ENJU, Encuesta Nacional de la Juventud (National Youth Poll), 255n61, 262n16; Jóvenes contra la Violencia (Youth against Violence), 258n90; municipal development committees, 259n5; music, 88; National Maya Youth Organization Network, 256n69; National Plan for Youth, 67; Red Nacional de Organizaciones de Jóvenes Mayas (RENOJ, National Network of Maya Youth Organizations), 256n69

Zapata, Adrián, 64, 224n14
Zepeda, Andrés, 142, 247n91
Zolov, Eric, 214n35
zotz', 125–26, 126fig., 128, 239n104

Founded in 1893,
UNIVERSITY OF CALIFORNIA PRESS
publishes bold, progressive books and journals
on topics in the arts, humanities, social sciences,
and natural sciences—with a focus on social
justice issues—that inspire thought and action
among readers worldwide.

The UC PRESS FOUNDATION
raises funds to uphold the press's vital role
as an independent, nonprofit publisher, and
receives philanthropic support from a wide
range of individuals and institutions—and from
committed readers like you. To learn more, visit
ucpress.edu/supportus.

www.ingramcontent.com/pod-product-compliance
Lightning Source LLC
Chambersburg PA
CBHW021337230426
43666CB00006B/319